The Civil Wars in U.S. Labor

The Civil Wars in U.S. Labor

Birth of a New Workers' Movement or Death Throes of the Old?

Steve Early

Haymarket Books
Chicago, Illinois

First published by Haymarket Books in 2011.
© 2011 Steve Early

Haymarket Books, P.O. Box 180165, Chicago, IL 60618
773-583-7884, info@haymarketbooks.org
www.haymarketbooks.org

Trade distribution:
In the U.S., Consortium Book Sales and Distribution, www.cbsd.com
In Canada, Publishers Group Canada, www.pgcbooks.ca
In the UK, Turnaround Publisher Services, www.turnaround-uk.com
In Australia, Palgrave Macmillan, www.palgravemacmillan.com.au
All other countries, Publishers Group Worldwide, www.pgw.com

ISBN: 978-1-60846-099-1

Cover design by Josh On. Cover photo of health care workers protesting outside the
Oakland office of the National Labor Relations Board in July 2009 demanding the right
to vote to determine whether they would leave SEIU; courtesy of National Union of
Healthcare Workers.

This book was published with the generous support of Lannan Foundation and
the Wallace Global Fund.

Printed by union labor in the United States.

Library of Congress Cataloging-In-Publication data is available.

2 4 6 8 10 9 7 5 3

MIX
Paper from
responsible sources
FSC® C012752

For Suzanne, Alex, and Jess

CONTENTS

Preface and Acknowledgments

This book reports on recent conflicts within the progressive wing of U.S. labor that negatively affected far more workers than the union dues payers directly involved.

Both of our national labor federations, the AFL-CIO (American Federation of Labor–Congress of Industrial Organizations) and its smaller rival, Change to Win (CTW), hoped that Barack Obama's election in 2008 would aid sixteen million recession-battered union members. Labor also looked to Obama to help improve the pay, benefits, and job conditions of America's nonunion majority (now 88 percent of the workforce and growing every year).

Unfortunately, this long-awaited political opening—or "new moment," as the *Nation* called it—coincided with unexpected turmoil inside organized labor. During the 2008 presidential campaign, a series of "civil wars" (as they were invariably described) erupted in and around the Service Employees International Union (SEIU), a founder of CTW and a key backer of Obama. With nearly two million members, SEIU is, by far, the nation's most highly visible and politically influential labor organization. No other union did more to get Obama elected and none had more initial access to him in the White House. No labor organization in America is a bigger bogeyman among right-wing foes of unionism in any form.

By the time the Democrats took power in early 2009, this widely acclaimed "social justice union" was proving to be a problematic vehicle for progressive social change. Its much-condemned organizational misbehavior alienated many rank-and-file members and angered past friends and admirers of the union. Concern about SEIU's overall direction developed almost apace with left-liberal disillusionment with Obama's presidency, particularly after real health care reform was amputated and, partly as a result, long-overdue changes in labor law were stalemated.[1]

The multiple union disputes described herein generated much national and local press coverage. Little of it was helpful at a time when labor's public standing was already dropping, and any pro-worker proposals faced powerful corporate resistance in Congress. Beset by Republican enemies on Capitol Hill and, per usual, getting less support than expected from "union-friendly" Democrats, the "House of Labor" could ill afford a costly family feud in what passes for its left wing. This book is an attempt to take a deeper look at the politics, personalities, and institutions involved in the trade union wars of 2008–10. It offers both historical context and personal commentary, drawing on my own political experience, past union work, and recent reporting.

Like other critical studies of controversial institutions—not to mention "unauthorized biographies" of politicians, literary figures, and Hollywood celebrities—*Civil Wars* was written with little or no "official cooperation." SEIU headquarters in Washington did not respond to my request, made at the time of the union's 2008 convention, to interview any of its top officials, including then President Andy Stern, Secretary-Treasurer Anna Burger, and influential board members like Eliseo Medina. Bruce Raynor, head of Workers United, SEIU, was equally unresponsive.[2] By the time Mary Kay Henry was sworn in as Stern's successor, I didn't even bother to make a pro forma request for a formal audience or phone chat with her. I have relied instead on the (not-always-tough-enough) questioning of others. More than compensating for this lack of access to top officials was the generous assistance I've received from SEIU members, staffers, and elected leaders, past and present, all over the country. Some of these folks have asked to remain anonymous for fear of jeopardizing their current staff employment, elected union positions, or future job opportunities in the labor movement.

When talking with sources in nonlabor organizations that interact regularly with SEIU or depend on it for funding, I encountered a similar reticence about being interviewed "on the record," so their identities have also been protected where necessary. Many proud SEIU members nevertheless spoke freely with me—if not always for attribution—because of their dismay about the direction of a union they have tried to serve well. As one anguished former headquarters staffer confessed in a personal email, recent developments in SEIU are "cause for profound sadness and discouragement." His greatest fear was that external threats to organized labor in general and SEIU in particular were being overlooked because of its focus on conflicts with dissident members and union rivals like the National Union of Healthcare Workers (NUHW) or UNITE HERE. His prediction was that "the strength and unity of working people will continue to decline and the percentage of workers who are part of the union movement as a whole will be lower next year than this year and lower still the year after that." (When the Bureau of Labor Statistics released union density figures for 2009, that forecast turned out to be accurate and probably will be again in 2010.)[3]

Like many other sixties radicals who migrated to union work forty years ago, this former SEIU official once "hoped to make a small contribution" toward reversing labor's fortunes. But that modest goal "no longer seems possible today given that the small forces left on our side" are "fighting each other rather than the larger enemy." While this particular correspondent removed himself from the fray—in part, to display personal disapproval of it—other combatants viewed the enveloping conflicts as a call to action. Labor civil warfare was not a condition of their choosing. But, when SEIU aided and abetted various forms of organizational mayhem, they tried to make the best of the adverse circumstances they found themselves in. Whether reforming their own SEIU locals, creating a new health care union, or defending a CTW affiliate or an unaffiliated union from SEIU attacks, these trade unionists somehow managed to confront labor's "larger enemy" (the employers) *and* deal with the fallout of SEIU dysfunction at the same time. It was a demanding assignment. And that's why SEIU reformers, NUHW supporters, UNITE HERE organizers, Puerto Rican teachers, and California nurses were often quite proud of their victories, large and small, over a union behemoth with far more resources and political clout. Most of them had no problem being publicly identified and quoted by name.

Via the very long list below, I want to acknowledge the assistance or insight I obtained from individuals on all sides (or caught in the middle) of SEIU-related disputes. Many people on the list below agreed to be interviewed and/or provided later fact-checking help. Others wrote (or were the subject of) email messages, blog postings, union documents and reports, books, and articles that shed considerable light on the subject matter of *Civil Wars*. Some union officials on the list, who wouldn't talk to me, were interviewed by other reporters and researchers whose informative work is cited in the book.

I have read more than a few flawed accounts of union activity that I was personally involved in over the years so I know how easy it is for an outside observer to get significant details wrong. I hope I've been able to keep such errors of fact and interpretation to a minimum. How many of the latter mistakes I've made will, I'm sure, depend on the eye of the beholder. My apologies to interviewees whose many illuminating labor and political experiences are not recounted in *Civil Wars* due to space limitations. I have another labor-related book project in the works that will hopefully atone for these omissions next time around.

For this project then, thanks go to: Stewart Acuff, Marilyn Albert, Catherine Alexander, Sylvia Alvarez-Lynch, Edgardo Alvelo, Michelle Amber, David Aroner, David Bacon, Harry Baker, Martha Baker, Morty Bahr, Tom Balanoff, Aaron Bartley, Judy Beck, Herman Benson, Elaine Bernard, Bruce Boccardy, Barri Boone, Eileen Boris, Ed Bowen, Joan Braconi, Larry Bradshaw, Mark Brenner, Jerry Brown, Ed Bruno, Gene Bruskin,

Joe Buckley, Paul Buhle, Anna Burger, Gene Carroll, Dan Clawson, Larry Cohen, Cliff Cohn, Pasquelino Colombaro, Christopher Cook, Angelio Cordoba, Carmen Cortez, Gladys Cortez-Castillo, the late Tim Costello, Catherine Cox, Carol Criss, Jeff Crosby, Brian Cruz, Ellen David-Friedman, Rebecca Davis, Russ Davis, Tom DeBruin, Rose Ann DeMoro, Yonah Diamond, Arturo Diaz, Chuck DiMare, Jennifer Doe, Mike Donaldson, Tim Dubnau, Ariel Ducey, John Dugan, Buck Eichler, Enid Eckstein, Jackie Edwards, Kay Eisenhower, Mike Eisenscher, Frank Emspak, the late Andy English, Bob English, Suzan Erem, Keri Evinson, Tess Ewing, Mike Fadel, Rick Fantasia, Liza Featherstone, Rafael Feliciano, Kim Fellner, Michael Fenison, Carl Finamore, Dick Flacks, William Fletcher Jr., Arthur Fox, Max Fraser, Tyrone Freeman, Paul Friedman, Marshall Ganz, Fernando Gapasin, Mel Garcia, Jose Garcia, Mischa Gaus, Hector Giraldo, Angela Glasper, Emily Gordon, Steven Greenhouse, Ryan Grim, Harris Gruman, Gary Guthman, Walt Hamilton, Jim Hard, Leslie Harding, Van Hardy, Lauree Hayden, Adam Dylan Hefty, Kennedy Helm, Tania Hernandez, Maria Herrera, Warren Heyman, Jamie Horowitz, Rick Hurd, Chuck Idelson, Joe Iosbaker, Harriet Jackson, Edgar James, Remzi Jaos, Nelson Johnson, Margaret Jordan, Lover Joyce, Mathew Kaminski, Esther Kaplan, Harry Kelber, Tony Kin, Greg King, Jennifer Klein, David Kranz, Paul Krehbiel, Gabe Kristal, Mike Krivosh, Monty Kroopkin, Paul Kumar, Chris Kutalik, Zev Kvitky, Elly Leary, Steve Leigh, Stephen Lerner, Paul Levy, Stephen Lewis, Nelson Lichtenstein, Steven Lopez, Stephanie Luce, Matt Luskin, Alec MacGillis, Nancy MacLean, Kris Mahar, Audra Makuch, Adrian Maldonado, Ken Margolies, Dan Mariscal, Frank Martin del Campo, Karen McAninch, Robert McCauley, Matt McDonald, Patrick McDonnell, Ken McNamara, Elvis Mendez, Craig Merrilees, Ruth Milkman, Mike Mishak, Joanna Misnick, Juan Antonio Molina, Kim Moody, Gene Moriarity, Maya Morris, Bob Muehlenkamp, George Nee, Ruth Needleman, Karen Nussbaum, Richard O'Brien, Peter Olney, Ken Paff, Mike Parker, Jennifer Peat, Warren Pepicelli, Jan Pierce, Sin Yee Poon, Eric Pourras, Peter Rachleff, Ella Raiford, Wade Rathke, Norma Raya, Krystyna Razwadowski, Dave Regan, Eloise Reese-Burns, Kurt Richwerger, Hector Rincon, Michelle Ringuette, Paul Rockwell, Holly Rosenkrantz,

Hetty Rosenstein, Robert Ross, Fred Ross Jr., Howie Rotman, Ed Sadlowski Jr., Ed Sadlowski Sr., Roxanne Sanchez, Mario Santos, Libby Sayre, Meredith Schafer, George Schmidt, James C. Scott, Ana Serano, Judy Sheridan-Gonzalez, Dana Simon, Jane Slaughter, Lorrie Beth Slonsky, Ben Smith, Matt Smith, Rex Spray, Andy Stern, Art Sweatman, Peter Tappeiner, Jonathan Tasini, Julia Tecpa-Molina, Greg Tegenkamp, John Templeton, Joyce Thomas-Villaronga, Lisa Tomasian, Michael Torres, Chris Townsend, Don Trementozzi, Andrew Tripp, Maria Vega, Kim Voss, Erik Wallenberg, Brenda Washington, Pilar Weiss, John Wilhelm, Sarah Wilson, Mike Wilzoch, Samantha Winslow, Dana Wise, Matt Witt, Charles Wood, Tom Woodruff, Ferd Wulkan, Glenna Wyman, JoAnn Wypijewski, Michael Yates, and Steve Zeltzer.

Special recognition goes to four SEIU member-bloggers, all of whom cling to varying degrees of protective anonymity. I am referring here to the formidable California quartet composed of: Tasty, who serves up many a juicy morsel at *Stern Burger with Fries*; Keyser Sose, proprietor of *The Red Revolt in Sonoma County*; the pioneer in the field but now sadly silent Perez of *Perez Stern*; and the equally inactive Sierra Spartan, whose *Adios Andy!* blog was always ahead of the curve. All four provided biting online commentary about SEIU's tragic takeover of United Healthcare Workers (UHW). They then kept rank-and-file rebels in California and elsewhere fully informed about every outrageous development afterward, while greatly aiding my own *Civil Wars* coverage. A tip of the red hat to all of you, whoever and wherever you are.

Cartoonist Ellen Dillinger, on the other hand, did not work undercover. Her UHW-related comic strip, called "Life Under SEIU Trusteeship," combined the insights of a thirty-year veteran of hospital work in Sacramento with satiric commentary on the indignities of international union occupation of her local. Ellen's informative and very funny work is archived at http://dillingertoons.dillwood.org.[4]

Manny Ness, editor of *Working USA, the Journal of Labor and Society* (*WUSA*), has been tremendously supportive of this project and published earlier versions of three chapters in *WUSA*. He was also an invaluable source of information about relations between unions and academics. Alexander

Cockburn and Jeffrey St. Clair at *CounterPunch*; Jeremy Gantz at *Working In These Times*; Emily Douglas at the *Nation*; Stuart Elliot at Talking Union; Yoshie Furuhashi at MRZine; Chris Spannos at ZNet; Chris Kutalik, Mischa Gaus, and Jane Slaughter at *Labor Notes*; Mike Eisenscher at Solidarity Information Services; Tony Budak at Community Labor News; and the moderators at Portside all published material from the book, in different form, in their respective online or hard-copy publications. To survive, all these outlets for labor journalism (and, in several cases, other kinds of writing) must have continuing financial support from readers. Just because something's online doesn't mean it's free. Please consider sending all of the above a contribution or, better yet, becoming a paid subscriber.

The writing and/or information sharing of the following SEIU/UNITE HERE–watchers was invaluable at every step of the way. Paul Garver's knowledge of SEIU, based on his longtime work as a local union activist in Pennsylvania, made his *Talking Union* commentaries very incisive. Mark Brenner has done double duty—as director of Labor Notes and as its correspondent covering the SEIU and CNA (California Nurses Association) beats for the magazine. Likewise, Herman Benson, the ninety-five-year-old founder of the Association for Union Democracy (AUD), has combined his continuing organizational work for AUD with many trenchant commentaries on Andy Stern and SEIU. Paul Abowd took a lot of heat, from various sides, for his excellent reporting on UNITE HERE controversies in *Labor Notes*. Lee Sustar's interviews with Sal Rosselli in *Socialist Worker* were the best anywhere, by far. Randy Shaw's *BeyondChron* blog has been an indispensable source of fast-breaking news and commentary for readers far beyond the Bay Area. Juan Gonzalez has covered labor's civil wars as both a columnist for the *New York Daily News* and cohost of *Democracy Now!* A long ago column by Juan about SEIU's trusteeship over Local 32B/J in New York City first got me thinking about "who rules SEIU." Thanks to Juan's reporting on the struggle of Puerto Rican teachers, I was able to meet some wonderful members of the FMPR (Federación de Maestros de Puerto Rico). Paul Pringle's Polk Award for his series of articles about local union corruption in Southern California was well deserved, if very much unwelcomed by SEIU. Cal

Winslow's great 2010 PM Press book, *Labor's Civil War in California*, helped get the story of NUHW out quickly, while placing the state's health care workers' rebellion in historical context. Along with Ellen David-Friedman, Cal has been a valued friend and coworker in NUHW fund-raising and solidarity activity in California and around the country.

I also want to thank Michael Schiavone, author of *Unions in Crisis: The Future of Organized Labor in America* (Praeger, 2008), for sharing his very insightful but not-yet-published manuscript about SEIU. Adam Reich's forthcoming account of SEIU and NUHW organizing in the same California hospital was extremely illuminating; look for it soon from Cornell ILR Press under the title, *With God on Our Side: Labor Struggle in The Catholic Hospital.*

Jack Getman sent me a very helpful prepublication copy of his definitive study of UNITE HERE, called *Restoring the Power of Unions: It Takes a Movement,* which is now available from Yale University Press. The authors of *Organizational Change at SEIU, 1996–2009*—Adrienne Eaton, Janice Fine, Allison Porter, and Saul Rubinstein—collected many useful facts and figures about the union's structural transformation in a report that few members and local officers have ever seen. (The four SEIU consultants based their internal report on interviews with "150 leaders and staff at the International and seven different locals" but, apparently, very few rank and filers.) As noted in chapter 8, my old United Mine Workers (UMW) colleague Don Stillman penned an authorized institutional biography, *Stronger Together: The Story of SEIU.* It draws on *Organizational Change,* but is intended for a broader audience.

I owe a big debt of gratitude to Jack Metzgar from Chicago, longtime professor at Roosevelt University, who was good enough to read and provide detailed feedback on original drafts of multiple chapters. The author of a wonderful memoir and union history, *Striking Steel: Solidarity Remembered,* Jack was a great editor at the now much-missed *Labor Research Review.* His editorial advice (particularly in the area of de-snarking) remains as sharp as ever.

I must also give special thanks to my long-suffering in-house editor

and spouse, Suzanne Gordon. Suzanne's years of experience as an author and, more recently, series editor at Cornell's ILR Press sure came in handy at deadline time. Her many comments, criticisms, and cuts in the copy helped make the book better and more readable. I want to thank my daughters, Alexandra Early and Jessica Early, for putting up with my crankiness during this project. As noted later in the book, Alex had the double burden of being a California health care union "warrior"—on the insurgent side. Among the many others involved in UHW prior to its trusteeship, I particularly want to thank Sal Rosselli, John Borsos, Paul Kumar, Dana Simon, Glenn Goldstein, Emily Gordon, Marti Garza, Fred Seavey, Sadie Crabtree, Laura Kurre, John Vellardita, Barbara Lewis, Dan Martin, Ralph Cornejo, Paul Delehanty, and Phyllis Willett. My longtime collaborator, Rand Wilson, provided many useful reality checks on some parts of this book, my previous one, and earlier published work, some of which he coauthored.

Last but not least, I am most grateful to all the great folks at Haymarket Books. Anthony Arnove, Rachel Cohen, Julie Fain, Elliot Linzer, Sarah Macaraeg, Jim Plank, Trey Sager, Sharon Smith, Dao Tran, worked together, along with Anne Borchardt at the Borchardt Agency, to make this fast-turnaround project possible. In publishing, no less than union organizing, teamwork is essential to the success of any campaign!

Organizations and Abbreviations

CCWU	Child Care Workers Union
CHP	Catholic Healthcare Partners
CHW	Catholic Healthcare West
CLRE	Center for Labor Research and Education at UC Berkeley
CNA	California Nurses Association
COPE	Committee on Political Education
CPPEA	California Professional Public Employees Association
CSRs	customer service representatives
CTW	Change to Win
CUHWU	California United Homecare Workers Union
CUJ	California United Janitors
CWA	Communications Workers of America District 1199
DDD	State Division of Developmental Disabilities
EFCA	Employee Free Choice Act
FHU	SEIU Healthcare Florida
FMLA	Family and Medical Leave Act
FMPR	Federación de Maestros de Puerto Rico, Puerto Rican Federation of Teachers
FOUR	Federation of Union Representatives
HCA	Hospital Corporation of America
HCAN	Health Care for America Now
HERE	Hotel Employees and Restaurant Employees
HSU	Health Services Union
HTUP	Harvard Trade Union Program
IAMAW	Known as IAM, International Association of Machinists and Aerospace Workers
IBEW	International Brotherhood of Electrical Workers
IBT	International Brotherhood of Teamsters, or Teamsters
IEB	international executive board
IFPTE	International Federation of Professional and Technical Engineers
IGI	Investigative Group International
IHSS	In-Home Supportive Services
ILGWU	International Ladies Garment Workers Union
ILWU	International Longshore and Warehouse Union

ILR	School of Industrial and Labor Relations
KP	Kaiser Permanente, or Kaiser
LAWCHA	Labor and Working Class History Association
LMP	Labor Management Partnership
LMRDA	Labor-Management Reporting and Disclosure Act
MAC	Member Action Center
MAPE	Marin Association of Public Employees
MASC	Member Action Service Center
MDU	Members for a Democratic Union
MMBA	Meyers-Milias-Brown Act
MMC	Maine Medical Center
MRCs	member resource centers
MROs	member resource organizers
MSRC	Member Strength Review Committee
NAGE	National Association of Government Employees
NEA	National Education Association
NHA	Nursing Home Alliance
NJEA	New Jersey Education Association
NLCC	National Labor Coordinating Committee
NLF	*New Labor Forum*
NLRA	National Labor Relations Act
NLRB	National Labor Relations Board, the board, the labor board
NMB	National Mediation Board
NNOC	National Nurses Organizing Committee
NNU	National Nurses United
NSUP	New Strength and Unity Plan
NUHW	National Union of Healthcare Workers
PCAs	personal care attendants
PERB	Public Employees Relations Board
PHS	Port Huron Statement
PNHP	Physicians for a National Health Program
PPI	Georgetown University's Public Policy Institute
PPACA	Patient Protection and Affordable Care Act
PRB	Public Review Board
PSSU	Pennsylvania Social Services Union

QPSU   Queensland Public Sector Union
ROTC   Reserve Officer Training Corps
SAWSJ   Scholars, Articsts, and Writers for Social Justice
SDS   Students for a Democratic Society
SEA   New Jersey State Employees Association
SEIU   Service Employees International Union
SEIU-UHW   United Healthcare Workers West
SJHS   St. Joseph Health System
SLAC   Student Labor Action Coalition
SMART   SEIU Member Activists for Reform Today
SRM   Santa Rosa Memorial, or Memorial
SWU   Service Workers United
SWOC   State Workers Organizing Committee
TANF   Temporary Assistance for Needy Families
TDU   Teamsters for a Democratic Union
UAW   United Auto Workers
UC Berkeley University of California, Berkeley
UCLA   University of California, Los Angeles
UCSB   University of California, Santa Barbara
UCSF   University of California, San Francisco
UDR   *Union Democracy Review*
UDW   United Domestic Workers
UE   United Electrical Workers
UFCW   United Food and Commercial Workers
UFW   United Farm Workers
UFT   United Federation of Teachers
UHW   United Healthcare Workers
ULTCW   United Long Term Care Workers
ULU   United Labor Unions
UMass   University of Massachusetts, Amherst,
            or UMass Amherst
UMW   United Mine Workers
UNAC   United Nurses Association of California
UNI   Union Network International
UNITE   Union of Needletrades, Industrial and Textile Employees
UNITE HERE Union of Needletrades, Industrial and

	Textile Employees and Hotel and Restaurant Employees
UPRT	Union of Puerto Rican Teachers
USAS	United Students Against Sweatshops
USAW	United Service and Allied Workers
USC	University of Southern California
USCCB	United States Conference of Catholic Bishops
USWA	United Steel Workers of America, or United Steelworkers
USWD	United Service Workers for Democracy
USWW	United Service Workers West
UUHS	Union of UNITE HERE staff
VISTA	Volunteers in Service to America
VSEA	Vermont State Employees Association
VWRP	Vermont Workers' Rights Project
WU	Workers United, SEIU
WMWA	Wal-mart Workers Association
WUSA	*Working USA, the Journal of Labor and Society*

Introduction

From the Sixties to San Juan

*"If you cannot relate your past, the history through which you lived
and that you helped make, to the present, then how can you expect
those whose total experience is in the present to relate it to a past
they do not know?"*
                                    —Al Richmond in *A Long View from the Left*[1]

It was a convention full of "contradictions," as radicals used to say (and
some still do). It evoked the glories of labor's past and excitement about
possibilities for the future. Held four decades after the penultimate year
of the 1960s, the gala 2008 gathering of delegates from the Service Employees International Union (SEIU) in San Juan, Puerto Rico, showcased
all that's good and bad, right and wrong, hopeful and unhelpful, about
sixties-inspired efforts to change American labor.

Long applauded as our "most dynamic, fastest growing, and (many
would argue) most progressive union," SEIU has certainly become the nation's most highly visible one.[2] Its own transformation began in the 1970s,
after thousands of veterans of antiwar activity, the civil rights movement,
feminism, and community organizing migrated to workplaces and union

halls with the professed goal of challenging the labor establishment. As I reported in the *Nation* in 1984, this generational cohort constituted "the largest radical presence in unions since the 1930s, when members of the Communist Party and other left-wing groups played a key role in the formation of the Congress of Industrial Organizations (CIO)."[3]

Among those who shifted from campus to labor activism, in the wake of the sixties, was SEIU president Andy Stern, who was by 2008 "America's most powerful union boss," according to the *Wall Street Journal*.[4] The son of a lawyer from West Orange, New Jersey, Stern entered the University of Pennsylvania to study business at the Wharton School but soon "discovered the civil rights movement, the anti-war protests, women's liberation, the environmental and consumer movements and the counter culture." Thanks to the events of that era and 1968 in particular, "Marketing turned out not to be my top priority," he explained many years later.[5] The future SEIU president ended up studying education and urban planning instead. After graduation, he became a welfare department case worker and member of the Pennsylvania Social Services Union (PSSU), affiliated with SEIU as Local 668.

In PSSU, Stern was a militant shop steward and critic of the union leadership, who supported a three-day wildcat strike "to reject a statewide contract as a 'sell-out.'"[6] Not long after that membership rebellion, Stern was elected PSSU president, a position later occupied by his fellow activist Anna Burger, later secretary-treasurer of SEIU. In 1984, Stern became SEIU organizing director and moved to its national union headquarters in Washington, D.C. There, according to *Business Week*, his background "as a bushy-haired young left-winger in the student movement led him to experiment with the in-your-face tactics that first put SEIU on the map."[7] In 1996, Stern became SEIU president and, a decade later, the driving force behind Change to Win (CTW)—a five-million-member union coalition that broke away from the AFL-CIO in 2005. Burger became CTW chairperson and the first woman to head a labor federation in America.

As Stern stood before 3,500 San Juan convention delegates and guests—most wearing purple, the union's signature color—he proudly reviewed

SEIU's singular success over the twelve years since his predecessor, John Sweeney, left to lead the AFL-CIO. During that time, SEIU nearly doubled in size and now claims 2.2 million members; in 2008, 21 percent of all the new union members recruited that year were organized by SEIU.[8] The union was widely hailed in the media as America's most savvy, well-funded labor player in politics. During Barack Obama's presidential campaign, there was even speculation that Stern might end up in his cabinet or become a candidate for public office himself.

In the course of the labor movement's 2005 split, Stern easily eclipsed Sweeney as labor's most visible (and frequently quoted) national spokesperson. In his 2006 book *A Country That Works* Stern outlined an agenda for getting the U.S. economy "back on track" that garnered far more attention than Sweeney's similar volume a decade earlier.[9] In the first flush of enthusiasm for the breakaway CTW, some academic boosters likened Stern's rival federation to the CIO during its Depression-era heyday. A few even compared Andy to John L. Lewis, the Mine Workers leader, whose industrial union challenge to the AFL seventy years ago led to millions of blue-collar workers finally getting organized. Stern had long cultivated progressive academics and intellectuals who could burnish his own reputation and help promote SEIU campaigns. One campus enthusiast, UCLA professor Ruth Milkman, particularly liked CTW's emphasis on organizational mergers and "a one-union-per industry model that would curb competition among unions and increase the organizing capacity of those that remain." Milkman informed readers of the *New York Times* op-ed page that Stern's "program offers labor's best hope—maybe its only hope—for revitalization."[10]

The battle cry of the CIO in the 1930s and SEIU/CTW today seemed to be much the same in 2008. Appeals to "Organize the Unorganized!" resounded from the walls of San Juan's new convention center, as SEIU delegates approved their union's bold plan to recruit another five hundred thousand workers—in health care, building services, and government jobs—by 2012. To help meet this goal, Stern won delegate backing for an expanded "SEIU Organizing Corps." This recruitment team would include idealistic young people working in a fashion similar to Peace Corps or

Teach for America volunteers. One of SEIU's biggest organizing projects, at that moment, involved forty thousand Puerto Rican teachers, a campaign championed by Dennis Rivera (who was born in Aibonito), longtime leader of SEIU health care workers in New York. Welcoming delegates on the first day of their meeting was Rivera's close friend, the governor of Puerto Rico, Anibal Acevedo Vila. Said Rivera: "We are here to celebrate… the wonderful homeland of a people of great strength and determination to prevail as a nation." He called SEIU's choice of meeting location, on his native island, "an affirmation of the importance of our global alliances."[11]

Delegates were also informed, proudly, that this would be "SEIU's first green convention." Convention planners pledged to "reduce the amount of solid waste generated by the meeting," plus eliminate any "use of toxic materials," as a way of educating those in attendance "about green practices that positively impact climate change." Delegates learned that their decisions could "set the stage for four years of the most historic progress working people have made in generations." With this in mind, they adopted resolutions calling for an end to the war in Iraq, closer ties with workers abroad (like embattled Burmese trade unionists), health care and immigration reform at home, and passage of the Employee Free Choice Act (EFCA).

The Employee Free Choice Act was a set of amendments to strengthen the 1935 statute, the Wagner Act, that did so much to aid CIO organizing by requiring employers to engage in collective bargaining with legally certified unions. According to Stern, enactment of EFCA under a new Democratic administration would lead to membership growth on a New Deal scale. It would enable SEIU to organize more than a million workers a year by demonstrating majority support for unionization through union card signing, rather than National Labor Relations Board (NLRB) elections. SEIU allies in low-wage worker organizing could also expand rapidly using this same "card check" process. Like Stern, convention guest Bruce Raynor, then president of UNITE HERE, painted a rosy picture of a post-EFCA future when he addressed the delegates.

Achieving such ambitious goals required, of course, that Republicans be ousted from the White House and their numbers greatly reduced on Capitol Hill. So, in San Juan, Stern unveiled plans to mobilize a hundred thousand members and spend $85 million on the election of a Democratic president and a "pro-worker majority in Congress" in November. SEIU's preferred candidate, Obama, addressed the delegates, via satellite, and was greeted with rapturous applause. (By election day, SEIU would spend $60.7 million on Obama alone, making "it by far the largest single PAC donor in the campaign."[12]) To free up additional resources for political races in the fall (and new organizing in general), Stern's second in command, SEIU Secretary-Treasurer Anna Burger, won delegate approval for shifting more day-to-day servicing of SEIU members to a nationwide network of call centers. These "Member Resource Centers" would, she assured the convention, handle workplace problems and contract grievances more expeditiously and in a manner befitting a "twenty-first-century union" availing itself of the latest technology.

Before their deliberations ended, delegates reelected Stern, Burger, and six other top officers to new four-year terms. They also backed an administration slate of candidates for sixty-five other executive board slots—adding many new faces to a national leadership body already proclaimed to be "the most diverse in the history of the labor movement."[13] Nevertheless, both inside and outside the convention hall—not to mention back on the mainland—there were signs of trouble ahead in the world of progressive labor. Several major controversies involving SEIU were about to emerge that would eclipse the high hopes and confident predictions of the San Juan convention. The first of these bad portents was the extraordinary security surrounding the meeting itself—circumstances required by a determined group of Puerto Rican teachers who were not fans of SEIU. They haunted its gathering like the ghost of union radicalism past.

Justice for All?

As SEIU delegates and guests were bussed in from their beachfront hotels each day, they entered a "convention center district" that was completely surrounded and cordoned off with metal barricades. Guarding the outer perimeter of this exclusion zone were scores of armed police (some on horseback), supplemented by private security guards. The inner ring consisted of numerous SEIU "sergeants-at-arms," union staffers in yellow vests who were stationed at each door with electronic scanning devices to check delegate ID badges. Despite the big purple and white banner that hung over the main entrance and proclaimed SEIU's commitment to "Justice for All," the huge local police presence made the event look like a locked-down meeting of the World Trade Organization. The security precautions were taken because of Acevedo Vila's visit to the convention and daily picketing by the Federación de Maestros de Puerto Rico (FMPR), an independent union of public school teachers.

The teachers' ongoing struggle with the governor—and SEIU itself—stemmed from a ten-day islandwide work stoppage in March 2008. FMPR members walked out to protest thirty months of stalled contract talks and Acevedo Vila's threat to privatize education (a policy usually opposed by public sector unions like SEIU and the American Federation of Teachers). The FMPR strike was strongly supported by teachers, students, and other community allies, but it was illegal under the island's public sector bargaining law. Even before the teachers stopped work, Acevedo's administration decertified the left-led FMPR—simply for taking a membership strike vote. The union was barred from any future negotiations on behalf of forty thousand Department of Education employees.

SEIU represents public school support staff in Puerto Rico and was thus well positioned to provide the usual forms of strike assistance to a fellow education department union. Instead, as *New York Daily News* columnist Juan Gonzalez reported, Dennis Rivera got the "green light from Acevedo Vila to replace FMPR with a new SEIU-backed group called the Union of Puerto Rican Teachers." As Gonzalez noted, the UPRT is "a subsidiary of the SEIU-affiliated Puerto Rico Teachers Association that has long represented principals and supervisors at island schools." Thus, with help from Rivera's union, school administrators were, in effect, creating a new union for their own subordinates.[14] At the time of the convention, Rivera was working with the government on a plan to hold a representation election in the fall of 2008, so teachers could switch to SEIU. Employee free choice was not part of the plan: SEIU would be the only union option on the ballot. The FMPR would remain legally disqualified from participating.

To many teachers I interviewed, SEIU's collusion with their employer was not just the shameful betrayal of solidarity exposed by Gonzalez. It was a form of North American "labor colonialism," involving a tainted local politician who doubled as a union-busting boss. Just three months before his SEIU convention speech, Acevedo Vila had been indicted on nineteen criminal counts, punishable by twenty years in jail, for tax fraud and campaign finance law violations—legal problems that put his own reelection in jeopardy. (He ended up being voted out of office in November 2008, but was acquitted of all charges the following year.) The governor's appearance at the convention made it a magnet for daily FMPR demonstrations. The high point of those protests involved the use of "mobile picketing" skills well honed during the teachers' militant strike. On Saturday, May 31, 150 FMPR members marched right up to a police barrier. After a few moments of brave scuffling, more than half the group burst through the checkpoint and made a successful dash toward the soaring arches of the convention center several hundred yards away. There were some casualties along the way. Teachers were tackled, clubbed, or arrested by the police.

Finally reaching the front door, the FMPR visitors were quickly contained by another layer of security. With sirens blaring, a convoy of police vehicles with black-tinted windows pulled up and unloaded members of Puerto Rico's notorious riot squad. Heavily muscled, carrying guns, wearing paramilitary garb, and brandishing even bigger batons than the regular cops, these fellows formed a long, menacing line to discourage any fraternization between protesters and delegates. The teachers, largely female and half the size of their picket-line adversaries from the strike four months earlier, simply ignored the "Fuerza de Choque." They quickly formed a chanting, singing, and hand-clapping circle that would have been hard to break up without further public embarrassment for SEIU. Led by FMPR's soft-spoken leader, a forty-nine-year-old science teacher and socialist named Rafael Feliciano, the protestors unfurled a hand-painted banner urging SEIU to "Stop Union Raids." The teachers proceeded over the next several hours to grant multiple media interviews and distribute as many flyers as they could to convention delegates who ignored SEIU staff attempts to herd them back inside the building. Moved by FMPR's courage— and unsettled by the police presence—one reform-minded delegate, Harry Baker from SEIU Local 1021 in San Francisco, even joined the informational picketing. "I just don't like us being here and the teachers over there—with all these cops in between," Baker told me.[15]

A Proliferation of Critics

Back on the mainland, SEIU was, at the same time, facing harsh criticism from a smaller rival on its home turf in the the health care industry. The California Nurses Association (CNA) is a union for RNs heavily staffed by left activists and led by a former graduate student in sociology from the University of California, Santa Barbara (UCSB), Rose Ann DeMoro. It was squaring off with Stern's union in organizing battles in California, Texas, Nevada, Ohio, and other states. In those fights, CNA, like FMPR, argued that SEIU was not any paragon of progressive unionism but, rather, its very opposite. "SEIU has become the union of choice for a growing number of corporate CEOs," the CNA charged. "What SEIU has to offer is a business partnership with a union that 'adds value to their bottom line' while sacrificing public protections, workplace improvements, and a voice for workers on the job."[16] Counterposing its own aggressively marketed brand of "social unionism" to Stern's "new corporate unionism," the 80,000-member CNA clashed with SEIU over health care reform strategy, issues related to patient advocacy, and whether or not RNs are best represented by a "craft" union or a "wall-to-wall" hospital workers' organization like SEIU.

Raising his own concerns about Stern—while keeping a discreet distance from FMPR and CNA—was Sal Rosselli, SEIU's leading internal critic. During the six months prior to the San Juan convention, his 150,000-member local, United Healthcare Workers (UHW), tried to stimulate debate about SEIU organizing and bargaining strategies, and the need for greater internal democracy. UHW began to criticize Stern because of disagreements over national union contract settlements that made too many concessions to management in return for union growth opportunities that UHW believed could be achieved through greater militancy and member involvement. In particular, Rosselli denounced SEIU deals in the nursing home industry that "hinder workers from advocating effectively on behalf of the people they serve, significantly limit the scope of collective bargaining rights, and frustrate workers' ability to participate in negotiations and vote on agreements that affect them."[17] In response, Stern sent Rosselli a letter in March of 2008 laying the groundwork for a headquarters seizure of UHW, long regarded as a model SEIU local. UHW, in turn, launched a highly unusual mobilization of its rank-and-file members and many allies to resist such a hostile takeover. By May 1, 2008, the dispute had attracted sufficient public attention for more than a hundred labor-oriented intellectuals to weigh in. They sent Stern an unusual public letter (reprinted in the *New York Times*), which urged respect for "legitimate and principled dissent." They warned that putting UHW under "trusteeship" would show that "internal democracy is not valued or tolerated within SEIU."[18]

Rosselli came to Puerto Rico as the de facto leader of several hundred opposition delegates, from his own local and others in California. By then, UHW members faced an additional form of SEIU retaliation: possible dismemberment of their local. In San Juan, UHW and its allies in an opposition group called SMART ("SEIU Member Activists for Reform Today") were unable to block Andy Stern's plan to force 65,000 long-term-care workers out of UHW, against their wishes, and into a Los Angeles local headed by a Stern loyalist regarded as more management friendly. While vastly outnumbered by Stern loyalists in San Juan, SEIU reformers did succeed in forcing some discussion of their proposals to create a national strike fund, hold direct elections for top officers, and provide members with a stronger voice in bargaining—before all these ideas were rejected. They also forced a rare contested election for the SEIU leadership by running fifteen candidates against Stern's hand-picked administration slate. A gay political activist from the Bay Area, Rosselli was still contributing "diversity" to the SEIU executive board right up until the convention's last day. In the final session, his independent bid for reelection as vice president was defeated by bloc voting for the entire Stern-Burger team. In an impassioned floor speech, Rosselli applauded the convention efforts of UHW members "and other delegates that stood with us and dared to disagree." He pledged that "we will never give up on the idea that members are the voice of our union."[19]

Like many others in the SEIU leadership, Rosselli was a Vietnam War protester, a former student leader, and community activist. As such, he shared a common political history—or at least the same generational trajectory—with Stern, Burger, and Raynor, Juan Gonzalez and Dennis Rivera, CNA director Rose Ann DeMoro and her inner circle, key militants in the FMPR, and the left-wing academics who signed the May Day letter to Stern opposing a UHW trusteeship. Almost all were veterans of the same social movement ferment that propelled thousands of other sixties radicals into lifelong involvement with labor and, in some cases, top positions in Change to Win or AFL-CIO unions. Yet, forty years later, some of these folks were about to find themselves on opposite sides of new barricades. They would no longer be confronting the cigar-smoking "pale, male, and stale" bureaucrats who ruled the labor movement of the 1970s and '80s. Instead, they would have the Pogo-like experience of looking in the mirror and realizing: "We have met the enemy—and it is us." Or at least some of us.

As 2008 came to a close, Sal Rosselli was unique in this cast of characters. In many ways, he was almost right back where he started, twenty years before in SEIU as a "union dissident" battling an earlier SEIU trusteeship in California. In fact, while his former colleagues at SEIU headquarters were basking in the glow of Obama's election victory and positioning themselves to be even bigger "inside the Beltway" players with the Democrats back in power, Rosselli faced the prospect of being ousted as local president. When this pivotal event finally occurred on January 27, 2009, one hundred other elected leaders of UHW were removed with him, in a Stern-imposed trusteeship resisted by thousands of rank and filers. The UHW takeover quickly triggered the formation of the National Union of

Healthcare Workers (NUHW), a rival organization that would soon be making common cause with John Wilhelm, an aggrieved founding father of CTW.

The New Terrain of Progressive Labor

Andy Stern's use of the union-equivalent of "martial law" against UHW put an unfriendly spotlight on SEIU. As Herman Benson of the Association for Union Democracy noted, SEIU's "rhetorical call for 'justice for all'—for the poor, the immigrants, the minorities, the oppressed—had long enabled Stern to rally round him a troop of social idealists in whose eyes the union has become an extension of civil rights campaigning and community organizing." But now, the trend "toward bureaucratic central control" in SEIU was clearly alienating "a whole other cadre of social idealists who want the labor movement to be a democratic movement of workers."[20] Thanks to its association with popular campaigns like Justice for Janitors, SEIU had also long enjoyed good press coverage. But, as the union's carefully cultivated liberal image began to get hazier—due to its deepening estrangement from members and past political allies in California—there was a related shift in its relationship with the press. The mainstream media, led by prize-winning *Los Angeles Times* reporter Paul Pringle, began delving into a series of embarrassing scandals involving SEIU officials close to Stern.

The worst stain on the union's reputation came from Tyrone Freeman, a Stern protégé, who embezzled more than a million dollars from Local 6434 in Los Angeles. This massive abuse of membership dues money occurred just ten years after the same local (then known as 434B) won the largest single organizing victory in SEIU history, among 75,000 low-paid home health care aides. Freeman's activities, plus related media disclosures about questionable financial dealings by other prominent SEIU officials, led Stern's top media advisor, Matt Witt, to propose an emergency damage control plan. In private email messages later leaked to the *New York Times* and *Wall Street Journal*, Witt warned of a growing public perception that SEIU's rapid growth had come "at the expense of ethics and democracy." (*Daily News* columnist Juan Gonzalez made the same point, less diplomatically, when he described SEIU as "the Roman Empire of the labor movement" because its president "is forever on the prowl for new workers to absorb into his empire and doesn't much care how he does it."[21])

Witt warned Stern that mounting negative publicity might endanger his own future job opportunities outside of SEIU, "whether with the [Obama] administration or a foundation or whatever." A veteran of past union reform efforts in the Mine Workers and Teamsters unions, Witt bluntly reminded the SEIU president that "if you leave while what you built is steadily eroding, the blame will fall on you, not your successor." The solution, proposed by Witt, involved a public act of contrition. In the fall of 2008, SEIU announced the creation of a "high-level ethics commission." According to Stern, this distinguished panel of outsiders would help him "place this union at the leading edge of the reform effort in the labor movement."[22] Unfortunately for SEIU, this PR effort was soon overshadowed by its disastrous intervention in the messy divorce between the garment workers and hotel employees, two unions that merged prior to becoming cofounders of CTW. By March 2009, Stern's poaching of UNITE HERE members had become so brazen that hotel workers leader John Wilhelm announced he was considering a return to the AFL-CIO.

SEIU's absorption of the "Workers United" faction of UNITE HERE, led by Bruce Raynor, unleashed a whole new round of labor civil warfare, adding hotels, casinos, and food service contractors to the list of battlefields that previously included Puerto Rican public schools and U.S. health care. SEIU's continuing repression of UHW members, its abandonment of several campus-based organizing campaigns (which left workers and students in the lurch), and published reports of "sweetheart contracts" covering cafeteria workers nationwide eroded its standing with solidarity groups like United Students Against Sweatshops (USAS).[23] Wilhelm, a former member of Students for a Democratic Society (SDS) at Yale and once a close ally of Stern, now joined Sal Rosselli as a major adversary. "Stern's messianic mindset has led him to seek membership growth by conquest," Wilhelm declared. "His undemocratic practices threaten the entire labor movement." UNITE HERE, along with CNA, poured money into the NUHW, with Wilhelm becoming a particularly strong backer of the new health care union. Only after Stern suddenly retired from office in 2010 was the huge legal and financial mess created by his organizational cannibalism finally resolved. It made CTW look a lot less like "labor's best hope" for anything.

Missing the Obama Moment

Labor's costly and distracting civil wars occurred at a very inopportune time—a moment supposedly pregnant with political possibilities. With Obama in the White House and big Democratic majorities in Congress, unions were looking forward to much-needed and long-overdue legislative gains. Among their key objectives were labor law reform, national health care, new rights for immigrants, modification of job-killing free trade deals, and emergency assistance for the millions of workers battered by the worst economic downturn since the Great Depression. Even before Obama took office in January 2009, union campaigning for workers' rights (in the form of EFCA) triggered a fierce business counter-campaign. Yet it also generated a rare public debate about the pros and cons of collective bargaining. This heated argument ranged far and wide, from talk radio to the halls of Congress, from newspaper op-ed pages to local union meetings, from labor marches and rallies to the multimillion-dollar corporate advertising campaign against the bill. A key assumption of this book— namely, that strong democratic unions are an essential feature of a healthy economy and just society—was much contested by EFCA foes, in their ultimately successful bid to maintain the legal status quo. EFCA backers argued, to no avail, that private sector labor law reform would help boost consumer purchasing power and raise living standards, just as the National Labor Relations Act did (in combination with labor's own mass organizing) during the New Deal.

That should be an argument that resonates widely now, since the vast majority of Americans go to work every day bereft of even the most basic due process protections. While they are covered by many state and federal antidiscrimination laws—which apply to union and nonunion workplaces alike—these are far harder to enforce in the absence of bargaining rights and union representation. Workers have no power to negotiate with their employers about the avalanche of recession-related pay cuts, freezes, furloughs, pension and 401(k) plan changes, and widespread reductions in paid time off. Yet organized labor suffers, at the same time, from a perceived inability to deliver anything substantially different for the two hours pay per month (or in some unions, like SEIU, much more than that) they collect in dues. In the last half of the last century, unions were widely viewed as an effective vehicle for securing material benefits and greater justice on the job. In America today, collective bargaining, as an institution, has acquired the doomed aura of "legacy benefits"—those burdensome relics of the past, like pensions, job security, and seniority rights—that older corporations and cash-strapped public employers are doing their best to shed. As the fiercely anti-union (and corporate-backed) Center for Union Facts repeats like a sacred mantra: "Labor union membership is an outdated concept for most working Americans. It is a relic of Depression-era labor-management relations."[24]

Clearly, globalization, corporate restructuring, deregulation or privatization, and myriad forms of outsourcing have created a new workplace terrain distinctly unfavorable to workers, here and abroad. In response, a few labor organizations, like SEIU, have tried to rethink their organizing and bargaining strategies, and how they're structured, nationally and internationally. However, as we see later in *Civil Wars*, Andy Stern essentially concluded, if you can't beat them, join them—corporations, that is. In the apt description of a leading Democratic Party consultant, Stern pursued a "strategy of adaptive cooperation."[25] At the same time that SEIU was battling other unions, left and right (but mainly to its left), Stern was searching for new business "partners." He invited Howard Schultz, the union-busting founder of Starbucks, to kick around ideas with the SEIU executive board.[26] He did joint health care lobbying with Lee Scott, the CEO of Wal-Mart and archenemy of the United Food and Commercial Workers (a fellow CTW union that didn't like this dalliance with their least favorite boss one bit).[27] He flitted from foundation board meetings, with billionaires like Eli Broad and George Soros, to brainstorming at the Aspen

Institute and hobknobbing in Davos. He became so enamored with a particular drug company during his last few years as SEIU president that he joined its board of directors shortly after leaving the union.

As this book went to press, top labor officials were understandably worried about what policy recommendations Stern might endorse, on labor's behalf, as its sole representative on President Obama's "deficit reduction" commission. In the past, Stern's bonding with right-wing politicians, like commission cochair Alan Simpson, has produced inappropriate praise for bitter enemies of labor. In *A Country That Works*, the SEIU president lauded the "smart and contemplative demeanor" of a noted "history scholar" named Newt Gingrich. After meeting and talking with Newt, Stern reported that, on matters related to "the change-making process" in America, "Gingrich's thinking reinforced much of my own." This is the same former Republican House speaker who now describes the White House as a "secular socialist machine" posing "as great a threat to America as Nazi Germany or the Soviet Union once did."[28]

Critiques of SEIU can easily focus on its protean former president. But the left (or at least that part of it so inclined) doesn't have Andy to kick around anymore. He has moved on, is "pursuing other projects," as they say in Hollywood, and has handed the gavel to Mary Kay Henry, long on the headquarters career track for "senior managers." Henry is, we're told, a kinder, gentler CEO of SEIU, Inc. Her official bio trumpets her pathbreaking role in "hospital-employer partnerships" and formation of the union's "Lavender Caucus." A good friend and former associate describes her as a "Catholic warrior for women's rights and gay and lesbian rights" who has "never even threatened to leave the church."[29] For thirty years, she has displayed similar loyalty and devotion to the hierarchy of SEIU. What its members remain saddled with—and what the breakaway NUHW resisted in California health care—is a deeply flawed, increasingly autocratic institution that doesn't deliver as advertised, no matter who is in charge.

The Stern/SEIU model (with some honorable local union exceptions) abhors rank-and-file initiative, shop floor militancy, and democratic decision making by workers themselves. In the name of "building power *for* workers," it embraces labor-management cooperation (from a position of weakness), bureaucratic consolidation, and top-down control. When this model faces internal criticism, members are told they must all speak with "one voice." To "win for workers," SEIU must pursue "justice for all" and can't afford to dwell on the workplace issues or concerns of "just us"— that is, existing members—because those just get in the way of more important big-picture goals. Just as large corporations pay lip service to "shareholder democracy" by having a single annual meeting and related proxy voting, SEIU observes the forms and conventions of union elections. But it does so in a context that renders workers about as powerless to change their local union leaders or policies as any small shareholder in a Fortune 500 company. As a result, SEIU often "settles short" in areas where it clearly has the potential to accomplish far more, for its own members and other workers.[30] But that would require a very different, more engaged relationship between the leadership and the led—and more leaders coming out of the ranks instead of just the union staff.

Our Generation: Then and Now

Like many others we meet in this book, I'm part of a generational cohort that went into unions to change the balance of power between labor and capital by first changing power relationships within unions themselves. In my own career as a college-educated, sixties-inspired "union troublemaker," I initially worked with reform-minded members of unions representing coal miners, steel workers, and teamsters. Then, I spent twenty-seven years as a Boston-based staffer for the Communications Workers of America (CWA). In 2007, I finished up that role as an assistant to the vice president in charge of CWA's largest district.[31] During my three decades as an organizer and international rep in New York, New Jersey, and New England, I handled a lot of contract grievances, helped workers deal with their employers in difficult bargaining and strike situations, trained shop stewards and local officers, and devoted much time to recruiting new members in both the private and public sector. I was part of an informal network of like-minded activists around the country who aided CWA's growth and diversification. Collective efforts to "engage rank-and-file workers in the project of labor revitalization" and create a culture of "membership mobilization" finally led, in 2005, to the long-overdue election of our friend Larry Cohen as the union's new national president.[32] Now on the high side of sixty himself, Cohen was shaped, in part, by his own campus activism in the 1960s and later work in a Pennsylvania psychiatric hospital and other human services jobs. Like Stern, Raynor, and Wilhelm, Cohen was "part of the new generation of progressive leaders" who rose to the top in the 1990s (or later) based on their dynamic role as organizing directors in their respective organizations.[33]

While serving on the CWA national staff, I also wrote many articles, book reviews, essays, and op-ed pieces about workplace trends, labor politics and culture, organizing and bargaining, strikes, and union democracy struggles. This freelance work appeared in major metropolitan dailies, liberal and left-wing magazines, official or unofficial labor publications, academic journals, and, as chapters, in five or six edited collections. In mid-2009, some of my labor-related essays/reviews were republished by Monthly Review Press in a book called *Embedded with Organized Labor*.[34] Beginning in the mid-1990s, some of my extracurricular scribbling began to address controversies related to union revitalization. By then, the role of former student radicals in labor was already much celebrated by their generational peers in academic circles. There seemed to be a glib assumption that any solid sixties political resume guaranteed laudatory results in subsequent labor work.

One typical anthology on organizing identified the "most innovative" architects of "new labor" as "activists from the 1960s and 1970s generation who cut their teeth in the New Left, the anti-Vietnam War movement, civil rights and the women's movement." Two leading sociologists welcomed this "influx of outsiders" who believed that "the decline of labor's power" gave them a "mandate to change."[35] In the 1980s and 1990s, some of these activists played "major roles in the organizing drives that laid the groundwork" for the emergence of John Sweeney as an AFL-CIO reformer.[36] The flurry of new programs launched by the AFL-CIO after Sweeney became president reinforced the perception that the successful restructuring of labor organizations tends to be "orchestrated from the top, contrary to the rather romantic view that only the rank-and-file can be the fount of democratic change."[37] Some academic supporters of labor—influenced by the success of SEIU—even embraced the idea that internal democracy is dispensable. In a period of labor movement crisis and declining membership, SEIU strategists like Stephen Lerner have argued that rebuilding "density" is far more important than union democratization. They have acted as if local union autonomy—along with membership control over locals—is a major impediment to recovering "union market share" and, therefore, must be swept away by any means necessary.

As both a union organizer and a longtime supporter of rank-and-file movements like Teamsters for a Democratic Union (TDU), I didn't agree that union strength and growth are incompatible with workers having a voice in their own organizations. I became increasingly concerned that some progressive trade unionists were not only abandoning "participatory democracy," a still-worthwhile sixties notion, they were also creating union structures that would disenfranchise workers to a greater degree than "old guard" unions do. As TDU national organizer Ken Paff told the *Los Angeles Times* in regard to SEIU: "When your union is less democratic than the Teamsters, you have to look in the mirror and ask, 'What happened?'"[38]

So, in various articles, I began to question why membership empowerment was so often missing from otherwise praiseworthy attempts at union renewal, like SEIU's Justice for Janitors campaigns. Why did the AFL-CIO Organizing Institute—much dominated, in its heyday, by SEIU, UNITE, and HERE—fail to promote "member-based organizing" instead of trying to turn "ex-college students into transient, disposable mobile organizers" with "little connection to the internal life of the institutions they serve"?[39] If our goal was to help "local unions re-invent themselves as membership organizations," why was SEIU creating so many "staff-dominated multi-state 'megalocals'" as part of a consolidation drive that reinforced "the dominant tendency of unions to act like insurance plans, bureaucratic and staff-run, dispensing services for a fee"? Was it really healthy to function like "public interest lobbying groups who relate to their 'dues payers' largely through direct mail, phone solicitation, or door-to-door canvassing"? Unions are, after all, supposed to be workplace organizations, run by and for workers, not controlled by lawyers, lobbyists, and professional administrators.[40]

Some Labor History Lessons

My disquiet with some progressive union trends was not the product of "romantic views" about union democracy. Nor did it reflect a knee-jerk preference for "bottom-up change," since I had helped introduce a few changes from "the top" at CWA. I just fervently believed that past struggles for democracy and reform, in unions like the United Mine Workers (UMW) and Teamsters, were still relevant today. When autocratic presidents of the UMW removed elected local and district leaders in the fifties and sixties—and appointed their successors—these open-ended trusteeships had bad consequences for coal miners.[41] Contract negotiations were conducted in secret. Working conditions deteriorated, while sweetheart deals with mine owners proliferated. Problems like black lung—a widespread occupational hazard—were downplayed by the UMW itself. There was little new organizing because the union's luster had dimmed in many coalfield communities. The lack of effective membership control over the UMW led to a dark descent into the worst sort of union racketeering and even murder (of an opposition candidate and his family).[42]

That same story was writ large in the Teamsters. Prior to 1991, when TDU-backed Ron Carey became president in the biggest reform victory since the triumph of Miners for Democracy in 1972, the Teamster bureaucracy was deeply calcified and corrupt. Teamster officials were often unresponsive, incompetent, and even more prone to violence and intimidation than their counterparts in the UMW. Working members paid the heaviest price for this organizational decay—since it was they, not any big employers, who were being muscled by the union leadership and staff. In the seventies, aided by deregulation, trucking employers launched an offensive that undermined job safety and health standards, increased employment insecurity, eroded pension and medical benefits, led to stagnant pay, and drew the union into debilitating labor-management cooperation schemes.

When rank-and-filers organized against these threats, they had to challenge union practices and policies, not just management behavior, in order to make the International Brotherhood of Teamsters (IBT) a more effective sword and shield. The UMW reformers and Teamster dissidents I met during this period learned the hard way that workers who lose their voice in the union don't have one at work for very long. None would have agreed with Andy Stern's later assertion that "it's hard to make the argument that unions with direct elections better represent their members."[43] Among the gains of rank-and-file struggle, in the UMW and IBT, were new structures and voting procedures that enabled members to hold national and local leaders more accountable. These changes invariably improved the quality of representation and, under some industry circumstances, also increased the union's appeal to nonunion workers.

When Andy Stern was first elected SEIU president in 1996, he confronted an "old guard" that included Teamster-types like Gus Bevona in New York City. To his credit, Stern properly used the trusteeship powers of his office to replace these bloated crooks and grifters.[44] Unfortunately, he didn't stop there—or return locals that were put under trusteeship to the members afterward. Instead, he kept taking over more locals for reasons that had nothing to do with corruption and couldn't even be justified in the name of more efficient organizing. He installed a "new class" of local union managers, drawn from his college-educated staff, who were personally loyal to him and lacked workplace roots (and sometimes even union experience). "While liberal in their politics and sometimes more diverse than the leaders they replaced, these former staffers lack what should be one of the key qualifications of leadership in a workers' organization—namely, experience as a working member in the local union they lead."[45] In 2004, some of these SEIU officials were already taking advantage of "the absence of financial accountability and transparency" that went along with being appointed rather than elected. Writing further on this topic, I warned that Stern's abuse of trusteeship powers would come back to haunt the union, via "corruption scandals that will erupt, sooner or later." I also predicted greater membership opposition to "SEIU's top-down, technocratic, transformation-by-trusteeship strategy."[46]

In light of subsequent developments, my 2004 forecast turned out to be pretty accurate. But it was not welcome by the AFL-CIO's most prominent in-house critic. In early 2005, SEIU president Stern wrote to CWA president Morton Bahr, his executive council colleague, with the accusation that I had unfairly assailed "SEIU, our programs and our leaders" in many different "printed and digital communications." Stern characterized my freelance writing as a "full-time campaign against SEIU"—even though it was confined, by the demands of my day job, to late nights and weekends. Stern demanded to know whether the author of so many objectionable articles was "speaking for himself or for CWA?" If the latter was the case, Stern was holding CWA responsible for "the misrepresentations, distorted characterizations, and personal attacks" published under my byline in the *Boston Globe*, *New Labor Forum*, *Working USA*, *Labor Notes*, and other journals. Fortunately for my own job security, Stern's missive—not the first such complaint CWA had received over the years—arrived just as Andy was threatening to set up a rival labor federation. Bahr was strongly opposed to that split. So, this time, scant notice was paid because the irate letter-writer was about to leave the AFL-CIO.

Having weathered Andy's fan mail (and "final warnings" from Morty on other occasions), I finally became pension eligible two years later. This freed me up for a real full-time campaign of research and writing about labor issues. My initial plan was to explore, through interviews, what my own New Left generational cohort set out to achieve in unions, what we have and haven't accomplished, and what useful lessons might be derived from this collective experience by younger activists more recently arrived in the "house of labor." Among the veteran organizers I interviewed were those whose original "turn to the working class" in the seventies involved getting blue-collar jobs in trucking, mining, steel-making, and manufacturing (where a hardy few survivors of deindustrialization remain to this day). Other interviewees had gone into white-collar fields like health care, education, or social work, where they were able to aid public and service sector union growth. Most people whose stories I collected had started out as rank-and-filers, often as part of a left-wing group. Now, they were either elected local leaders or appointed union organizers, contract negotiators, researchers, educators, lobbyists, or communications specialists.

The Book and Its Contents

Many of my most colorful interview subjects proved to be connected, in one way or another, to labor's emerging civil wars. That story seemed to be a more urgent one, in need of firsthand reporting, so the earlier left-labor history project was set aside and remains a work in progress. I was drawn to scenes of current conflict because so many labor-oriented intellectuals, students, community activists, and public officials were being asked to get involved in matters traditionally regarded as "internal" to the labor movement. As someone with past experience in union democracy struggles—who had written extensively about the challenge and complexities of Teamster reform—I became particularly intrigued by the emergence of SEIU reform efforts that were anchored, for a time, by a local union (UHW) with enormous resources. I had worked for years on "bargaining to organize" campaigns in the telecom industry so I was no stranger to the debate, raging in SEIU and UNITE HERE, about "contract standards" versus "union growth." I had seen quid pro quos involving card check/neutrality become a source of internal tension within CWA. One public sector campaign I assisted in New Jersey was a virtual knockoff of the "political organizing" responsible for so much SEIU growth. As a union spokesperson in many strikes and organizing campaigns, I was also an admirer of SEIU's exceptional media savvy, reflected most often in the successful positioning of Andy Stern as a "visionary labor figure" in the minds of many editors, reporters, and columnists.[47] While I didn't much like the man or his vision, it was hard not to be impressed by his marketing success. As *Civil Wars* shows, it came with a hefty price tag and a huge downside for workers.

Finally, in 2008, I had a family member actually working for SEIU—or rather the only SEIU local in America where her last name wasn't an obstacle to employment! My older daughter Alex was a former member of the Student Labor Action Coalition (SLAC) at Wesleyan University in Connecticut. As an undergraduate, she had worked, in prototypical fashion, with both SEIU-represented janitors and Wesleyan cafeteria workers who belong to UNITE HERE. (With Alex translating for me, we even collaborated on several unofficial steward-training sessions for Wesleyan janitors, who felt much abandoned by their New York City–based Local 32BJ.) Relocating to California after graduation and a six-month tour of social justice duty in El Salvador, Alex ended up as a UHW representative for nursing home workers in San Francisco, on the front lines of their anti-trusteeship struggle. By early 2009, Alex was working as a volunteer organizer for NUHW. Both before and after she was fired by SEIU, she served as an invaluable window into the world of young labor organizers today. Like the sixties-inspired activists who preceded them, these young men and women are still trying to narrow the gap between the real and the ideal in organized labor. That task didn't get any easier amid the strife described herein, which produced no shortage of personal disillusionment and burnout.

In chapter 1, *Civil Wars* explores why and how sixties radicals who ended up in SEIU (or among its friends, foes, and critics) initially came to embrace the cause of labor, after being "politicized" in struggles against war, racism, and the oppression of women. Most unions didn't roll out the red carpet for former student activists, as was the case several decades later. Those that were more welcoming—like the United Farm Workers (UFW), SEIU, and its now affiliated New York City hospital workers union, District 1199—soon got the benefit of much youthful energy, political idealism, and community-based organizing. In SEIU, some newcomers also got a taste of future problems.

Chapter 2, "Taking the High Road to Growth?" describes the challenges facing unions as they struggled, throughout the eighties and nineties, to find ways to neutralize management interference with organizing drives in health care and other industries. It examines the development of labor campaigns to "bypass" the National Labor Relations Board and secure union recognition based on "card check" or "free and fair" election deals. I also describe the downside of "organizing rights" agreements that add more dues-paying members but sacrifice the interests of existing members and limit the ability of new ones to make gains after they've won union representation. The chapter concludes with a case study of "high road" unionism turning into collusion with a union-busting employer.

Chapter 3 reports on the scramble to organize home-based workers—the biggest source of labor movement growth in recent years. The sometimes dicey political deal making necessary to win union recognition for workers doing publicly funded home health care and child care spawned intense competition, followed by forced cooperation in some states. Making sure these new bargaining units are more than just a dues-collection device requires significant investment in real organization-building. Nontraditional workplaces don't lend themselves to traditional forms of collective action, so unions have been forced to come up with something different. In Fresno County, California, competing visions of home care worker unionism clashed sharply in 2009 in a $10 million slugfest that prefigured a costlier battle ahead at Kaiser.

Chapter 4 explores the brave new world of call center servicing. SEIU's centralization and modernization seeks to create a "21st Century unionism" that is "less focused on individual grievances, more focused on industry needs."[48] Instead of traditional workplace structures like steward councils, SEIU locals are now using "Member Resource Centers" (MRCs) to handle workplace problems and complaints so more staff resources can be devoted to politics and organizing. In this section, we visit the MRC operated by SEIU Local 1 in Chicago, and hear from its proponents. The chapter also recounts the membership backlash against call center use in locals where MRC servicing has become such a hot political issue that incumbent officers have been ousted over it.

Chapter 5 asks "Who Rules SEIU" and then profiles the union's international executive board, a group that is quite diverse except in one respect: few workers need apply. To a greater degree than in most other unions, the majority of SEIU board members are completely beholden to the union's top officers. As such, they can't easily question leadership decisions or prevent costly organizational mistakes—of the sort Andy Stern made with increasing frequency late in his reign. The union's culture of political conformity and fear of political retaliation from the top also infects local union life. Long applauded as labor's "best and brightest," SEIU's cadre of installed local union leaders showed signs of growing dysfunction in 2008–10, as reported herein.

Chapter 6, "The Mother of All Trusteeships," chronicles the rank-and-file revolt that developed among California's health care workers, and SEIU's elaborate but not unprecedented countermeasures against it. Andy Stern's retaliatory takeover of UHW spawned NUHW and a protracted insurgency not fully anticipated by either side. Its total cost now runs to many tens of millions of dollars. This section describes how the new health care union emerged as a dogged but underfunded rival of SEIU, even as the California Nurses Association, an initial NUHW benefactor, suddenly changed course, declared a truce with Stern, and fell silent as a fellow critic of his union.

Chapter 7 examines SEIU's new relationship with its one-time friend and ally, UNITE HERE. Its president, John Wilhelm, broke with Andy Stern in 2009, left the Change to Win coalition his union helped to form just four years earlier, and returned to the AFL-CIO. During UNITE HERE's competition with Workers United—the membership faction that Bruce Raynor led into SEIU—Wilhelm began to articulate his own scathing critique of SEIU organizational practices and influence on the labor movement. Just one-tenth the size of SEIU, Wilhelm's union defended its turf successfully while becoming a major funder of NUHW. There were, however, a few casualties along the way, in the form of young organizers with conscientious objections to UNITE HERE's methods.

Chapter 8 describes the "progressive quandary" among union-oriented intellectuals about how to relate to labor's civil wars. For several decades, SEIU has been wooing students, professors, labor educators, and journalists. As the landscape of progressive labor shifted dramatically and a less appealing side of SEIU emerged, its relationships with allies of all types became increasingly strained and harder to maintain. Left/liberal intellectuals were forced to reexamine their views and, in some cases, take difficult new stances on inter- and intra-union disputes. Others, influenced by SEIU's considerable largesse, continued to advocate on its behalf, while sometimes failing to disclose which side they were on (financially speaking).

In chapter 9, I recount SEIU's important Washington role in the political tug-of-war over health care and labor law reform. In 2009–10, SEIU used its strategic industry position, access to the White House, and employer partnerships to help keep single-payer health insurance "off the table," as a serious policy option, while other sixties-inspired labor activists, who favored "Medicare for All," actively resisted that effort. The result was legislation, finally enacted in March 2010, which leaves many low-wage members of SEIU, plus millions of other union members, still trapped in a costly, inefficient, and crumbling system of job-based private insurance coverage. Chapter 9 also shows how this high-profile political battle proved fatal to labor's hopes for passage of the Employee Free Choice Act. Thanks to the toxic entanglement of EFCA and "Obamacare," labor's only consolation prize from the Democrats (for the third time in the last thirty-five years) is a more "union-friendly" NLRB, the same agency that dragged its feet interminably when thousands of California workers wanted to switch from SEIU to NUHW.

Chapter 10, "*Labor Day: The Sequel*," opens with Andy Stern's resignation from the union he led for fourteen years. His sudden departure sparked a contested leadership contest—but one only involving the top-level officials profiled in chapter 5. Mary Kay Henry's selection as Stern's successor raised hopes, in some quarters, that a course correction was under way at SEIU. Henry did settle up with UNITE HERE, if only to curtail its support for NUHW. But, as I report, thousands of workers at Kaiser saw more continuity than change as Henry simultaneously spent millions of dollars and unleashed hundreds of staffers to block any exodus from SEIU. That "David versus Goliath" contest, in October 2010, was the biggest and most costly engagement in labor's civil wars so far.

Civil Wars concludes with a brief summary of lessons to be learned from all this. It assesses where the failure of labor law reform leaves the leading practitioners of "bargaining or organize" who fell out among themselves in 2008–10. The conclusion argues for a single standard regarding "employee free choice" because, as an exercise of workplace rights, changing unions is no different than forming or joining one in the first place. Nowhere is it decreed that once workers have made their initial unionization decision, they are condemned to remain captive members of the same labor organization forever. The book also ends with a call for more "bottom-up"—and less "top-down"—methods of building a "new workers movement," whether one emerges from the ashes of recent conflagrations or conflicts yet to come.

A Note on "Participatory Labor Journalism"

Let me add a brief comment about journalistic objectivity. As C. Wright Mills once said, "I try to be objective but I don't claim to be impartial." For more than thirty-five years, I've been writing about organizing, strikes, union reform struggles, and labor strategy debates that I've often played a role in. As explained in a previous book, my "embedded" condition as a labor movement participant/observer means that I'm neither a "neutral" academic researcher nor a typical labor journalist (not that there are many of those left anymore). In addition to being a committed trade unionist, I support three different socialist groups, and always back union democracy causes. So I obviously have lots of minority opinions, which I've rarely been shy about expressing, in print or in person. In the period covered by *Civil Wars*, I helped organize opposition to the UHW trusteeship and, afterward, became a solidarity campaigner for NUHW. Nevertheless, as noted in the preface, I have always tried to talk to a wide range of people, in and around SEIU, who hold divergent views about its strengths and weaknesses, good points and bad.

Not surprisingly, some interviewees have changed their views in recent years. For example, when I first started writing about his union, an officer of SEIU Local 509, who lives nearby, reacted quite defensively—out of institutional loyalty and mounting exasperation with me. Reacting to some recently published provocation, he blurted out one day: "Boy, you must really hate SEIU!" Over time, his personal annoyance began to recede, in direct correlation to his growing concern about the fate of his own local union, whose near death experience is recounted in chapter 5. My

SEIU neighbor's remark was not without precedent, however. It echoed complaints sometimes heard when I was writing about the Teamsters for the *Nation*, the *Progressive*, *Working In These Times*, and other publications. In the IBT—particularly at union headquarters, before and after the reform presidency of Ron Carey—my reports on racketeering, corruption, and undemocratic practices were regularly denounced as "anti-Teamster." All I could ever say in response was "How can I be anti-Teamster? Some of my best friends are Teamsters!" Clearly, commentary that's critical of the history, politics, structure, or leadership of any national union— whether SEIU or the IBT—shouldn't be mistaken for a blanket condemnation of the institution. My reporting on the Teamsters was rooted in many years of supporting embattled rank-and-filers and reform-minded locals. Their goal was to make the IBT less corrupt, more democratic, and, thus, stronger in its dealings with management. Thanks to the efforts of TDU and Carey, Teamsters were able to make considerable progress on many fronts in the 1990s. Despite perennial accusations to the contrary, no outside critics aligned with TDU—or the group itself—have ever undermined any legitimate activity of the IBT or publicized its failings for any anti-union purpose. The same is true of my writing about SEIU.

I should note that top SEIU functionaries do not agree. One sign of their disapproval was the union's refusal to issue me press credentials so I could cover its 2008 convention. Several publications had asked me to write about that gathering in San Juan, including *Working USA*, *Counter-Punch*, and *Union Democracy Review* (*UDR*), newsletter of the Association for Union Democracy. SEIU had no problem admitting representatives of the *Wall Street Journal*, Associated Press, Bureau of National Affairs, the Huffington Post, and even *Labor Notes*, a monthly publication then-bristling with pro-UHW coverage and criticism of Stern. When *UDR* editor Herman Benson spoke with SEIU strategic affairs director Michelle Ringuette about her refusal to credential me, she assured Benson that even he was welcome to fly down to Puerto Rico and attend the convention, but I was beyond the pale. According to Ringuette (as reported by Benson), I was "biased," "not really a journalist," an "enemy of SEIU," and (more accurately) had "helped get a whole group of academics to sign a letter to President Stern about UHW."

My Michael Moore Moment

Not the least deterred by this rebuff, I made my way to San Juan anyway. I checked into a hotel full of friendly and chatty purple-clad convention-goers. Along with two colleagues from Labor Notes—its director Mark Brenner and University of Massachusetts professor Stephanie Luce—I boarded a union-chartered shuttle bus for the trip from Condado Beach to the heavily policed and barricaded convention center zone, where a number of preconvention sessions were being held. When we got off the bus, Mark went in to get his credentials. I waited with Stephanie outside the main entrance to the convention center, using this opportunity to talk to various SEIU local delegates and hailing other dignitaries that I knew from a distance (including SEIU general counsel Judy Scott and her law partner Ed James). Among the people we ran into was Maya Morris, a hospital worker from California and an elected board member of UHW, who was soon to be a leader of the reform forces on the convention floor when the meeting officially opened a day later.

As we were chatting with Maya, who should come striding out of the closely guarded front door but President Stern himself, with a young aide trailing in his wake. Ever the genial host (and good politician), Andy stopped to shake hands and say hello to everyone in our little group, including me, before continuing on his way. A few minutes later, one of the taller sergeant-at-arms checking credentials at the door came over as well. I immediately sensed that I was about to have my own *Roger and Me* moment, SEIU-style. With the same awkward bearing as the corporate lobby rent-a-cops so familiar to Michael Moore movie fans, this bearded SEIU staffer asked if I was Steve Early. My identity confirmed, he told me that I had to leave immediately and asked how I had gained access to the premises in the first place. I was deliberately vague about the ease of getting on a shuttle bus for delegates, hoping to use that method again. But I did acknowledge not having press credentials, like the ones Mark was now wearing, which granted him (but not me) access to the convention center. Why, I asked, should there be an objection to my just hanging around outside where I could talk to SEIU members who were coming and going, sitting in the sun, having a smoke or a cup of coffee during breaks in their busy meeting schedule?

The problem, I learned, was this: SEIU had rented the whole convention center zone, not just the hall itself. According to this particular sergeant-at-arms, I was not welcome anywhere inside the outer perimeter, which was a good quarter of a mile from where we stood while discussing this matter. I was being expelled to a place you couldn't even see—to a faraway intersection where the FMPR was camped out (but not for long). Just as our discussion reached the point of impasse, I noticed that Andy was returning from wherever he had been outside the hall and was walking right past us again, headed back toward the front door. I decided to appeal directly to the international president. "Hey Andy," I shouted, as he strode briskly by. "Your sergeant-at-arms is trying to throw me out. Is there anything we can do about that?" This time, Stern didn't stop to exchange pleasantries. Without even looking back, he merely shrugged and said, "I'm not in charge." A second later, with the same dutiful aide trailing him, Stern was in the building and out of sight. However, for the next five days, until the SEIU convention was over and the last police barricade taken down, Andy Stern was definitely the man "in charge." But in charge of what? And headed where? And leaving behind what kind of legacy for SEIU members? All are questions explored in the rest of this book.

Chapter 1

The Quest for Union Renewal

"When the civil rights, anti-war and women's movements were born, most unions (with some notable exceptions) didn't embrace, support, or, in the end, grow with them. Unions missed an incredible opportunity to support progressive change."
—Stephen Lerner, SEIU organizer and IEB member, July 15, 2008

When Andy Stern, Anna Burger, Bruce Raynor, Dennis Rivera, Sal Rosselli, and John Wilhem first embraced the cause of labor, it was to do battle with corporate bosses. They wanted to make unions stronger as a voice for all working people, not fight with each other, because organized labor was already on the skids. Four decades ago, when unions still represented nearly a quarter of the U.S. workforce, the AFL-CIO was cautious, complacent, and insular. The great industrial union upsurge of the 1930s was already a distant memory, the subject of labor history celebrations and commemorations. It no longer animated the thinking of most union leaders, either veterans of that era or their younger organizational successors. Only among labor radicals, recently arrived from campus and the community, was there any sense of urgency about reversing the steady decline in union density that began in the early 1950s, when the labor movement reached its postwar membership peak of about 35 percent. Public sector union agitation—and accompanying changes in state and federal labor law covering teachers and other government employees—provided an infusion of new blood in the late 1960s and '70s. But, as traditional bastions of union strength like mining, manufacturing, transportation, utilities, and even construction were all eroded, the overall level of unionization continued to fall, year by year, until it was just 12.3 percent in 2009.[1]

In early 2010, as private sector labor law reform efforts failed for the third time in thirty-five years, the Bureau of Labor Statistics reported a 10 percent loss of private sector union membership during the previous year—Barack Obama's first in office. This was the largest single year decline in more than a quarter century and reflected huge union job losses in manufacturing and construction. The UAW (United Auto Workers), USWA (United Steel Workers of America), IAM (International Association of Machinists), and CWA lost nearly two hundred thousand members, with my alma mater, CWA, accounting for about 10 percent of that number due to telecom industry downsizing. The five more fortunate AFL-CIO affiliates with the greatest net growth in 2009 were all, like SEIU, heavily involved in the public sector. For the first time in U.S. history, government-employees represented by unions (7.9 million) outnumbered dues payers in private industry (7.4 million).[2] Adding to labor's challenges, a Pew Research Center poll reported a drop in union favorability ratings that reflected labor's waning workplace clout and community influence. Surveying a sample of 1,383 adults reached by phone in early February 2010, Pew found that only 41 percent of respondents had a favorable opinion of unions, while 42 percent expressed an unfavorable view. Just three years earlier, the same pollster claimed that 58 percent of those polled had a positive view of unions and only 31 percent had a negative impression. This reported decline in public standing was consistent with the trend discovered in earlier Pew studies of what proportion of the population thinks unions are essential for worker protection. In 2003, 74 percent of those polled still believed that unions were essential for that purpose. In 2007, that was down to 68 percent. And, by April 2009, only 61 percent agreed with the state-ment "labor unions are necessary to protect the working person."[3]

Thirty or forty years ago, this was not where most sixties-inspired labor activists hoped or expected unions would be today, membership-wise or in public opinion polls. Organizers from the civil rights, antiwar, and women's movements detested the political conservatism of labor's old guard, but they gravitated toward grassroots labor activity anyway. Their union solidarity work was largely ignored by the media, which preferred to focus instead on a few high-profile clashes between "hard hats and hip-pies" over the Vietnam war.[4] Even the "Port Huron Statement"(PHS), the famous founding document of Students for a Democratic Society (SDS), was quite worker friendly.[5] The PHS politely thanked union members for "making modern America a decent place in which to live" before chiding their leaders for failing to project a broader political agenda and for "losing much of the idealism that once made labor a driving movement in the 1930's." Trade unionism was already in a state of "profound crisis" in 1962, according to SDS. It faced two possible scenarios:

> Either labor continues to decline or it must re-constitute itself as a mass political force demanding not only that society recognize its rights to organize but also a program going beyond desired labor leg-islation and welfare improvements. Necessarily this latter role will re-quire rank-and-file involvement...greater autonomy and power for political coalitions of the various trade unions in local areas.[6]

Even where unions still had muscle, SDS found the "labor bureau-cracy" to be "cynical toward, or even afraid of, rank-and-file involvement in the work of unions." Proposing a healthy dose of "participatory democ-racy," the PHS recommended "reductions in [labor] leaders' salaries or ro-tation from executive office to shop obligations, as a means of breaking down the hierarchical tendencies which detached elite from base and made the highest echelons of labor more like businessmen than workers." If unions could revitalize themselves, SDS thought they could again become a force for "new politics"— this time based on a "synthesis of the civil rights, peace, and economic reform movements." To that end, SDS pledged to promote labor causes on campus "through publications, action programs and new curricula." In turn, its founders hoped that labor would (despite their comradely criticism) welcome campus participation on picket lines and in political campaigns—and offer student internships![7]

As noted above by Stephen Lerner, most trade unions did not sympathize with 1960s social movements nor were they eager to have radical student interns. Top leaders of the AFL-CIO were an integral part of the cold war establishment. They had worked with employers, the FBI, and Congressional witch-hunters to purge the old left from unions in the late 1940s and '50s. They were particularly hostile to protests against the Vietnam War, whether organized by wayward liberals or radicals suspected of "enemy sympathies."[8] Then federation president George Meany and his AFL-CIO executive council "supported American policy in Southeast Asia without reservation."[9] At the 1967 AFL-CIO convention, on the eve of defections by leading Democrats from the pro-war camp, an antiwar resolution was voted down 2,000 to 6 among union delegates.

Nevertheless, in the spirit of Port Huron, many campus activists who opposed the war and the draft also strongly embraced labor causes. Among them were people who later became influential figures in SEIU, CNA, UNITE HERE, CWA, and other progressive unions forty years later. Because they were critical of the AFL-CIO's cold war anticommunism, and the spotty civil rights record of most unions, ex-students often felt most comfortable with left-leaning survivors of McCarthyism like the United Electrical Workers (UE) and District 1199 in New York. Many labor-oriented students became supporters of the UFW, an organization widely viewed in its early years as an inspiring model for social justice unionism. Other campus activists aided struggles like the 1968 Memphis sanitation workers' strike, a fight for union recognition that grew directly out of African American civil rights struggles and helped expand public sector unionism in the South.[10]

On campus, student radicals tried to win recognition for pioneering unions of teaching assistants and other university employees. These campaigns linked the cause of students and workers in ways that reflected not just idealism but economic self-interest as well. Some decided to stay on—or left and later returned to—the academic track. Years later, they ended up as tenured sociologists, historians, political scientists, or women's studies specialists—but retained a working-class orientation. Their influence on a new generation of undergraduates and graduate students helped foster the anti-sweatshop movement and other campus-labor alliances that survive to this day. In 1995, as discussed later in the book, some of these same intellectuals created Scholars, Artists, and Writers for Social Justice (SAWSJ) to aid union campaigns during the AFL-CIO presidency of John Sweeney. Many continue to do so today under the banner of the Labor and Working Class History Association (LAWCHA). Over the last two decades, the focus of much solidarity activity, on and off campus, has been the very same "poor workers—day laborers, low-wage clerical and service workers, welfare recipients, and the marginally employed" whose plight so engaged New Leftists during their original forays into urban community organizing.[11]

Bankrolling the Left

Independent union ventures became necessary because most AFL-CIO affiliates cared so little about contingent labor, predominantly female workplaces, organizing the South, or organizing anybody, for that matter. "Social movement activists launched a wave of economic organizing initiatives," writes Vanessa Tait. "While they didn't necessarily carry the label 'labor,' hundreds of campaigns for equal employment and workplace rights flourished during the civil rights, New Left, and women's movements of the '60s and early '70s." These efforts "brought the voices of marginalized poor workers into the struggle for economic justice" and began "expanding the labor movement in crucial ways."[12] To its credit, SEIU was one of the few AFL-CIO unions willing to bankroll "outsiders" whose politics might be suspect, but whose enthusiasm for organizing could help the union grow.[13]

One such adoptee was the National Association of Working Women, or "9to5," then a little-known group organizing against the mistreatment of clerical workers. After attending the University of Chicago, 9to5 founder

Karen Nussbaum took a job as a clerk-typist at Harvard so she could "pay the bills." Her previous passion had been "compelling political work" related to the war in Vietnam and equal rights for women. She had supported the Black Panther Party and traveled to Cuba, as part of the Venceremos Brigade, and to Vietnam, with the Indochina Peace Campaign, then headed by Tom Hayden and Jane Fonda. Nussbaum and other 9to5 founders soon decided that helping their coworkers deal with pay discrimination and other job-related issues could be just as "compelling." 9to5 was born at a conference to stop the war and help women organize in white-collar workplaces then largely ignored by male-dominated mainstream unions. Their labor feminist campaign was publicized first in a short PBS documentary that hailed the new "insurgent consciousness among working women." Just a few years later, 9to5 really hit the publicity jackpot with a feature film from Hollywood, named after itself and starring Fonda, Lily Tomlin, and Dolly Parton. Nussbaum was able to get SEIU to charter a new affiliate—Local 925—that could function more like a union and formally represent workers initially recruited through 9to5's issue-oriented activity.[14] Soon, SEIU-backed clerical worker organizers were operating nationally as SEIU District 925.[15]

Nussbaum's union sponsorship looked good to me. Since I was a man with an organizing plan too, I sought my own personal audience with sixty-five-year-old George Hardy, then national president of SEIU. In the summer of 1976, I traveled all the way to Washington, D.C. from Vermont, where I had been a campus antiwar activist. I carried with me what I thought was a very persuasive ten-page proposal for SEIU financing of a "workers center" that I had set up in Montpelier six months before. The Vermont Workers' Rights Project (VWRP), as it was called, was up and running. In fact, it was already active enough to be much resented by the Vermont AFL-CIO, a sleepy little outfit headquartered just down the street. The project was very low on funding, which consisted of several small foundation grants and the unemployment benefits I was still collecting from my previous job at the UMW. I was the only full-time staffer of the VWRP, but had a law degree and a passing grade on the state bar exam. I was still in the middle of satisfying my six-month clerkship and residency requirement so I could be sworn in as a full-fledged member of the Vermont bar. In the meantime, I cheerfully welcomed any aggrieved worker who came through the door with a job-related legal problem that needed pro bono solving. Who knew which worker contact might lead to a major organizing drive? Already, I had referred some of my "clients" to the UE, Teamsters, and American Federation of Teachers (AFT) who proceeded to launch campaigns of varying quality at a local beer distributor, a daily newspaper, the Cabot Creamery, and the Vermont Council of Girl Scouts. So my mission in our nation's capital was to convince George Hardy that the VWRP could make SEIU—not any of these other outfits—the premier union in Vermont. I proposed that he charter an "organizing local" that "would have broad jurisdiction to organize health care and other service workers." The VWRP would then generate leads for SEIU organizing in much the same way that 9to5 was already steering workers toward Local 925 in Boston.

As things turned out, I was a man ahead of his time, workers' center–wise (and coming from the wrong state as well). My "face time" with President Hardy was arranged by Joe Buckley, the sympathetic SEIU official from Boston who had previously connected 9to5ers to the union. Hardy was a crusty, no-nonsense kind of guy—a veteran of West Coast janitor and public employee organizing who personally trained hundreds of SEIU recruiters. When he retired a few years later and turned the reins over to John Sweeney, he toured the country giving farewell speeches and left SEIU locals with the following command: "If they're breathing, organize them."[16] Unfortunately, my "pitch meeting" with Brother Hardy lasted about as long as one in Hollywood between a studio head with a very short attention span and a fledgling screenwriter with a not very marketable movie idea. After listening to my quick presentation, Hardy couldn't get beyond the name of the state in which I was proposing to spend his members' money. "Vermont?" he scoffed. "Why, there's nothing up there but cows!" In reality, as I pointed out, the number of people had recently overtaken the number of cows. And as more native Vermonters left their milking cans behind for jobs in the state's rapidly growing but low-wage service sector, they really did need a union.

Alas, organizing in Vermont didn't get funded by Hardy. My timing was obviously off. In the mid-seventies, Ben & Jerry, Bernie Sanders, Howard Dean, and other recently arrived "flatlanders" had not yet turned the Green Mountain State into the well-known center for social and political experimentation that it is today. It would be another thirty years before SEIU finally sent some organizers up to Montpelier—for an unsuccessful affiliation campaign involving the (still-independent) Vermont State Employees Association (VSEA). By then, lots of nurses and university workers were organizing in Burlington (which boosted the membership of the UE and AFT). The original VWRP was long gone, but replaced by a far more effective Jobs with Justice affiliate. And I had left Vermont for steadier work elsewhere, returning only much later as a Boston-based organizer for CWA.

More strategically positioned young organizers (with better schemes than mine) did succeed in gaining the patronage of Hardy or his successor, John Sweeney.[17] Wade Rathke had a late sixties encounter with Saul Alinsky that led him away from Williams College in western Massachusetts and, eventually, into an association with SEIU that lasted more than twenty-five years. In Rathke's recollection, he was already on "long-term parole" from Williams, so he could march on the Pentagon and become a draft counselor when he met Alinsky. The legendary founder of the Industrial Areas Foundation in Chicago and author of *Rules for Radicals* reinforced Rathke's own pragmatic inclination to focus on concrete local issues in order to build lasting organization. By the fall of 1969, the future founder of ACORN (Association of Community Organizations for Reform Now) was mobilizing welfare mothers in Springfield, Massachusetts, before relocating to Arkansas to pursue a "southern strategy on welfare reform." ACORN "went national" a few years later with a much broader program for low-income community empowerment, which included workplace organizing through its network of United Labor Unions (ULU). The eventual absorption of ULU chapters by SEIU landed Rathke on the union's national executive board. ULU's early campaigns involved hard-to-organize workers in hotels, fast food, and home care. "We needed help" Rathke explains today. "We were out-gunned and didn't have the resources. So SEIU made a deal with us....We came in with 2,000 members and the investment paid off in spades for them."[18] As part of the package, SEIU gained a network of ULU organizers, some of whom remain active in the union today, in either local or national positions.[19]

Lessons of the United Farm Workers (UFW)

A far larger gateway organization for progressive labor activists was the UFW. In SEIU and UNITE HERE particularly, there are many organizers whose lives were changed and subsequent careers shaped by their initial involvement with the UFW. Even at its 1980 peak, this relatively small labor organization never represented more than a hundred thousand workers. (Its membership today is less than 10 percent of that.) Yet, in the sixties and seventies UFW founder Cesar Chavez commanded the loyalty of hundreds of thousands of strike and boycott supporters throughout the United States and Canada. As Randy Shaw documents in *Beyond the Fields*, there is a strong historical link between the UFW in its heyday and later progressive activism. "UFW alumni, ideas, and strategies" have greatly influenced Latino politics, immigrant rights protests, union organizing strategy, and labor coalition-building with student, community, and religious groups. In the 2008 presidential campaign, the union's old rallying cry (or, at least an anglicized version of it) was appropriated by a former community organizer from Chicago. Both at pep rallies for Barack Obama and innumerable protests involving Spanish-speaking immigrants, the determined cry, "Sí, se puede!" still "reverberates across the nation's political landscape."[20]

Like SEIU several decades later, with its Justice for Janitors campaigns, the UFW generated public sympathy and support because it championed low-paid, much-exploited workers—people of color courageously struggling for dignity and respect on the job.[21] Prior to his thirty-year career as a trade unionist, Chavez spent almost a decade knocking on doors as a community organizer and voting rights activist in Mexican American barrios throughout California. His mentor was Fred Ross, an apostle of Saul Alinsky–style grassroots organizing (and father of Fred Ross Jr., who later worked for both SEIU and UNITE HERE). Chavez succeeded in mobilizing tens of thousands of Mexican Americans to register to vote and use their newly acquired political clout to deal with issues ranging from potholes to police brutality. In 1962, he set aside political agitation to organize farm workers in a state with a long history of failed unionization efforts in agriculture during the first half of the twentieth century.[22]

California agribusiness did not come to the bargaining table quickly. In fact, powerful growers had every reason to believe they would never have to negotiate with Chavez's fledgling union because farm workers lacked any rights under the National Labor Relations Act, which covers most non-agricultural workers in the private sector. Prior to 1975, this left UFW supporters in California with no way of securing union representation elections and no legal protection against being fired for union activity, a penalty that also included eviction if you lived in a grower-owned migrant labor camp. When grape or lettuce pickers walked off the job to join UFW picket lines, they faced court injunctions, damage suits, mass arrests, deadly physical attacks by hired guards, and the widespread hostility of racist local cops.

How Chavez, his union, and their diverse allies overcame such formidable obstacles was not only inspirational. The UFW provided useable models for later campaigning by other "poor workers' unions," operating in sectors of the economy where Spanish-speaking immigrants migrated in large numbers, when their choices were less limited to agricultural labor. More than any other union in the past half century, the UFW employed recognition walkouts, consumer boycotts, hunger strikes, long-distance marches, rallies, vigils, and creative disruptions of all kinds to win its first contracts. California farm workers became a national cause célèbre that attracted college students, civil rights activists, liberal clergy, and political figures like Robert Kennedy, who conducted U.S. Senate hearings on working conditions in the vineyards of Delano. Chavez's own public persona contributed much to the union's appeal. Deeply religious, the UFW president was, like Reverend Martin Luther King Jr., a homegrown Gandhian who opposed the Vietnam War (although much later than King).[23] In 1968, as strike-related confrontations swirled around him, Chavez embarked on the first of many widely publicized fasts to demonstrate the power of moral witness and nonviolent action.

The UFW's initial gains were nearly swept away when some growers signed sweetheart contracts with the IBT to avoid dealing with the dreaded "Chavistas." Ironically, the Teamsters of today are CTW colleagues of the UFW and SEIU. In the sixties and seventies, the Teamster bureaucracy was corrupt, gangster-ridden, and quite prone to using violence and intimidation for a variety of purposes (including keeping its own rank and file in line). One of those indigenous UFW militants who faced down Teamster goons was Eliseo Medina. When Medina first showed up in a UFW hiring hall, he was merely seeking work as a grape picker. Instead, the nineteen-year-old was recruited by Dolores Huerta to help win an upcoming representation vote at DiGiorgio Corporation, a grower that favored the management-friendly Teamsters. "Though inexperienced, Medina was sufficiently effective to prompt the Teamsters to beat him up badly during the run-up to the election."[24] The UFW won anyway, by a vote of 530 to 331. This crucial victory helped propel Medina into a multifaceted forty-five-year union career. As one of the most prominent members of the UFW diaspora, Eliseo spent time working for CWA in Texas and then returned to California when offered a local union leadership position by SEIU. He later became executive vice president of SEIU, its chief public advocate for immigration reform, and, in September 2010, secretary-treasurer of the national union.

The inter-union mayhem in California agriculture forty years ago finally forced state legislators to act. After UFW-backed Democrat Jerry Brown became governor (the first time) in 1974, he created an Agricultural Labor Relations Board (ALRB) to referee farm labor disputes. Before the ALRB was eventually subverted by Brown's Republican successors, UFW victories in government-run elections drove the Teamsters out of the fields, while briefly stabilizing job conditions in California's central valley. At long last, some farm workers were finally getting a living wage, health benefits, better housing, and protection against dangerous pesticide use. Unfortunately, the UFW fared worse than most unions during the ensuing

Reagan-Bush-Clinton-Bush era. Nonstop grower opposition, the massive influx of undocumented workers from Mexico, and the union's overreliance on boycott activity and its longtime failure to back that up with ongoing organizing in the fields all led to a thirty-year decline in membership and influence. The union also suffered from a very undemocratic internal structure. Virtually all power was concentrated in Chavez's hands, leaving members with little ability to curb his autocratic behavior when it began to tarnish the union's past glory and make future gains impossible.

This painful but important detail has been airbrushed out of all official portraits of Chavez. Since his death at age sixty-six in 1995, the UFW founder has been posthumously transformed into "a national icon," while his darker side has "been minimized or ignored."[25] The aura of secular sainthood that surrounds him obscures one major reason for the terminal dysfunction of a union once so widely respected and dynamic. As UFW historians like Randy Shaw, Miriam Pawel, Marshall Ganz, and Frank Bardacke have all shown, Chavez was not accountable to anyone within the UFW. As Bardacke notes, this was due, in part, to the union having "its own source of income, separate from dues." (Between 1970 and 1985, payments from workers represented less than 50 percent of UFW income; the majority of its revenue was generated by direct mail activity or contributions from wealthy individuals, church groups, and other unions.[26])

Rank-and-file critics of Chavez were purged with no internal union recourse, then blacklisted and driven from the fields in truly disgraceful fashion. In *The Union of Their Dreams*, Pawel recounts this story most poignantly by profiling Mario Bustamante, a lettuce strike leader from Salinas. Bustamante bravely challenged Chavez over the issue of elected ranch committee leaders, whose role Chavez wanted to curtail; he also tried to expand worker representation on the UFW executive board by supporting several opposition candidates.[27] The opposition slate was ruled ineligible to run at the UFW's 1981 convention. Bustamante, his brother Chava, and their supporters walked out forever to shouts of "*Bajo a los traidores!*" (Down with the traitors!) and "*Muerte a los Bustamantes!*" (Death to the Bustamantes!). Chavez made sure his critics were unemployable in the fields. Mario became a taxi driver and, later, was even denied a small UFW pension.

"Union of Their Dreams" Becomes a Nightmare

Other potential rivals like Medina, a UFW vice president, and key staffers like Ganz had already left the union in dismay (although neither aided the UFW rebels in 1981). Both witnessed Chavez consolidate his rule by employing, at union headquarters in La Paz, a bizarre and destructive group therapy exercise known as "the Game." Chavez borrowed this tool of control from Synanon, a cultish drug treatment program already controversial in California. The Game required participants to "clear the air" by launching personal attacks against one another, an experience that created much anger, bitterness, and emotional trauma. As former UFW research director Michael Yates describes with great vividness in his recent memoir, *In and Out of the Working Class*, these exercises were manipulated by Chavez personally to humiliate, isolate, and then cast out staff members he disliked or distrusted.[28] In 1977, Yates saw "a screaming mob of 'Game' initiates" purge "enemies of the union" at La Paz. When one victim had the audacity to ask for a formal hearing on the trumped-up charges against him, Chavez called the police, and had the volunteer arrested for trespassing and taken to jail.

In *Why David Sometimes Wins*, Ganz describes how Chavez used union centralization, more systematically, to crowd out constructive criticism and political pluralism. "Control over resources at the top and the absence of any intermediate levels of political accountability—districts, locals, or regions—meant that potential challengers could never organize, build a base, or mount a real challenge to incumbents."[29]

> [T]he UFW was not giving workers any real power or responsibilities in setting the union's direction...Chavez's decision that the UFW would not have geographically distinct "locals" left the union without the vehicles traditionally used by organized labor to obtain worker input. [As early as 1978] the UFW's executive board had no farmworker representation, leaving those working in the fields with no way to influence the UFW's direction.[30]

Over time, Chavez further stifled "creative internal deliberation" by replacing "experienced UFW leaders with a new, younger cadre, for whom loyalty was the essential qualification."[31] The result was a dysfunctional personality cult.

How UFW veterans have processed their cruel experience varies widely. Reconciling proud memories with the profound sadness and political disillusionment that sometimes followed farm worker duty is not easy, particularly amid contemporary union conflicts that contain distinct echoes of the past. SEIU critics in California today see similar unhealthy trends in their own, much larger labor organization. Like the dissident Chavistas who raised the banner of democracy in the UFW long ago, only to be crushed and expelled, some SEIU members have joined local reform groups or, when driven out by the UHW trusteeship, helped to build the NUHW. In either case, they hope for a better outcome this time. In California health care facilities where NUHW and SEIU have contested for bargaining rights, just as the UFW and IBT once did in the fields, workers complain of Teamster-style bullying by SEIU staffers. Within UHW, since the 2009 trusteeship, hundreds of elected UHW stewards have been purged because of their "disloyalty" to leaders who have little or no structural accountability to the membership.[32] Not all UFW alumni are repelled by these trends, of course. Some who later found their way to SEIU—like Eliseo Medina, Stephen Lerner, and Scott Washburn—are now among its leaders. In California, they either helped suppress rank-and-file opposition to Andy Stern or provided ideological cover for his takeover of UHW. In a reversal of roles, Mario Bustamante's brother Chava went to work for the UHW trusteeship and removed shop stewards who were not sufficiently loyal to SEIU.[33] Dolores Huerta, who personally fired Mario and sided with Chavez when he pushed out Medina and others, became a champion of worker dissent within SEIU today.

One former UFW staffer who sees political parallels between then and now is Monterey County social worker Wren Bradley, a reform leader in SEIU Local 521. Bradley was radicalized in high school while working as a nursing home aide in New Jersey. She attended a hospital-run nursing school in nearby Philadelphia, where her public support for a District 1199 organizing drive cost her the honor of being named Pennsylvania student nurse of the year in 1969. She moved to California to work for Cesar Chavez in medical clinics set up by the UFW for farm workers and their families. "I loved Cesar dearly," Bradley recalls. "But I was naïve, young, and thought we were all working for the same cause, and in the same direction, with no issues about power or control coming between us." Bradley became concerned for the future of the organization when Chavez suddenly decided to close the much-used clinics. The staff, including Bradley, had been drawn into conversations with their patients about internal UFW problems and controversies. Now they were politically suspect in a union with little tolerance for disloyalty. Bradley and other clinic staffers tried to resist the closings based on the important services they provided to members with little access to affordable health care. Chavez was more concerned that facilities were not under his personal control.[34] By then, according to Bradley, the UFW president was surrounded by a small circle of loyalists and wasn't listening to anyone else.[35] The UFW clinics did not survive.

In a 2009 interview, Bradley was struck by the many similarities between the UFW as it began to unravel and SEIU today. She is mystified that "people who were around Cesar then and became very critical of him don't see that Andy Stern is doing some of the same things now."[36] One twenty-three-year SEIU staffer who got his start with the UFW raised similar concerns directly with Stern. In a letter sent nine months before the UHW trusteeship, Mike Wilzoch urged him to end his "destructive conflict with UHW" so SEIU could fulfill its potential as "the best Union in the country." "I remember all too well what happened to the UFW in the 1970s after it devolved into loyalty oaths and vicious personal attacks on anyone asking pesky questions," Wilzoch wrote. "They burned their culture and so many top flight organizers that it did permanent internal and external damage to the union and the dreams of the workers."

"History is replete with tales of radicals and reformers who became what they once despised," Wilzoch reminded Stern. "Even the smartest and bravest fuck up sometimes. Tragically, few had the raw courage to pull back in time, find the best in themselves that had gotten sidetracked some-how, and repair the damage." In an email to Stephen Lerner and Mary Kay Henry, Stern asked whether Mike's message was "worth a call or answer?"[37] Wilzoch ended up getting a brief note from Andy acknowledging his serv-ice to the union and assuring him that his concerns would be addressed at the upcoming SEIU convention in Puerto Rico.[38]

A New School of Hard Knocks

While SEIU provided welcome refuge for UFW alumni, their new union could also be a school of hard political knocks. Sal Rosselli has rebounded from them not once but twice in his thirty-year career—both times rallying a similar group of aggrieved SEIU members. A native of Albany, New York, Sal ended up in the Bay Area after some youthful dissent at a Catholic col-lege. The future SEIU reformer and NUHW founder wanted to attend Al-bany State but enrolled instead, under parental pressure, at Vincentian-run Niagara University. There, in 1967, male student participation in the Reserve Officer Training Corps (ROTC) was still mandatory. So Rosselli and "a group of other antiwar folks, over a two-year period, through heavy conflict, successfully forced the university to take ROTC off the campus." In retalia-tion, he was booted out as well. "One Sunday morning, the university pres-ident, a priest, calls me into his office and there's my father sitting and crying because they had convinced him I was being expelled for undermining the Church. It was a terrible period—my father didn't talk to me for a couple of years afterwards."

Unable to return home, Rosselli left for New York City and moved in with pacifist Dorothy Day at her Catholic Worker House of Hospitality on the Bowery. He stayed for almost a year, cooking for hundreds of homeless people every day and selling the *Catholic Worker* newspaper on the steps of St. Patrick's Cathedral to raise money for the organization. "The day-to-day experience there was profound for me, it affected my life and social justice consciousness," Rosselli says today. "House of Hospitality was also a haven for draft dodgers. We took in people on the run so there was lots of FBI activity and surveillance all the time. The women's movement inside this struggle was extraordinary in terms of fighting the war." While serving at the Catholic Worker House, Rosselli also aided UFW boycott activity.

After a brief stint with Volunteers in Service to America (VISTA) in Indiana and a cross-country motorcycle trip to San Francisco, Rosselli became an undergraduate again, hoping eventually to enroll in medical school. He became a student leader at San Francisco City College and, off campus, joined the gay and lesbian rights movement, rising to the presidency of the Alice B. Toklas Club, a well-known group of San Francisco Democrats. While working his way through school, Sal got a night job as a janitor, became a member of SEIU, and, through a college friend, met its recently retired president George Hardy, who had just returned to California. Hardy took Rosselli under his wing and arranged for him to work full time for the union. Sal was soon involved in a long janitors' strike at the city's United Artist theaters, which occurred when the film *Making Love* was just opening in San Francisco. His first task—no small challenge—was to build community support for boycotting theaters screening one of the first sympathetic Hollywood portrayals of a gay romance. "I really believed that the labor movement and the gay rights movement had so much in common and just had to work together," he told me twenty-five years later. "If we couldn't do it in San Francisco, where could we do it?" Rosselli's strike support work led local gay and lesbian Democratic clubs to establish labor caucuses and work more closely with unions. Rosselli found himself getting sworn in as a local union delegate to the San Francisco Labor Council. Because of his high-profile activity in "the Alice Club," everyone present knew who he was. When he walked in and sat down, all the union men got up and moved to the other side of the room. "Because I was gay, right. In San Francisco, can you imagine? All except Stan Smith, the head of the building trades back then, who befriended me. After a while, other people got to know me and that's how you break down homophobia, just like any other prejudice."

In 1983, Rosselli moved across the bay to become an organizer for Oakland-based Local 250. Three years later, a seven-week strike at Kaiser left the local broke and defeated. Afterward, the existing leadership agreed to step down and accept a "voluntary trusteeship" imposed by then-SEIU

President John Sweeney. Members who were not health care workers were transferred elsewhere so Local 250 could rebuild with a better industry focus. "Sweeney took it over, sent in his team of people and they actually did some good things the first year in terms of reorganizing the union," Rosselli recalls. Then, in December of 1987, when SEIU headquarters was getting ready to hold elections and take Local 250 out of trusteeship, Rosselli decided to challenge Mark Splain, a national union staffer hand-picked by Sweeney to become its new president. Rosselli and several allies were immediately fired from the union payroll. The trusteeship was extended to give Splain additional time to consolidate membership support. Rosselli got certified as a nursing assistant and went to work in an Oakland nursing home and as a home care worker so he could maintain his membership in the local. He describes the experience of being a working member again as "wonderful."

Running for office in 1988 was a marathon, uphill all the way. Rosselli and his rank-and-file supporters were campaigning in a local with thousands of widely dispersed members and a paid staff of fifty. Among those working for Splain was Local 250 staff director Mary Kay Henry, a graduate of Michigan State, originally hired by SEIU in 1979 as a researcher. Rosselli's rank-and-file slate and their supporters had none of the advantages of de facto incumbency. Some quit their jobs to work full time on the campaign; others sold their cars to raise money, gave up their own apartments, and slept on basement floors. Their campaign platform called for greater member empowerment, union transparency, and accountability to the rank and file. Only in an outfit with the emerging diversity of SEIU would you find an Alice B. Toklas Club member successfully bucking the national union, while the young lesbian staffer destined to become its leader twenty-two years later sided with the union establishment. Nevertheless, somebody on Mary Kay's side was so desperate to defeat Sal that they tried to make an issue of his sexual orientation. As Rosselli recalled angrily in 2007, "Two weeks before the election, they mailed out a gay hit piece on me to every one of our members who lived outside of San Francisco and it was such extreme stuff." In Alameda County, which includes the city of Oakland, this cut-and-paste job from Bay Area gay newspapers was sent to African American UHW members along with a flyer announcing that local Black ministers backed Splain.

When the vote count began, it didn't go well for the gay-baiters. Rosselli's slate was leading when Gerry Shea, the John Sweeney appointee in charge of the election, suspended the process. "For the next month," Rosselli recalled, "they tried to steal the election in a very systematic way by disqualifying ballots from hospitals that we won. So we organized our members, big time, to call Sweeney every minute of the day, twenty-four hours a day." Finally, the headquarters-backed candidates threw in the towel and Sweeney permitted Rosselli and his running mates to be sworn in. They won by a few thousand votes but the executive board of the local remained badly divided. "It took us the better part of the year to really unite everyone into one program and direction," Rosselli said. "And then we started making a lot of progress building the union."[39]

At the time of Rosselli's election, Local 250—later to become UHW—had about twenty-five thousand members. Over the next two decades, it grew six times larger, through a merger with another local and the successive waves of health care organizing described in the next chapter. Few people who were involved on either side in the 1988 fight over the future of Local 250 expected to have a rematch twenty years later. And, certainly, no one foresaw how much union blood would be shed, in the multiple rounds of the second bout, by some of the same combatants.

Chapter 2

Taking the High Road to Growth?

"We've got to get to know each other. We want to convince you that we are the best thing that could ever happen to you and your institution."
—SEIU Health Care Division leader Dennis Rivera appealing to nonunion hospital CEOs in Boston during an interview with the *Boston Globe*[1]

"Some of Andy Stern's critics on the left complain that he is replacing class struggle with class snuggle."
—Former SEIU researcher Clayton Nall, in the *Washington Post*[2]

When employers don't want to "snuggle"—because they're not convinced that unionization is "the best thing that could ever happen" to them—they make it very hard for workers to win through struggle. Hundreds of thousands of union supporters have faced bitter defeat in union representation votes conducted by the NLRB that were vigorously contested by management. Many key activists have been fired or suffered other forms of job discrimination because of their union activity.[3] Most NLRB election victories these days are in bargaining units with only a few hundred employees or less. The bigger a workplace is, the harder it becomes for workers to prevail in any no-holds-barred fight over bargaining rights with a well-funded corporate adversary. As two academic supporters of EFCA summed up the situation:

> Current laws are an impediment to union organizing rather than a protector of workers' rights. The rules are stacked against workers, making it extremely difficult for even the most talented organizers to win elections. Under current National Labor Relations Board (NLRB) regulations, any employer with a clever attorney can stall elections, giving management time to scare the living daylights out of potential recruits.[4]

During my twenty-seven-year career with CWA, I often flattered myself by thinking I was among those "talented organizers" who knew how to help workers beat union-busters. The formula for success was fairly simple on paper (if hard to follow in practice). You had to build a strong and representative "in-plant" committee, encourage collective action around workplace issues to bring the union to life on the shop floor, inoculate workers against the inevitable anti-union propaganda from management, and sign up 70 to 80 percent of all eligible workers on union authorization cards, even though 50 percent plus one was all that the law required to win. Even if we started out with a big "card majority," the employers always had a good six to eight weeks before an election to whittle it down.

To win these contests, most employers inundate workers with anti-union messages throughout the working day. With total access to the workforce, supervisors can—and often do—call one-on-one and group meetings that workers must attend. Management is then able to discuss, with little opportunity for rebuttal, every conceivable negative consequence of unionization. The fine legal line between employers merely speculating about the future of their enterprise and making coercive threats of retaliation (in the form of lost jobs or benefits if union organizing succeeds) is continually blurred. Union representatives have no equivalent access to the workplace. If they don't have a strong committee of inside supporters, they're reduced to standing at the end of a driveway or the edge of an employee parking lot, trying to hand out information there. They can try to visit workers at home or call them on the phone. But an accurate list of their names, home addresses, and phone numbers can take weeks and, in some cases, months to assemble, with the painstaking help of union committee members. The list of eligible voters that unions are entitled to get from the NLRB is available only right before an election—and contains only names and addresses, not phone numbers. In theory, the labor board protects employees from discrimination because of their union activity. In reality, when retaliatory suspensions or dismissals occur, this management misconduct is rarely remedied in time to rescue the organizing campaign from defeat born of fear. If the employer loses a representation election, its lawyers can easily delay negotiations on a first contract for months or even years, by filing postelection challenges and legal appeals. The financial penalties for unfair labor practices—such as being forced to offer reinstatement and back pay (minus interim earnings) to illegally fired workers—don't act as a deterrent at all. As Richard Freeman, a labor economist, has noted, management in the private sector has "much to gain and little to lose from fighting unions."[5]

Thanks to this extremely uneven and forbidding playing field, I often found myself attending emergency meetings held on the eve of NLRB elections to assess the damage done by employer union-busting. Anti-union mailings to workers' homes, "captive audience" speeches delivered by the employer (or his "clever attorney"), and intimidating one-on-one conversations with supervisors were indeed scaring "the living daylights out of potential recruits." At last-minute meetings convened for damage control purposes, I've seen the fear and foreboding in the faces of CWA committee members as they tally up the number of their coworkers who are no longer planning to vote "Yes." We, the outside organizers, and they, the inside supporters, would usually have only a few days or hours left to shore up a slim union majority already on its way to becoming a minority.

So, the tense atmosphere at an organizing meeting in South Portland, Maine, in late August 2000, was very familiar, even if the union involved was not my own. A textbook anti-union campaign was nearing its peak at the Maine Medical Center (MMC). The pressure was clearly on both pro-union workers and their professional helpers from SEIU. The outcome of this MMC drive and many others like it illustrates why, in the last decade, SEIU has sought a different path to boosting what is still less than 10 percent "union density" in its core private hospital jurisdiction.[6] Along with other "organizing unions," SEIU has tried to persuade employers to sign agreements that would obligate management to remain neutral and enable workers to win bargaining rights whenever a majority of them sign union cards in a previously agreed-upon unit. In other versions of these "organizing rights" deals, unions agree to participate in a second (and unnecessary) step of the recognition process—namely, a secret-ballot vote—but only if it's "free and fair," as in devoid of union-bashing.

Management's Anti-Union Campaign

At Maine's largest hospital, administrators were not interested in neutrality. Instead they hired high-priced lawyers and anti-union consultants and pulled out all the stops to fight SEIU. This meant the union's only option was to meet with workers outside the hospital either in their homes or at meetings like the one I attended in a rented function room at a local Holiday Inn. The after-work crowd of about fifty nurses, mainly middle-aged, from the MMC was part of a proposed SEIU bargaining unit of 1,250 RNs who were scheduled to vote on unionization shortly after Labor Day. Standing in the back of the room was a group of full-time staffers, largely from out of state. The organizers under their supervision were checking Blackberries and card signer lists and conferring in whispered tones among themselves. Per SEIU's dress code at the time, all the young men wore ties. Yet, even nicely dressed, some looked young enough to be the sons or daughters of the nurses on the organizing committee.

The gathering had been scheduled so pro-union RNs and the SEIUers assisting them could review their pre-election strategy, after getting pep talks from two other out-of-town visitors. The evening's inspirational speakers were Martha Baker, president of SEIU Local 1991 in Miami, and

Suzanne Gordon, a Boston-based journalist and author of numerous books about nursing.[7] Baker went first, bringing greetings from SEIU-represented RNs around the country and speaking on their behalf as a national leader of the SEIU "Nurse Alliance." She described some of the wage, benefit, and work rule gains made by her local in Florida and how unionized nurses can be a stronger voice for RNs when dealing with public policy and professional issues as well. Citing the accomplishments of RN unions in Massachusetts and California, Gordon pointed out that "by lobbying for safe staffing ratios, minimum length of stay rules, and patient bill of rights protections, organized nurses have been able to resist hospital cost-cutting that threatens patient care."

In a sophisticated bid for union preemption, MMC had created a "Nurse Advocacy Board," so nurses could discuss their workplace concerns. Nurse managers tried to discredit the idea that collective bargaining could ever be more effective than these "roundtable" talks, conducted in house and without the assistance of a "third party." As one head nurse explained, "the most important fact we have tried to convey is that, while there are workplace issues here that need to be addressed, a union is not the answer." Big-picture problems like "the nursing shortage" are national in scope, this manager argued, "and unions have not been able to solve them." In a widely distributed message to nurses (and their families), MMC executives equated unionization with increased labor strife:

> We want to keep Maine Medical Center free of conflict and divisiveness. We also want to keep our community free of the threat of strikes that could affect the vital services we provide. We do not want our friends and neighbors to be unable to receive care because of a picket line. We do not want nurses who are concerned enough about their patients to cross a picket line to be demeaned as "scabs."... The rancor of a strike would take a long time to heal, if ever, in a community this size.[8]

Workplace reports from nurses at the Holiday Inn indicated that SEIU was losing ground, due to this daily dose of union-bashing and the "high road" appeal of the Nurse Advocacy Board. When the union petitioned for an NLRB vote in early July, 62 percent of the nurses had signed

SEIU cards because of their dissatisfaction with pay and working conditions. Now, just seven weeks later, pro-union RNs were on the defensive, spending a lot of time at work answering questions from coworkers about SEIU dues, strikes, fines, and "adversarial bargaining" that, according to management, wouldn't produce pay and benefits any better than MMC already provided. As Gordon and I noted shortly thereafter, in a pro-SEIU op-ed piece that appeared in Maine's largest newspaper over Labor Day weekend, the hospital was delivering its anti-union message via "mailings, newsletters, and lengthy 'captive audience' meetings that robbed harried nurses of time with their patients." SEIU was being unfairly depicted as a meddlesome "third party" with its own agenda. Yet MMC was, at the same time, employing its own high-priced outsiders—lawyers and anti-union consultants who "worked, day and night, to deny workers their democratic rights."[9]

At the Holiday Inn meeting, it might actually have been a good idea to do some brainstorming about union responses to hot button issues like strikes. For better or worse, strike activity had just received lots of Portland-area press coverage, due to local telephone worker participation in a two-week Maine-to-Virginia work stoppage at Verizon.[10] But SEIU organizers clearly felt pressed for time. One nervous staff member warned Gordon before her speech not to mention "the 'S' word" at all. The staff wanted to focus instead on the critical work of updating employee lists, contact information, and "assessment" sheets, which showed the current pro- or anti-union leanings of 1,250 soon-to-be voters. SEIU was about to launch another round of intensive phone-banking and house visiting. It was trying to get a majority of the MMC nurses to sign a public letter, to be released right before the election, bravely declaring, "I'm voting Yes!" The resulting staff-run "blitz" produced signatures from more than 50 percent of the RNs eligible to vote. Yet, SEIU lost the election a few days later by a 622 to 568 margin. Numerous postelection objections were filed, citing unlawful behavior by MMC. The NLRB dismissed them all so no second election was held. The RN unit at MMC remains nonunion to this very day, along with the rest of the hospital.

Lessons of the MMC Defeat

Several months later, a staff member of SEIU in Boston prepared a confidential memo, based on interviews with MMC nurses, about what went wrong and what the union might do better next time. Rand Wilson, who is now employed by the national AFL-CIO, found that SEIU supporters "were simply overwhelmed by the hospital's opposition" and their "committee wasn't able to stand up to it." As one RN reported, "People were shocked by the extent of management's campaign, taken aback by the anti-union films and the voluminous amounts of literature. We were always caught off guard and playing catch up." One nurse praised SEIU for its "training sessions on what to expect from management, that really helped." But she bemoaned the fact that "not enough people were given this inoculation and then it was too late." Said one union backer: "Management picked apart SEIU contracts. The comparisons demoralized people and made them think unions can't make a difference. We needed to have our supporters better educated." Another attributed defeat to nurses being swayed by "the announcement of pay and benefit improvements right before the vote." According to this union activist, "People were bought off by the raise." More than one SEIU committee member recalled that their coworkers felt "bombarded" from all sides—SEIU staff, the hospital administration, and RNs who favored the Nurse Advocate Board approach but appeared to be urging a "No" vote independently of management.

In his postmortem on the campaign, Wilson noted that SEIU itself came in for some "pretty scathing criticism." The rank-and-file feedback he collected, as reflected in his 2001 memo, highlighted campaign mistakes that would have been fatal for any union. The organizers had moved to the card-signing stage of the campaign too quickly, without building a pro-union network that was strong enough and covered all departments. When this workplace weakness was exposed by MMC's anti-union offensive, SEIU tried to compensate by bringing in even more outside staffers, twenty in all. But this had the effect of reducing rank-and-file "ownership" over the drive. "We should have been better organized inside the hospital," one nurse said. "The union office was never really ours. It was SEIU's. The staff muzzled us. How come we were never allowed to really say to the public and the press that patient care was threatened?" Another RN agreed that "a better structure" was needed inside the hospital "so that people could get their questions answered on the job. It hurt us to have people who were strangers coming unannounced to nurses' homes or making phone calls to someone they had no relationship with." The frenetic staff activity, unleashed in the home stretch, irked even some ardent union advocates." People value their privacy," said one committee member. "The phone calls were too aggressive. That bugged people. There was too much of an SEIU sales approach and not enough emphasis on the value of nurses themselves."

Taking the High Road Instead

Wilson hoped that, by circulating this feedback, he could make the case for stronger committee involvement in future campaigns involving the nation's fourteen million health care workers.[11] But SEIU was already in the process of rethinking its approach, reaching somewhat different conclusions. A year before its defeat in Maine, the union produced a fifteen-page guide for SEIU organizers called *The High Road: A Winning Strategy for Managing Conflict and Communicating Effectively in Hospital Worker Organizing Campaigns.* The unidentified author of this document based his or her recommendations on more generic polling and focus groups, not interviews with the battered survivors of one particular campaign. The SEIU manual offered advice about what works—and warnings about what doesn't—when organizers try to win over nervous undecided voters during hospital election campaigns. According to *The High Road,* hospital workers would "prefer to have a cooperative rather than confrontational relationship with their supervisors." That's why "concerns about conflict often outweigh their desire for a voice on the job," even when the latter is "presented in the context of protecting patient care and professional standards." Noting that hospital workers "are somewhat skeptical" about union claims, *The High Road* found "they are quick to recognize the value of working together with their co-workers to solve problems. The biggest detractor, even more than concerns about dues or strikes, is their distaste for conflict—which they believe unions inherently bring to the workplace."

SEIU's organizing guide contained little practical advice about how to get people "working together" with their coworkers "to solve problems" and, thus, demonstrate how a union might actually function for the betterment of its members. Instead, *The High Road* cautioned against "confrontational tactics," particularly if accompanied by "anti-management rhetoric" that might "reinforce the perceived negatives of unions." Union supporters were advised to adopt "a moderate rather than strident tone" and avoid "agitational messages." SEIU staff should emphasize that "conflict ends when the campaign ends" and "the ultimate goal of unionization is to foster a cooperative relationship with the hospital administration." This particular assertion seemed unlikely to appease anti-union managers intent on using workplace tension and division to discourage unionization. Would worried hospital employees be comforted by union assurances about future labor peace? SEIU believed they would. Thus, "organizing campaigns must stress—as a core value—the importance of working together with management to meet mutual goals and make the hospital a better place for all."[12]

Bargaining to Organize

Not all union organizers, inside or outside health care, embraced *The High Road* after reading it. Some SEIU rivals, like CNA, strongly disputed its advice.[13] Nevertheless, whether you favored softer union "messaging" or remained a true believer in shop floor struggle and "inside committee"-building, there was an emerging consensus about one thing: avoiding the NLRB. At the time of SEIU's bid for bargaining rights at MMC, the labor board still conducted about three thousand elections a year. A decade later, that number was down to thirteen hundred. Labor's reduced use of the NLRB reflected both the general decline in private sector organizing and, where unions are still alive and kicking, the turn toward negotiated agreements that provide alternative methods of union recognition. By 2009, so few petitioners were using the NLRB anymore that the total number of workers annually involved in representation elections was only seventy thousand; in 1997, almost one quarter of a million participated in Maine Medical Center–type balloting. During roughly the same period (1995 to 2008), unions lost 1.1 million private sector dues payers.[14] Where labor had any large-scale success offsetting those membership losses, it was usually the result of "bargaining to organize"—which meant bypassing the Board in some fashion.

Unions like SEIU, UNITE HERE, CWA, UAW, UFCW, and the Teamsters used their bargaining leverage to discourage employers, already partially unionized, from interfering with membership recruitment at their nonunion subsidiaries or facilities, whether in health care, hotels, telecommunications, auto parts manufacturing, meatpacking, or trucking.[15] The terms of their "organizing rights" deals have varied, along with the degree of employer compliance with them.[16] At the wireless company now called AT&T-Mobility, CWA has been able to organize more than forty-two thousand workers using a "card check" process that comes with a management commitment to remain neutral and not try to sway workers against unionization. AT&T is also obligated to turn over employee lists and give non-employee organizers access to workplaces from which they would normally be barred. The scope of possible new bargaining units is agreed upon in advance, and the existence of majority support for unionization is verified by the American Arbitration Association (AAA), a neutral third party that checks signed authorization cards that organizers have collected against employee lists obtained from the company. In other union settings, a secret ballot election may still be required as a second step after union card signing, but under mutually agreed upon "free and fair" conditions. Typically, the employer agrees not to hire union-busting lawyers or mobilize supervisors against unionization, as the Maine Medical Center did. Both sides refrain from criticizing each other in their written and verbal communication with employees prior to the vote.

In his 2006 book, *A Country That Works,* Andy Stern described how SEIU has pursued this non-adversarial approach with a combination of carrots and sticks and savvy use of political action. Taking things a step further down the high road, philosophically, he argues that neutralizing

employer interference with union organizing requires that our side aban-
don any vestige of a "class struggle mentality."

> We realized that our biggest strategic challenges came down to two
> basic questions. First, how could we build relationships with employ-
> ers that added value to their businesses as well as to our workers' pay-
> checks? Second, with labor laws so archaic, how could we find ways
> for workers to make free and fair choices about union representation
> without shedding blood at their workplaces?[17]

Stern's proposed "value added partnerships" have been more appealing to some employers than others. The ability of SEIU, or any union, to
offer most private firms material incentives sufficient for them to accept
unionization—while, at the same time, extracting meaningful gains for
workers—has definite limits. In his book, Stern chides corporate America
for its manifest "lack of creativity and courage" in finding ways to reduce
organizing campaign bloodshed. He bemoans management's failure to
embrace the "paradigm shift" from "confrontation to cooperation" that
could lead to "a new model of labor-management relationships." In SEIU,
he declared, "we have reinvented ourselves but it takes two to tango."[18]

In health care, SEIU has been able to find dance partners because so
much of the industry is dependent on Medicare and Medicaid. When
SEIU locals approach a hospital or nursing home chain, they can credibly
offer—as one major quid pro quo for organizing rights—their services as
a lobbying partner equally interested in better funding of patient care. In
the public sector itself, some labor-friendly politicians can even be enticed,
with the help of campaign contributions, to create new bargaining units
for home health care aides and child care providers.[19] The unionized workforce that emerges from "political organizing" of these home-based workers can also be mobilized, at the state level, to defend home care and child
care funding, in a "win-win" for everybody.

The Partnership Approach

In his book, Stern describes the impressive union growth in both acute care
and long-term care that has resulted from this approach. Once a hotbed

of more "traditional 'class struggle' attitudes," District 1199 in New York took a new direction under its president Dennis Rivera in the nineties. After Rivera's union affiliated with SEIU, "1199 taught us a great deal about how to tango," Stern writes. 1199 had created a "paradigm-busting collaborative relationship with major hospitals in the New York metropolitan area," based on its members becoming "the champion of their employers' need for fair hospital reimbursement rates."

> [A] fixture in Albany, SEIU 1199's record-setting political contributions and members, who could flood the legislative corridors when needed, gave them the clout to be the legislators' best friend or worst nightmare. Dennis and hospital industry leaders used their coordinated efforts to win billions for the hospitals, which translated into stable balance sheets for the employers and excellent wages and the gold standard of benefits for their workers, including multi-million-dollar training and upgrading funds.[20]

The equivalent "paradigm-busting" relationship, which established the "gold standard" for California hospital union contracts, was forged between SEIU and Kaiser Permanente (KP). Now a giant, multistate health maintenance organization and hospital chain, KP was founded as a pioneering prepaid medical plan. It was embraced by California unions to such a degree that it became known as "the HMO that labor built." By 2007, KP's nationwide workforce was 130,000 strong, and its 96,000 union members made it one of most heavily unionized "not for profit" health care providers in the nation. But its own labor-management relations did not always reflect or respect its union roots. From the late 1970s to the early 1990s, KP was the scene of a series of disruptive walkouts (including the 1986 strike that bankrupted SEIU Local 250 and led to its first trusteeship). KP employees were angry about contract concessions, management cost-cutting, and unilateral decision making based on hospital "reengineering" studies. In 1995, SEIU and twenty-six other KP unions formed a coordinating council, with help from the AFL-CIO, and began developing a joint strategy for more effective bargaining and strike activity. At the time, KP was losing $250 million a year and facing pressure from competing HMOs with lower cost structures. The 1996 KP contract was settled without a work stoppage and created an elaborate management-funded joint program for reducing workplace tension and increasing employee involvement. Sal Rosselli recalls this change of course:

> The Kaiser "partnership"—and the Kaiser contract—exists because of struggle, not because Kaiser is some benevolent employer. There were huge strikes in the late '80s and early '90s that forced Kaiser to the brink. Then, some enlightened leaders in Kaiser sat down and said, "Okay, we've got to do something different or we're going to go out of business." That was the birth of the Labor-Management Partnership.[21]

Union and academic proponents of the Kaiser Labor Management Partnership (LMP) point to subsequent gains in the areas of job security, pension coverage, and standardized wage rates, plus opportunities for workers to participate in decision making about issues beyond the scope of normal collective bargaining.[22] One undisputed benefit of the partnership—if you were part of it—was membership growth. Overall, between 1997 and 2006, KP coalition unions grew from about 55,000 to 86,000 members, via card check recognition, bargaining unit accretion, and additional hiring. Kaiser's pledge of non-interference with new organizing led to a union success rate of 80 percent, in twenty-nine campaigns involving 7,400 workers—a record that would have been hard to reproduce if there had been contested NLRB elections. At a 2009 forum in Washington, D.C., AFL-CIO president John Sweeney celebrated nearly fifteen years of the partnership. He applauded Kaiser for its "improvements in patient outcomes, reductions in medical errors, better preventative care, cost savings, and a better, more satisfying work environment." In particular, Sweeney cited the "significant work" of "unit-based teams" in "bringing doctors, nurses, technicians, pharmacists, and other caregivers together on behalf of patients."[23]

The Kaiser LMP also attracted critics. Many Kaiser nurses in California do not participate in unit-based teams or the partnership because of CNA's official opposition.[24] CNA has also objected to incentive pay schemes that might compromise patient care. In 2002, for example, KP began to reward SEIU-represented clerical staff for reducing the amount of time they spent on patient calls and for limiting referrals to advice center RNs.[25] CNA argued that these "morbidity bonuses" put patient safety at risk. The nurses union also reproached SEIU and other LMP participants for backing Kaiser's legislative agenda to the detriment of consumer interests. In spite of a huge consumer backlash against some managed care practices, LMP unions, including SEIU, supported the HMO industry goal of requiring patients to agree, in advance, to compulsory arbitration of malpractice disputes. In contrast, CNA defended the right of patients to sue for negligent denial of care or other acts of medical malpractice.[26]

Another downside of the LMP was its disrespect for employee free choice, if workers opted for a non-partnership union (like NUHW in 2009–10). In those organizing situations, Kaiser has behaved like any other anti-union health care employer. In 2002, a group of Kaiser call center representatives in Alameda, California, contacted the Communications Workers of America and asked for assistance with various workplace problems. They called CWA because many of its members in telecom are customer service reps who do similar jobs. After a series of meetings and discussions with CWA organizers, the Kaiser reps formed an organizing committee. In 2003 and early 2004, they signed up a majority of their 160 coworkers. Despite its "union friendly" reputation, Kaiser would not recognize their union, based on a card check. Instead, in more typical union-busting fashion, management sought additional time for "Vote No" campaigning by insisting that the NLRB hold a representation election. After losing that vote, KP continued to spend heavily on a law firm specializing in "union avoidance." Kaiser bargained in bad faith for twenty-one months, refusing to agree to contract terms that were standard in its LMP union agreements covering other call centers. By early 2006, the workers were frustrated, demoralized, and not strong enough to strike. They voted down a tentative agreement that one CWA organizer described as "inferior in many ways." Then, in a narrow vote encouraged by management and employees who had always been anti-union, the Alameda call center workforce decertified CWA in February 2006, almost four years after the campaign began. During this whole ordeal, not a single partnership union protested Kaiser's blatant union-busting; in fact, CWA officials believe that Rosselli and SEIU helped to exclude these CWA-represented workers from the KP union coalition (even after CWA sought to join the LMP). SEIU's stance clearly gave Kaiser the green light to make union recognition and first contract bargaining as difficult as possible for CWA.[27]

Growth versus Standards at CHW and Tenet

For the two California SEIU locals representing Kaiser workers—Local 250 in Oakland and Local 399 in Los Angeles (which later merged and became UHW)—the big challenge in the late 1990s and early 2000s was organizing Kaiser competitors like Catholic Healthcare West (CHW) and Tenet. For decades Local 250 had represented three hospitals that are now part of CHW. But as CHW morphed into a big statewide chain, it grew to thirty-two facilities in all, with the other twenty-nine being nonunion. The unionized minority "knew that they had to organize the whole CHW system," Sal Rosselli said. "They sacrificed wages and other things to win organizing rights. And in the late '90s, over a five-year period, we organized twenty-seven other hospitals throughout the state. In just two contract cycles, CHW is now the second-best hospital contract in the country, right behind Kaiser's, with a master agreement for fifteen thousand workers." For UHW leaders, this campaign of community activism and workplace mobilization was a positive example of "bargaining to organize." CHW workers bought into the strategy and helped implement it, after much debate and discussion, because they understood what was required to maintain and then raise their own contract standards. For Rosselli, this success was proof that the union's pursuit of "justice for all"—at CHW or anywhere else—was not incompatible with using its bargaining clout to defend the interests of existing members.

In her official SEIU biography, Mary Kay Henry is extolled as the architect of "groundbreaking agreements" with CHW and Tenet Healthcare Corp.[28] In fact, both campaigns required extensive collaboration with UHW and not everyone involved, from the national union staff and leadership, reached the same conclusion as Rosselli about how to achieve growth and better contract standards at the same time. Henry's controversial 2006–07 work with UHW members at Tenet helped lay the groundwork for escalating conflict between UHW and the national union over the next two years, and the bitter post-trusteeship rivalry between SEIU and NUHW. According to John Borsos, then head of UHW's hospital division, union officials in Washington "signaled to the employer that SEIU was seeking a deal at all costs, which gave Tenet the power to ratchet SEIU down." UHW was not against tradeoffs to win organizing rights for twelve thousand nonunion Tenet workers so the union could grow and be stronger outside of California. "Our position was that the leaders can't decide that," Borsos explained. "They can't manipulate behind people's backs. If you want workers to make concessions to win long-term power, you have to ask the workers, explain the issues, answer questions, have a debate, and have it be their decision."[29]

Tenet operated nine hospitals in California, but was bargaining nationally with SEIU on contract issues affecting nine thousand members there, in Florida, and in Nevada. In December 2006, SEIU negotiators announced a tentative agreement making organizing easier at twenty-three nonunion Tenet hospitals throughout the United States. In the process, they not only undermined attempts to make pension and retiree health care improvements for existing UHW members at Tenet,[30] they agreed to give up the right to strike in California for ten years (making any such gains in the future harder to achieve); they allowed the company to subcontract up to 12 percent of the workforce at any time; and they weakened other job security provisions. Tenet workers who belonged to UHW weren't happy about the bargaining process or its outcome. As labor historian (and NUHW ally) Cal Winslow reports, Tenet was soon "faced with the opposition of thousands of mobilized UHW members in California" and, in the end, "withdrew its concessionary demands" during further negotiations.[31] Henry was among those accused of bypassing locally elected negotiators to reach the tentative agreement. "SEIU was not looking out for the interests of its dues-paying members, but was looking to expand its membership," contends Tony Aidukas, a rehab specialist at Tenet's Desert Regional

Medical Center in Palm Springs, who served on the UHW bargaining committee in 2006. "Mary Kay has a fundamental lack of respect for workers in deciding the course of their union and their contract." As the person in charge nationally, Henry insisted that she kept everyone fully informed about any tradeoffs and personally opposed the subcontracting concession. In an interview three years later, Henry blamed an unidentified "rogue bargainer" for creating the Tenet contract controversy—a temporary glitch that she quickly corrected.[32] "I have never at any time bargained anything behind anybody's back," she told the *Los Angeles Times*.[33]

Former UHW organizer Barbara Lewis shared an office with Henry for seven of the nearly thirty years she spent on SEIU national and local union payrolls. She believes the Tenet bargaining experience revealed a deeper, more troubling set of SEIU headquarters blinders. During the negotiations, Tenet wanted to limit the scope of shop steward activity, including union use of workplace bulletin boards to keep members informed about contract issues and union programs. At Tenet, UHW also had contract language that enabled stewards to get paid time off, not just for grievance handling, but for training, education, and political action. At one point in the union's internal caucusing, Henry asked Lewis whether it was really that important for stewards to have bulletin board access and so much time off the job for union work. Lewis had to explain to her that, for shop stewards, the power to communicate with coworkers—and the capacity to blow the whistle on management misbehavior, when necessary—is central to their effective functioning. Lewis was shocked at the willingness of SEIU headquarters "to strip anything out of the contract that would give workers the ability to alter the balance of power in the workplace."[34]

A Nursing Home Alliance

By 2007, after more than a decade of Andy Stern's presidency, SEIU was not displaying great institutional capacity for accommodating local union criticism of its growth strategy. Like the bargaining breakdown at Tenet, the national union's attempt to overcome obstacles to organizing in long-term care facilities led to further tensions between UHW and SEIU. The problem in long-term care was the difficulty of unionizing nursing homes one by one, rather than on a chainwide basis, under the terms of organizing rights agreements like those SEIU had negotiated with Kaiser, CHW, or Tenet. Between 2000 and 2010, SEIU added only about six thousand new nursing home members a year in the entire country. This increase in union market share lagged far behind industry growth during the same period.[35] To boost its organizing volume in a sector still less than 11 percent unionized, SEIU began to experiment with a partnership concept known as the Nursing Home Alliance (NHA). "We joined that alliance because of twenty years of not being able to organize nursing homes," Rosselli explained later. "These were sweatshop employers, squeezing every dime, and nothing had worked up to that point. We felt we needed to get more money in the system. But we ended up leaving too much money on the table with the employer."[36]

Nursing home operators who joined the alliance had to grant union organizing access to some of their facilities in exchange for SEIU meeting various "political benchmarks"—mainly involving its lobbying for better Medicaid reimbursement of patient care costs. Another quid pro quo was union support for state laws limiting the right of nursing home patients to sue over mistreatment. For example, in the 2004 version of the California alliance agreement, SEIU access to workers in thirty nonunion nursing homes was tied to enactment of this industry-backed "tort reform" legislation.[37] In Washington State, SEIU Local 775 negotiated a pioneering ten-year NHA deal that promised "no strikes" and "let nursing-home operators—not the union or workers—decide which homes are offered up for organizing." Local 775 agreed to limit its overall membership recruitment to no more than "half of a particular company's non-union homes."[38] The terms of the "template agreement" covering these new members were worked out in advance of union recognition; there was little or no opportunity for input from the affected workers after they became unionized.

According to the *San Francisco Weekly*, "employer friendly" model contracts in California prevented SEIU members from reporting "health care violations to state regulators, to other public officials, or to journalists, except in cases where the employees are required by law to report egregious cases of neglect and abuse to the state."[39] In late April 2007, the SEIU state council, then still headed by Rosselli, also took heat for working with for-profit nursing home chains to help block a "Nursing Home Residents Bill of Rights." Among other things, this bill in the state legislature would have increased government oversight of nursing home staffing levels. Jamie Court, a well-known California consumer advocate, condemned the NHA (and SEIU's related lobbying) as a betrayal of nursing home workers and patients. Said Court: "Nursing homes are a sector where caregivers are the eyes, the ears, and the witnesses when there is patient abuse...I've never seen a labor union except for the SEIU enter into a top-down, industry-friendly agreement that binds the hands of the workers. To tie their hands and tie their tongues is to let people die."[40]

As this negative publicity mounted, reflecting growing concern among California union allies, the reaction at SEIU headquarters in Washington was not to rethink its NHA strategy and come up with a better one. Instead, Andy Stern and his leadership circle simply became more focused on how to remove any potential internal obstacles to a strategy they had already decided was the only way to boost "union density" in nursing homes.

Internal Criticism Grows

Stern could hardly ignore the fact that the downside of his approach (the potholes in the "high road") were beginning to trouble longtime allies within SEIU. Among them was Jerome Brown who spent thirty-five years building 1199/New England into a well-regarded and effective 20,000-member health care affiliate of SEIU. As Don Stillman writes, "one of SEIU's toughest fights came in Connecticut in 2001, when 4,500 nursing home workers in 1199 New England conducted a four-week strike at 39 nursing homes. Republican Governor John Rowland deployed National Guard troops to escort strike-breakers to work and spent $20 million of taxpayer dollars to help owners pay replacement workers."[41]

Not long after he retired as president of this militant local and from the SEIU executive board, Brown circulated an assessment of *A Country That*

Works to his former colleagues on the SEIU international executive board (IEB). This thoughtful review of Stern's book raised important questions about where SEIU was headed in nursing homes and health care generally. Brown wrote and spoke with particular authority because he was no stranger to hard-fought (and sometimes disappointing) organizing rights campaigning. His Connecticut-based local waged a sophisticated, multifaceted ten-year struggle to protect 1,800 workers at Yale-New Haven Hospital from union-busting activity of the Maine Medical Center sort. After thwarting Yale's plans for a $430 million expansion, 1199 finally won what it thought was a "free and fair" election commitment. Management engaged in massive unfair labor practices anyway, violating the deal in such a way that 1199 was forced to withdraw from the vote. Afterward, it was able to invoke an unusually strong penalty clause in the organizing rights agreement. In 2007, even though the hospital remained unorganized, an arbitrator ordered Yale-New Haven to pay Brown's local $2.3 million for its organizing costs, plus another $2.2 million to 1,700 workers themselves—an amount equal to what management spent on union-busting consultants.[42] This well-deserved but extraordinary financial penalty was "20 percent more than the $3.6 million that the labor board awards on average each year to all workers nationwide for all back pay for being retaliated against for supporting a union."[43]

So, in principle, Brown wasn't opposed to "institutional peace pacts" that might spare any workers the decade-long ordeal of Yale–New Haven Hospital workers (who remain nonunion). The problem, according to Brown, was that "even when we are allowed to organize [in nursing homes] unbeknownst to the members, there is often a pattern agreement or 'template' in existence which hinders or even makes impossible the growth of a workplace organization that can make decisions for itself." Brown warned that, if workers see themselves as a "third party in a collective bargaining relationship brokered by labor and management bosses, SEIU was spawning "the very antithesis of true rank-and-file unionism." SEIU needed to ask itself whether such "methods can produce a real, democratic workers organization" or if such arrangements will lead to a dues-paying membership largely alienated from the union. Brown urged non-retired SEIU leaders—at least those who "really believe in the fundamental dignity of union members"—to grapple with this question along with the related challenge of preserving "effective democratic processes" in ever-expanding SEIU megalocals.[44]

In California, Jerry's old friend Sal Rosselli and others in UHW were having second thoughts of their own about the NHA. Several years into the NHA experiment, and in anticipation of it being up for renewal in 2007, UHW prepared a detailed assessment of the pros and cons of this partnering. (This was an example of constructive internal criticism/self-criticism rare in the labor movement, in my experience.) The UHW report indicated that only 83 of 284 homes covered by the alliance had been organized. Even if all of them had been unionized, the industry as a whole would still be 75 percent nonunion. While SEIU lobbying had secured $120 million for participating nursing home chains, only $20 million found its way into union contract improvements.[45]

In May 2007, UHW's 150,000-member executive board met to discuss these findings. The local's elected leaders adopted a formal resolution opposing any further NHA-type deals that would prevent SEIU members "from advocating effectively on behalf of the people they serve, significantly limit the scope of workers' collective bargaining rights, and frustrate healthcare workers' rights to participate in negotiations and vote on agreements that affect them." UHW board members demanded that any future NHA-type agreements negotiated by SEIU meet three substantive and procedural conditions. First, "healthcare workers' ability to make their voices heard on matters of patient/resident/consumer care…must be furthered, not frustrated." Second, "to advance workplace democracy," the rank and file "must have a seat at the bargaining table," be "fully informed of the terms and conditions of any proposed agreement," and have the right to ratify or reject it. Third, any agreement that deprives health care workers of "full collective bargaining rights, including the right to engage in concerted action," must be very limited in duration.[46]

In a follow-up letter to UHW long-term care workers, Rosselli disclosed that their elected local union representatives had been excluded from nursing home talks by SEIU. Rosselli warned that home care workers might be the next group to be similarly disenfranchised. "If we cannot ensure that our nursing home members have a voice at work, it's only a matter of time before we, as homecare workers, lose our voice and ability to negotiate contracts that move us forward," the letter said. To prevent this from happening, UHW members were urged to sign petitions, circulated by UHW stewards, demanding "a voice for quality care," "union democracy," and "full collective bargaining rights."[47] Within a month, Andy Stern responded to the rising clamor by announcing he had terminated the alliance deal in California. Stern left the door open for later renegotiation of the NHA agreement, saying SEIU would return to the table if the nursing home chains "have some new ideas."[48] In the meantime, Stern was developing a few ideas of his own about how to deal with his pesky critics in UHW. When implemented over the next twenty months, these measures had the effect of turning them into organizers of a rival union.

Taking the Low Road in Santa Rosa

At its 2008 convention in San Juan, SEIU set ambitious new organizing goals for all its "core jurisdictions" to meet over the next four years. As projected in a convention-approved "Strategic Unity Plan and Program to Win," most of the new members the union hoped to recruit—350,000 out of 500,000 overall—were health care workers of one sort or another. "We don't believe that the way we get to 350,000 is the way we've done it previously, which is NLRB elections," said soon-to-be Executive Vice President Dave Regan, from SEIU 1199 in Ohio. "We have to look to employers in the health systems, long-term care industry, and emerging healthcare industries across this country."[49] The union's strategy of "looking to employers" for new or expanded neutrality deals did succeed at the Caritas chain in Massachusetts and HCA in Texas and other states, as reported later in the book. But that was not the only direction SEIU took in 2008–10 under leaders like Regan and Mary Kay Henry. In California, due to circumstances of its own creation, SEIU continued to be very involved in NLRB elections—of the three-way sort (with two competing unions and "no union" as the choices on the ballot). Its own campaigning in these contests mimicked the worst behavior of anti-union employers and made a mockery of the "free and fair election" standards that its community allies have been asked to promote in the health care industry around the country.

SEIU's self-destructive tactics began, bizarrely enough, in a major hospital organizing campaign where it stood to gain members itself. In August of 2008—six months before NUHW was even formed—UHW had a big organizing drive under way in Palo Alto among 1,500 nonunion workers at Stanford Medical Center and Lucile Packard Children's Hospital. At the time, in preparation for its later takeover of UHW, SEIU headquarters was bombarding UHW members with mailings about why their local should be dismembered and/or put under trusteeship. This was not a reassuring topic for workers about to choose whether or not to join UHW. Nevertheless, SEIU Secretary-Treasurer Anna Burger obtained a copy of the NLRB voter list at Stanford and sent each employee on it a letter echoing the anti-union propaganda of their own employer. Burger's mailing claimed that UHW leaders were under investigation for engaging "in a pattern of financial malpractice and fraud involving the diversion of millions of dollars of union treasury monies and property, in possible violation of federal law." She explained that help was on the way from Washington, in the form of a trusteeship that "will allow us to appoint strong and stable leadership to oversee the union and ensure that it continues to serve its members and their best interests during this investigation." Despite Burger's meddling, the workers voted 3 to 1 to join UHW under its existing leadership—and not because they wanted to see it removed. The main organizer at Stanford was Michael Krivosh, a veteran of SEIU campaigns around the country, who quit in protest when UHW was later put under trusteeship. Writing to Burger after the Stanford vote, he expressed shock and amazement over her letter. "We prepare and inoculate workers for the employer's message and tactics," he noted. "But, in my 36-year career as a union organizer, I have never had to inoculate and prepare workers for the international union's message and tactics."[50]

SEIU's low-road messaging at Stanford paved the way for even more outrageous conduct at Santa Rosa Memorial Hospital (hereafter referred

to as "Memorial" or "Memorial Hospital") after the UHW trusteeship
was imposed. Workers there had been trying for five years to persuade
the Sisters of St. Joseph, the Catholic religious order that controls the
hospital, to refrain from anti-union activity prior to any NLRB vote.[51]
In 2004, Local 250—soon to become UHW—ran a strong but traditional
"hot shop" campaign in Santa Rosa. In short order, nearly 70 percent of
the Memorial workers signed up, just like at Maine Medical Center four
years earlier (although no nurses were involved this time because they
already had a union). A majority publicly identified themselves as union
supporters prior to the scheduled NLRB election in February 2005. Then,
the same combination of carrots and sticks that defeated SEIU in Maine
began to work their dark magic in California. In Memorial's propaganda
blitz, Local 250 was soon transformed into a big bureaucratic, strike-
happy interloper. Workers were told that the union only cared about collecting hundreds of thousands of dollars a year in dues and would not,
as promised, provide a more effective voice for employees than their own.
Management induced rising workplace tension, which contributed to
card-signer defections. Unlike the SEIU organizers in Maine in 2000,
Local 250 saw the handwriting on the wall and withdrew its petition before the vote.

A Different Approach

A different approach was obviously required for the next round of this
unionization struggle, to neutralize such damaging management interference. Working together, SEIU local and national staffers launched a sophisticated, multifaceted campaign to pressure Memorial Hospital to agree
to a "fair election agreement" (which the administration immediately
likened to "unilateral disarmament"). Organizer Fred Ross Jr., who began
his union career with the UFW in 1970, coordinated the effort. He put together a Sonoma County coalition that linked issues of health care quality
and community access to the union struggle. By 2007, SEIU's local allies
had grown in number and its leverage campaign was interfering with
Memorial's planned takeover of a nearby Sutter-owned facility.

What ultimately brought the drive to the brink of success was appeals to religious conscience, combined with various forms of local and national shaming. The Sisters of St. Joseph of Orange have a history of social justice work. While their order has been guilty of much institutional anti-unionism in health care, some of its activist members were early supporters of the UFW. Others backed SEIU Justice for Janitors activity in Los Angeles and aided solidarity campaigns involving the people of El Salvador.[52] The St. Joseph Health System (SJHS) controlled by the order (if no longer directly managed by it) is a prominent player in the larger world of Catholic health care systems, which SEIU was targeting nationally. As Ross notes, "SJHS was very profitable" and, thus, far less vulnerable to economic pressure than other SEIU corporate campaign targets. Drawing SJHS into a discussion of fair election ground rules in Santa Rosa required a well-organized, multiyear refresher course in Catholic social teaching about the rights of labor.

The Sisters of St. Joseph were prodded and/or embarrassed by events like a weeklong vigil, involving workers and their supporters outside the headquarters of their order (or "Motherhouse") in Orange, California. California's then attorney general (and now governor again) Jerry Brown joined Dolores Huerta and other well-known figures in this vigil, which featured nightly interfaith services. The vigil culminated in a thousand-person march that was covered in the *New York Times* and *Los Angeles Times*. To make sure Catholic readers knew about the dispute, the union ran three full-page ads in *National Catholic Reporter*, highlighting the disconnect between the Sisters' past support of the UFW and their more recent resort to union-busting in SJHS hospitals. Although the campaign was orchestrated by staffers like Ross and UHW organizing director Glenn Goldstein, it developed strong support among the many religious figures, Latino leaders, and elected public officials who met directly with Memorial workers and heard their stories. By the summer of 2008, SJHS was feeling pressure. The Catholic Bishops of California privately urged a negotiated settlement. In the fall of 2008, Ross and Goldstein had a preliminary meeting with the CEO of Memorial Hospital. Both had hopes that any agreement they reached would eventually help twenty thousand other SJHS workers organize at more than a dozen hospitals in California, New Mexico, and Texas. "We were on the path to a breakthrough," Ross recalls. "And then it got blown up by the trusteeship."[53]

When SEIU seized control over UHW, 60 percent of the workers at Memorial had already signed union cards—again. Some made repeated phone calls to national union staffers to determine the status of SEIU support for their drive. Overwhelmed by trusteeship work elsewhere, SEIU officials simply abandoned the organizing committee in Santa Rosa, apparently thinking that would end its activity. All campaign staffing was withdrawn and the local UHW office closed. However, as Ross points out, there are two divergent models for seeking organizing rights agreements. One is the "workerless" approach typified by the Nursing Home Alliance. This model tends to be a staff-dominated, with "lots of bells and whistles, smoke and mirrors, but not many workers." And then there is the "worker driven" comprehensive campaign model that Ross, Goldstein, and the pretrusteeship UHW patiently pursued at Memorial over five difficult years. It requires making a long-term commitment to rank-and-file leadership development, while simultaneously building outside pressure on management—both of which were missing ingredients in SEIU's campaign at Maine Medical Center in 2000. With the latter kind of campaign background, training, and encouragement, Memorial workers were able to take charge of their own campaign going forward. They were assisted, of course, by UHW staffers who had quit or been fired and were now working as volunteers for the newly formed NUHW.

Respecting the "Just Rights" of Workers?

By April of 2009, Ross had resigned from SEIU himself, citing its emerging attacks on UNITE HERE.[54] By then, a majority of the 675 workers at Memorial petitioned the NLRB to hold a vote so they could join NUHW instead of SEIU. Their resilient inside committee did the hard work of getting hundreds of people to sign union authorization cards for the third time since 2004. SEIU immediately returned to Santa Rosa and launched a ten-month campaign to delay and disrupt any secret-ballot vote. That effort began with the filing of frivolous unfair labor practice charges known as "blocking charges" (because their effect is to block any vote while the NLRB investigates and determines whether it should issue a formal complaint based on the charges).[55] The local community-labor response to SEIU's behavior was overwhelmingly negative. A majority of Memorial workers signed a public statement supporting NUHW and urging SEIU to get out of their hospital. In a highly unusual intervention, the North Bay Labor Council, representing sixty unions in four counties, sent a similar appeal to UHW cotrustees Dave Regan and Eliseo Medina (who originally hired Fred Ross as an SEIU organizer in the nineties). "It is clear that Memorial workers have chosen NUHW as their union," the central labor council said. "We ask that SEIU-UHW respect these workers' choice and withdraw so they can finally have the successful election they have worked so hard and risked so much for."[56] In June of 2009, the U.S. Conference of Catholic Bishops (USCCB) issued a long-awaited report entitled *Respecting the Just Rights of Workers: Guidance and Options for Catholic Healthcare and Unions.* The labor signers of this accord included John Sweeney and SEIU's own health care division chair Dennis Rivera. As one of its key principles, it urges both employers and unions "to refrain from harassing, threatening, intimidating, and coercing workers."[57]

The USCCB document gave further impetus to NUHW efforts to get Memorial to restrain its own anti-union campaigning. Under pressure from local religious leaders, like Monsignor John Brenkle, a parish priest in the Santa Rosa diocese, the hospital finally "expressed willingness to sit down and negotiate ground rules leading to a fair election agreement." But now, much to the dismay of Brenkle, not only was SEIU "misusing labor law as a means of delaying an election for as long as possible," it was also refusing to come to the table with the other parties.[58] In an open letter to Brenkle and other Santa Rosa religious leaders, Medina defended SEIU's actions at Memorial, where an election was finally scheduled for December 17–18, 2009. Medina said he was "deeply troubled by the prospect of Santa Rosa hospital workers making a choice based on the promises of individuals with whom they are familiar—without considering that NUHW has no real membership base and its future viability is questionable at best." According to Medina, SEIU would not participate in any three-way discussions on election campaign guidelines because "that would suggest that 'NUHW' is a legitimate alternative" to SEIU in a situation where only a "bi-lateral agreement with the employer" was appropriate.[59]

This condescending attitude outraged workers at the hospital. Monsignor Brenkle offered to break the deadlock by acting as a mediator in the dispute. He was joined by former U.S. secretary of labor Robert Reich, now a professor at Berkeley. (Reich's role was arranged by his son, Adam, who had worked with Ross on the Memorial campaign prior to the UHW trusteeship.)[60] When he and Reich were both rebuffed by Medina, Brenkle wrote a guest editorial in the *Santa Rosa Press Democrat* denouncing SEIU for behavior that "flies in the face of Catholic social teaching and contradicts its own national advocacy for exactly the types of agreement it is now trying to thwart."[61] SEIU was, indeed, undermining years of its own community organizing work and coalition building among labor, clergy, and Catholic hospital workers at a time when these efforts were finally paying off, locally and nationally, with workers rights' initiatives like the USCCB report.[62]

In Santa Rosa, Monsignor Brenkle joined sixteen other religious leaders, local academics, labor officials, and politicians on a hastily formed Fair Election Oversight Commission that tried to monitor the Memorial vote. Even with such backing, workers had to run one final gauntlet of SEIU interference before the ballots were cast, counted, and then legally challenged in December 2009. As indicated by its own election showing—a paltry 13 votes out of a possible 675—SEIU had virtually no support inside the hospital.[63] The real battle raged between NUHW supporters and foes of unionization who enjoyed the full backing and encouragement of management. In a preelection letter distributed at the hospital, Ross accused SEIU in Washington of secretly trying to sabotage Memorial worker organizing six months before the UHW trusteeship.

> The International union made a decision in August 2008 to no longer support workers at SJHS or put pressure on the system, because they

did not want you to have the opportunity to vote for a union led by Sal Rosselli. SEIU broke faith and trust with you by deserting you when you most relied on them. This misconduct seriously undermined the opportunity you had to win a fair election agreement with SJHS in the fall of 2008.

Ross urged NUHW supporters to "keep your eyes on the prize." He predicted they could "withstand SJHS's anti-union campaign" and "overcome SEIU's campaign of smear, fear, and futility."[64] Ross was proven right, but just barely. NUHW received 283 votes versus 263 for "no-union," a narrow victory that did not require a runoff because, after challenged ballots were disposed of, NUHW retained its simple majority lead.

In the days prior to the election, SEIU did everything it could to help the hospital avoid this outcome. It sent dozens of full-time staffers to Santa Rosa. They unleashed a door-knocking, phone-banking, and home-mailing blitz that seemed, in this case, to be solely designed to create a worker backlash against both unions. While hospital administrators conducted MMC-style "one-on-one meetings with workers to pressure them into voting against the union and forced them to sit through anti-union speeches," they also "gave SEIU space to circulate anti-NUHW messages inside the hospital, most notably by delivering two sheet cakes to every department encouraging workers not to vote for the upstart union."[65] SEIU's campaign culminated with a rally outside the hospital. Three hundred union staffers and loyal members from other work locations were bussed in to march around with picket signs, in a raucous simulation of the strike activity Memorial was warning workers about inside. Not a single employee from the hospital participated.

If SEIU had been on the ballot by itself, it would not have flouted a fundamental rule of *The High Road* by conducting such a protest just a few days before a hospital election. An action like that would only highlight the possibility of future labor-management strife. In this case, the picketing merely confirmed that one of the two unions was a disruptive outsider. "It's a vendetta," NUHW activist Nancy Timberlake sadly observed. While not fatal to the hopes of Timberlake and others, the damage inflicted by SEIU was still considerable. In typical employer fashion, Santa Rosa Memorial filed ten postelection objections and refused to recognize the new union or begin bargaining on a first contract. In its NLRB appeal, the hospital claimed that NUHW engaged in coercion and intimidation that prevented "the free expression of the employees' choice." A labor board hearing officer dismissed these bogus objections and recommended that NUHW be certified immediately. That was in May 2010. In November, ten months after the election, Santa Rosa Memorial workers were still waiting for the NLRB in Washington to affirm the election results.

After NUHW is finally certified, hospital administrators may still balk at negotiating a first contract. In that case, the whole NLRB appeal process might have to begin all over again, on a different track. NUHW would have to file an unfair labor practice charge and, in response, the NLRB regional director would have to issue a complaint alleging that Memorial's "refusal to bargain" constitutes a new violation of federal law. A labor board administrative law judge (ALJ) would then hold a hearing on that complaint. Any hearing decision in favor of NUHW could be appealed by the hospital to the full five-member labor board in Washington. In response to any ALJ ruling being upheld there, the employer could then seek relief from the U.S. Court of Appeals. A final order to bargain could be delayed for two to three years in all (on top of the five required to get an election in 2009 that workers were able to win, despite the double whammy of labor and management misconduct).[66]

The organizing at Santa Rosa Memorial became, over time, a model campaign. Nevertheless, it only narrowly avoided becoming one more monument to the frustration and failure of U.S. labor law. The main party responsible is Memorial management. But the "just rights" of Catholic hospital workers were also flagrantly abused by SEIU, which abandoned its own supporters and then tried to undermine their independent union.

Chapter 3

A Scramble for New Members

"SEIU has long been home to workers that other unions didn't want—women, immigrants, and people of color."
—Andy Stern, May 6, 2010[1]

"The future of the labor movement isn't industrial workers, it's homecare workers: people of color making seven dollars an hour with no insurance."
—Robert Craig, SEIU Wisconsin Political Director[2]

In the parched landscape of American labor, where few unions can claim much membership growth, SEIU's recruitment record has been the envy of all. SEIU organizers have been rightly applauded by labor activists and academics alike for their innovative campaigns to create new bargaining units for home-based workers, most of whom are women, immigrants, and/or people of color. After a ten-year effort, SEIU was able, in 1999, to win bargaining rights for a huge group of home health care aides in Southern California who had been previously treated as "independent contractors." This victory, among seventy-five thousand caregivers, was even compared to the triumph of UAW over General Motors in the 1937 Flint Sit-Down Strike.[3] Organizing of home health care aides or child care providers in a dozen states has resulted in overall unionization of six hundred thousand workers. They are the labor movement's largest source of new members lately—even if their newly created, quasi-public "employers of record" are nothing like GM or any other giant corporation, where industrial workers once had such social weight because of their capacity for collective action.

By 2005, it was no longer true, if it ever was, that only SEIU wanted to provide a home for the working poor. In some parts of the country, the potential membership gains in this sector of the population were so tempting that a union free-for-all ensued. The competition between SEIU and AFSCME (American Federation of State, County and Municipal Employees) in Illinois and California become particularly intense and costly, right before and after the AFL-CIO split. And AFSCME wasn't the only AFL-CIO union trying to emulate SEIU's success with low-paid, direct care providers at the bottom tier of government employment. Other labor organizations with a public sector presence—AFT, UAW, and my own alma mater, CWA—all launched their own home-based worker campaigns. Depending on how this new union-building was done, it could be seen as the culmination of the admirable "poor worker" organizing started thirty years ago by sixties-inspired welfare rights advocates and community activists or it could just be a mad scramble for new members—in any place where the management hostility of the Memorial or MMC sort was thankfully missing.

I found myself wondering which form this new organizing would take for CWA, during a meeting at a Newark, New Jersey, union hall in September 2005. A group of CWA organizers had convened for the purpose of brainstorming about our bid to represent six thousand home-based child care workers. Hosting the meeting was Local 1037, then headed by the fiery and indefatigable Hetty Rosenstein, a past critic of SEIU for failing to "engage rank-and-file workers in the project of labor revitalization."[4] Rosenstein's local already represented more than eight thousand workers. Most were employed by the state of New Jersey or worked for nonprofit social service agencies.

Under Rosenstein's leadership, Local 1037 had been very successful in organizing. It was also committed to follow-up leadership development and steward-training in new (and old) bargaining units. For Hetty, the big challenge facing CWA in state-funded child care was how to build something resembling a real union among workers lacking a traditional workplace. In a high-turnover workforce that included many part-timers, would it be possible for child care workers to be active and engaged and not just passive dues payers? Was there a way to structure representation so they would have a steward system like the one 1037 had developed over the years in state agencies? Should we do this organizing together, with another union, or on our own, possibly in competition with others? Either way, Rosenstein believed that doing this right would require an enormous commitment of resources. Otherwise, any day care group in New Jersey would turn into what she called a "1-800-GRIEVANCE operation"—and that was not the kind of union that 1037 strived to be.

A History of Union Competition

Rosenstein first joined CWA in 1981, the same year a majority of her fellow state employees embraced CWA rather than AFSCME or the AFT. CWA's public sector growth spurt in the Garden State owed a lot to an illegal strike by fifteen thousand white-collar state employees in 1979. In Trenton, Newark, and other cities, these union members walked off the job to protest an unpopular contract settlement negotiated by the then independent New Jersey State Employees Association (SEA). The strikers were denounced by the governor (a liberal Democrat), criticized in the media, enjoined by the courts, and undermined by leaders of both SEA and AFSCME, which ordered its members to ignore any picket lines.

Forced back to work, rank-and-file strike leaders joined forces with CWA organizer Larry Cohen. In the late seventies, Cohen helped form the State Workers Organizing Committee (SWOC), while recruiting new members for CWA in local government jobs. SWOC's goal was to replace the SEA, which later affiliated with the AFT. As Cohen envisioned it, the new CWA-backed state workers' organization, would be militant, democratic, and run by "elected stewards and active members who understand that the union is a vehicle for rank-and-file mobilization, not just servicing."[5] With CWA financing and staff help, SWOC members signed up twelve thousand of their coworkers to trigger representation votes among New Jersey's thirty-four thousand clerical, administrative, professional, and supervisory employees. When the balloting was over in 1981, CWA became the largest public employee union in the state. The eight new CWA locals spawned by the SWOC campaign have had their ups and downs since then. Rosenstein's Local 1037 remained the most consistently committed to workplace activism, a strong steward system, and member-based organizing of nonunion workers.

SEIU represents only a handful of public workers in New Jersey and is mainly a presence in health care and building services. In its search for home-based worker growth opportunities around the country, the Garden State was not neglected, however. When Democrat James McGreevey became governor, SEIU secretary-treasurer Anna Burger personally decided to ingratiate herself with McGreevey by supporting privatization of public employee pension fund management. This scheme was opposed by CWA, AFSCME, and the New Jersey Education Association, so Burger's lack of solidarity on the issue was widely resented.[6] Her real play was not about pensions and investing. SEIU hoped that McGreevey would—out of gratitude and in return for future campaign contributions—transform thousands of state-funded "independent contractors" into workers eligible for collective bargaining rights and, thus, membership in SEIU.

Unfortunately, SEIU placed its bet on a politician soon forced to resign. But SEIU's ability, in Illinois, to join forces with an even more troubled governor, and then outmaneuver AFSCME, the state's largest public employee union, in a contested campaign for forty-eight thousand home care providers, was a second wake-up call for CWA. In March of 2005, Larry Cohen, then executive vice president of CWA (and soon to be its new president), sent an urgent email to other executive board members about the "need to create opportunities like this" in New Jersey. Otherwise, he warned, the state "will definitely be a battlefield" and, if CWA didn't "move very quickly, SEIU will scoop up thousands of members there as well."[7]

Our political challenge was positioning CWA to become the more deserving beneficiary of a union-friendly executive order, signed by a new Democratic governor, Jon Corzine (who was then in the process of spending $40 million of his own money to move from a U.S. Senate seat to the governor's mansion in Princeton). This order would be drafted to cover state-funded home day care providers, many of whom are women enrolled in Temporary Assistance for Needy Families (TANF), the welfare-to-work program introduced by Bill Clinton. Their workfare assignment consists of taking care of their own or other TANF-recipients' children, in their homes. For that work, they received average annual compensation of about $17,000 in 2005, which doesn't go far, either in inner-city New Jersey or its less visible pockets of rural poverty. It was our plan to have Corzine, the former chairman and CEO of Goldman Sachs, take note of the child care providers' plight and make a public commitment to helping them after he became governor, with CWA's help.

A Jump Start from ACORN

Present at Local 1037 to advise us on the mechanics of all this was a wily independent contractor of a different sort, Wade Rathke. The cowboy boot–wearing Williams College dropout who founded the Association of Community Organizations for Reform Now (ACORN) was accompanied by several young ACORN canvassers. The New Jersey branch of his group was already receiving CWA funding (that eventually exceeded $200,000) to collect authorization cards needed to demonstrate that a majority of state-subsidized family day care providers wanted a union. Dedicated ACORN organizers like Kate Atkins were able to jump-start our campaign due to the overlap between ACORN's dues-paying membership in inner-city neighborhoods and child care provider lists obtained from the state by both CWA and AFSCME.

In the wake of Hurricane Katrina, which had just swept through his own neighborhood, Brother Rathke was still juggling a bewildering array of responsibilities. He was functioning as the "Chief Organizer" and key national fundraiser for ACORN, his labor of love for thirty-five years. He was the senior staff member and de facto leader of Local 100, a multistate SEIU affiliate based in Louisiana and originally part of the ACORN-initiated United Labor Unions we met in chapter 1. And he had, until the year before, even been a national executive board member of SEIU—the union still viewed as a potential contender for the affections of child care workers from Trenton to Camden. None of these roles yet carried the slightest whiff of controversy to come—in the form of disclosures about the embezzlement of one million dollars from ACORN by Rathke's brother, which would lead to his resignation from the organization. Within just a few years, this scandal would be followed by right-wing media demonization of the group, leading to its bankruptcy, dissolution, and local chapter reorganization and rebranding in 2009.[8]

At the time, in the ACORN founder's mind, it was apparently not a conflict of interest, union-wise, for him to be dispensing insider advice, for a price, to a "rival union" still wary of possible SEIU organizing competition on its biggest piece of public sector turf. Rathke was at the peak of his influence as the Johnny Appleseed of home-based worker organizing. He had worked out a highly entrepreneurial arrangement with SEIU, which, as he later explained to me, gave his own union "first refusal" on partnering with ACORN in any particular state. On the other side of the Hudson, he obtained SEIU's approval to persuade Randi Weingarten, then president of the United Federation of Teachers (UFT) (and now national AFT president), that her local should work with ACORN to recruit twenty-eight thousand New York City–area child care providers. In New York, the day care turf would be divided in half, with the union representing most state workers—AFSCME's Civil Service Employees Association organizing upstate providers and AFT/ACORN pursuing the downstate group.

In New Jersey, our situation was a little more unsettled, given the possibility of a three-way labor squabble. Our old adversary from 1981, AFSCME, was already signing up the same child care providers as us, with a similar Corzine deal in mind. In a scenario vividly described to us by

Rathke, his own union was still lurking about, marshaling its forces for an imminent invasion of New Jersey. SEIU might be appearing at any moment with a horde of out-of-state staffers, a huge advertising budget, and the unbeatable momentum of its latest child care win in Illinois. (There, SEIU Local 880, headed by former ACORN and ULU organizer Keith Kelleher, had bested AFSCME.) What CWA needed to compete with this impending onslaught was "a much more robust program," the chief organizer insisted. By that, he meant giving more money to ACORN. Plus, he had another budget-busting idea: we should not even consider working together with AFSCME.

Instead, CWA should do battle until our union rival was forced to butt out, just like in Illinois. Cooler (or more cost-conscious) heads prevailed on both questions. In CWA circles in New Jersey, there was not much enthusiasm for working with AFSCME, after years of bargaining-related tension and mistrust. But, given the political realities in Trenton (the state capital), it was hard to imagine that the new governor would deliver a whole new bargaining unit to the biggest state worker union at the expense of the second largest one (also a supporter of his campaign), without the latter screwing up the deal somehow. Furthermore, CWA organizers Anne Luck and Tim Dubnau wanted to inject programmatic content into the campaign—something harder to do if it degenerated into a competitive "blitz" of door-knocking, phone calling, and mud-slinging mailings.

Beyond just getting the child care workers signed up and a contract negotiated, Rosenstein believed there was a daunting second layer of complexity to address, involving the work itself. Namely, how should child care ideally be organized and funded? How should providers be registered, trained, and supported? How can parents, providers, and low-income communities work together to influence public policy in this area? What could be done to create a career path out of home-based work into better-paying and more secure state employment for any woman on TANF who didn't wish to remain (what union literature always calls) a "*professional* child care provider"? Here, Rosenstein was raising concerns more normally the province of academics who write about home-based work.

Among the most prominent researchers in that field are Jennifer Klein and Eileen Boris, professors from Yale and UCSB, respectively. Their forthcoming book, *Caring for America*, describes how SEIU affiliates have tried to improve the work lives of child care providers and home health aides. In one of their already published articles on home care unionization, the authors describe the challenge of "empowering care workers" within the new organizations that have been built for and with them. While appreciative of the economic gains made, Klein and Boris warn that if SEIU and other unions simply "become providers of services, rather than educators and mobilizers" and stop trying to "revalue caring labor," the result will be "bureaucratic unionism that reinforces the old racialized gender distinctions of care work and stymies the advancement of rank-and-file women."[9]

In New Jersey, CWA tried to link community and labor concerns about child care by releasing a research report called *Our Children, Our Future*, modeled after a similar study done by SEIU in Illinois. It made the case for better pay and conditions in a way that also emphasized the need for greater access to quality subsidized day care. Local 1037's existing cadre of stewards assisted the drive and some served on the organizing committee with child care workers themselves. They knocked on doors and made phone calls to obtain the four thousand union cards ultimately submitted to the state in 2006. (Fortunately, SEIU never showed up to collect a single one.) Later that year, newly elected Governor Corzine signed the executive order recognizing both CWA and AFSCME as the Child Care Workers Union (CCWU).[10] On the CWA side, Local 1037 then converted its organizing committee members into "neighborhood shop stewards," who could, wherever possible, try to represent other day care workers in the same communities. Neighborhood stewards helped get bargaining surveys filled out. They carpooled coworkers to meetings to elect negotiating committee members and, in the fall of 2007, encouraged rank-and-file participation in contract ratification voting.

That CCWU agreement increased annual per child payments to providers; a worker caring for five children would be earning $7,200 more annually by the end of its four-year term. The contract obligated the state to provide parents with seniority lists so, when choosing a child care worker, they would know who was experienced and who was new to the job. A grievance procedure was created, which included arbitration of unresolved disputes about contract violations. Compared to the thick benefit-studded agreement covering regular state workers, it was a bare-bones contract that did not improve health coverage. (That problem was to be surveyed and addressed later on, if possible.)

Future progress would depend on Local 1037's ability to do even more labor-intensive work to promote day care provider activism. That task proved to be difficult while juggling the competing challenge of mobilizing thousands of other 1037 members for their own subsequent contract fights with Corzine and, now, his extremely anti-union Republican successor, Chris Christie. Improving the conditions of a contingent workforce of direct care providers at the bottom tier of public employment when "regular" state workers are under attack is not easy. And the respective workplace worlds of these new and old members remain as different as the union contracts that cover them.

An Organizing Boost from Blago

As joint union ventures go, the AFSCME-CWA alliance in New Jersey had to be deemed an initial success, if only for dodging the bullet of labor civil warfare. As we shall see in the case of Illinois, inter-union conflict is not the only potential risk—or obstacle to overcome—in politician-assisted public sector organizing of this sort. To recruit thousands of home-based workers in the land of Lincoln, SEIU helped saddle millions of people with a governor so bad he ended up becoming the latest Illinois chief executive to be indicted or jailed for corruption. (There have been four in the last thirty-five years.)

To be fair, SEIU's 2005 child care election victory, involving forty-eight thousand workers, required years of work by Local 880, a sister organization of ACORN that affiliated with SEIU in 1984, along with other ULU chapters. For more than a decade before Democrat Rod Blagojevich became governor, 880 had organized and supported a nonbargaining, community-based association of day care workers. Using direct action tactics and hand collection of dues, these workers lobbied for and won increases in the state's contribution to their subsidy payments.[11] Blagojevich's Republican predecessor, George Ryan, refused to sign a bill backed by SEIU granting these workers bargaining rights.

"Blago," as he is popularly known, was a member of Congress from Chicago when he first sought the Democratic gubernatorial nomination in 2002, with backing from both SEIU and AFSCME. As SEIU state council leader and Local 1 president Tom Balanoff later explained, "We told our members we had to build up our political arm, in order to grow, so we increased the locals payments to our state council. And we took a huge risk with Blagojevich." SEIU "provided roughly 1,000 precinct walkers in the [2002] primary campaign's final weeks, with an estimated 400 coming from Wisconsin and Ohio…Blagojevich eked out a one percent victory."[12] SEIU money was also critical. As one longtime political observer noted, "the moment Blagojevich transitioned from a backbench kind of nobody congressman was when he filed with a million dollars…After that, the thing that made people come to him, to advise him or advocate on policy or whatever—your advice was only as good as how much money you could raise."[13]

Soon after his general election win, Blagojevich issued an executive order allowing twenty thousand home health care workers to unionize. A year later, they had a first contract that raised starting pay from $7.15 per hour to $9.35 over three years. The governor also appointed Balanoff to the Illinois Health Facilities Planning Board, which oversees hospital construction projects, a position that could be used to aid "leverage campaigns" to win organizing rights.[14]

In 2004, Local 880 stepped up its child care worker organizing, putting several dozen additional staffers on the project. When Blagojevich issued a second executive order in February 2005, covering the proposed day care unit, SEIU was ready with eighteen thousand provider-signed cards demanding a representation election. This vote was scheduled to take place within forty-two days. As was true later in New Jersey and other states, the governor's order limited the scope of bargaining; day care workers were not eligible for regular state worker health insurance or pension coverage. This infuriated an already outmaneuvered AFSCME. Said Henry Bayer, its state director: "We've been representing state employees for 30 years and now SEIU has created a [new] class of employees and signed away their benefits...They came in here and cut our standards!"[15]

Dozens of AFSCME organizers from around the country were quickly dispatched to Illinois, where they collected enough cards to win a place on the ballot with SEIU. Andy Stern was just several months away from launching Change to Win, but that didn't stop him from invoking the organizing dispute resolution procedures of the AFL-CIO constitution. SEIU demanded an immediate hearing aimed at ousting AFSCME from the field before any vote took place. The gist of SEIU's jurisdictional claim was that 880 had worked for years to lay the groundwork for this day care worker election. If it became a full-blown inter-union slugfest, Tom Balanoff predicted that "SEIU and AFSCME will each spend over a million dollars on something that shouldn't be happening." An AFL-CIO-appointed umpire ruled in favor of SEIU, forcing its unhappy competitor to bow out during the balloting period. (AFSCME still received 16 percent of the vote statewide.) To boost its own turnout in the home stretch, "SEIU marshaled 500 organizers from Local 880 and other locals, allied unions, and ACORN to knock on 4,000 doors a day...nearly 17,000 workers [out of 49,000 eligible] mailed in ballots, with more than 80 percent of them voting for SEIU."[16] In December 2005, after 880 negotiations with the Blagojevich administration, SEIU's new day care members obtained a $250 million, thirty-nine-month contract designed to raise providers' daily rates an average of 35 percent and eventually provide them with some health coverage.[17]

The Price of "Pay to Play"

Helping home care and child care workers didn't come cheap in the "pay to play" world of Illinois politics. SEIU pumped $1.8 million into Blagojevich's campaign coffers between 2001 and 2008, becoming his top contributor when he ran for reelection in 2006. "It wasn't long into his first term that articles began to appear about questionable state hires and no-bid contracts connected to Blagojevich donors." Barack Obama, sensing trouble and showing better sense than SEIU, "began keeping his distance from Blagojevich long before scandals started to accrete around the governor."[18] Being part of the governor's team increased SEIU's entanglement with him after Obama was elected president and the union's closest political friend in Illinois got to fill his seat. The governor sought to use his appointment power to gain personal favors for his wife and himself, either from the administration or other well-heeled Washington allies with an interest in influencing his decision about Obama's replacement in the Senate.

In various conversations wiretapped by the FBI, Blagojevich professed interest in getting a top job at CTW (or some other well-endowed nonprofit group) after he left office in 2010. Tom Balanoff was among those political supporters whose conversations with the governor, on this and other topics, were recorded or discussed. For awhile, Blagojevich quite liked the idea of becoming CTW director because, based on what he knew about Tom's neighborhood in Chicago, a union job in Washington, D.C., might be very lucrative. "He lives on the North Shore," the governor noted in one taped conversation. "You gotta think he makes more than the governor, right?"

Later, Blagojevich decided CTW pay wouldn't meet his requirements— a salary of at least $300,000 a year. Plus, toiling for a labor coalition with an uncertain future seemed to be too speculative a reward for the political jewel he had to trade here and now.[19] One day before the 2008 election, Andy Stern and Balanoff discussed these matters directly with Blagojevich—at a point when a Democratic presidential win seemed assured and the governor was, according to federal prosecutors, actively peddling Obama's Senate seat to the highest bidder.[20] Blago's crude, convoluted, and often comical scheming was part of a larger pattern of state government corruption that was simply "breathtaking," according to the *Nation*.[21]

Federal prosecutors accused him of shaking down road construction companies, racetrack owners, a children's hospital, and other targets as early as 2003. The governor's December 9, 2008, arrest along with several associates (who later pleaded guilty and testified against him) led to weeks of wrangling in the Illinois legislature over his impeachment. After the Democrat-controlled state Senate voted to convict him on January 29, 2009, he was removed from office by a vote of 59 to 0. Meanwhile, the state faced "a crisis of confidence in government, a $4 billion budget gap, and a record level of unpaid bills to day care and healthcare providers"—the same low-paid workers SEIU won the right to represent with Blagojevich's help.[22]

The union's very close, once useful, now extremely embarrassing connection to the governor proved to be a propaganda jackpot for right-wing foes of organized labor and their drive to defeat EFCA. Headlines like the one in the *New York Times* on December 9—"Union Is Caught Up in Illinois Bribe Case"—quickly found their way into big anti-EFCA ads, as critics of labor law reform recycled every tawdry detail of Blago-gate. "Connect the Dots, Chicago-Style," urged one full-page spread in the *Washington Post*. "SEIU has given more cash to Rod Blagojevich than any other group in America," the Center for Union Facts informed readers of the *New York Times*. The bottom line in both messages: "Call Your United States Senators Today! Tell Them To Oppose the deceptively-named 'Employee Free Choice Act!'"[23]

When Blagojevich finally went to trial, Tom Balanoff was a stand-up guy—for the prosecution. As promised when the governor was arrested, the union whose funding was so critical to electing the defendant twice fully cooperated with the feds when it was time to put him in jail. In August 2010, the jury deadlocked on twenty-three out of twenty-four counts against Blagojevich, agreeing only that he lied to the FBI (an offense carrying a sentence of up to five years). A mistrial was declared on the rest. Blago said he would appeal his conviction, and the government made plans for a retrial in January 2011. This delay minimized further distractions for Illinois Democrats while they tried (unsuccessfully) to hold onto Obama's Senate seat during the November 2010 elections.[24]

Trying to help them recover from the scandal was SEIU. The union quickly cemented its relationship with former Lieutenant Governor Patrick Quinn, who replaced Blagojevich after his impeachment, and then ran for his own full term as governor. In February 2010, SEIU contributed an astounding $1.7 million—25 percent of all the donations made—to Quinn's primary election campaign. His win was one of four statewide primary races where an SEIU-backed candidate emerged victorious. "The union's successes culminated a long push for prominence that has seen it become the biggest financial contributor to Illinois political campaigns. Its campaign committees, which were only bit players in local politics a decade ago, have spent more than $10 million across Illinois in the past six years."[25]

Before getting elected in 2010, Quinn remained a bit gun-shy about signing any executive orders that might be viewed as overly friendly to SEIU. At the time of his arrest, Blagojevich was about to create a home-based bargaining unit for three thousand people who care for the disabled. Quinn acted on this in 2009, but AFSCME also got on the ballot. Unlike four years earlier, SEIU's rival campaigned to the bitter end. The caregivers choosing between AFSCME, SEIU, and no union mainly worked in their own homes for a family member. More than half elected to remain nonunion. Some reportedly voted no because they didn't think either union would be able to lift a legislative cap on their state reimbursement rates.[26]

SEIU versus AFSCME in California

With 1.6 million members of his own, Gerry McEntee, the president of AFSCME, is no slouch when it comes to political spending. ("We're the big dogs, not that we brag," he said in the fall of 2010, when AFSCME showered $90 million on endangered Democrats around the country.)[27] Nor is seventy-five-year-old Gerry a stranger to the disappointment that occurs when "friends of labor" fail to deliver once in office. Yet, even after the "pay to play" scandal in Illinois left SEIU splattered with mud, McEntee was still miffed about the better treatment Andy Stern got from Blago. "SEIU had a special relationship with the governor," McEntee told the *Wall Street Journal*, when Blago was facing impeachment. "We never did. We weren't involved in their plans so we can't speculate on what was worked out."[28] Given the bruised feelings involved, it took some months for AFSCME to get things "worked out" with SEIU.

Delaying that reconciliation was Stern's brazen interference with United Domestic Workers (UDW), a troubled AFSCME affiliate based in San Diego. Representing about sixty thousand Southern California home care workers, UDW had a history of being democracy challenged. Founded in 1979, it went for twenty-four years without holding a single membership election for its top officers, based on the claim that it was not a local union but rather an "intermediate" body that was entitled to have just a few union delegates elect the leadership. The U.S. Department of Labor (and AFSCME itself) finally forced the husband-and-wife team who led UDW since its inception to change these illegal election rules that enabled them to run the local with little accountability to its widely dispersed, poorly informed, and atomized rank and file.[29]

This undemocratic arrangement led to questionable spending, just as it would in SEIU's largest home care local only a few years later. According to AFSCME, UDW was near bankruptcy despite collecting $1 million a month in dues from its low-wage members. So McEntee announced that it was time "to stop bad actors within the UDW leadership from misusing workers' hard-earned money." He removed all fifteen officers and board members of UDW, and put the local under trusteeship.[30] Enter Andy Stern, but this time in the unprecedented role of trusteeship opponent.

SEIU embraced the ousted founders of UDW, Ken Seaton-Msemaji and his wife, Fahari Jeffers. It began collaborating with them in a fashion quite ironic in light of Stern's later grounds for seizing UHW and filing a $25 million lawsuit against organizers of NUHW. At first, UDW tried to arrange a quickie vote to merge with SEIU, cutting all ties to McEntee's union. When this affiliation attempt was blocked by a court injunction, the deposed UDW leaders urged their supporters to decertify, unit by unit, and become part of SEIU that way. Using what AFSCME claimed were purloined membership records, SEIU organizers began calling and visiting UDW-represented workers to sign them up on petitions seeking elections so they could switch unions. In Riverside County, where AFSCME officials who took over UDW were trying to negotiate a new contract, SEIU signed up nearly thirty-five hundred workers. SEIU Local 434B president Tyrone

Freeman, an ambitious young protégé of Stern's, joined Seaton-Msemaji in calling for an immediate election to determine which union should represent home care workers in contract negotiations with the county.

This time, AFSCME struck back by invoking AFL-CIO no-raiding rules in the nick of time. A federation hearing was held and, just one week before SEIU left to form CTW, President John Sweeney informed Stern that his union was in violation of article 20 of the AFL-CIO constitution. SEIU was ordered to stop poaching members of AFSCME. Six weeks later, after their own direct negotiations, SEIU and AFSCME announced that they had reached a "breakthrough agreement" enabling them to "devote their energies to strategically uniting workers in childcare and homecare"—rather than spending hundreds of thousands of dollars, if not millions by then, competing with each other. Henceforth, the two unions would cooperate, in several states, on joint ventures in child care worker organizing.[31]

This Southern California home care peace treaty had one unfortunate effect. It helped expand the reach of Tyrone Freeman and his own subsequent opportunities for thievery. Under the terms of Stern's settlement with AFSCME, Freeman's Local 434B and UDW/AFSCME retained their separate jurisdiction. But twenty-five thousand other caregivers whose bargaining rights had been in dispute became the unwitting members of an organization jointly affiliated with SEIU and AFSCME, called the California United Homecare Workers Union (CUHWU). Freeman was named president of CUHWU and then, thanks to subsequent Stern-directed mergers within SEIU, he also emerged as the appointed president of 160,000-member Local 6434, the successor to 434B. Home care workers in both CUHWU and 6434 would eventually pay a big price for Tyrone's multiple union roles as we'll see in chapter 5.

At War with the Nurses

While SEIU was able, even outside the AFL-CIO, to patch things up with AFSCME, its relations with the California Nurses Association got even worse after the CTW split. Once SEIU left the "house of labor," the previously independent CNA suddenly found it far more attractive to be part of the federation. Now, the AFL's "no-raiding" rules and jurisdictional complaint procedures (of the sort invoked by SEIU against AFSCME in Illinois and by AFSCME against SEIU in California) could no longer be used by Stern to block CNA overtures to SEIU-represented nurses anywhere. Plus, with Andy Stern gone, CNA's politically ambitious director Rose Ann DeMoro hoped to move the federation in a better direction on health care reform, unimpeded by the greater policy clout of a fellow affiliate with far more hospital worker members, 1.6 million per capita dues payers, and little enthusiasm for single-payer solutions.

After CNA joined the AFL-CIO, DeMoro became a rare female member of its executive council. There, she didn't refrain from criticizing her recently departed rival or other unions for their partnership agreements and general political timidity. "I think that one tremendous success of neoliberalism, the neoliberal agenda, has been to get unions to define themselves as part of the corporation," she said in one typical interview. "It's just so chilling that unions today can't even envision a different type of world or a different type of model, where the corporations are there to serve society, rather than the workers being there to serve the corporation."[32] With rhetoric like this, the CNA encouraged a rethinking of past left-wing assumptions about the merits of "wall to wall" hospital unionism versus an organization that championed members of a single health care occupation. In the past, professional unions, particularly for nurses, had been more conservative than "industrial" ones. But if this particular "craft union" was now more militant, "anti-partnership," and progressive-sounding than SEIU, perhaps it was the better choice for RNs and left-liberals alike?[33] The continuing fights between the two unions—in California, Nevada, and then Ohio—were nevertheless distressing to many friends of labor and, in the case of Ohio, particularly hard to fathom.

CNA-SEIU differences in the Buckeye State gained a national spotlight at a conference of labor activists held in Dearborn, Michigan, in April 2008. The sponsor of this biannual event was Labor Notes, a thirty-year-old Detroit newsletter and labor education project always on the cutting edge of union controversy. In the fall of 2007, Labor Notes conference organizers invited Rose Ann DeMoro to speak at their "Troublemakers Award" dinner, a major fundraising event for the group. Two months before her scheduled appearance, DeMoro dispatched organizers from the CNA-backed National Nurses Organizing Committee (NNOC) to Catholic hospitals in Ohio to dissuade RNs there from voting for SEIU on the aforementioned grounds that it was a "company union." SEIU had spent three years engaged in "corporate campaigning" (and some inside committee building) directed at Catholic Healthcare Partners (CHP), the largest hospital system in the state. The goal of this statewide campaign was to get CHP to accept representation elections free from the coercion employed by management in previous organizing battles at several individual facilities. As journalist Esther Kaplan reported:

> SEIU activists mailed out literature about fair unionization rules to elected officials, clergy, and advocacy groups. They had hearings before the state legislature. They got community members and hospital workers to sign open letters, held protests over layoffs and wage-and-hour violations, and met with priests and bishops. They issued reports criticizing the chain for inadequate charity care and bloated CEO pay.[34]

The result was a highly unusual process, seemingly detached from any workplace activity by SEIU organizing committees where they still existed. In February 2008, CHP management petitioned the NLRB to hold a representation vote—a step usually taken by unions, not employers. The election ground rules that were worked out in advance by CHP and SEIU sharply limited campaigning on the job and mailings to workers' homes by either side. "The employees were informed of the election two weeks in advance by means of a letter co-signed by CHP and SEIU, a jointly written fact sheet and a broadside from each party arguing for and against the union. Each side set up a toll-free number for questions and that was that."[35] Only SEIU was on the NLRB ballot, but without the usual showing of signed authorization cards indicating worker support for any union. NNOC national organizing director Ed Bruno charged that "employee discussion about the union and the election was specifically forbidden by managers, with the agreement of SEIU...a significant violation of the rights of association and speech and the [NLRA] Section 7 right of self-organization."[36]

CNA managed to unravel this arrangement simply by sending its own organizers to visit CHP facilities to talk to nurses about joining CNA/NNOC instead. CHP clearly abhorred any intervention by a labor organization not on the ballot and very much intent on stirring up workplace controversy about SEIU's "back-room deal." So the employer withdrew its petition, canceling statewide balloting that would have covered eight-three hundred workers in many different potential bargaining units, in nine out of twenty-one CHP facilities. (As of 2010, not a single one has been organized by any union.) This setback infuriated SEIU District 1199—which covers Ohio, West Virginia, and Kentucky—and SEIU national union officials. An enraged Andy Stern directed all SEIU locals still affiliated with AFL-CIO central labor councils to stop paying dues to them until John Sweeney imposed sanctions on the CNA, one of his newest affiliates.[37] Sweeney, of course, pointed out that the established internal procedure for settling such disputes (used in the Illinois and California home care cases involving AFSCME) would have been available to SEIU if Stern's union had not abandoned the federation three years earlier.

Organized around the theme "Rebuilding Labor's Power," the Labor Notes meeting in Michigan would have been the perfect venue for SEIU partisans to engage their CNA critics about the Ohio controversy. For a modest registration fee, anyone was welcome to attend. Labor Notes conferences are a rare place in the labor movement where rank-and-file activists, union officers and staff, friends of labor, and foreign trade unionists all come together for freewheeling exchanges of information and opinion, unfettered by union protocol or party lines. At one session that I chaired in 2008, organizing rights agreements—including the SEIU-CHP deal—were hotly debated. Among those attending were SEIU staffers (part of a small group who did register for the conference), nurses from CNA/NNOC, and UHW members, plus organizers from UNITE HERE, CWA, and other unions. The crowd of about a hundred spent several hours weighing the tradeoffs between contract standards and growth that were becoming increasingly controversial, as we saw in the previous chapter. The panel had been provocatively titled, "Neutrality Agreements and Organizing Deals: Salvation or Sell-Out?" Most people—with the exception of a few revolutionary party members—no doubt left the session concluding that the reality of these agreements lies somewhere in between. As one panelist, then UHW political director Paul Kumar, reported afterward: "Many participants, who can fairly be described as members of the labor left and generally suspicious of top union leaders, were actually very sympathetic to the SEIU's grievance against CNA surrounding the events in Ohio."

SEIU decided that it would deal with DeMoro's scheduled appearance through direct action, not further discussion. On Saturday morning of the conference, hundreds of participants found a flyer under their hotel room doors. Addressed to DeMoro personally, this SEIU handbill asked: "How can you talk about rebuilding labor's power when you're busting unions and taking away the rights of thousands of workers?" SEIU highlighted the fact that DeMoro "and her husband Robert rake in over $330,000 in salaries from the California Nurses Association and front groups CNA funds." (By 2009, DeMoro's salary was more than $280,000 and her husband—whose name is actually Don—was making about $140,000 from the union.)[38]

This leaflet drop was just a warm-up for the main event on Saturday night. As Labor Notes' big fundraising and awards dinner got started in the hotel ballroom, five or six busloads of SEIU members and staff from Cleveland and Detroit pulled up outside the Hyatt. They unloaded and set up an informational picket line. DeMoro got wind of this rumored demonstration the day before and decided not to come. So she was not even present at the banquet being picketed (although she did address the crowd via videoconference from the safety of her union headquarters in Oakland). The protest organizers were, of course, welcome to picket—as UAW and Teamster officials have done in the past when they objected to a Labor Notes conference speaker or participating dissident group. But, this time, there was more to the protest plan. The organizers intended to enter the hotel and burst into its crowded ballroom, where nine hundred conference-goers had just been seated for a dinner honoring UAW strikers, immigrant taxi drivers, and living wage organizers.

A group of hastily assembled Labor Notes volunteers stood in front of the doors leading to the ballroom to prevent anyone from entering who was not registered. A staffer for SEIU, who was a conference participant, opened one of the locked lobby doors from the inside, and that was the signal. Part of the picketing crowd surged into the hotel, knocking over literature tables in its rush toward the ballroom. Some involved in the charge used their purple bandannas to conceal their faces; others started pushing, shoving, and throwing punches when their path was blocked, nonviolently, by the linked arms of the Labor Notes marshals. Among those injured was Dianne Feeley, a retired UAW member and Labor Notes volunteer. She ended up with a bloodied head requiring a trip to the hospital and stitches. In the ranks of SEIU, the fracas took a more tragic toll. After the melee, David Smith, a heavy-set African American home care worker from Detroit, collapsed on the sidewalk, dying of a heart attack, as Dearborn police, hotel security, and several ambulances descended on the scene.

While the repelled protestors were still milling around outside the hotel, some Labor Notes supporters went outside to talk with them. From these conversations, it became clear that few SEIU members involved knew anything about the gathering they had just picketed—other than it was a "meeting of union-busters," or so they had been told by their local unions. Like Smith, many participants were home health care aides and nursing home workers from SEIU Michigan Healthcare, the 55,000-member local headed by Stern appointee Rickman Jackson. Some of the female home care workers even brought their children on this union outing, unaware that the scenario included charging into a tightly packed ballroom to deliver SEIU's anti-CNA message. As SEIU staffers herded everyone back onto their buses, some protesters were clearly confused by the discovery that fellow trade unionists were in the hotel, including nearly one hundred from UHW and other SEIU locals. A team of EMTs labored over David Smith until his purple-clad body was moved from the sidewalk to a stretcher and driven away. The next day, his coworkers were informed on the local's website that "he passed away…during a rally to give healthcare workers the right to organize in Ohio."[39]

This whole appalling scene, particularly SEIU's manipulation of home care workers, generated much national publicity, all of it negative for the protesters. The *New York Times* covered the brawl and ran an unflattering picture of it. The left press and labor-oriented listservs were soon buzzing with disapproval as well. In his capacity as head of the AFL-CIO, SEIU's own former president John Sweeney issued a statement saying: "There is no justification, none, for the violent attack orchestrated by S.E.I.U. Violence in attacking freedom of speech must be strongly condemned."[40] A social worker in Cleveland, who belonged to Regan's local and whose dues money helped pay for the outing, immediately sent him an email expressing her shame and outrage about the union's behavior at Labor Notes. "I work with angry teenagers day in and day out to teach them 'anger management' skills," she wrote. "Apparently some SEIU staff need a crash course…Please explain to me and other members what you are doing to ensure this doesn't continue to happen." In his reply, Regan saw no need to apologize. He assured this concerned member that, in the face of provocation by the "disingenuous, dishonest, and unprincipled" CNA, "we conducted ourselves appropriately and with composure."[41]

"A Butt-Whipping They Will Never Forget"

Fourteen months later, the same well-composed Dave Regan mounted a stage at the Fresno County Fairgrounds to welcome a different SEIU contingent to California. This time, the threat to his union was internal and would take more than a day trip to Dearborn to quell. It came from dissident home care workers who were trying to take their bargaining unit of ten thousand out of SEIU in mail balloting that was just getting under way. Arrayed against them (and a group of about 150 volunteer organizers from the new NUHW) was an expeditionary force of nine hundred SEIU staffers and local union "lost-timers." They were flown into Fresno, given generous per diem allowances, issued rental cars and GPS devices, and housed for several weeks or more in the best local hotels. It was their job to go door-to-door and persuade workers to stick with SEIU, not switch to NUHW. After his Labor Notes invasion attempt, Regan had received not one but two big promotions from Andy Stern. He was named executive vice president of SEIU, a job paying $200,000 a year, and then made cotrustee of UHW. So a lot was on the line for him personally in this struggle to defeat what his fellow trustee Eliseo Medina called the "contras" of NUHW. Rallying the troops in Fresno with both of them were future SEIU president Mary Kay Henry and Gerry Hudson, another SEIU EVP originally from District 1199 in New York.

The jowly, gray-haired forty-three-year-old Regan, a graduate of the Cornell School of Industrial and Labor Relations and a former algebra teacher, addressed the crowd with his shirt collar open and sleeves rolled up. For the moment, he was in blue-collar tough-guy mode—speaking frankly to those he called his "old school friends." In order to prevent any future home care worker defections, SEIU needed to demonstrate, once and for all, that "it is hopeless, you can't win." He told the assembled canvassers that "this is not an election we want to win by a few hundred votes. We have to put them in the ground and bury them." In other words, "what we gotta do here is administer an old-school ass-whipping over the next two weeks. I know everybody knows what that means. We gotta give a butt-whipping they will never forget."[42] Regan's choice of venue for this high-minded speech about the future of home care unionism in Fresno didn't have great historical vibes; seventy years earlier, the fairgrounds were used to confine Japanese Americans before they were shipped off to internment camps for the duration of the Second World War.

As a contemporary union battlefield, this sun-baked corner of the Central Valley was not a happy place in June 2009. Several years earlier, metropolitan Fresno—which has a population of one million—placed first among America's fifty largest municipalities in the category of "concentrated poverty."[43] Thanks to the national recession, the region soon ranked high in unemployment and home foreclosures as well. The saddest local symbol of those two trends was several hundred homeless people living in homemade shacks and tents, plus some city-provided aluminum huts, all located in parking lots just a few blocks from the city center. As state and local tax revenue declined, affordable housing was not the only thing in short supply. Other social services were being squeezed as well—including the In-Home Supportive Services (IHSS) program, which employed Norma Raya and thousands of her coworkers at an hourly rate of $10.25.

Part Native American and looking older than her years, Norma was a founding member of the home care workers union in Fresno and served on its first bargaining committee. She was among those who struggled in 2002–03 to unite its diverse workforce of Anglos, Chicanos, Filipinos, African Americans, Hmong, and other Asians in the campaign for bargaining rights and a first contract. Along with her coworker Flo Furlow, a native of Arkansas and veteran of the southern civil rights movement, Norma was among those who marched, picketed, protested, and got arrested to help build the union, with the help of community allies like Dolores Huerta, the eighty-year-old founding mother of the UFW. When Norma's local was taken over by Stern appointees like Regan and Medina, she helped sign up 2,500 fellow members to vote SEIU out. Now, she was out knocking on doors again in every imaginable setting—suburban subdevelopments, gated communities, urban barrios, and dusty rural trailer parks—because "we do our own union bargaining and don't need any outsiders, from out-of-state, telling us what to do."

In their understandable enthusiasm for low-wage worker organizing, some academic boosters of SEIU have downplayed the economic realities that still dominate long-term care. One frequently quoted professor, Harley Shaiken at University of California, Berkeley, has claimed, for example, that SEIU has "transformed a whole class of jobs—from janitors to home health-care workers to nursing home workers—into middle-class jobs by helping them unionize and negotiate contracts."[44] In fact, Eileen Boris's assessment of the typical provider-client relationship is much closer to the mark: "It's the poor caring for the poor."[45] About a third of all home health aides in Fresno—providers like Raya and Furlow—work in other peoples' homes, while the rest care for an aged parent or disabled child of their own. Only a small number in this latter category could be considered "middle class"—and they achieved that status long before becoming a primary caregiver, certified and paid by IHSS. As Raya noted, "People give up jobs, good jobs, to take care of family members because they don't want them to be in a facility somewhere, but they have no life. And some don't even know they are in a union." The wages, benefits, and pension coverage now enjoyed by health care workers at major hospital chains like Kaiser took decades to achieve; in long-term care, contract standards remain much lower and recent gains are very fragile. As Sal Rosselli acknowledged prior to the UHW trusteeship, "Some of our members make a fair and decent living, but not most of them. Our nursing home members have to work two jobs just to make ends meet. We have a long way to go with long-term care workers."[46]

In early 2009, the Fresno board of supervisors made that "long way to go" even longer by cutting a home care worker wages to $9.50 an hour, effective July 1. Many providers already had difficulty getting enough hours to qualify for the negotiated health plan; now, their meager income was threatened as well. The UHW contract—negotiated with the help of organizer Dana Simon before he moved to Boston—gave the union the right to challenge the scheduled pay cut in arbitration. Unfortunately, the SEIU deputy trustee who handled the union's grievance was not familiar with the contract. Despite Simon's helpful participation as a union witness, the arbitrator ruled in favor of the county. Adding insult to injury, when forty rank and filers, including past bargaining committee members like Flo Furlow, showed up to attend the arbitration hearing, the same staffer barred them from entering. "I have decided it's not in the best interests of the workers for you to be here," SEIU's Rebecca Malberg informed the group. Later, she refused to let home care workers see a copy of the arbitrator's decision.

Disgusted by Malberg's behavior and heartsick over "the destruction of the organization, rights, wages, and benefits of workers I struggled alongside for years," Simon returned to Boston and quit his 1199/SEIU job.[47] He soon went back to Fresno to aid the decertification campaign.

For workers like Furlow and Raya, the pay cut case confirmed their worst fears about being trapped in a union controlled by appointees with no elected officers or stewards. In a pro-NUHW message to her coworkers, Furlow linked the struggle against SEIU in Fresno to the voter registration drives in the 1960s that changed the South. The civil rights movement operated on the principle, "No decision about us without us," she wrote, and home care workers deserved a union that functioned the same way.[48]

Activists like Furlow and Raya were particularly concerned about SEIU's plan, not yet implemented, to transfer them out of UHW and into what Eliseo Medina claimed would be "the nation's largest and most powerful organization of long-term care workers," a 240,000-member California-wide SEIU "local" created by merging all or part of three existing affiliates, including Local 6434 in Los Angeles.[49] This scheme was never mentioned during a costly TV, radio, and newspaper ad blitz that SEIU launched to win the Fresno vote. As local labor activist and NUHW volunteer Pam Whalen noted during the campaign, "SEIU would absolutely lose if there was any whisper of that...But the fact that these workers are so isolated makes them very vulnerable to exploitation and manipulation."[50]

The message that SEIU delivered—in person, via billboards, sign trucks, phone-banking, and over the airwaves—was basic fear-mongering. Over and over, workers were told that if they changed unions, their contract would "become null and void" and they would "lose their SEIU Health Insurance Plan."[51] (As Simon pointed out in an affidavit supporting NUHW's post-election appeal, negotiated medical coverage would "remain a term and condition of employment, regardless of which union prevailed in the representation election." Furthermore, under state law, public employers are barred from changing wages or benefits because workers chose to unionize or change unions.)[52]

Dolores Huerta tried to overcome these fears in personal appeals to Fresno home care workers. Just a few years before she had been invited down to Florida by Medina to help persuade University of Miami president Donna Shalala that campus janitors should be allowed to organize, free of coercion, during a campaign that included UFW-style fasting and appeals to local religious leaders.[53] Now the two former Cesar Chavez associates (and fellow honorary cochairs of the Democratic Socialists of America) were battling it out on opposite sides of the NUHW versus SEIU struggle. "I am a witness to how hard you fought to build this union," Huerta told a preelection rally with Sal Rosselli. "I know it takes a lot of courage and determination to do this…But you are the ones who should make the decisions about your own work and the standards you have struggled so long to maintain."[54]

When the ballots were finally counted in Fresno, there was no big "asswhipping" of Norma Raya, Florine Furlow, or Dolores Huerta. In fact, with a budget of only $200,000, their side lost by just several hundred votes—2,938 to 2,705—an outcome that was still being contested by NUHW a year later.[55] Based on SEIU's estimated total spending on the campaign (about $10 million), victory was not cheap. In fact, it was purchased at a price of about $3,300 per vote, which has to be an all-time union record in such a large unit. Nevertheless, SEIU EVP Tom Woodruff—who first hired Dave Regan as an SEIU organizer in 1990 after he answered a help wanted ad—pronounced himself pleased with the results. "This election harkens back to the great struggles of the '30s," Woodruff declared. "This is the kind of effort we need to use in our fights to win healthcare for all, achieve card check recognition for all, and in our broader fight to win economic justice for everyone in the country."[56]

In reality, SEIU's costly mobilization of its loyalists in Fresno was, if anything, a major diversion of resources from these other fights in 2009. And the election itself did not hark back to "the great struggles" of the past in any way other than faintly resembling some of the lopsided battles in the early thirties between much-reviled, left-led "dual unionists" and their conservative business union opponents. As important as home-based workers are to the recent growth of SEIU and other unions—and as much as they deserve greater "economic justice"—they are not the modern-day equivalent of the millions of factory workers who formed industrial unions via strikes like the famous GM sit-down. "Home healthcare and nursing home workers are not the commanding heights of the economy," retired SEIU board member Jerry Brown has pointedly observed. "We're right to organize them and improve their conditions. But to think that's going to be the basis for rebuilding the labor movement, you have to be out of your mind."[57]

Chapter 4

Dial 1-800-MY-UNION?

"The special gift of this union has been its ability to do things differently."
—Andy Stern, in the *Washington Post*, April 14, 2010

In the recession of 2008–09, some moviegoers sought humorous relief watching a film that spoofed corporate America's love affair with outsourcing and its often insensitive handling of laid-off workers. In *Up in the Air*, George Clooney plays Ryan Bingham, a human resources consultant who works for a highly specialized firm based in Omaha. Bingham racks up millions of frequent flier miles as he travels around the country informing people they have been fired. Clooney's character is quite skilled in this line of work, which requires deft one-on-one handling of each worker's anger or emotional distress when he or she gets the bad news. At each "exit interview," Bingham hands out glossy information packets about whatever severance pay and "employment transition services" his corporate client is offering. But, more importantly, Bingham delivers a carefully customized pep talk about how dismissal is actually a great opportunity for personal growth and career development—elsewhere.

Bingham's smoothly delivered spiel strikes some as insincere, but at least he's sitting in the same room with them, looking them in the eye, talking face to face, ready to offer a tissue if any tears begin to flow. The film's main plot twist—and there are several—revolves around his own firm's decision to reduce costs by using videoconferencing instead of on-site visits. In a memorable scene, we see a skeptical Bingham returning from a business trip and getting a quick tour of the new call center created for this purpose. The firm's "termination managers"—their new job title—are now working with headsets on in small cubicles. We see them talking in highly scripted fashion to fired workers on their computer screens. Bingham is so aghast that he rebukes the smug young executive (played by Natalie Keener) who designed the new system. "I don't think a MySpace page qualifies you to rewire an entire company," he tells her. "You know nothing about the way I do things." By the end of the film, her melding of call center servicing and HR outsourcing has collapsed in disarray. And Ryan Bingham is back on the road again, terminating workers the old-fashioned way.

Maybe I'm just "old school" (like Dave Regan and the character played by Clooney), but if anyone had told me twenty years ago that call centers were a way to rebuild the labor movement, I would have said they were crazy. The idea might work as a funny plot twist in a Hollywood spoof of unions. Not that Hollywood has ever paid much attention to workplace representation, as traditionally provided by union shop stewards. Even in *Up in the Air,* all the fired workers are white collar and, thus, presumably nonunion; none have a coworker at their side to advise them of their rights or provide other assistance in any of the meetings about their termination. The idea that a union might want to embrace a corporate model of "customer service"—using call centers for critical interaction with members who have job problems or questions—is strange indeed. But that's where SEIU seemed to be headed in June 2008 at the San Juan convention center, where the delegates were debating and voting on this very question.

Getting Away from Grievance Handling

On the eve of SEIU's convention, Andy Stern pressed hard for delegate approval of more Member Resource Centers, as the union's call centers are known. "We have a 1930's teletype model of representation in the 21st century world," Stern told the *New York Times.* "You can Google almost anything. But then you call your local union office and you have to push 1 or 2 and then you can't find someone who speaks the language you speak."[1] Since unreturned phone calls is a widespread union member complaint—among native born workers as well as immigrants—anything improving customer service in this area sounds like a good idea. However, Stern put a slightly different spin on it when addressing business audiences.

In 2007, for example, Stern informed the *Wall Street Journal* that SEIU wanted to develop "a new model [of unionism] less focused on individual grievances, more focused on industry needs."[2] His downplaying of grievance-handling was also at odds with his past criticism of union democracy as a distraction from day-to-day representation. "It's hard to make the argument that unions with direct elections better represent their members," he has said. "Our members are more concerned about being serviced. That is what I hear about."[3] To improve servicing, while freeing up more resources for organizing and political action, Stern and Anna Burger proposed that:

> During 2008 and 2009, we will work together to evaluate, test, and pilot member resource centers (MRCs). We will determine the most effective and efficient manner in which to implement MRCs and to provide high quality member representation…across the union.
>
> By 2012, a majority of members will have 24/7 access to quality information and services from member resource centers…MRCs will meet union-wide standards for cost, quality of service to members, ease of access, multiple language capability, support available to member leaders and staff, and quality of data to support SEIU programs and strategies.[4]

Prior to the vote on MRC Resolution 204, all convention delegates, plus guests and reporters, got a clever invitation printed in Spanish and English on pink telephone message slips. It asked: "Are you tired of talking to machines? Leaving voice mail messages? Getting put on hold? Visit the

MRC exhibit to find out how SEIU locals can improve member service and support stewards and other member activists." Those who inspected the mock call center became eligible for a prize "just for visiting," plus they could don headphones themselves to hear a sample exchange between a member/caller and an MRC staffer. Computer screens displayed the kind of contract information that MRC reps would supposedly have at their disposal to handle individual queries, while performing other useful functions, like updating the union's membership database with personal information provided by callers.

Every delegate also received a glossy thirty-page document entitled *The Union of the Future: Membership Action and Leadership to Win for Working People*. This was the report and recommendations of a fifteen-member SEIU committee, chaired by Burger, that spent three years exploring ways to enhance "local union strength." Burger's panel was aided by union advisors and an impressive array of CEOs, corporate consultants, pollsters, and business school professors (hailing from the Boston Consulting Group, the Beneson Strategy Group, X2 Technology, QB International, MIT's Sloan School of Management, and Peter Hart Research). To "take a deeper look" at "the member experience," SEIU also contracted with a Palo Alto firm called IDEO, "a world leader in innovation and design…known for working on products such as the Macintosh mouse and the Palm Pilot."

An Import from Australia

Burger's *Union of the Future* report included a much-cited section on the "near-death experience" of organized labor in Australia. There, the rightwing governments in power prior to a Labor Party victory in 2007 introduced draconian legislation to curtail collective bargaining, dues check-off, and union density. "The combined effect of the conservative attack was that many unions lost half their membership within a very short time period." As part of their comeback strategy (as recounted by SEIU), the Aussies "reorganized representation using modern call center technology" so workers with a weakened shop-floor union presence could call "a central location for critical information and to file grievances."

Aided by advisors from Australia, SEIU public sector locals on the West Coast began working with the international union in 2006 "to create the largest most technologically advanced MRC yet." Two years later, according to the Burger report, this facility in Pasadena was "serving more than 200,000 members from California locals 221, 721, 521, and 1021," with a high level of customer satisfaction. Citing organizational synergies achieved in Australia, the report projected a rosy future in which members would be "so strongly supported" by call centers that stewards and field staff could then "focus on building the union: identifying and developing leaders; organizing around workplace issues; fighting for better contracts, uniting more workers, and winning politically and in the community."[5]

An accompanying promotional video extolled the same possibilities, plus additional ones. Jenny Yang, Local 721's enthusiastic young MRC project coordinator, explained that call centers were critical to SEIU becoming "this really, you know, kick-butt organizing union for the 21st century." Annelle Grajeda, the Stern-appointed leader of Yang's local, predicted that MRCs would allow SEIU "to be more creative, to partner with our employers to bring innovation and quality to public service."

Rank-and-file members from several California locals, including 721, strongly disagreed with Yang and Grajeda. They spoke out against Resolution 204, on and off the convention floor. Mel Garcia, a thirty-year SEIU activist at Kaiser, told reporters that no union can function well without elected stewards who are "known, respected, and trusted" by their coworkers. "With call centers," Garcia argued, "you take away that face-to-face connection. If members have to pick up a phone and call an 800 number, how can they feel protected and supported, particularly in a discharge situation? That, to me, is not a union…If a member calls me or comes to my desk, they're going to say, 'Get back to me.' If you call someone on the phone in this big call center system, it will be very easy for your message to get lost and your call not returned."[6]

Delegate Leslie Harding, a Kaiser HMO surgical technologist from Redwood City, California, expressed her opposition on UHW's daily convention blog. There, she wrote: "I never dreamed I'd see my own union imitate credit card companies, the IRS, and major insurers and try to turn us into 'dial a union.' Having a union is supposed to help us stand up to management, not just give us the ability to pick up a phone and call a 1-800 number. A union is not about long-distance representation from someone who's never set foot in your work-place, who doesn't know you or your manager, and who doesn't have any understanding of what goes on where you work."[7]

UHW also prepared a formal critique of Burger's report. Entitled *"Justice for All" or "Control for Just Us?"*, the document explained why shop steward functions shouldn't be outsourced:

> Throughout SEIU's history, we have learned that powerful unions require trained and effective workplace leaders, strong shop-floor organization, and a culture of solidarity and action among members…[They] require stewards and member leaders who can organize their co-workers, interpret and defend their contract, conduct issue fights, handle grievances and resolve problems. This combination of people, skills, organization, and culture allows members to build worker-led unions.

UHW warned that MRCs would be used by SEIU "to dispense with workplace conflict administratively and re-construct the union as an issue advocacy organization to pursue priorities and execute campaigns in which workers would have little say." Emulating the AARP (American Association of Retired Persons) or MoveOn.org, SEIU might then "become the biggest, strongest, and best-funded issue advocacy organization in America," but it would no longer resemble, in any way, "an organization of workers, by workers and for workers."[8]

On the convention floor, UHW tried to amend Resolution 204 to clarify that new MRCs were designed to enhance the work of stewards, not replace them. "We're not against new ideas for being more innovative and effective, as long as they work," Sal Rosselli explained.[9] But the effort was defeated. A large majority of the delegates supported the leadership recommendation to expand call center coverage. One of the dissenters, Michael Fenison, a UHW delegate from Inglewood, California, angrily disputed Stern's claim that MRCs were still being introduced as a pilot project. "This resolution is being forced down our throat and we're going to get call centers whether they work or not," he predicted.[10]

A Teletype Model of Representation

My own call center skepticism (and sympathy for UHW's losing side of the argument) was not born of any great attachment to mainstream labor's "teletype" model of representation. That model didn't empower stewards enough either. And it rarely encouraged membership action on the job to put pressure on employers to resolve problems quickly and more favorably to workers. Instead, full-time union officials file grievances on behalf of individual members, who then passively watch a long and legalistic slog through the multiple steps of the contract grievance/arbitration procedure. Some cases are won, many more are not, and others just disappear along the way—leading to considerable frustration at the rank-and-file level in many unions.

Still, I couldn't help wondering whether SEIU officials infatuated with call centers—as a 21st century alternative to our last century grievance morass—had ever visited the real thing, since the model they were adopting was so obviously corporate inspired. As a union rep myself, I spent more than a quarter century in and around telecom industry call centers run by giant firms like AT&T and Verizon. There, thousands of CWA members service a "customer base" far larger than SEIU's. Over the years, I helped unionized customer service representatives (CSRs) joust with management about work organization and scheduling; training and equipment; coaching, monitoring, and changes in their sales scripts; performance standards and "productivity" incentives; and the use of "foreign language queues" to better assist non-English speakers. I was also involved in many disputes about service quality, as phone companies made CSR work more computer-paced, highly scripted, and often less helpful to customers.[11]

One of the local unions I assisted began tackling such issues in 1980 after an NLRB election victory in three phone company offices in New Hampshire. Back then, only one hundred and fifty customer service reps out of three thousand were unionized in New England. As a result of successful strike action by CWA and IBEW (International Brotherhood of Electrical Workers) over the next two decades—and much membership mobilization in support of "bargaining to organize"—the rest got organized eventually. By 2003, CWA Local 1400 had about eighteen hundred dues payers spread out over four states in a dozen Verizon call centers ranging in size from fifty to five hundred workers.[12]

Unfortunately, under an increasingly domineering and undemocratic local president, 1400's steward system became badly atrophied. Critical information was hoarded among the four full-time officers who worked out of union headquarters in New Hampshire, where all grievance handling was centralized and tightly controlled. The top leadership no longer recruited, trained, or maintained a network of stewards and chief stewards. Rank and filers were not involved, to the degree they should have been, in the presentation of grievances to the company. As a result, some stewards quit in frustration or disgust, while others felt poorly equipped to answer questions about the contract or handle day-to-day issues in their offices.

As CWA's shop floor presence diminished, more members with a question or problem began to think of "the union" as just the four full-time officers tucked away in New Hampshire. Being customer service reps who worked all day on the phone, they began to pick up the phone themselves and call the local's 800 number on their breaks and lunch hours. Throughout Local 1400, the habit of dealing directly with the union office—or, more often, just the president herself—began to spread. As the volume of member calls increased, more and more requests for help or information were not answered in a timely fashion, if at all. As the CWA staffer assigned to Local 1400, I began to get more of what (in phone company jargon) is called "overflow calls." Members would contact the national union to determine the status of backlogged grievances, arbitration appeals, hardship transfer requests, missing FMLA (Family and Medical Leave Act) paperwork, or other matters the local was supposed to handle or keep them better informed about. Few callers were happy about the amount of time they had already spent "in queue" during previous phone contact with the local.

This membership dissatisfaction reached the boiling point in late 2002. It became the deciding factor in a hotly contested election for Local 1400 officers. The twenty-year incumbent president, a founder of the local, was ousted, along with most of her executive board allies. The new president was Don Trementozzi, a service rep from Rhode Island who had two decades of prior union experience in the Machinists and AFSCME. The first thing his slate did, after getting sworn in, was reestablish and strengthen the local's workplace steward network. This required recruiting and training new stewards, making sure they knew the contract, and giving them the chance to enhance their skills and self-confidence by participating in worksite meetings with management.

Mobilizing for Power with Stewards

The local's rank-and-file executive board—previously underutilized in the grievance procedure—was redeployed to do more contract enforcement work alongside the stewards and elected chief stewards. A new system was developed to keep members better informed about the status of their grievances at each step of the process. For the first time in the local's history, workers who filed a grievance were invited to participate in all three pre-arbitration steps of the grievance procedure (a change in practice that Verizon labor relations reps particularly disliked). Workplace activists began to get a steady flow of information about their legal and contract rights. For the first time, CWA's internal organizing manual—*Mobilizing for Power*—was put in the hands of any member who wanted a copy. This sixty-page guide includes the following self-criticism of the "servicing model" of unionism as it evolved over time. It makes the case for doing things differently, with a much bigger dose of direct action on the job:

> CWA, like most unions, was organized on the basis of member involvement. Fundamentally, a union's power at any point in time is nothing more than the total energy and support of its members who can be mobilized. The basic premise of "mobilization" is that we must return to our roots and commit to a strategy that rests on increasing our power through membership education and involvement. We have

become too reliant on the crafty union negotiator, the clever chief steward, and the experienced local president to solve our problems. We can no longer solely rely on grievances, arbitrations or labor laws to achieve workplace justice.[13]

Trementozzi didn't hunker down in the Local 1400 office like his predecessor during the waning days of her old regime. Instead, he and other officers remained highly visible and accessible (just as they had been while campaigning for office, on their own time and at their own expense).[14]

They made frequent worksite visits to help lay the groundwork for the local's participation in a 2003 contract campaign at Verizon that involved seventy-five thousand IBEW and CWA members from Maine to Virginia. One building block of that campaign was an improved union communications network, utilizing members' personal email addresses; these were collected, one by one, in each workplace as stewards talked to their coworkers about the importance of receiving regular mobilization and bargaining updates via an electronic newsletter called *Unity@Verizon*. Union sticker-wearing, group grievance-filing, informational picketing, and other displays of workplace solidarity (like wearing red to work every Thursday) also became the order of the day. During local negotiations with Verizon, the Local 1400 bargaining committee was expanded to include board members as well as officers. For the first time in the union's twenty-three-year history, working members were also invited to attend as observers, on their own time.

During this rebuilding process, Trementozzi delivered the same message in every office he visited: "If you have a problem, don't call the local—go to your steward first." The local's four elected full-timers (plus their experienced office manager) continued to get plenty of calls, of course, but not as many from members directly. Far more of their phone conversations were now with stewards, chief stewards, and elected vice presidents calling on behalf of a coworker in their own office, seeking information or advice about how they themselves should handle the problem on the scene. For contract enforcement and membership mobilization purposes in 2003, Local 1400 ended up with nearly one hundred newly empowered workplace activists, many of whom had previously been sidelined by the union.

Gradually, the old dysfunctional division of labor was replaced by a new and more effective one. Local 1400 utilized members for all kinds of union-building work—either as volunteers or on a "lost-time" basis, in which case they were paid by the company (where possible under the contract) or, more frequently, by the local or national union. During Trementozzi's second term in office, 1400 was able to expand its external organizing activity, using the same member-based approach. A rank-and-file committee recruited several hundred new members at customer service centers or mobile phone retail stores. In these new bargaining units, the local went through the same process of promoting rank-and-file participation in first contract bargaining and/or labor-management meetings. Patient steward recruitment and training enabled these newly organized workers to become familiar with their contracts and, with backing from the local, develop confidence in their collective ability to deal with management at the worksite level.

With members in three different telecom bargaining units covering four states, Local 1400 now conducts regular conference calls involving up to one hundred and twenty stewards. They are encouraged to schedule an after-work party at someone's home, MoveOn.org-style, and participate in the call together as part of a local group. Local 1400 also has a Facebook page for its activists and the highest level of CWA COPE (Committee on Political Education) participation in its history. (20 percent of the membership now donates to COPE, as opposed to only five workers in 2002.) By 2009, the new leadership had restored sufficient confidence in the union to get a dues increase passed (from 1.3 to 1.6 percent of base pay); now it can fully participate in multiple central labor councils and local Jobs with Justice coalitions.

The challenges facing Verizon workers today are daunting. They include a long-term corporate de-unionization strategy that has reduced union density within the company to about 30 percent. Local 1400 has been in the forefront of resistance to one form of Verizon's downsizing—its dumping of rural landlines. Along with the IBEW, it waged a vigorous campaign to block the sale of Verizon operations in northern New England. The deal was approved by state utility regulators anyway. As predicted by both unions, the successor employer, FairPoint Communications, soon went bankrupt.[15] After difficult bargaining, Local 1400 was able to keep most of its old Verizon contract intact, while the company reorganized under Chapter 11.[16]

When reformers first took over 1400, they could easily have continued the de facto call center servicing model inherited from their predecessors. As trained, experienced, energetic young CSRs, they were well equipped to upgrade the union's own "customer service." All they had to do was keep their Verizon headsets on, sit in a new office all day long, and handle Local 1400 "call volumes" more efficiently than their jaded predecessors. But they chose not to. "I don't see how a call center for members could ever be effective because that's not what having a real union is all about," Trementozzi said. "There's no personal interaction or relationships of trust—it's like calling Verizon about your phone bill. What gets management's attention is people doing things together at work and building an organization, from the bottom up."[17]

"Our Call Center Is a Little Different"

In SEIU's brave new world of "megalocals"—described further in the next chapter—Don Trementozzi's organization wouldn't count for much. In fact, it might not even be allowed to exist at all. According to SEIU, an affiliate the size of Local 1400 doesn't have the "scale" necessary to support massive new organizing and more effective political action. Local 1400 dues are too low and it doesn't have any unelected full-time staff (other than a single clerical person). The highly competitive elections it holds every three years (with 40 to 50 percent of the members participating) is just a dangerous distraction from the challenge of "building power for workers." In addition, SEIU strategists would say, the culture of this CWA affiliate is much too focused on "local union interests"—that is, the workplace problems of "just us"—rather than the sweeping objective of "Justice for All." As SEIU board member (and former CWA organizer) Stephen Lerner has argued, "servicing and defending remaining islands of unionization" (like Local 1400 at Verizon) is simply not viable anymore. That's

why, in Lerner's view, SEIU's use of MRCs is a truly "radical development."
By embracing more call centers, SEIU members are "changing the world,
not just their worksites."[18]

In big locals on both coasts and in the Midwest, SEIU has been using
MRCs not just to free up resources for politics and organizing, but to assist
members who don't have traditional "worksites." As we saw in the last
chapter, hundreds of thousands of the union's newest recruits work in
their own homes or someone else's. In such settings—far removed from
the cubicle-filled world of a big white-collar employer like Verizon—
there's no way to have easy access to a shop steward; there aren't even other
union members around, unless they happen to be doing home care or
child care in the same neighborhood. So one reason for SEIU's shift to call
center servicing is the very real challenge of being responsive to dues payers
who work in relative isolation from each other. According to Anna Burger's
convention report, MRCs are already providing "great service" to "home
care locals in California, Washington, Oregon, and Illinois…in an industry
without common worksites."

The eighty thousand janitors and security guards in Local 32BJ, which
is headquartered in New York City, also have access to a regional call center.
By 2008, it was reporting half a million calls a year from members in workplaces from Hartford, Connecticut, to Washington, D.C. As a result of
switching to this system, 32BJ claims, more union staffers could be reassigned
to "organizing the largest contract action team ever in the commercial jani-
torial division" and "dramatically increasing member participation in
COPE." In the Midwest, a similar multistate property services local reported
that it now had "a strong system of representation in place" thanks to a call
center launched in 2004 and a companion "grievance center." At Local 1, "not
only have services improved," according to Burger's report, but more resources are now available for "crucial campaigns, including organizing 5,000
janitors in Houston."[19]

While visiting Chicago, I was able to talk to Local 1 president Tom
Balanoff about his MRC experience. "Our call center is a little different,"
Balanoff insisted, when I mentioned the criticisms I had heard from SEIU

members in Puerto Rico and California. The Local 1 MRC grew out of the merger of three SEIU locals that were undergoing demographic changes. Under the old system of servicing, field reps handled all their own calls from members in their assigned buildings, filed all the grievances, and made workplace visits. "Reps like to be lawyers," Balanoff observed. As a result, an estimated 60 percent of local resources were being consumed by contract administration. Little staff time was left for what the Local 1 president calls "moving program" or "mobilizing workers." Plus, there were still "a lot of problems and complaints from members" about servicing. According to Balanoff, some staffers couldn't speak the language of the foreign-born members they represented. In Chicago, Local 1 used to have many dues payers from Poland; now members are just as likely to be Latino or from the former Yugoslavia. Local 1's call center serves workers in English, Spanish, Polish, and Serbo-Croatian because "members like getting phone calls answered in their own language," Balanoff said. The local itself has fifty thousand members spread out over seven states and eleven cities, including Indianapolis, Detroit, Milwaukee, Cleveland, Cincinnati, St. Louis, Kansas City, and far off Houston.

My tour of the Local 1 MRC was conducted by Krystyna Razwadowski, a tall, blond, and friendly Polish immigrant who is Balanoff's member resource coordinator. She and Ed Bowen, the union's grievance director, explained how the seventy or more staffers working for the organization have been redeployed. Local 1 has multilingual "Member Resource Representatives" on duty and fielding calls from union headquarters on East Wacker Drive in downtown Chicago. Its "grievance center" operation is staffed by "grievance representatives" who work in the same Chicago office and other Midwestern cities within Local 1's expanding jurisdiction. The remaining staffers are called "field representatives" and, as their title implies, are still deployed in workplaces but not for grievance-handling purposes. When a member contacts the union, MRC personnel, under Razwadowski's supervision, do the initial intake and end up answering most questions themselves. "We found that 60 percent of the calls coming into the local weren't about filing a grievance," Balanoff explained. Instead, janitors and security guards just wanted basic information about benefits, their next wage increase, or other contract entitlements. To answer such questions, the call center reps, some of who used to be Local 1 administrative/clerical employees, consult either hard copies of contracts or a database with relevant contract information. They use each conversation to update member contact information, whether they are talking directly to Local 1–represented workers or family members calling on their behalf. If computerized records show that the member calling has not yet signed up for COPE or volunteered for any other Local 1 activity, the call center reps encourage such participation.

If the caller is complaining about a contract violation—like mistakes in pay—that are fairly simple to resolve, the call center reps will try to straighten things out with an employer. Bigger or more complicated problems, like being disciplined or discharged, get referred to the grievance center, where grievance reps (some of who used to work in the field) make a determination about whether or not to file an individual or group grievance. These "dispute" calls also trigger "action needed" email notification of the relevant field rep and Local 1 departmental director. (The union has different departments for allied/industrial shops, security firms, and different types of building service contractors.) The standardized intake work of the call center and its coordination with the grievance center enables grievance cases to be logged in, tracked, and closed out, with less paperwork, and greater organizational capacity "to at least quantify the work, measure how quickly reps resolve grievances, how many are resolved," Balanoff said. If the union decides not to pursue a member complaint, Bowen said that the staff tries "to educate stewards and members on the reasons why that case will not be successful." Local 1 directors also use MRC-generated data to flag reoccurring problems involving contract interpretation that may need to be addressed in future negotiations with management.

Nothing But Positive Feedback?

Stocky, goateed Ed Bowen is a former security officer at an Illinois nuclear power plant, where the workers are represented by SEIU. He became a full-time union rep back in the days when "we were all jacks of all trades." Now,

Bowen believes that his own job performance suffered because he "was so bogged down in grievances," particularly about pay issues. Today, he told me, the Local 1 staff has a more efficient division of labor and contracts are better enforced than under the old system because of the MRC. Bowen explained that, in a few large Local 1 units—like the McCormick Place convention center, a major Chicago hospital, the Navy Pier complex, and several nuclear power plants—there are enough members working in one place (with fewer language barriers) to permit a traditional structure of workplace representation. There, stewards and chief stewards can handle grievances themselves with little or no reliance on the MRC. But, in Bowen's view, the challenge of steward recruitment among janitors or security guards in three hundred downtown Chicago buildings made MRC servicing an absolute necessity.

Since the MRC was introduced, the function of both stewards and field reps has been redefined. According to Bowen, the stewards still "police the contract" but "they are brought into the grievance procedure more as a witness," when there is a grievance meeting with management. The rest of the time they are encouraged to help field reps with COPE sign-ups and turnout for rallies. The field reps are, in turn, responsible now for what Balanoff calls "building the union, identifying leaders, moving program, and organizing fightbacks." Bowen does not believe there is a tension between mobilizing members around union-defined contract and political goals and the higher priority that workers might place on having Local 1 deal with their day-to-day problems. "I've gotten nothing but positive feedback from most stewards," Bowen said, except for a few "who don't want to change."

This claim was vigorously disputed by a former Local 1 staffer and one-time coworker of Bowen's. This source was also hired from the ranks and has many relatives and friends who are still Local 1 members. He now works for another Chicago-area union and asked to remain anonymous. When the MRC was first introduced in 2003, he said, Local 1 staffers loyally tried to adapt to their new roles as call center–bound grievance reps. Instead of working with an assigned constituency of stewards and members they knew well and had developed long-term relationships with, these reps were now sitting at a desk eight hours a day, waiting for localwide calls from workers they didn't know and whose contracts were sometimes unfamiliar to them. Their previous mix of duties—workplace visits, signing up new members, enforcing and negotiating contracts—had certainly been challenging and, at times, quite stressful. But, at least then, reps had ongoing face-to-face contact with the rank and file.

One experienced Local 1 rep was fired when he tried to propose changes in the new system during several meetings with Balanoff in which the objections of fellow staffers and members were aired. Management claimed he was guilty of "disloyalty and insubordination." Two years later, a three-member NLRB panel (that included the board's current chairperson, Wilma Liebman, and her Bush-appointed predecessor, Robert Battista) disagreed. They ordered the rep's reinstatement because his right to engage in "protected concerted activity" had been violated.[20]

The former Local 1 employee I interviewed believes that "the 800 number has made members less engaged" than before and definitely more resentful of workplace visits by the new field reps, who are seen as "the guys coming to get your COPE money who don't know shit about your building." On balance, and while still a fan of SEIU in other respects, this former staffer believes that Balanoff's MRC "is bad on many levels and does more harm than good." He notes that SEIU has invested heavily in a new Detroit-based regional call center and worries that more Midwestern locals will be forced to utilize its services in a manner similar to Local 1's operation. An immigrant himself, this source dismissed the idea that Local 1's multilingual workforce required MRC servicing. Instead, he theorized that the new system had more to do with insuring that "Tom would remain president for life." In his view, the MRC system was designed, in part, to ensure that all membership loyalty, such as it was, would flow directly to the top. No Local 1 steward or full-time rep would ever again be able to develop enough of a political base to challenge the leadership, given the restructuring of those two union roles and the huge geographical scope of the local.[21]

Local 1 says it hasn't done a survey of membership satisfaction with the MRC (although a systematic study of its functioning is now being conducted by Bob Bruno, a University of Illinois labor relations professor.) For Tom Balanoff, the deciding factors in favor of call center servicing are being able to "free up half the resources previously devoted to grievance-handling" and finding "ways to put more resources into building a bigger movement," that can raise contract standards. The Local 1 president acknowledged that call center servicing might work better where a local is administering a limited number of master contracts. If Local 1 was "a big amalgamated local, with a hundred different contracts, the [new] system wouldn't work as well," Balanoff said. Razwadowski noted likewise that, "based on our membership and structure, it works for us. That doesn't mean it will work for other unions."

Some California Complaining

If the past, present, and future of call center servicing seemed bright (to some) in the Windy City, there was much discontent with it in sunny California, the epicenter of SEIU's call center experiment. At a statewide gathering of SEIU reformers—held in Berkeley in the spring of 2008—the MRC in Pasadena (which refused my request for a tour) was much reviled. Among its critics at that time were state, county, and municipal workers whose already large locals had, in four instances, been restructured and consolidated into new SEIU affiliates with appointed leaders and expanded membership of up to eighty thousand. Mike Donaldson, who works at Laney College in Oakland, explained that his 35,000-member Local 790 had a Bay Area focus, a "relatively democratic structure," and a history of rank-and-file involvement. Despite being promised new "communication tools" like the MRC, he was concerned that workers in his new 55,000-member Local 1021, which covers all of Northern California, wouldn't have the same "connection to the union" as before. "It's not just the aspect of losing local control," he said. "We're becoming spectators in our own union, passive consumers of the union product—and that's a serious problem."

Catherine Alexander, a Santa Clara County librarian shifted from Local 715 to 521, was first briefed on SEIU's call center project well before the merger, but not told what it might cost. But then, in the summer of

2007, she and other members learned that the MRC was being introduced at great expense to their new local. In fact, money had to be diverted from 521's already depleted strike fund to pay for its initial contribution to the MRC in Pasadena. By 2008, the local's annual budget indicated that it was costing 521 members $1.2 million at a time when the local faced a deficit of nearly $2.8 million. "I felt the whole thing was a slap in the face," Alexander said. "As stewards, we've taken classes, learned to empower ourselves, and helped our coworkers exercise their rights in the workplace."[22]

According to state corrections department worker Joyce Thomas-Villaronga, a member of Local 1000, "SEIU doesn't have a good history of day-to-day representation, of handling the problems that we, as stewards and local officers, have to deal with...A lot of our longtime leaders have gotten frustrated and walked away." She reported that the labor reps working full time for her local would no longer handle grievances when that work was shifted to the MRC. Instead, the reps were going to focus on internal organizing—trying to sign up more of the non-members in state government units. She questioned the effectiveness of this redeployment, arguing that working members, like herself, would be more effective signing up their coworkers than paid staffers. "Members need to be more engaged and they should be the ones organizing other state workers while the staff should be doing professional representation work and mentoring stewards on how to write effective grievances," she said. "We're not teaching enough of them how to write grievances."[23]

Another call center critic, who came to the meeting from Southern California, was Arturo Diaz, who voted against Resolution 204 in San Juan as a convention delegate from Local 721. Diaz works as a computer programmer for Los Angeles County and was a rank-and-file executive board member of Local 660 before it was dissolved and merged into a new seven-county entity. After that consolidation, 721 was run by an "interim president," MRC booster Annelle Grajeda, the former staff director of 660 who had never been a working member of any component part of 721. As of March 2008, unhappy members estimated that their local had already spent $360,000 on the Pasadena MRC. Like Catherine Alexander in 521,

Diaz doubted that the MRC would be an adequate substitute for trained stewards and some of the experienced 660 staffers who lost their jobs when that local was merged into 721.[24]

One such layoff victim was Paul Krehbiel. As a Local 660 field rep and organizer, Krehbiel focused on building large steward committees and promoting member activism on the job—goals that Grajeda cared little about, in his view.[25] So Krehbiel and more than a dozen other "popular, effective and active staff members were let go," Diaz complained. Members were then told to pick up the phone and talk to newly hired staffers at the MRC who "never had a real job and don't know anything about labor." Diaz assured me he didn't "have anything against young people, but a lot of them are getting a big check now so their attitude [toward Grajeda] is 'Whatever you want me to do, boss.'" When you're speaking with someone on the telephone, Diaz noted, "it's just too easy for them to say, 'You don't have a grievance.' And that's the end of the story."[26]

Dan Mariscal, a supporter of SEIU Member Activists for Reform Today (SMART) is a Los Angeles city worker and longtime shop steward. Like Diaz, Mariscal doubted whether call center personnel would ever be as responsive to members as an elected (or even appointed) steward who is their coworker. But he tried to keep an open mind about the idea. In early 2007, he was part of a "transitional representation committee" that brought together stewards from his Local 347 and several others that were being merged into 721. The stewards were assured that the MRC would streamline communications between members and their new local, plus "free up" its fifty to sixty field reps (who would now be called "worksite organizers"). "On its face, this sounded like a pretty good idea" to Mariscal, until he sought assurances that the worksite organizers would still be "helping us assist members with their grievances." Mariscal was worried that any city employee who invoked the right, under L.A.'s labor relations ordinance, to have a "representative of his/her choice" in grievances and disciplinary actions might end up with less, rather than more, access to union representation.

Mariscal and other stewards raised these concerns during several visits to the Pasadena MRC in the summer of 2008. By then it was operating with about twenty-three member resource organizers (MROs) and its director, Rodney Bullock, boasted of his ability to track how many calls were coming in per hour, how long the callers were on hold, the duration of the calls, and the average call handling time. Within the MRC itself, Mariscal discovered that calls were being routed to the "right people," in terms of their second language skills, but "not necessarily anyone knowledgeable about your particular contract." The newly minted MROs had never worked as members or staffers in any of the bargaining units they were fielding calls from. They only received three weeks of training and were employed by the SEIU International union, not any of the four locals funding the center. For Mariscal, this arrangement raised obvious questions about their accountability: "In the former Local 347, the staff was accountable to the member-elected executive board. If a staff member wasn't 'cutting it,' the board could fire him/her and also approve his/her replacement. That was obviously not the case now."

The six-local merger that created 80,000-member Local 721 had been touted by SEIU as the pathway to a "bigger, better, and stronger union." But Mariscal and other stewards expressed mounting frustration over 721's apparent "disconnect" from the realities of life in the hundreds of far-flung worksites, now included the merged local. In their view, the transfer of traditional field staff functions from worksite organizers still in the field to call-center-based MROs had not provided any additional staff support for shop stewards. Supervisors now "regarded SEIU stewards as a mere nuisance," Mariscal reported. "Members were losing confidence in the union at an alarming rate."

The Membership Backlash Against MRCs

Local union election results in 2009–10 indicated that membership discontent with MRCs was not limited to SEIU reformers. Several local presidents, sensing that a membership backlash was brewing, were forced to distance themselves from the call center concept for their own political survival. Those who didn't—in Massachusetts Local 888 and California Local 1021—were voted out of office.[27] In 888, there were multiple reasons for membership dissatisfaction with Susana Segat, an incumbent originally installed by Stern and Burger. On their Change888 website, her opponents highlighted one major rank-and-file gripe: "Segat's 'Member Resource Center' is just a computerized voicemail system." In his campaign against Segat, Boston City Hall worker Bruce Boccardy charged that widespread steward demoralization, combined with high staff turnover, had created a representation void affecting many of the local's ten thousand members. According to Boccardy, the old leadership "[D]ecided to do away with as many [field] staff as possible by implementing the call-in MRC. But that only made the problem worse. How can a few staff people, stuck in a statewide union office, with a pile of 200 different contracts possibly figure out what is going on in workplaces that they've never visited? They can't. It is a ludicrous system."

Boccardy pledged to scrap this system and replace it with "the traditional model of representation: individual staff who are assigned to units and are responsible for, and to, the membership of those units." Yet Segat's opponent was no union traditionalist himself. Boccardy is a former sixties radical whose seven-point program to "bring the union back to the members" was actually red-baited by a few members because it opened with a quote from *Catholic Worker* founder Dorothy Day and ended with one from socialist Eugene V. Debs (neither of whom are much cited in union campaign literature these days).[28] Boccardy won by a two-to-one margin in his second bid for the presidency.

In early 2010, ten months after Segat's defeat, another MRC defender fell on her purple sword. Damita Davis-Howard, the Stern-appointed "interim president" of Local 1021 and, like Segat, a member of the SEIU executive board, had glowingly introduced the call center servicing video at the San Juan convention. As noted above, Local 1021 extends all the way from San Francisco to the Oregon border. During three years of de facto trusteeship, its dues payers discovered that bigger does not necessarily mean better. "Philosophically, politically, I think the merger [of seven locals into one] was a good decision," said Roxanne Sanchez, president of Local 790, whose members are now part of 1021. "But the way they handled it was atrocious…the

International was so unreceptive to anything we, as rank-and-file people, brought to the table."[29] By early 2010, some workers were so estranged from their dysfunctional and ineffective "megalocal" that they were petitioning for a decertification vote (just as smaller groups of disgruntled 888 members did during the waning days of the Segat regime). Other dissidents decided to stay and fight. Their "Change 1021" team challenged Davis-Howard and defeated her whole incumbent slate by a substantial margin, winning twenty-six out of twenty-eight elected positions in the local.

Like Bruce Boccardy in 888, the San Francisco reformers—including Sanchez, Sin Yee Poon, Larry Bradshaw, and Harry Baker—argued that "a strong, democratic, and effective union is built on a solid foundation of stewards and local chapters," not a faraway call center. "To the degree we lose focus on representation and workplace issues, the members feel the union is working off its own agenda," Poon said, citing her own neglected disciplinary case as an example. Prior to her election as 1021's new "CEO," or chief elected officer, Poon was the chairperson of a 1,700-member chapter of 1021 in San Francisco. When Poon's agency tried to suspend her for seven days for alleged misuse of the city's internal email system, no one from the local union came to her workplace or even made a phone call to management about the suspension grievance, which she ended up handling herself. The Change 1021 slate promised to improve on that sorry performance. It's platform pledged:

> We will ensure member representation is the first priority...Local 1021 has seen a revolving door of union staff with no consistency... Staff's first responsibility will be to train and mentor chapter officers and stewards. We will foster increased communication between chapters, industries, and bargaining units. The most effective means of communication is face-to-face. We will require staff and officers to regularly visit work sites.[30]

In two other California locals, incumbents who were once equally enthusiastic about MRC servicing changed their tune in time to avoid the fate of Davis-Howard. In early 2008, Kristy Sermersheim, the Stern-appointed leader of Local 521 in San Jose, issued an upbeat report to her executive board about the initial rollout of MRC coverage for her 55,000-member local. The Pasadena facility was "fully staffed," "fully trained," and "capable of communicating in four languages," she promised.[31] Two years later, Sermersheim was facing, for the first time, the expanded electorate of 521 as a candidate for president. To improve her chances of winning, she announced a pullout from the MRC that had cost her local an estimated $1.5 million. In Local 521 meetings held prior to the February 2010 election, "complaints about the MRC came up over and over again," recalls Wren Bradley, who ran on an opposition slate called "Voices of the Members."

Like Paul Krehbiel in Local 660, Bradley was fired when her smaller local was merged in 2007 with four others to create Local 521. At the time, she predicted the consolidation would lead to "a reduction in services" and "the participatory democracy that existed in Local 535." She returned to her old job as a social worker and began to organize her coworkers against what she called "the Wal-Martization of SEIU."[32] When Bradley's slate challenged the Local 521 leadership, they heard many complaints from members about grievances not being filed in a timely fashion. "Workers would tell their story to the person at the MRC who would tell them, 'I'll call your worksite organizer,'" Bradley said. "Then, they'd never hear back from anyone. People at the MRC couldn't figure out the right contract someone was covered by when they called and had no understanding of concepts like 'past practice.' Kristy knew it was a disaster. She saw the writing on the wall."[33]

In San Diego Local 221, interim president Sharon-Frances Moore had a similar revelation on the eve of an election that was later overturned by the U.S. Department of Labor. Faced with a challenge by county worker and SMART member Monty Kroopkin, she announced plans to withdraw from the Pasadena MRC, citing the cost. Kroopkin and his Reform221 slate ran on a twelve-point platform that included a pledge to: "Abolish the 'Call Center' because 'workers with grievances or contract questions should be able to talk to a steward or union staffer, IN PERSON, not at some distant call center.'" Kroopkin believes the MRC just "undermines the steward system" in 221, which has already been weakened because Moore refused to post a directory of all stewards on the local's website.

While campaigning, Kroopkin "heard people say the same thing every-where: it just wastes time getting in touch with your steward through the resource center, which doesn't have good answers to members' questions anyway." Among stewards themselves, the system has been "totally debil-itating," he contends. "A lot of stewards are just quitting because of lack of communication or call-backs from the local, and the fact that staff don't show up enough at our worksites."[34]

Megalocal Disengagement

If one MRC goal was to boost membership involvement in the union, one area where it did not succeed was rank-and-file participation in local union elections. Voter turnout in 221, 521, and even 1021 and 888, where reform-ers won, was extremely low. According to MRC critics, this reflected deep-ening rank-and-file alienation from locals that had become too big and/or disconnected from the membership. In Local 888, 22 percent of its ten thousand members voted in the Boccardy versus Segat contest in 2009—less than half the regular turnout in CWA Local 1400 elections. In 7,500-member 221, only 9 percent of the eligible members voted—a number at least larger than the fifty-six who voted for convention delegates the year before. In 521, less than three thousand voted out of fifty-five thousand. In what, by trade union standards, was a hotly contested election in 1021—taking place in the middle of a public sector fiscal crisis with wages, bene-fits, and thousands of jobs on the line—only 5,360 valid ballots were returned out of more than forty-two thousand workers eligible to vote and a claimed membership of fifty-four thousand.[35]

When 721, the huge Southern California public service employees local, finally held its first election in March 2010, the Members for a Dem-ocratic Union (MDU) slate included call center critics Arturo Diaz and Dan Mariscal. They assembled a team of forty campaign volunteers who worked hard in their spare time to publicize MDU's call for "member em-powerment" and "actual worksite representation." During his workplace visits, Mariscal "heard a lot of member complaints about the MRC." The challengers were limited in their ability to reach many of the local's sixty-seven thousand members to discuss this or any other issue. No candidate forums were held and the local refused to include candidate statements with the mail ballots sent out to members (as several predecessor locals, 347 and 660, had always done so voters would have biographical and platform information). The incumbents used their resource advantage to do three expensive mailings of their campaign literature to the entire membership; they also had the active or tacit support of the entire local staff. Only 9 percent of eligible workers bothered to return their ballots and just one MDU candidate was elected. (As of the fall of 2010, the U.S. Department of Labor was still investigating MDU's post-election appeal of the results.)

Five months after defeating MDU, even president Bob Schoonover acknowledged that Local 721 had a problem with members being disengaged. In August 2010, Schoonover held an invitation-only weekend brainstorming session for one hundred newly elected officers, board members, rank and filers, and staff. Called "Imagine 721," the stated purpose of the gathering (and related "scientific polling") was to figure out "why some people participate in the union, but many do not" at a time when union-negotiated wages and benefits are under attack. "It is hard to protect these gains if more people on our side are not involved," Schoonover noted. "One of the things I've heard some of our most active members say many times is that we don't pay enough attention to members already in the union. We spend a lot of time on organizing campaigns, but the perception is that once someone becomes a member they don't get as much attention."[36]

Up in the Bay Area, the reformers who won in Local 1021 were also searching for ways to reconnect members to the union and address long-ignored workplace problems. Weeks after his election, new 1021 vice president Larry Bradshaw was still dismayed at how few workers turned out to vote in the election that the Change 1021 slate had, nevertheless, won overwhelmingly. "Our union was mired in inertia and inactivity," he observed. "It just shows the sad state of these megalocals, where members have become so disengaged and demobilized." Upon taking office, the new 1021 officers had hoped to unplug from the Pasadena MRC and use the money they saved for union rebuilding programs. They did arrange for the MRC to make outbound calls to aid their emergency mobilization of members in San Francisco to fight budget cuts, furloughs, and layoffs. But, as soon as possible, they wanted to restore MRC functions to a Bay Area facility, "staffed with our own people, who know our contracts," Bradshaw said. Unfortunately, after being sworn in by Andy Stern himself, the new leadership found that the Pasadena MRC was a bit like "Hotel California" (in the Eagles's famous song); once you checked in, it was very hard to leave. Local 1021 members were locked into a contract, requiring them to pay $54,000 a month for MRC services. For another whole year, they were prisoners of Andy Stern and Anna Burger's call center dream, whether they wanted to be or not.

A Resource Center Reassessment?

But Local 1021 is not alone in feeling saddled with someone else's costly experiment that hasn't quite worked out as planned. In late 2010, a five-person internal committee, mainly composed of SEIU board members and chaired by the union's new secretary-treasurer Eliseo Medina, sounded the alarm about the rising cost and mixed organizational returns from call center servicing. The Medina-led "Member Strength Review Committee" (MSRC) found that more than 835,000 SEIU members are now covered by some kind of MRC-type arrangement. More than half have their calls funneled to an MRC operated by their own local. Five locals in California are still plugged into the MRC in Pasadena (referred to within SEIU as a "MAC" or Member Action Center), while two, including a janitors' local in Boston, now contract with a new Member Action Service Center (MASC) near Detroit to handle their grievance intake calls. In addition to grievance processing, the MASC was supposed to be a full-service "mega-center," providing participating SEIU locals with centralized dues processing, financial accounting, and other administrative help.

The problem, identified by the MSRC, is that few locals have utilized the MASC for any purpose. To establish its Michigan facility, SEIU received local tax abatements, plus a five-year, $2 million tax credit from the state's economic development agency (based on a promise to create several hundred new jobs). After spending "nearly $14 million in setting

up and operating the MASC in its first year," SEIU was still far from achieving its "highly optimistic enrollment of 402,000 members by December
2011." In fact, Medina and his committee found there was no scenario in
which "SEIU's investment would be recovered in the foreseeable future."[37]

Operating with a staff of only thirty—far below the original projected
employment level—the MASC "would require an additional allocation of
$900,000 through 2011 and by December 2011, a monthly subsidy of ap-
proximately $130,000." According to the MSRC, "Even a good idea can't
be underwritten indefinitely when there is little apparent interest among
the intended 'customers.'" The authors of the MSRC report listed several
options for keeping the MASC afloat, including moving SEIU's headquarters dues-processing operation to Michigan. In the meantime, they also
urged new president Mary Kay Henry "to develop a contingency plan for
shutting the operation down, if necessary."[38]

The MSRC concluded that: "[C]reating the MASC has been all con-
suming at the expense of a well-developed and executed member engagement program. Even if all local unions had enrolled in the MASC, we
believe we would be no further along on actually achieving our member
engagement goals." Although "widely adopted as a tool for representation
in SEIU," local MRCs have not lived up to their original expectations either.
At the SEIU convention in 2008, delegates were told that "participating in
MRCs...would free up money spent on representation and administrative
tasks that could be redirected to member engagement programs in the locals." Two years later, "none of the locals spoken to or surveyed said that
creating the MRC in their local has freed up any resources. Several locals
with longer experience report spending more—not less—on operating
their MRC. Similarly, locals in California who are participating in a collective MRC (the Pasadena MAC) don't report savings."[39]

In *Up in the Air*, management quickly learned from its mistake of trying to make call center servicing (of corporate downsizers) a one-size-fits-
all outsourcing solution. In SEIU, course corrections apparently take
longer because the union is less sensitive to "customer" concerns. Even if
its MRC spending spree is brought under control, SEIU's reliance on call
centers will still be an obstacle, not an aid, to real "member engagement."

Chapter 5

Who Rules SEIU (and Who Doesn't)

"Workers want their lives to be changed. They want strength and a voice, not some purist intellectual, historical, mythical democracy."
—Andy Stern on "Democracy in Unions," a March 15, 2004, blog post[1]

"When your union is less democratic than the Teamsters, you have to look in the mirror and say, 'What happened?'"
—Ken Paff, Teamsters for a Democratic Union, quoted about SEIU in the *Los Angeles Times*, August 2008[2]

"Smart people do stupid shit."
—Jane McAlevey, SEIU official, referring to dissident members of her own local in an interview with the *Las Vegas Sun*[3]

John Templeton is a feisty, white-haired social worker, now retired in western Massachusetts, who spent twenty-three years working for the Department of Human Services. Always a fixture at Boston-area labor and political events, John rarely left home without his SEIU T-shirt or button, plus a stack of flyers under his arm, touting some upcoming rally or cause.

For more than ten years, he served as president of SEIU Local 509, well-known statewide for embracing almost every progressive cause, from gay rights to labor-based protests against American military intervention abroad. Rare among SEIU locals—and unions generally—509 imposes term limits on its top officer and chapter leaders. They are restricted to two consecutive terms, which must be followed by at least a one-year break. Even more unusual, the local's constitution limits top officer pay to the earnings level of the highest-paid working member. (Before Templeton stepped down from the presidency for the last time in 2005, he made about $65,000 a year.) "In our local," he proudly recalled, "we have a lot of dissent. If you don't allow for that, people get really disillusioned and they don't participate. What we should be doing at every level of SEIU is encouraging people to participate more and to speak freely, and even to change the union. If you can't keep the members interested and involved, we're not going to be able to make the union movement grow."[4]

As Templeton sadly discovered over time, his national union had no problem with encouraging membership participation—but only if that worker activity was staff directed and "on message." Speaking freely and trying to change the union, in unapproved fashion, was a different matter entirely, particularly if you were the elected president of a 10,000-member local. Initially, Local 509 was a strong supporter of Andy Stern's "New Strength and Unity Plan" (NSUP), the sweeping reorganization scheme that was adopted in 1996, four years after Stern took office. In Stern's view, local, regional, and national labor organizations should mirror the market scope and corporate structure of business. Smaller-scale union bodies—no matter how participatory—are simply anachronistic "in an era of corporate mergers." According to Stern, a traditional "local union structure" may have "made sense years ago" but "now does more to handicap workers than it does to help." Even Local 509 field rep and organizer Ferd Wulkan—who later became a Stern critic—agreed that "some sort of reorganization made sense." Wulkan favored uniting "workers with similar interests" in the same SEIU local, so they could better coordinate their organizing and political programs and deal with common employers.[5]

In Massachusetts, implementation of the NSUP led to a complicated 2003 realignment of thousands of SEIU members from Boston to the Berkshires. This reshuffling was accompanied by merger- or trusteeship-created opportunities for SEIU appointees to replace elected officials in three of the five largest locals in the state. As part of this process, 509 loyally coughed up 1,650 new members, professional employees recently organized at the University of Massachusetts, Amherst (UMass), so they could be united with three other UMass SEIU bargaining units in a single local. All were transferred, unfortunately, to Local 888, a newly created public sector entity, whose appointed "interim president," Susana Segat, was a staff protégé of Anna Burger.

When a rising star in SEIU, a fellow much favored by President Stern, came to Boston, Templeton and other 509 leaders gladly met with him. The young man in question, Tyrone Freeman, proved to be "a Bible-thumping kind of a guy" and quite an "effective speaker," John recalls. His message from the international union was that Local 509 members should "tear up their grievance forms and start working things out differently with management." While open to alternative forms of workplace problem-solving, Templeton found Freeman to be overly detached from the job problems and concerns of dues paying members. He also regarded Freeman's ideas about "non-adversarial" labor relations to be unrealistic and unlikely to succeed. To this day, John Templeton insists that he doesn't want "to sound completely negative" about SEIU. "I really like the way they've organized janitors," he says. "We were one of the first locals in the country to start devoting 20 percent of our dues to organizing. I think the progress they've made with organizing, especially low-paid workers, is marvelous."

But eight years into Andy Stern's presidency, the president of Local 509 began to have doubts about giving Stern "more power to reorganize and trustee locals" so he could install non-members (including relatively inexperienced staffers) to run them. Previously, "there had to be corruption, malfeasance or undemocratic activity but, after New Strength Unity, they could trustee for almost any reason." Templeton believed this trend was headed in a bad direction. It was a formula for trouble, sooner or later, because the people installed—even if competent and hardworking—would always be more accountable to Stern than to the membership. In 2004, Local 509 delegates came to the SEIU convention in San Francisco with four constitutional changes recommended by their executive board. When Templeton tried to have information about the proposals sent to all delegates, SEIU headquarters said such material could only be distributed "if someone was running against Andy." In order to publicize his reform ideas, John announced his candidacy against Stern, only to withdraw his name from consideration before any contested vote was held. In the meantime, he lobbied for rank-and-file voting on top SEIU officers in the future, rather than the convention election method still in use that gives incumbents such an overwhelming advantage. Templeton also urged adoption of the following safeguards against the abuse of Stern's trusteeship powers:

> *SEIU shall establish clear and consistent guidelines for placing local unions under trusteeship. Trusteeships shall be used only as a last resort in the case of corruption or serious malfeasances and never for political reasons.
>
> *SEIU shall encourage the process where rank-and-file members are encouraged to run for top leadership positions.
>
> *SEIU shall not interfere in local elections by arranging for trustees, interim appointed officers, staff or any other persons not currently or recently employed within the local's jurisdiction to run for local offices.
>
> *Any provisional local officer shall serve in that capacity for no more than one year, and shall not be eligible to run for office unless that person is a member by virtue of being currently or recently employed within the bargaining unit jurisdiction of the local.[6]

All these proposals were easily defeated at a convention controlled by the SEIU leadership and staff (who also dominated the next one in San Juan four years later). The only idea that garnered much support was membership election of top officers. In the context of SEIU politics, and in light of what occurred within the union over the next five years, Templeton was a man ahead of his time, sounding an alarm that few wanted to hear. Like UHW, after its public agitation for similar reforms in 2008, Local 509 soon found its own existence threatened. Following the San Francisco convention, SEIU dispatched a key operative to Boston, Tom Balanoff from Chicago (who owed his Local 1 presidency to a series of trusteeship and merger-related appointments by Stern).

SEIU Mergers and Consolidations

Balanoff's mission was "to review jurisdiction, including possible merger and/or transfer of bargaining units, for state workers in Massachusetts." Translation: he was coming to Boston, on Stern's behalf, to hold a hearing on whether 509 members would be better off in another local. As noted in a 2009 study by four union consultants, it is not necessary under the SEIU constitution "for local unions to ratify the structural changes mandated through the hearing process." Restructuring can be imposed from above after a formal period for membership comment is observed. In their report, the SEIU consultants found that there were 136 local reconfigurations— involving either total mergers or the transfer of some bargaining units— between 1997 and 2007. Due to this trend, the fifteen largest SEIU locals, each of which collects dues from 50,000 to 350,000 workers, now represent 57 percent of the total national union membership. More than forty locals have 10,000 to 50,000 members. Under Stern, the total number of SEIU affiliates dropped to 140 from 373 while their average size increased sixfold. Local 509 was a surviving smaller local and, thus, a candidate for consolidation.[7]

SEIU's preferred repository for Massachusetts social workers was a sprawling 45,000-member organizational oddity called the National Association of Government Employees (NAGE). NAGE also represents some Massachusetts state workers along with government employees, like police officers, in Florida, Georgia, Hawaii, and forty other states. Not surprisingly, its president, gruff, six-foot-three David Holway, was the product of a Stern trusteeship. Holway's predecessor, Kenny Lyons, led NAGE for many years when it was an independent union. Lyons eventually worked out an affiliation agreement with John Sweeney to gain raiding protection as SEIU Local 5000. After Stern became president, Lyons's behavior—like that of

Boston janitor's local president Eddie Sullivan Jr.—became a public embarrassment. So Stern ousted Lyons (and Sullivan too).[8]

Unfortunately, Stern's choice of Holway as Lyon's successor did not enhance labor's image either. In his previous incarnation, Holway was a Beacon Hill lobbyist and top aide to a speaker of the Massachusetts House of Representatives who was forced to resign because of unpaid federal income taxes. An enterprising lawyer, Holway had multiple sources of income to report himself (plus homes in Cambridge and Martha's Vineyard). As *Boston Globe* columnist Steve Bailey reported in 2005, Holway made $229,455 as president of NAGE/Local 5000. He also got another $10,692 for being a Stern appointee to the SEIU executive board, or $240,147 in all—a total even greater than Stern's own pay at the time. For several years after Holway became Local 5000 president, he received payments of about $100,000 annually from the Massachusetts Thoroughbred Breeders Association, a racetrack lobbying group that continued to employ him as its executive director.[9]

Resenting Democracy

In short, a forced merger of Locals 509 and 5000 was not a good match, given the activist history of one and the business union practices of the other. During the jurisdictional hearings, SEIU organizer Ferd Wulkan was struck by how much the international union seemed to resent Local 509's democratic traditions. Under the leadership of John Templeton, the local had done everything Stern ever asked in the area of organizing, political action, and volunteering to help other SEIU affiliates. Yet now, 509 defenders feared that their union's rank-and-file committees and contract action teams (with up to seven hundred members) would be dismantled after a forced merger with NAGE/Local 5000. To avoid this fate, 509 stewards and members mobilized in large numbers. They testified against any takeover at Balanoff's hearing, where their cause was aided by the bad publicity Holway was generating in the *Boston Globe*.

In the end, they succeeded in fending off megalocal absorption. (In subsequent years, however, NAGE was awarded a bigger role in the coordination of Massachusetts state worker bargaining.)

Local 509 activists were joined in their anti-merger protests by former 509 members now trapped in Local 888. These UMass employees were transferred to their new local in 2003, only to find that its appointed leader, Susana Segat, was extremely unresponsive to rank-and-file concerns. They sharply criticized the SEIU-installed leadership of 888 and appealed for creation of a higher education local of their own. (When this request was ignored and the UMass group was also barred from returning to 509, Wulkan began organizing a decertification campaign. He and several thousand others were then allowed to leave SEIU and join the Massachusetts Teachers Association).[10]

The post-Templeton leadership of 509 learned the lesson that it doesn't pay to anger SEIU headquarters. By the time SEIU's next convention rolled around in San Juan in 2008, all the delegates from 509 kept their heads down and eyes averted from the struggle waged by UHW and allied reformers on the convention floor. They had no desire to incur the same official wrath that Templeton attracted after the previous convention when he raised similar issues. The message of the 2004 jurisdictional hearings in Boston was clear: becoming a leadership critic, however constructive, can have bad consequences for your own union career (if you're a full-time official) and/or result in SEIU interference with the normal functioning of your local. At a time when many SEIU local officials already had their hands full dealing with public sector budget crises, privatization schemes, and employers seeking concessions, few sought the additional challenge of fending off powerful enemies within their own parent organization.

Over time, under Andy Stern's presidency, the fear of political retaliation fostered a culture of organizational conformity. By 2009, a longtime SEIU local officer in Massachusetts could only "marvel at Andy and Anna's ability to crush anyone who gets in their way." This same left-wing activist once led protests against worker repression by U.S.-backed governments in El Salvador and Guatemala in the eighties. Now, faced with an authoritarian regime in his own national union—albeit without the capacity to imprison or physically harm anyone—he felt powerless to resist. Even though speaking out in SEIU today is a far cry from dodging death squad bullets in Latin America, few local officials want to take the political risks involved or subject their members to the possible consequences. What happened to trade unionists under military rule abroad three decades ago was something you could protest without rocking the boat too much here at home. Abuses of power in SEIU are occurring today—at home—making the dynamic of dissent a lot different, even if the need for mutual aid and protection is very much the same.

Andy Stern's Management Team

The internal tensions described above rarely intrude on the official SEIU narrative about how the union has successfully restructured itself for the benefit of its own members and all workers. Yet the composition and functioning of the top leadership produced by restructuring enabled Andy Stern to wreak havoc inside and outside SEIU, with little internal objection. SEIU's seventy-four-member executive board is the union's top decision-making council (except when its convention is in session once every four years). In very corporate fashion, Andy Stern transformed this body into a high-level "management team," mainly charged with carrying out policy, rather than formulating it along with the officers.[11] A union executive board is supposed to provide oversight, checks, and balances. SEIU's was continually expanded in a way that discouraged any questioning of presidential decisions. By the end of his reign, Stern had packed the IEB with loyalists who favored his agenda, no matter how costly or destructive it became for workers in SEIU or other unions.[12]

Under Stern, SEIU board members had as much real independence as corporate directors handpicked by a powerful CEO. In the union version of this setup, if anyone asks too many questions or disagrees with official policy too much of the time, he or she can be dropped from the "administration slate" at the next convention, as Sal Rosselli was in 2008 in San Juan. That's because the entire CEO-assembled slate in SEIU (except for its four Canadians) is elected "at large," under circumstances in which an independent candidate has about as much chance of winning as a dissident shareholder running for director of General Electric at its annual meeting.[13]

Only after Stern retired was the board's rubber-stamp tendencies even acknowledged. Said one SEIU leader after a single IEB gathering without Stern in charge: "This is the first time in two years that I've said anything in a board meeting. Before, it was the Andy and Anna show. All of us were called on to execute, but not all of us were asked to form the policy." Interviewing other board members after Mary Kay Henry took over, Hal Meyerson found that most still "acclaimed Stern's leadership." But they "expressed almost a sense of relief that Stern's acknowledged genius no longer dominated their proceedings."[14]

Fourteen years of "genius" rule left an enduring and unhealthy structural legacy. Even though the SEIU board spurned Stern's recommended successor, most IEB members—including Henry, the current president—owe their careers to him. They are products of the leadership development system Stern inherited from John Sweeney and further shaped himself. A UHW analysis of SEIU board members, released just before the 2008 convention, found that "the majority are Stern appointees or staff. Out of [what was then] 67 members of the IEB, well over half are either SEIU International Union staff, or local leaders who were originally appointed to leadership positions in their local by Stern, rather than being elected by their members."[15]

Opportunities for such upward mobility abound in SEIU, to a degree unparalleled in the rest of organized labor. During his presidency, Stern put nearly eighty local unions under headquarters trusteeships or reorganized them under new leaders named by him. They served for periods ranging from eighteen months to three years, and sometimes longer, before any election was held. If parachuted in from elsewhere, these SEIU trustees or "interim presidents" always became members of their assigned locals. Then, they entrenched themselves politically before facing a membership vote conducted under rules they devised. Running as de facto incumbents, with the support of fellow payrollers they hire or decide to retain, headquarters-installed staffers are nearly impossible to beat in a megalocal.

This new class of local union managers has become the talent pool for the IEB. At last count—and the number is always expanding—SEIU has (in addition to its two top officers) six executive vice presidents, twenty-six vice presidents, and thirty-four other executive board members, plus a related eight-member International Board of Auditors. As IEB vacancies were filled by Stern, and more promotions to VP and EVP slots were announced, the patronage loop was complete; the rewards for loyalty and service to the bureaucracy became more abundant than ever before.[16]

The Abuse of Trusteeships

Outside of SEIU, national union trusteeships have never been employed so systematically to remake a union, and, in the process, reduce the proportion of former rank-and-file members in the leadership of what is supposed to be a workers' organization. Trusteeships are, in most unions, a method of rooting out corruption, straightening out a troubled affiliate's finances or functioning, and then holding elections within eighteen months or less to restore membership control. In some unions, trusteeships have been used and abused for political purposes. In the Teamsters and other mob-dominated unions in the fifties, they were a favorite method of rewarding friends and punishing rank-and-file enemies. In the United Mine Workers, under John L. Lewis and his benighted successors, trusteeships over UMW districts became a near-permanent form of martial law over large swaths of the union, depriving coal miners of the right to vote for years.

Such abuses of union democracy were highlighted in Congressional hearings that led to passage of the Labor-Management Reporting and Disclosure Act (LMRDA) in 1959. The LMRDA contained a union member "bill of rights" that has compelled unions to be more democratic and transparent in their handling of dues money, officer elections, contract ratification votes, and other internal matters.[17] Progress in all these areas required a huge amount of litigation. Most of these lawsuits were filed over the years by union reformers like the Miners for Democracy and Teamsters for a Democratic Union, with assistance from the Association for Union Democracy (AUD). Unfortunately, Title III of the LMRDA, which deals with trusteeships, provides insufficient protection against retaliatory local union takeovers—a weakness in the statute that John Templeton tried to remedy through SEIU constitutional changes in 2004. As union democracy lawyer Arthur Fox points out,

> Title III contains a loophole or booby trap. The moment a trusteeship is imposed, the law proclaims that it "shall be presumed to be lawful for a period of 18 months." As a consequence, even assuming that a trusteed subordinate union has the resources to retain counsel to file a lawsuit to challenge the trusteeship, the courts will rarely look beyond the union president's statement of reasons for its imposition, reasons that have been crafted by his lawyers, regardless of the real underlying facts, to fit within the framework of the LMRDA language allowing the imposition of trusteeships.[18]

In other words, if a union like SEIU claims to be imposing a trusteeship "to restore democratic process" or "correct financial malpractice," it gets the benefit of the doubt for a year and a half, even if its real goal is ousting dissenters and installing headquarters loyalists in their place. When elected leaders are replaced as part of a union merger/reorganization scheme, their appointed successors can run the show even longer—a full three years.

As noted in the introduction, taking over and remaking locals has acquired a different aura in recent years. Leading labor-oriented academics decided that trusteeships were an essential tool for progressive union transformation from the top down. In their 2004 book *Hard Work: Remaking the American Labor Movement,* sociologists Kim Voss and Rick Fantasia applauded the work of SEIU's appointed, rather than elected, "senior managers" and college-educated staffers because they were "trying to build a new labor movement in the shell of the old." Voss and Fantasia noted that such operatives were sometimes a bit too "brash and overconfident," and often "give off an air of arrogance and exclusivity," just like "Silicon Valley entrepreneurs." But what mattered most was SEIU's "zero tolerance" for any local union that failed to organize, as required by its NSUP or later benchmarks. Any local leaders who didn't go along deserved to be purged, merged, and replaced by Stern appointees who would get the job done.[19]

More recent applause of this sort was heard from three Rutgers professors and a Washington, D.C., labor consultant who produced the internal report called *Organizational Change at SEIU, 1996–2009*. Authors Adrienne Eaton, Janice Fine, Allison Porter, and Saul Rubinstein praise Stern, who funded their report, for assigning "talented staff to key leadership positions inside local unions, sometimes as a trustee and sometimes as senior staff." Not surprisingly, they found that "these new leaders were more ideologically in line with the national leadership and more comfortable with the concept of a strong, central organization." They are also "younger, more likely to be female or Latino, more likely to have been a union organizer, more likely to have gone to college, and more likely to be a close ally of the Stern administration than those they replaced." One outstanding example of this leadership type is Javier Morillo-Alicea, a Yale graduate and former Macalester College history instructor. He became president of Local 26 in Minneapolis after he left academia and worked for SEIU briefly as an organizer of janitors. Morillo-Alicea is young, energetic, gay, and Latino; within a few short years, Stern appointed him to the IEB, named him to the union's ethics commission, and made him a national coordinator of SEIU work on immigration issues.

A few SEIU leaders still serving on the IEB, like Diane Sosne from Seattle, have a longer history in the union and slightly more independence. They have a base in locals (usually smaller ones) that they developed themselves after emerging from the ranks of fellow government employees and hospital or nursing home workers. In their own communities, they are, like Morillo or Tom Balanoff in Chicago, well known in progressive circles. Among those old enough to be sixties movement veterans, some were once even communists, socialists, or union dissidents themselves. Today, they're understandably proud to be part of an executive body that is by far the most diverse in labor, in many categories that are usually underrepresented (that is, women, African Americans, Asian Americans, Latinos, gays, and lesbians). Unfortunately, this "diversity" was manufactured as part of a leadership selection system that leaves top officials largely unaccountable to the membership—if not in their own locals, certainly at the international union level.

In other labor organizations, it's rare to find so many board members who are appointed union staffers and department heads. At SEIU, vice presidents Dennis Rivera, Tom DeBruin, and Eileen Kirlin all direct or assist headquarters programs. IEB members like Justice for Janitors strategist Stephen Lerner, UHW deputy trustee and former international affairs staffer Debbie Schneider, former chief of staff Kirk Adams, and Workers United/SEIU staffer Mark Fleischman also work under the direction of national officers or EVPs. Several other union payrollers—such as John Tanner from Los Angeles and Celia Wcislo from Boston—are involved in SEIU locals but hold no elected positions. In SEIU, those who report directly to the national officers on a day-to-day basis have even less inclination to function independently on the board, when it meets, than IEB members who still have a local union base (however they obtained it) outside union headquarters. (In late 2010, for example, Lerner had an organizing-related dispute with his new headquarters boss, Scott Courtney, who had not yet been promoted to the IEB. Courtney reportedly disciplined Lerner by putting him on what became a three-month paid "administrative leave." If Lerner was fired or forced out as an SEIU employee, he could still retain his anomalous position as an elected board member until 2012.)[20]

Upward Mobility in Other Unions

In most unions—UNITE HERE being one major exception—national executive boards are primarily composed of former working members.[21] It's not easy to rise from the ranks anywhere in the labor movement, but a talented and politically ambitious worker has a much better chance of making it into the top leadership of almost any other union than SEIU. Three-quarters of its current officers and EVPs have never been working members, just as almost no building services local presidents have ever been employed as a janitor or security guard. (EVP Mitch Ackerman, who has directed SEIU's Property Services Division, did major in "third world" studies at Oberlin.)

In other union settings, candidates for national board positions usually start out at the bottom, as an elected or appointed shop steward. Later, they become a bargaining committee member, serve on a local union executive board, and then get elected president or secretary-treasurer. If the national union likes them, they may get promoted to serve on the national staff, in the field, or at union headquarters in Washington, D.C. Later on, they might run for a seat on the national executive board, as an independent or, more likely, as part of an administration slate. In big unions like the Teamsters and United Steelworkers, some candidates run for at-large positions—unionwide office, like the presidency. But most executive board hopefuls have to compete for fellow members' votes in regional constituencies where they have lived, worked, and are well known.

This traditional system of upward mobility is certainly no guarantee of militant, rank-and-file leadership. Left-wing critics of the labor movement, from C. Wright Mills to Stanley Aronowitz, have chronicled the trajectory of many a "working-class hero" from shop floor militancy to labor statesmanship, with a few disappointing stops in between.[22] The transition from working member, serving as a steward or committee person, to full-time local union official inevitably distances a leader from his or her former coworkers who remain "in the shop." That distance can get even greater when union activists move up the organizational ladder and become an international rep or headquarters official, elected or appointed. At that point in their career, they are not only much further away from the day-to-day workplace concerns of the rank and file; they may also be earning a big salary and enjoying benefit coverage and job perks that provide them with both a standard of living and even a new social circle quite different from that of ordinary dues paying members. So the question has always been what type of union structure keeps leaders at every level more connected to members at the base? If union officials have never even had the formative (but apparently still easily forgotten) experience of working as a rank-and-file member, how close to the rank and file will they remain?

In unions like my own former employer, CWA, the top officers and executive board are elected, SEIU-style, by convention delegates chosen by the members. There is no referendum vote involving the entire membership or some part of it (except among Canadian members and those who belong to the Newspaper Guild). But, regardless of whether voting is direct or indirect—and no matter how bureaucratized a union may have become—the allocation of executive board seats to different constituencies (smaller than the entire union) tends to make board members more politically accountable to those at the bottom rather than just the top. In CWA, the board is composed of some vice presidents who represent multistate districts (ranging in size from 20,000 to 175,000 members). Others are elected from occupational groups such as manufacturing workers, flight attendants, public employees, or journalists. (In 2007, CWA also created "four at large diversity seats representing four geographic areas of the union, with the goal of having at least three of the new members be people of color and at least two women" who would provide a "greater voice to local leaders" on the board.)[23]

Competition for seats on the CWA board is quite common. Independent candidates can even oust incumbents backed by the national president and fellow board members, as a challenger did in the CWA/Newspaper Guild in 2008. When then organizing director Larry Cohen was first elected EVP of CWA in 1998, he faced stiff competition from a conservative former telephone worker. This incumbent board member, a woman, campaigned vigorously for the same open position, with the support of CWA's female secretary-treasurer, other board members, and 47 percent of the convention delegates. Cohen's narrow victory made him just one of three national officers elected "at large," by the convention as a whole.[24]

What's striking about SEIU is the limited opportunity for competitive elections for open board or officer positions.[25] (The 2010 board vote to replace Stern with Mary Kay Henry, instead of his designated successor, Anna Burger, was a rare event indeed; it was preceded by a flurry of campaigning by both candidates, within a rather exclusive electorate.) Structurally, the SEIU board now resembles the ruling body of the IBT, *before* that union was democratized through decades of reform movement activity, aided by federal court intervention in the late eighties. During the IBT's mob-dominated past, its members had no right to elect top officers in a nationwide vote or elect, from their own region, the Teamster vice presidents who make up the rest of the executive board. The only successful IEB candidates were all elected at large, by several thousand delegates at leadership-dominated conventions, as part of slates formed by Teamster presidents (four of whom were indicted and three of whom were jailed for corruption). Each of these pre-1989 Teamster chiefs would add or drop people from their leadership "team," as needed, to ensure executive board conformity with their wishes (using the additional carrot of a full salary, on top of any others, just for attending board meetings).

Beginning in 1991, thanks to the presence of TDU and the settlement of a federal racketeering lawsuit, the IBT has had a series of contested elections for the top leadership. (The role of convention delegates is now limited to candidate nominations.) In each race, the president, secretary-treasurer, and some VPs have run at large, with all 1.4 million Teamsters eligible to vote for them. All other board members, representing regional constituencies, have had to campaign for election among a smaller number of rank-and-file voters who live and work in the same area they do. Almost all successful IEB candidates, whether liberal or conservative, "old guard" or "reformer," started out in the union as working members, not appointed staffers. With the notable exception of current president James P. Hoffa, all previously served in lower-level elected positions.

Reflecting the IBT's local union roots (and a protective clause in the Teamster constitution), a bigger Teamster local can't take over a smaller one without members of the latter voting to approve the merger. Although trusteeships were often used in the IBT's bad old days to crush dissent, since 1989 they have mainly been used under court supervision to oust crooks. Tom Leedham, the progressive leader of a Portland, Oregon, local, has campaigned for the Teamster presidency three times as a TDU-backed candidate. He has always sharply criticized Hoffa's leadership and garnered between 35 and 40 percent of the vote each time he ran. Within the Teamster officialdom, Leedham has faced considerable political hostility for his reoccurring role as a high-profile standard-bearer for TDU. Unlike Sal Rosselli after he emerged as Andy Stern's leading foe in SEIU, Leedham has never had his local put under trusteeship by Hoffa in retaliation for his dissent.[26]

Not the Best and Brightest

Nothing illustrates the downside of installed leaders better than what happened to a significant minority of them while serving in international union positions after the San Juan convention in 2008. Of those elected to SEIU's executive board on the Stern-Burger slate, 12 percent left amid controversy within eighteen months. The reasons for their departure included repudiation by their own members (in two contested local union votes) or, more commonly, allegations that they mishandled dues money, failed to stop others from stealing it, or behaved improperly during local union elections. (During the same period, one other IEB member from Local 49 in Oregon fled to Switzerland. Alice Dale, who now represents SEIU at Union Network International (UNI), was unscarred by local scandal or electoral defeat, but wanted to escape headquarters disapproval of her sympathy toward UHW.)[27]

The fate of these SEIU officials reveals the weakness of a managerial class whose career advancement now has more to do with Washington connections than any past achievements or a mandate from the membership.[28] Their rise and fall also reflects a culture of conformity that began to bother one 25-year SEIU leader in Southern California when he went to "state and national meetings and the only question you ever heard was, 'Are you on program?'" Increasingly, he told me, "the only thing SEIU seems to value is 'yes men,' who will just say: 'program, program, program.'" Despite his obvious pride in the union and "the effectiveness it has achieved," this now retired local official was deeply concerned about the concentration of power at the top. "Workers need to have a real voice in their union," he said. "The top needs to be anchored to the bottom. If it's not, sooner or later, we're bound to lose our way." His own well-functioning four-thousand-member public employee local is a former independent association. As such, it had an affiliation agreement, dating back to the eighties, that prevented SEIU from forcing it to merge, against the members' wishes, and also provided some degree of trusteeship protection. Every other public sector local in the region was consolidated, regardless of the consequences for day-to-day representation and leadership accountability to the rank and file. As this California source observed: "SEIU leaders have convinced themselves that the ends justify the means. In order to make our big omelet, we have to break a few eggs. But, in the end, an ends-justifies-the-means approach doesn't serve our members well."[29]

Another former SEIU local president pointed out that it's no longer just "brilliant organizers" who are breaking eggs in SEIU's kitchen. Some grifters, bumblers, and overreachers are wearing purple toques as well. According to this critic, SEIU has fast-tracked "folks who did not earn their status—they were handed it and that leads to dependence on who handed it to you. The union's leadership bench is actually very shallow today...A person's talent and skill and upward mobility now seem to be in inverse proportion in SEIU."[30]

No one fit that description better than the now-disgraced former president of Local 6434, the second largest SEIU local in North America. At the San Juan convention, just two months before his downfall, Tyrone Freeman was given a prominent speaking role, along with Monica Russo, a board member from Florida. Standing together on the platform, they denounced the shady dealings of private equity firms and other greedy corporate predators. When the *Los Angeles Times* first published an exposé of his own greediness, Freeman chided the paper for "failing to inform readers that our elected executive board and its committees—which are composed of 55 long-term care workers—review all of our expenses and vendor contracts." Every bit of union spending questioned by reporter Paul Pringle, in what became a Polk Prize–winning investigative series, was made "in the context of fighting poverty," Freeman insisted.[31] Home care provider Barri Boone was one of many Local 6434 members who doubted this claim.

An experienced labor and political activist, Boone has belonged to many different SEIU affiliates in California over the past forty years. She served briefly on Freeman's executive board after her smaller local merged with his, an experience she likened to joining a megachurch dominated by a single flamboyant preacher. Because Local 6434 members are scattered throughout the state, the board didn't meet face-to-face once a month; instead, some rank-and-file representatives, like Boone, had to participate via videoconferencing. Meetings began late and ended early, with the high point, for those physically present, being the union-provided lunch. On any particular agenda item, Tyrone would speechify for forty-five minutes or more, leaving just five minutes for questions and discussion.

Despite Boone's repeated requests for information about how dues money from 160,000 members was being spent, she never heard Freeman or his handpicked secretary-treasurer Amanda Figueroa, a fellow SEIU executive board member, give a financial report. All board committees were appointed rather than elected; the communications committee once convened to consider which of three different pictures of Tyrone should be used in Local 6434 literature. During Boone's time on the board, dues were increased from $20 to $30. This meant that workers, who often have less than full-time work, were being charged the equivalent of three hours pay per month to the union. "Their mantra was we should always 'speak with one voice,'" Boone recalls. "Any dissenters were too intimidated to do anything but just say, 'OK.' The kind of people who stayed on the e-board would just go with the flow."[32]

A Charmed Existence

Forty-one-year-old Tyrone Freeman's charmed existence on the SEIU payroll began far from California, after he picked up degrees in political science and business administration. According to one former SEIU board member from the South, "Tyrone made a mess of Local 1985 in Georgia, including the money," the handling of which "has been a consistent problem with him, throughout his career."[33] Nevertheless, in 1996, Stern made Freeman the youngest person on the IEB in the union's history. Four years later, Freeman was promoted to international vice president as well. He was moved to Los Angeles and given control of the local that won bargaining rights for 75,000 home care workers in 1999 and later, through mergers, became Local 6434 in 2006. During that time, the warning signs became clear again; Freeman was spending too much money on perks for himself, his family, and favored lieutenants.

In his investigative reporting, Pringle alleged that SEIU officials first became aware of Tyrone's questionable behavior in 2002. Their only response was to develop a media strategy "to keep the allegations from embarrassing SEIU at a time of epic membership growth."[34] SEIU staffer Steve Trossman was among those who tried to keep the lid on things; when questioned about this in 2008, his memory was poor. "I don't remember exactly what happened," he told Pringle. According to Trossman, SEIU might have performed an audit of 6434, but he couldn't be sure. Trossman claimed he never talked to Freeman directly about any problems with his local and couldn't recall whether Stern was informed about them. (When Freeman's thievery was finally exposed, the private reaction of a longtime SEIU staffer in Los Angeles was quite different. Jono Shaffer is the real-life Justice for Janitors organizer played by Adrien Brody in *Bread and Roses*. In an email about Freeman's misconduct to friends at SEIU headquarters, Shaffer told them: "I wish I could say this is unbelievable, but for those of us in Southern California, the only surprise is that it took so long to make it to the public."[35]

As noted in chapter 3, by 2005, Tyrone started wearing two hats after SEIU negotiated its Southern California home care war truce with AF-SCME. By the time of his removal in 2008, he was taking home $213,000 a year from Local 6434; $30,000 a year as president of the CUHWU, a 30,000-member organization affiliated with AFSCME and SEIU; and also $2,500 per month from a nonprofit housing corporation, along with a $14,500 lump sum payment from the same union-sponsored group.

To hold onto his multiple salaries, Freeman secured SEIU approval of bylaws, which guaranteed, in effect, he would always run for office unopposed. Later challenged by the U.S. Department of Labor, 6434's election rules gave candidates for the presidency three weeks to collect and submit nominating signatures from a mere 4,800 fellow dues payers![36] This requirement was no problem for an incumbent with an army of paid staffers at his disposal, plus a rank-and-file patronage network that included the 6434 executive board and other members whose "lost time" for union trips, meals, and meetings was all reimbursed by the local. In a union of home-based workers—who may not see five coworkers in an entire month—such a barrier to candidate eligibility was illegal on its face. It would have been an unfair and farcical nomination petition requirement even in a steel mill or auto plant where all members of the same local union worked, in traditional fashion, under one roof.

Unfortunately for his low-paid members, Freeman's own traditional tastes led to embezzlement, not just Teamster-style triple-dipping. The total cost of his financial malfeasance was well over $1 million. SEIU claims to be still trying to recover this amount from him personally, his wife, mother-in-law, or various other friends and confederates. As SEIU's own belated investigation revealed, Freeman spent hundreds of thousands of union dollars on day care and videomaking ventures run by his relatives, $10,000 at the Grand Havana Room (a "members only" cigar bar in Beverly Hills), $8,100 on his own lavish Hawaiian wedding, $3,400 on a trip to the NFL Pro Bowl, and so on down the menu to $250 bottles of wine and $175 glasses of cognac.[37] Among the past or present staffers implicated in this scandal was Freeman's former chief of staff Rickman Jackson, another up-and-coming young SEIU leader whose new local in Michigan sent protesters to the 2008 Labor Notes conference. Freeman's nonprofit housing corporation improperly paid $33,500 to lease Jackson's Los Angeles residence and use it as a business address.

More Problems in L.A.

Los Angeles Times reporting on SEIU focused next on its highest-ranking official in the state, Annelle Grajeda, and her former boyfriend Alejandro Stephens. Stephens was the longtime president of SEIU Local 660 in Los Angeles before it was merged with others to form Local 721; Grajeda, an ex–garment worker organizer and 660 staff director, became the Stern-appointed "interim president" of the eighty-thousand-member merged local. In 2007, SEIU paid Stephens nearly $90,000 in "consulting fees"—as part of a severance agreement that was supposed to compensate him for the loss of his union presidency. Contrary to the terms of the agreement, Stephens continued to collect additional sums from the union, adding up to about $180,000, plus a salary from Los Angeles county during the time he remained on the SEIU payroll. Stephens was fired by the county when this arrangement (and Grajeda's possible role in it) came under investigation.

Stephens was also implicated in a scheme to pocket $50,000 from bogus consulting contracts he received from a nonprofit group created by the L.A. County Labor Federation. That money was used to finance his campaign for reelection as president of Local 660 in 2004, when Grajeda was in charge of the local's staff. In September 2008—just three months after she became one of six SEIU national EVPs—this additional scandal forced Grajeda to take a paid leave of absence from all her jobs, including being head of SEIU's state council (a position she secured, with Stern's help, when Sal Rosselli was purged from it). Nevertheless, 2008 continued to be a good year, financially, for Annelle. Her total compensation from Local 721 and the international union was later reported to be $366,000.[38]

Similar merger- and trusteeship-related maneuvering in the Midwest created the context for SEIU board member Byron Hobbs's lower-profile pilfering. As in California, it was long-term care workers who got ripped off. Hobbs became executive vice president of SEIU Healthcare Illinois Indiana, when that merged local of eighty thousand members was created by depositing all hospital, nursing home, and home care workers from both states into Local 880, under the leadership of Keith Kelleher. Hobbs was also entrusted by SEIU with running its trusteeship over Local 2000 in St. Louis. While juggling his three jobs, Hobbs found time to run up $9,000 in personal charges on his union-provided credit card. Hal Ruddock, the Stern-appointed secretary-treasurer of SEIU Healthcare Illinois Indiana while this theft occurred—and thus responsible for preventing unauthorized union spending—was soon on his way to California to help straighten out the finances of UHW as trusteeship staff member.

Like Hobbs and SEIU vice president Damita Davis-Howard from California Local 1021, Susana Segat owed her local and national union jobs to Stern and Burger. In 2004, when John Templeton bravely challenged Stern over trusteeship abuses, Segat was still serving as the appointed interim president of Local 888. Before workers in this newly created Massachusetts public employee local could choose their own leaders, new bylaws had to be adopted. But Segat was in no hurry to complete that process, which meant that Local 888 could not fully participate in the 2004 convention. Nevertheless, she brought forty handpicked convention "observers" to San Francisco. This was twice the number of voting delegates the local would have been entitled to send, based on its membership size, if 888 was operating under elected leadership.[39]

The real purpose of the convention junket was to reward those who would play a role in electing Segat two years later. But the cost to the membership was enormous and typical of the local's spending during her six-year reign. As the economy worsened in 2008 and Massachusetts public employees faced pay, benefit, and job cuts, Segat awarded herself a whopping 19 percent salary increase. By early 2009, she was making $123,000 a year, while 888's own finances deteriorated. The local was laying off staff and coming apart at the seams. Angry members in some of its two hundred state, county, and municipal bargaining units were petitioning to decertify the union. During Segat's tenure, her local had already lost a major growth opportunity when Massachusetts voters defeated a proposal to grant bargaining rights to state-funded child care providers.[40]

In Local 888 on the East Coast and Local 1021 in Northern California, SEIU members were fortunate to have the election competition that was described in the previous chapter. In 2009, Segat was defeated after one term in office and, ten months later, Damita Davis-Howard, the San Juan convention defender of call centers, was ousted as interim president of 1021 for similar reasons. Neither Stern appointee heads any SEIU local today.[41]

Hurricane Jane Hits Nevada

Faced with similar challenges to their control of Locals 1107 and 221 respectively, IEB member Jane McAlevey and new SEIU auditor Sharon-Frances Moore both triggered federal investigations and other controversies that helped curtail their union careers. Like many others fast-tracked to the top by Stern, McAlevey and Moore were hired from outside—and had never been a shop steward, committee member, local leader, or SEIU-represented worker of any type. McAlevey at least had a background in

environmentalism and community organizing, plus she was well connected to the liberal foundation world and had worked for the AFL-CIO.[42]
An attorney, Moore had no prior experience as a union administrator or
contract negotiator when she was put in charge of seven thousand members in San Diego at a salary of $130,000 a year. She was previously em-
ployed as a Senate staffer, corporate litigation manager, senior advisor to
the CEO of the Girl Scouts of the USA, and director of a lower Manhattan
nonprofit called the Tribeca Organization.

At age forty, Jane McAlevey was parachuted in to Nevada in 2004 to
be Andy Stern's agent of change. She became the top staff person in a health
care and public employees local with nine thousand members and bargaining rights for another eight thousand non–dues payers.[43] As reported
later by the *Union Democracy Review*, she was initially welcomed at 1107
as a "shrewd and effective organizer," whose frenetic activity earned her the
nickname "Hurricane Jane."[44] According to Jerry Brown, the 1199 leader
from Connecticut who served as her unpaid advisor, McAlevey initially
"inspired a large number of members to participate" in what was "a totally
dead business union." During her first two years in Las Vegas, Brown says,
"Jane did a phenomenal job of organizing, increasing the membership in
open shops and in new facilities, bargaining and political work. Brown at-
tributes McAlevey's subsequent problems, in part, to resistance from "incumbent rank-and-file officers who liked the old model of paid time off
for a few to 'service' the many and were threatened by her program of activism and militancy."[45]

McAlevey's mission to remake Local 1107 soon led to conflict with its
elected president, Vicky Hedderman, and members of the executive board
aligned with Hedderman.[46] As executive director of 1107, McAlevey was an
employee of the local, supposedly working under the direction of its member-elected board and officers. So she aroused bitter opposition when she
recruited and supported candidates to run against Hedderman (unsuccessfully) in two disputed local elections in 2007. In the first election, Hedderman backers won a significant number of board seats, despite McAlevey's
deployment of 1107 staffers against the elected leadership. One young or-

ganizer, who left to attend law school, was so upset about the campaign role he was pressured to play—which included spying on Hedderman—that he wrote to Stern directly. "Jane's actions and influence are detrimental to the local," warned Matt Stafford. "Her exploitation of staff and workers has led to a larger rift in the organization and is inexcusable."[47] Stern never replied to Stafford. Instead, SEIU pushed for a re-run election that was, according to the AUD, "far more badly flawed than the first." As the *Las Vegas Sun* reported, "Staff members, who have traditionally stayed neutral during elections, used vacation time or were given time off to campaign in favor of the pro-McAlevey slate. Staffers phone-banked from McAlevey's home and rented vans to transport workers to the voting sites."[48]

Hedderman won again but more of her allies were defeated. So, this time, they took their election complaints to the U.S. Department of Labor (DOL). The DOL's investigation led to a preliminary finding "that the pro-McAlevey slate used local union resources in support of its campaign, that it received $5,000 from another SEIU local, and that it received employer funds for printing and mailing its literature."[49] An opposition group, called Members for Union Democracy, began organizing protests against McAlevey, claiming she had rigged the election. On October 30, 2007, a crowd of clapping and chanting members descended on the Local 1107 union hall during a board meeting. McAlevey and her faction were forced to flee to the safety of a side office known, fittingly enough, as the "War Room."[50]

While her relations with members were deteriorating in general, McAlevey faced major rank-and-file defections to the CNA. Under CNA pressure, her handling of the media helped contribute to her undoing. When 1107 suffered what the *Las Vegas Sun* called "a clear vote of no confidence" in a decertification election at St. Rose's Hospital in May 2008, McAlevey was pressed to explain why hundreds of nurses there and at St. Mary's Regional Medical Center in Reno had voted to leave SEIU. In Reno, SEIU claimed that CNA organizers misled RNs about the meaning of decertification cards they signed to get an NLRB election. Asked by the *Sun* "how so many nurses were fooled again," McAlevey told the reporter:

"Smart people do stupid (expletive)."[51] As one angry RN responded on the *Sun*'s website, after this remark was published: "McAlevey's dismissive and condescending comment is indicative of the leadership of SEIU. Local 1107 is out of touch with nurses' needs." Another nurse wrote: "Smart people do stupid $#@% everyday—like let Jane McAlevey stay in Las Vegas. If she represents the best of what SEIU has to offer then SEIU's days are numbered."

In fact, it was Jane whose days were numbered. Just one month after being reelected to the national executive board in Puerto Rico, McAlevey was forced out as Local 1107 staff director. Her exit was a compromise—brokered by a high-ranking emissary from SEIU headquarters. As part of the same deal, Vicky Hedderman also stepped aside "in order to give union members the opportunity to have new leadership and unity moving forward."[52] Hedderman turned over the reins to a McAlevey ally on the board and McAlevey was replaced, on an interim basis, by another SEIU staffer who was a former nurse. In a face-saving move—unpopular with Members for Union Democracy—McAlevey continued to serve for a short period as a "consultant" to the local.

More Election Misconduct in San Diego

In San Diego, it took even less time for Sharon-Frances Moore to go from being an appointed president to an elected one (for just six months before she quit and her election was overturned) and then a would-be "consultant" to a local that, by then, just wanted her to go away. Moore's high-handed managerial style was similar to McAlevey's and just as unpopular. During her own short career as a Stern-installed leader, Moore had none of McAlevey's initial success in organizing, bargaining, or member involvement. Instead she spent her time battling Local 221 employees (who belong to CWA Local 9509). They filed a series of unfair labor practice charges, alleging that Moore harassed 221 field reps who participated in staff union contract campaign activity. Efforts by the local to mobilize San Diego County workers, prior to a two-year contract extension in March 2009, were desultory in comparison; the Local 221 settlement introduced two-tier wages and benefits for new hires. Moore used her interim presidency to shape a new constitution and bylaws for the local, with little rank-and-file input. When that secretive process was complete, Moore finally stood for election in July 2009, along with her fellow appointees to the interim executive board. Her campaign was run McAlevey-style by her chief of staff Eric Banks.

As opposition slate members, including Monty Kroopkin, complained to the DOL afterward, "a large section of the membership never got ballots, observers were not permitted to watch the count, paid staff campaigned on union time, and administration candidates had the use of membership lists that were denied to their rivals."[53] While the DOL was investigating these charges in the winter of 2009–10, rumors began circulating that someone had also filed an internal complaint against Moore with SEIU's new "ethics review board," a body created in the wake of the Tyrone Freeman scandal. In January 2010 Moore suddenly resigned for "personal reasons."

Tallying Up the Damage

Where did the troubled one-eighth of SEIU's top leadership end up after the personal and political mishaps chronicled above? Tyrone Freeman was banned from holding SEIU office for the rest of his life. The union litigation against him, to recover the funds he embezzled, has languished while SEIU has been far busier spending millions of dollars on its lawsuit against former leaders of UHW.[54] Freeman has tried to become a sports agent, while remaining under criminal investigation by the Justice Department for his massive theft from $9-an-hour workers. Freeman's secretary-treasurer, Amanda Figueroa, was forced to resign from her local and national posts; she received a three-year ban on her possible return to office. The rest of the fifty-five-member board of Local 6434 was also removed when the local was put under trusteeship, along with several top staffers.[55]

Freeman's junior partner in peculation, Rickman Jackson, relinquished both the presidency of his Michigan health care local and his IEB membership. (In 2007, Jackson received $178,405 in pay and benefits from

Local 6434 and $18,000 from the national union.) He was ordered to return the $33,500 in improper lease payments he received from Freeman's housing corporation in Los Angeles. Then, he was exiled to Canada, where he remained on the SEIU staff. (Initially, Mary Kay Henry tried to transfer him to SEIU headquarters until others in Washington objected; by mid-2010, Rickman appeared to be making a U.S. comeback, of sorts, under the forgiving wing of EVP Gerry Hudson, a former leader of 1199SEIU in New York.)

After her lucrative seven months of paid administrative leave, Annelle Grajeda resigned from all three of her jobs—interim president of Local 721, California state council president, and SEIU executive vice president. A spokeswoman for SEIU explained that Grajeda "opted to step down after 'sitting and reflecting' on what she wanted to do next."[56] SEIU absolved her of deriving any benefit from the wrongdoing of her former boyfriend. She was then reassigned to work in the SEIU secretary-treasurer's office in Washington, D.C., a strange place to stash someone who had just suffered a triple demotion due to a financial scandal. A year later, Grajeda quietly retired from SEIU and returned to California, where Alejandro Stephens pled guilty to federal income tax and mail fraud charges.

In September 2010 he was sentenced to four months in prison, followed by three more in home confinement.[57] That same month, "the Associated Press and the *Los Angeles Times* reported that the FBI and Department of Labor were investigating Stern's role in the SEIU consulting fees paid to Stephens, as well as the $175,000 contract Stern received from Simon & Schuster for his book, *A Country That Works*."[58] Stern denied being the target of any federal investigation and his press spokesperson, Michelle Ringuette, shifted all blame back on the former president of Local 660. "We believe Stephens violated the terms of his separation agreement with our union," she told the *New York Times*. "We have aggressively been seeking repayment."[59]

Byron Hobbs was removed from his Stern-appointed positions in two Midwestern locals and was, of course, purged from the IEB too; he promised to pay back what he stole. After their defeat by angry rank and filers in Massachusetts and California, Susana Segat and Damita Davis-Howard similarly disappeared from the roster of SEIU board members. Jane McAlevey's ouster as executive director of Local 1107 in Las Vegas was followed by her withdrawal from SEIU activity, including any board role. (Now living in California and recovering from a serious illness, McAlevey refused to be interviewed about the circumstances surrounding her departure.)[60]

Sharon-Frances Moore's sudden resignation was followed three months later by an agreement between SEIU and the DOL to hold a government-supervised rerun of her election. To ease her exit, the Local 221 executive board initially approved severance pay of $107,850 and a sixty-day "consulting" contract for her; when members learned about this, there was a major uproar and the deal was rescinded. Even SEIU headquarters, notoriously generous in such matters, discouraged Local 221 from paying Moore what she was originally promised.[61] Moore no longer reviews SEIU finances as a member of the union's Board of Auditors, but she is suing Local 221 for "breach of contract."[62]

A Megalocal Success Story?

Not all SEIU locals are like those headed by the former leaders we just met. One highly regarded health care affiliate is now the largest "local union" in U.S. labor history and, according to many observers, a continuing success story. The multistate entity known as 1199SEIU United Healthcare Workers East (1199SEIU) started out as a small left-led union of New York City pharmacists. It later branched out into other health care occupations to become an influential statewide union, was wracked by internal conflict during the eighties, and then got back on track after a long reform struggle waged by the "Save Our Union" movement. Under the leadership of Dennis Rivera, District 1199 finally merged with SEIU in 1998, becoming the largest component of its national health care division. In June 2010, 1199SEIU added another 10,000 members by taking over SEIU's Florida Healthcare Union (FHU), a statewide local of nursing home and hospital workers. 350,000-member 1199 now extends all the way from Boston and Buffalo to Miami, due to the recent addition of other members who previously had their own locals in New Jersey, Maryland, and Washington, D.C.

Why would a labor organization in Florida—very large by regional standards and, according to its admirers, already quite successful—need to merge with a New York City local that's bigger than all but a handful of national unions in the AFL-CIO? The FHU—also known as "SEIU Healthcare Florida"—is headed by Monica Russo, a former garment union organizer and Jobs with Justice activist. She was originally installed in her local by Stern and later elevated by him to the SEIU executive board. Between 1997 and the time of the 1199 merger, FHU grew from about 1,500 members to 7,500 (with bargaining rights for another 8,500 nonmembers), in a state that ranks near the bottom in union density.

As a statewide local, the FHU was much praised by labor educator and author Bruce Nissen, who teaches at Florida International University. In 2009, Nissen conducted a survey of more than four hundred FHU members to determine levels of "political and civic understanding and engagement" within their union. Although some activists expressed the need for stronger workplace organization, particularly in newer bargaining units, there had been "a number of positive transformations" in their lives. "Few other institutions can claim a similar record on so many fronts," Nissen concluded."[63]

Nevertheless, in early 2010, Russo worked out a deal with Dennis Rivera's successor at 1199, George Gresham, for FHU to become the southernmost appendage of United Healthcare Workers East (unless, of course, Puerto Rican SEIU members are the next to be absorbed). When the merger was approved by a 97 percent vote in favor, Russo reported that the union in Florida "just grew 30 times more powerful."[64] She became regional 1199 EVP. Her new boss, George Gresham, pledged to bankroll "significant struggles with employers" in Florida that would yield better pension and health care coverage and more industry participation in the union's joint training fund. One of Russo's main selling points was the progress made by ten-thousand-member, Boston-based Local 2020 since it merged with 1199 in 2005 and tripled its membership.

There was, of course, more to that Bay State story—and a downside to merging with 1199—that Russo didn't mention. Headquartered in Boston, 2020 traded local control for greater organizing and political action resources. This assistance could have come from the national union directly, but SEIU made it contingent on Local 2020 affiliation with 1199.[65] Tall, bearded, and soft-spoken Mike Fadel was 2020's organizing director at the time of the merger. He believed that Massachusetts health care workers were "in desperate need of a stronger voice in the major hospitals, both across the city and state."[66] As promised, the members who formerly belonged to 2020 did gain access to bigger organizing and job training grants. But union officials like Fadel, who were no longer elected locally, found it much harder to distance themselves from SEIU misbehavior nationally. When Fadel tried, he ran afoul of 1199 leaders and staff in New York who were more "on program."

The Price of Dissent in Boston

In Massachusetts, the original acquisition of 2020 by 1199 was marketed as a way to improve workers' political clout, training opportunities, and contract standards. Two years after 2020 voted to merge, Fadel, Enid Eckstein, and other local organizers got the state legislature and newly elected Democratic governor Deval Patrick to create a bargaining unit for Medicaid-funded "personal care attendants" (PCAs). In a mail ballot vote involving twenty-two thousand of these home health aides who had previously been classified as independent contractors, 1199 won by a vote of 6,135 to 135. A year later, PCAs, who had been earning $10.84 an hour with no benefits, won a 15 percent raise in their first contract, sick days, and expanded health coverage.[67] At the same time, Dennis Rivera—then still president of 1199—tried to forge an alliance with Massachusetts hospital officials modeled on 1199's longtime partnership with the Greater New York Hospital Association. Dennis came to Boston with a big flurry of publicity and a display of influential cultural and political allies ranging from Senator Ted Kennedy and Mayor Tom Menino to Hollywood actor Ben Affleck and the Dropkick Murphys, a popular local band. Rivera told the *Globe* he wanted to work cooperatively with Boston hospital executives and addressed them directly via the newspaper. "We've got to get to know each other," he said. "We want to convince you that we are the best thing that could ever happen to you and your institution."[68]

Unfortunately, Rivera's overture was rebuffed by the teaching hospitals, despite his joint training fund pitch and offers of labor help with lobbying for better Medicare and Medicaid reimbursement rates. Five years later, the city's two big bastions of anti-unionism, Beth Israel Deaconess Medical Center and Mass General (a subsidiary of Partners Healthcare), remain adamantly opposed to any organizing rights deals. Where 1199 did make progress in the meantime was at Caritas Christi Health Care, a smaller Catholic hospital chain. Caritas officials came under concerted labor-community pressure similar to that applied to the Sisters of St. Joseph in California. Even before the U.S. Conference of Catholic Bishops issued its 2009 guidelines for respecting workers, Caritas Christi CEO Ralph de la Torre, 1199 president George Gresham (Rivera's successor), and 1199 Massachusetts division EVP Mike Fadel all signed a negotiated election procedure agreement. It enabled the union to win a series of elections at Caritas hospitals in the Boston area. The first was at St. Elizabeth's in Brighton, Massachusetts, where several earlier drives had failed. This time, the pro-union vote there was a lopsided 453 to 168. "If there's not the incredible, intense, unlawful campaign that's waged in most nonunion workplaces, it's a no-brainer," Fadel said. "Our margins of victory were huge."

By the end of 2009, 1199 was able to negotiate a new master contract with Caritas Christi, covering three thousand workers. Some of the lowest-paid among them went from earning $8 to $12.62 an hour, immediately. With that victory as a model, the union resumed its now five-year effort to persuade Boston's larger, more powerful, and still-nonunion teaching hospitals that the tens of thousands of workers employed there deserved "free and fair" elections too. "Our goal is to organize Partners Healthcare—the General Motors of our industry," Fadel explained. "There are only five or six cities in the U.S. with as great a concentration of health care workers as in Boston. Organizing this sector is essential to raising standards for everyone else in the city."[69]

While Caritas workers certainly benefited from the single most successful SEIU hospital campaign anywhere in the country in 2009, Mike Fadel's role in that victory did not ensure his own job security. In February 2010, Gresham called Fadel about the slate he was assembling for the 1199-wide officers and executive board election that would soon be held. Fadel was informed that he was no longer the administration candidate for EVP representing the fast-growing Massachusetts division. Mike was offered a lesser position, but the political message was clear. Union headquarters was not happy with his opposition to sending 1199 staffers to California to fight NUHW or his objections to Andy Stern's raid on UNITE HERE in Massachusetts. 1199 in New York perceived Fadel's dissent to be a form of disloyalty. Clearly, Massachusetts needed a division manager who was a better team player on union policy questions, organizing strategy debates, and dealings with management as well.[70]

This sudden demotion of a well-respected, highly accomplished organizer was very demoralizing for other 1199 activists. As EVP, Fadel chaired 1199 leadership bodies within Massachusetts and was the union's top administrator in the state. Some coworkers urged him to run for reelection as an independent candidate, so he could continue representing them on the board. Fadel was concerned that such a challenge to the New York leadership might become a distraction from the unfinished work of unionizing Boston's major academic medical centers. Furthermore, if he ran and lost, Mike would no longer have full-time employment with 1199. And there was little doubt he would lose—because 1199 board members are elected just like SEIU IEB members. All of them run for office at large unionwide (in an electorate that, in this case, totals 350,000). Fadel could only count on winning a majority of the votes from the 34,000 members of 1199 in Massachusetts. As a candidate unknown outside the state, he would certainly lose to any Gresham-backed candidate for his old EVP slot. Since the biggest concentration of 1199 members is still in New York, that voting bloc ultimately decides who leads the union everywhere. In the end, Fadel bowed to the changed political realities of health care union-ism in Massachusetts. After being demoted, Mike was removed from hos-pital work and reassigned to nursing homes (where one former colleague says he was left "marginalized and undermined"). In August 2010, he re-signed from 1199SEIU and went to work for the Massachusetts Nurses Association, an affiliate of the National Nurses United (NNU).

Ironically, the creators of 1199's current megalocal structure were once defenders of union democracy when it was threatened by the dicta-torial regime of Doris Turner three decades ago. Back then, Dennis Rivera, his later successor as 1199 president George Gresham, and other progres-sive activists were part of the "Save Our Union" movement. Some, like Rivera, were purged from the 1199 staff as a result. When Gresham was an X-ray technician at Columbia-Presbyterian Medical Center in the early eighties, he argued for bylaw reforms that would improve representation by making union elections more competitive. ("Right now," Gresham wrote in one flyer, "elections in 1199 don't make any sense because people vote for slates, not knowing most of the names they are voting for.")[71]

"Save Our Union" supporters finally defeated the corrupt and incom-petent Turner. Their long struggle is recounted in *Upheaval in the Quiet Zone*, Leon Fink and Brian Greenberg's definitive history of 1199.[72] Run-ning a reform slate to change the dysfunctional 1199 leadership of that era was no easy task. The membership was only seventy-five thousand then, but it was concentrated in and around New York City. As Save Our Union organizer Moe Foner recalled in his memoir, "Turner had a hun-dred staff people to use as campaign workers. She had uninterrupted ac-cess to the members. She had lots of money and considerable management support. She used the local publication as a puff sheet."[73]

If Turner-style dysfunction should ever again require a similar oppo-sition challenge, saving 1199 will be a lot more difficult. Twenty-five years ago, Foner, Rivera, Gresham, and other dissidents just had to rally workers in the five boroughs of New York City. To hold any wayward officials ac-countable today, health care workers from Boston, Buffalo, Newark, Bal-timore, Washington, D.C., and Miami would have to build a reform network spanning the entire East Coast. They would face obstacles to running for office that have proved daunting in local unions only a fraction of 1199's current size.

But then, as Andy Stern himself so often reminded us, SEIU's structure was never designed "to make it easier or harder to elect or re-elect leaders." In Stern's view, organizational effectiveness has no relation to members' ability to choose their own leaders and replace them, as needed, based on their performance in office. The union should stay focused on helping workers "unite, fight, and win together."[74] To the extent that it matters (and some day it might matter a lot), who rules 1199 is not subject to worker control. And the same is true for SEIU, only far more so.

Chapter 6

The Mother of All Trusteeships

"These were people who were old-time union bullies who were masquerading under the name of democracy."
—Andy Stern on why SEIU had to remove a hundred elected leaders of United Healthcare Workers West and replace them with his own appointees[1]

"We knew SEIU was coming and we wanted to be there to make our stand, and let them know that the members don't want this, don't want them to destroy the union that was the citadel of our hopes and dreams."
—Kaiser worker Emily Ryan testifying in federal court about why she and other UHW members slept in their local union hall for three nights before it was seized by SEIU[2]

SEIU's invasion and occupation of United Healthcare Workers West in January of 2009 created the second largest local union trusteeship in U.S. labor history. But it was not without precedent. As we saw in the previous chapter, SEIU trusteeships (often in combination with forced mergers) are a key tool in the union's top-down restructuring and leadership reshuffling. The scale of the UHW takeover may have been bigger than anything attempted before, but the blueprint was quite familiar. Like Pentagon counterinsurgency planners, the Washington, D.C.–based architects of this tragedy had past interventions to guide them, while ignoring many of their most salient lessons.

Dissident janitors in San Francisco and Providence, Rhode Island, were among Andy Stern's earlier takeover targets. They both became an obstacle to "New Strength and Unity" in much the same way that UHW ended up on the wrong side of the false dichotomy between "Just Us" and "Justice for All." The offending local union leaders, having been elected, simply paid too much attention to what their own members wanted them to do, as opposed to what SEIU headquarters strategists decided was best for them. If anyone wanted a smaller-scale preview of what was in store for the 150,000 members of UHW in 2008–09, one only had to recall the respective legal ordeals of Locals 87 and 134 just a few years before.

San Francisco Local 87 was once headed by George Hardy, the gruff old guy who brushed aside my mid-seventies scheme for SEIU organizing in Vermont. In 2002, after jurisdictional hearings at which many janitors strongly objected, Local 87's 3,500 members were merged against their will into a statewide California local. Their new organizational home was Local 1877, headed by Mike Garcia, a leader installed after a John Sweeney–imposed trusteeship in 1995. According to Local 87 officer Ahmed Abozayd, San Francisco janitors were concerned that their pay and benefits would be adversely affected. "Our pay rate was $15.25 an hour, 1877's was between $7 and $9 an hour. We had full benefits, they had little or none."[3] Faced with rank-and-file resistance, SEIU didn't even put the merger to a pooled vote. Instead, an international union team that included Eliseo Medina placed Local 87 under trusteeship and removed all its elected officers and staff. The forced merger with 1877 that followed was supposed to boost union power in the industry. But the "master contract," covering more members in a larger geographical area, was negotiated by Garcia rather than a committee locally elected. Medina assured rank-and-file members in San Francisco that they wouldn't lose pay or benefits, despite their loss of control over contract negotiations. Post-trusteeship, the bargaining results were not satisfactory; workers ended up with health care givebacks and what many viewed as inadequate wage increases. Plus, they were now in a local less willing to fight layoffs.[4]

In response, ousted Local 87 president Richard Leung and others began organizing United Service Workers for Democracy (USWD). For a time, this small, underfinanced, independent union managed to unify a workforce prone to factionalism and ethnic division. "SEIU helped galva-nize these different constituencies, who all felt their democratic rights were being trashed," recalled Leung, who now works for the CNA. In August 2004, USWD supporters challenged Local 1877 in a labor board election that produced a major defeat for SEIU in a unit of nearly 1,700 workers. By a vote of 947 to 573, San Francisco building service employees voted to change unions—despite a huge deployment of SEIU organizers who tried unsuccessfully to avert decertification. (Their efforts were backed by the San Francisco Central Labor Council, which issued a letter warning that, if the janitors joined USWD, they "would no longer receive support from other unions during strikes and organizing campaigns."[5])

Winning the NLRB election, hard as that was, proved easier for USWD than surviving as an independent union. While SEIU's appeal of the elec-tion results was still pending, its officials encouraged building service con-tractors to withhold recognition from the new union. SEIU even sued USWD's lawyer Dan Siegel (who would later represent NUHW) to recover legal fees paid by Local 87 to fight the original trusteeship. With no treasury and little ability to collect dues or deal effectively with local employers, some USWD leaders sued for peace, using the leverage of decertification to wrest important concessions from SEIU. In February 2005, a member-ship meeting attended by four hundred janitors approved a "Unity Agree-ment" that restored Local 87 as a separate SEIU entity. As a result, the janitors reclaimed the treasury, union hall, and other property that had been seized by Andy Stern three years earlier. Equally important, the San Francisco janitors won some protection against future forced-merger or trusteeship attempts by the International Union. (As of mid-2010, Local 87 was still functioning on its own, within SEIU, but faced a major external threat: hundreds of its members were being dismissed because of their immigration status.[6])

Rhode Island Rebellion

In 2002–03, seven hundred janitors, campus maintenance workers, and librarians in Rhode Island became a similar fly in the ointment of SEIU regional restructuring. Andy Stern had just put the old janitors' local in Boston under trusteeship, appointed new leaders, and now wanted members of Local 134 in Providence to become part of newly reorganized New England–wide Local 615. When the vast majority of Local 134 dues payers signed a petition seeking to keep their own local intact, their wishes were ignored. So they sent a letter to Stern informing him that "we may be a small local in a small state but we have a big heart and will fight this to the end. You are mistaken if you think we will just lie down and let the International kick us around."[7] Like the San Francisco janitors, they created an independent union. It was called the United Service and Allied Workers (USAW) and proved to be more durable than USWD. SEIU believed that Local 134's only salaried employees—ex–Providence College mechanic Charlie Wood and former Brown University library worker Karen McAninch—should squelch the new union, bound by their fiduciary relationship to the international. Wood was the local's elected secretary-treasurer and McAninch its elected business agent.

Putting their own continued employment at risk, Wood and McAninch felt obliged to respect the democratic decision of their coworkers. "I supported Andy Stern for president, I thought he was a good guy," McAninch explained. "But I couldn't go along with this awful thing that was happening." As a result of their stand, she and Wood were fired by SEIU, locked out of their own office, blamed for nonexistent financial improprieties, and accused of "conspiring to keep contracts from being signed so they could secretly form a new dues guzzling machine."[8] Under the trusteeship imposed by Stern, all the other elected officers and stewards were removed along with them. Plus, in 2004, SEIU trustee Peter Rider, a former United Labor Unions organizer and future Local 615 secretary-treasurer, went after Wood and McAninch personally by suing them for damages in federal court. (SEIU had already tried, unsuccessfully, to prevent them from collecting state unemployment benefits.)

In its punitive lawsuit, SEIU accused the two defendants of "misappropriating trade secrets"—information about Local 134 bargaining units and members that anyone who served them faithfully for years would know well and not need to "steal." SEIU sought to recover $240,000 in lost revenue, resulting from members switching to USAW (which more than five hundred workers did as soon as they could file for NLRB elections). And Rider even tried to force Wood and McAninch to repay thousands of dollars in wages they had earned prior to the trusteeship. Aided by publicity in *Labor Notes* and the AUD, friends of Karen and Charlie raised more than $4,000 for their legal defense. Before SEIU's case was dismissed in 2006, USAW's total expenses related to the lawsuit were more than $25,000. This was a considerable financial burden for workers whose own accumulated dues money had been seized and was now being used against them in trusteeship-related legal fights. Despite SEIU attempts to blackball USAW from local community-labor coalitions like Working Rhode Island and Jobs with Justice, the new member-controlled union survived and was able to organize 150 workers at the Providence City Library. Far from being a "dues-guzzler," USAW managed to rebuild a local strike fund with a dues structure more modest than SEIU's. By 2008, its treasury was three times the size of the one commandeered by Andy Stern five years earlier and then squandered on litigation against the membership.

Win or lose in court, SEIU remained confident, based on these smaller encounters with restive members, that it could merge or dismantle affiliates anytime it pleased, installing its own "managers" in place of elected leaders and preventing most disgruntled dues payers from escaping to any other union. In the case of UHW, tens of thousands of workers tried their best to make their voices heard within SEIU, while sending it millions of dollars a year in per capita dues—money that, in 2008–10, was often used against them. When that affront became too much to bear, they headed for the exits, hoping to escape Andy Stern's Hotel California on a scale larger than ever before.[9]

An Old-Time Union Bully?

In the fall of 2007, when I first interviewed Sal Rosselli there were few signs that he wanted to be the next local officer ousted, slandered, or sued in federal court for disobeying orders from SEIU headquarters. In fact, at that point in Sal's career, he seemed optimistic about the possibility of "working within the system" to improve the union he had helped to build for most of his adult life. We met in what was then his small, second-floor office at the statewide headquarters of UHW on Thomas Berkley Way in downtown Oakland. If Rosselli really was an "old-time union bully" already scheming to hijack SEIU's third-largest local (as Andy Stern would later claim), his masquerade was pretty convincing. Over the years, I've been in the plush office suites of many a top union bureaucrat and most feel compelled to remind themselves of their own self-importance with big displays of plaques, citations, awards, and photos. In Sal's modest workspace, there were no "Mahogany Row" furnishings, no grip-and-grin shots with big-name politicians, and none of the tight security that would later sadly envelop the same union hall after it was seized in 2009, the locks changed, and dissenting members evicted from the building.[10]

In the fall of 2007, Sal Rosselli's political differences with Andy Stern were still being expressed discreetly and internally, for the most part; few would have expected his criticism of the national union leadership to result, fourteen months later, in a total parting of ways. In the view of many observers then (if not now), SEIU was still America's "most progressive union." It was run by people who bore little resemblance to the blue-collar thugs and bad guys who tried to crush union reformers in the United Mine Workers, Steelworkers, or Teamsters in the seventies and eighties.[11] Certainly SEIU could accommodate a loyal opposition composed of past Andy Stern supporters and allies who were, after all, fellow progressives. When Stern ran his own reform campaign for the SEIU presidency in

1996, Sal Rosselli was one of his leading West Coast backers. To become John Sweeney's successor, Stern had to defeat the union's conservative secretary-treasurer Dick Cordtz. The latter quickly fired Andy as organizing director after Sweeney left to head the AFL-CIO. Cordtz then launched his own bid for the presidency, backed by the most retrograde elements in SEIU. Sal, Jerry Brown, and other younger local leaders joined forces to help Stern win and keep the union's organizing program on track. Like Karen McAninch from Local 134 in Rhode Island, and many others, they had high hopes that the candidate from their own generational cohort would, in a slogan popular then, "make the best better."

When Stern triggered a wide-ranging public debate about the future of the AFL-CIO a decade later, Sal echoed his call for "structural change" and new federation leadership. He touted SEIU's own internal restructuring and financial commitment to membership recruitment as a model and supported its plan to "identify lead unions in each industry with the focus, resources, and strategy to win—instead of letting unions divide workers strength and undercut each other through overlapping organizing." In the same *Labor Notes* opinion piece, he wrote that "from the perspective of our local, it is hard to imagine why we would stay [in the AFL-CIO] unless basic changes are made."[12]

When we talked in November 2007, Sal argued in favor of local union consolidation to deal with common employers from a position of greater strength. But he contrasted the process of creating 150,000-member UHW, which was formed by merging Local 250 in Northern California and Local 399 in Southern California, with the other megalocal mergers that proved to be less popular, as we saw in chapter 5. In 2004, the executive boards of both Local 250 and 399 voted unanimously to merge. Officers, stewards, and staff members on both sides then spent almost a year holding rank-and-file meetings to discuss the merger and how the different cultures of the unions would be integrated. Unlike Locals 1021, 721, 521, and 221 later on, the proposed merger partners developed a constitution for UHW before that new entity was formed so members voting on the merger would know, in advance, how their new local would be structured.

Finally, the merger ballots were counted separately, not pooled, because the disparity in membership size—Local 399 had 20,000 dues payers and Local 250 had 70,000—meant that higher turnout in 250 would have been determinative. (The merger was ultimately approved by a 90 percent vote in both groups.) Rosselli had no problem with smaller locals having veto power over multilocal mergers. "We really believe in democracy, in empowering people and educating them," he said. "If some local votes no and the merged local proceeds to do a great job, they'll see the benefit and maybe change their mind then."

In our conversation, Rosselli emphasized how much UHW had cooperated with and benefited from coordinated organizing projects involving Tenet, Catholic Healthcare West, and Hospital Corporation of America. Between 2001 and 2006, Local 250 and then UHW added nearly 65,000 new members, making it one of the fastest growing SEIU affiliates in the entire country. Sal told me that the Nursing Home Alliance agreement (terminated in May of 2007 after UHW complaints about it) would be reviewed by an IEB committee examining a broader range of employer relationships. He intended to be part of that committee discussion, leading to proposals for the union's 2008 convention. If differences between UHW and SEIU over bargaining and organizing strategy weren't resolved by then, UHW delegates would state their case in a more public way at the convention. Rosselli was adamant about raising contract standards for California home care workers. Now that SEIU had achieved such great home care density, the union needed to improve benefit coverage and standardize wages, which still varied widely from county to county. He also argued for keeping long-term care workers united with hospital workers because "the challenge of having deeper participation of our home care members is huge" and UHW was willing to commit significant resources to that goal.

From Private to Public Criticism

Little of Rosselli's hopeful scenario materialized in the months after our conversation. Instead, relations between UHW and SEIU took a serious turn for the worse. First Sal broke with Stern over the latter's backdoor dealings with Governor Arnold Schwarzenegger about health care. In 2007, the governor vetoed single-payer legislation and another bill, based on the Massachusetts health care plan model, that was supported by the state AFL-CIO and California SEIU locals. "Stern jetted in to work with Schwarzenegger to mold a third, even more compromised bill, which required Californians to buy care but set no caps on rates and no floor for minimum coverage."[13] The Stern-Schwarzenegger scheme was rejected by the local labor movement, including UHW.

Stern responded by arranging to have Sal purged in the middle of his elected term of office as president of the SEIU state council, which represents seven hundred thousand workers. (Andy's handpicked successor was Annelle Grajeda, whose scandal-scarred tenure in the same position would last less than a year.)[14] In February of 2008, Rosselli decided to step down from the union's twenty-member national executive committee, a subset of the IEB, so he could express policy disagreements more freely. In his resignation letter, he reiterated UHW objections to the way recent SEIU bargaining with Tenet and CHW was handled. He also accused Stern of trying to realign long-term care jurisdiction in California so UHW would be stripped of its existing nursing home and home care members, thereby eliminating any future opposition to a revived NHA deal. Restating UHW's lengthy 2007 critique, Rosselli charged that: "The Nursing Home Alliance agreement and others negotiated by the International Union appear to relegate entire categories of workers to permanent second-tier status, without basic rights and standards to be expected in a union contract or any reasonable hope of achieving them. This transactional exchange of members' rights and standards for greater numbers contradicts the core mission of SEIU."[15]

Soon the UHW president's public criticism of Stern was appearing in publications ranging from the *New York Times* to *Labor Notes*. To reach other SEIU members, UHW launched a lively and informative website (www.seiuvoice.org) to stimulate internal discussion about the need for "real member participation" and a more democratic, bottom-up approach to building the union. Other SEIU leaders did not react well to Sal's outspokenness or call for debate. In a posting on the progressive political website

Calitics, Mary Kay Henry said there was "a legitimate, healthy debate to be had in the labor movement about our strategies and shortcomings." But, according to Henry, this wasn't the right moment for it because "the lives of workers should always come first" and their "standards of living" were now at greater risk because "too many union leaders have adopted the business model of unionism—focusing exclusively on their own members." She accused Rosselli of giving aid and comfort to multiple SEIU enemies while "distracting his own local from upcoming contract negotiations" and diverting "massive resources" to "divisive attacks" on the national union. "By criticizing the same employer neutrality agreements he once fought for alongside his members, he is giving employers ammunition to use against workers who dream of having what UHW members have," Henry claimed.

Henry's riposte appeared one day after Andy Stern sent a letter clearly designed to lay the legal groundwork for a takeover. It accused UHW officials of unethical conduct, financial irregularities, and failing to meet their fiduciary duties. Stern claimed that UHW was "developing a secret plan to destabilize and decertify bargaining units." As part of this conspiracy, UHW members would become part of a breakaway "independent union" formed in alliance with the AFL-CIO and the CNA. As a further sign of "sabotage," Stern said that UHW was hindering SEIU's campaign to replace the Puerto Rican teachers' union. He charged that dues money was being diverted to a nonprofit UHW "Patient Education Fund," set up to finance rebellious activity, not conduct legitimate political education and outreach.

After the arrival of Stern's threatening letter, UHW members awoke on March 27 to a headline in the *San Francisco Chronicle* that read: "SEIU Leader Moves to Oust West Coast Dissident." The following day, UHW elected leaders and staff organized what became the first in a series of highly unusual anti-trusteeship demonstrations—events that became bigger and bigger over the next ten months. At the first such gathering, several hundred African American, Asian, and Latino hospital workers, nursing home employees, and personal care attendants jammed their Oakland union headquarters for a raucous pep rally and press conference. Arriving

by bus, on the BART, on foot, and by car, the crowd chanted, clapped, whis-
tled, and made an enormous racket with union-issued yellow plastic clack-
ers. Almost everyone wore the signature purple T-shirts and jackets of
SEIU. A few of the home care workers even wheeled in the disabled people
they were caring for in nearby neighborhoods. Their call-and-response
chants got right to the heart of the matter. "What do we want?" a staffer
with a bullhorn asked. "Democracy!" the crowd responded. "When do we
want it?" The answer, delivered by all present, was a thunderous "Now!"
And then in a spirited chant, reminiscent of Bay Area protests past, they
began to shout: "Hey hey, ho ho—Andy Stern has got to go!"[16]

In his statement to the press that day, Rosselli disclaimed any intention
of decertifying from SEIU. While he acknowledged "profound disagreements" with its current direction, Sal insisted that "leaving is not an option.
SEIU is our union, that's why we're fighting to change it." As one sign of
UHW's continued commitment to building SEIU, Rosselli proudly introduced an organizing committee member from St. Francis Medical Center
in Lynwood, California, where six hundred service and maintenance workers had just voted to join UHW. As the rally broke up, I happened to run
into one of UHW's newest staff people who looked very familiar. It was
my twenty-four-year-old daughter, Alex. She had recently moved to the
Bay Area, after a six-month postgraduate tour of duty with a social justice
group in San Salvador. Her first choice of West Coast employment was a
"workers' center" job where she could continue to use her Spanish language
skills. When she discovered that all the cash-strapped groups aiding immigrant workers weren't hiring at the moment, she interviewed with HERE
and SEIU, the two unions whose members she had supported on campus
while majoring in Latin American studies. Her job offer from UHW came
with a staff union contract and longer-term prospects (or so she thought),
while all that was available at Hotel Workers Local 2 was a three-month
organizing internship. She had just spent her first several days on the job
organizing what we in CWA used to call "electronic picketing." Only this
time the target was not a recalcitrant employer. Even before she handled
her first grievance, helped out with contract negotiations, or signed up a

new member, Alex had been handing out Andy Stern's and Anna Burger's phone numbers in Washington, D.C., so UHW members could personally deliver the simple message: "Hands Off Our Union!" I told her she was already having a very unusual experience as a local union representative. However it might end, Alex was destined to learn a lot; her main tutors would be rank-and-file activists under attack from their own international union.

The Anti-Trusteeship Campaign

Unlike the much smaller and more politically isolated groups of workers who formed USWD and USAW, UHW members had no shortage of allies, locally and nationally, in their anti-trusteeship fight. One of the first who spoke up was Mike Casey, leader of the San Francisco Central Labor Council and president of UNITE HERE Local 2. Casey ignored the usual protocol that "members or leaders of other unions should not interfere in the internal disputes of another union." He released an open letter recalling the help his local received from UHW during the lockout of San Francisco hotel workers in 2004–06. Noting the mounting SEIU attacks on UHW now, Casey defended Sal personally and the right to dissent in general. "The Sal Rosselli I know is anything but shameful, unprincipled, and dishonest," Casey wrote. "Such a union and leader has more than earned the right to air objections to union practices without being vilified or demonized." Casey argued "that there must always be room within organized labor for legitimate and principled dissent...The questions and issues raised by Sal meet the threshold of such dissent...[These] are matters that must be addressed by any union looking to organize on a large scale."[17]

If the leader of a key central labor council could weigh in on an emerging controversy of this scale and importance, where, I wondered, were the voices of other concerned progressives? The disturbing dustup at the Labor Notes conference in Dearborn a month later made it easier to get the attention of labor-oriented academics. UMass sociologist and faculty union leader Dan Clawson was one of the Labor Notes supporters who locked arms with others to repel SEIU gate-crashers. Dan had been blogging about the UHW situation but, like Herman Benson at the AUD, seemed to have resigned himself to the inevitability of a Stern-imposed trusteeship. I suggested to Clawson that we should at least try to stay SEIU's hand for as long as possible, if that was possible. Our little ad hoc committee came to include Clawson's UMass faculty colleague Stephanie Luce, Robert Ross at Clark University, and two West Coast activists, former Vermont Education Association organizer Ellen David-Friedman and labor historian Cal Winslow, whose daughter Samantha was employed, like my daughter Alex, on the UHW staff.

Lifting from Casey, Dan and I drafted an open letter that campus friends of SEIU would hopefully be comfortable sending to Andy Stern. We decided to leave past critics of SEIU (like Benson, me, and non-academic Labor Notes activists) off the signatory list. As subsequent appeals did as well, the letter emphasized that some endorsers had "longstanding ties to SEIU" based on "research, writing, or labor education work involving its members, organizers and local leaders." More than a few had steered graduate students or undergraduates toward "internships or full-time job opportunities with SEIU." The letter explained that Stern's past friends and admirers in academia now felt "deep concern about SEIU's threatened trusteeship." The signers warned that:

> Putting UHW under trusteeship would send a very troubling message and be viewed, by many, as a sign that internal democracy is not valued or tolerated within SEIU. In our view, this would have negative consequences for the workers directly affected, the SEIU itself, and the labor movement as a whole. We strongly urge you to avoid such a tragedy.

Using a variety of email contact lists (and drawing heavily on former members of Scholars, Artists, and Writers for Social Justice), we quickly lined up about a hundred signers. More trickled in after our message was sent to Stern on May 1, 2008, and simultaneously publicized on the Internet with the help of an accompanying press release drafted by Dan. Among the writers, activists, and academic luminaries who put their names on the statement were Stanley Aronowitz, Elaine Bernard, Eileen Boris, Noam Chomsky, Mike Davis, Bill Fletcher Jr., Fernando Gapasin, Robin D. G. Kelley, Jennifer Klein, Nelson Lichtenstein, David Montgomery, Frances

Fox Piven, Adolph Reed, Steffi Woolhandler, and Howard Zinn. Readers of the *New York Times* opened their paper on Saturday, May 3, to find the same open letter reproduced as a full-length ad, thanks to a $75,000 splurge by UHW.

SEIU responded with not one but three different letters of its own. The first, from Stern himself, reassured us that "SEIU values the ideas, opinions, and views of the many people who work with labor from the progressive community." In their own more testy message, SEIU EVPs Gerry Hudson and Eliseo Medina faulted the academic signatories for taking sides "without engaging in honest consultation with us or 56 other members" of "the most diverse Executive Board in the history of the labor movement" (many of whom were soon pressuring signers to retract their support for the anti-trusteeship statement). A third letter soon arrived from forty-seven other SEIU leaders, most of them board members also. They claimed there was "no retaliatory trusteeship under consideration nor would we ever vote to approve one." (In January 2009, almost every IEB member listed on this last letter did, in fact, authorize the takeover of UHW.)

UHW Takeover or Dismemberment?

The stirrings of external concern about the consequences of trusteeship was one of a number of factors (and far from the most important) that led SEIU to postpone any final assault on UHW until early 2009. In the meantime, Andy Stern pursued a multitrack strategy for achieving his ultimate goal: eliminating an unprecedented source of internal dissent. Clearly, removing one hundred elected leaders of UHW on the eve of SEIU's June 2008 convention was not well advised. That would be seen as a blatant attempt to keep a significant block of opposition delegates from being seated in San Juan.[18] Furthermore, there was the pressing matter of the U.S. presidential election, then still in its primary season. How could SEIU deliver on its promise of ground troops for the Democrats if scores of national union staffers were tied down in California, running a 150,000-member local whose own elected leadership had just been decapitated? Last but not least, there was the thorny issue of how to make this beheading appear legally justified. (In the 1500s, King Henry VIII grappled with the same dilemma in England.)

Normally, internal union proceedings against UHW would have been conducted by a Stern loyalist to guarantee the outcome in advance. The May Day letter to Stern put pressure on SEIU to come up with some form of liberal cover from outside the union. At the same time, Stern's other objective—forced dismemberment of UHW—could be pursued, on a parallel track, in the run-up to trusteeship. If that card was played right, it might even produce some additional grounds for declaring martial law and moving in, posthaste.

At the San Juan convention in June, Andy got the ball rolling by ramming through a resolution paving the way for sixty-five thousand home care and nursing home employees to be transferred from UHW. Their new home would be Local 6434, then still headed by Tyrone Freeman, a convention star who (as we saw in the previous chapter) was about to crash and burn, big time, back home in Los Angeles. Just a few months earlier, UHW long-term workers had been polled, with the help of an outside agency, on whether they wished to remain part of UHW. With a very high level of participation—35 percent—they voted by 97 percent to stay put. But their preference was simply ignored in San Juan. After the convention, key members of Stern's brain trust conferred about SEIU's next moves against UHW, whose persistent but easily defeated convention floor challenges (described in the Introduction) further infuriated the leadership.

Presidential assistant Bill Ragen sent a memo to three IEB members who also doubled as headquarters staffers—Stephen Lerner, Tom DeBruin, and Kirk Adams—and an outside attorney, Edgar James, who is SEIU general counsel Judy Scott's Washington law partner. Ragen provided them with a summary of "post-convention UHW work" that needed to be done (and decisions made) in the area of communications, member outreach, and legal strategy. His memo suggested that further softening up might be possible in Southern California where "pockets of dissatisfaction" could be exploited after long-term care workers were removed from UHW. "Trusteeship would be difficult," Ragen predicted, expressing concern that "some key senior staff may want to get out of a suicide mission" of that sort. "It's like Iraq, easy to get in and then a slog," he wrote. "Implosion might be a better outcome, but what will it take?"[19]

UHW members experienced SEIU's "implosion" campaign as a never-ending barrage of phone calls, mailings, and emails, largely directed at the long-term care workforce Stern wanted to hive off and hand over to Tyrone Freeman. This extraordinary staff-intensive effort did nothing to help the seventy-five thousand UHW members who had contracts up for renego-tiation in 2008. In high turnover, low-wage workplaces where the structures of unionism are particularly fragile, SEIU headquarters deliberately sowed confusion and, in some cases, demoralization.[20] When my daughter Alex visited nursing homes during contract campaigns, she would ask the stew-ards whether they had received the latest bargaining update or protest pe-titions from UHW. Often, an embarrassed or exasperated worker would have to hunt through a big stash of recent "mail from the union" to find the missing flyers. Most of the material in the pile was anti-UHW propa-ganda carrying the Washington, D.C., return address of SEIU.

For those who did bother to read it, SEIU's message was that nursing home and home care workers would be better off in Local 6434. That was not appealing to those who knew Tyrone Freeman personally or had tried to work with his local in bargaining with common employers. Even before Freeman was exposed as a crook, UHW nursing home activists regarded him as a glib con artist and weak negotiator. Local 6434 did not uphold contract standards as well as the long-term care division of UHW.[21]

In July 2008, Stern proceeded with a two-day "jurisdictional hearing" aimed at delivering sixty-five thousand unwilling UHW members into the arms of Freeman. It was held in Manhattan Beach, California, with less than two weeks' notice to the affected workers. Nevertheless, after a costly mobilization effort, more than five thousand UHW members laid siege to the hotel where the hearing was held, protesting any decision by the outside hearing officer that would tear their local apart. The hearing was conducted by Leonard Page, a former NLRB general counsel and, more relevantly, an ex-coworker of SEIU's top lawyer, Judy Scott. Among those friends of SEIU arguing for keeping UHW intact was Charlene Harrington, a professor of sociology and nursing at the University of California, San Francisco (UCSF). In a letter introduced at the jurisdictional hearing, this nationally known expert on nursing home financing noted that SEIU lobbying for the NHA had increased "payments to nursing homes for taking care of Medi-Cal beneficiaries." Yet, Harrington's research showed that: "The nursing home operators spent too much of the money increasing their own profits and too little increasing staffing and raising workers' wages and benefits to improve resident care."

Harrington applauded UHW for opposing renewal of the alliance agreement—"unless it was changed to allow caregivers real freedom to advocate for themselves and their residents and ensure that operators spend more money on providing quality care." She cited a recently negotiated UHW contract with Mariner Health Care facilities in Northern California as a much "better path to improve nursing home quality" because it "empowers care-givers to stand up for their residents." She warned that SEIU's attempt to push UHW out of long-term care lobbying and bargaining "would have serious negative consequences for nursing home residents and for quality care."[22] As everyone knew he would, Page ignored this plea, along with reams of worker testimony against the dismemberment of UHW. Page dutifully upheld the international union's position that "California long term care members should have their own SEIU local union devoted exclusively to the needs of these workers."

The Ray Marshall Show

On August 25, Anna Burger confirmed that SEIU's takeover plans hadn't been abandoned either, just delayed. In a letter sent to all 150,000 UHW members, Burger announced that an even more prominent outsider—labor economist, author, arbitrator, and former U.S. secretary of labor Ray Marshall—would be coming to California to hold trusteeship hearings in late September. UHW responded to this new challenge by mobilizing thousands of members again, along with outside supporters, at its annual education conference in San Jose. There, members could choose among fifty workshops and training sessions offered for leadership development purposes. One that caught my eye was "Reform Movements Through History," a session where SEIU stewards, from UHW and other locals, discussed ways to promote greater rank-and-file involvement in union-building activity. "One challenge we face," explained John Borsos, who was a UHW vice president at the time, "is creating a culture of solidarity in nontraditional worksites, where there may not be the traditional kind of union consciousness. So we have tried to be very conscious about instilling a sense of history and institutional culture. We want to demonstrate that what we are doing has been done before."

One of the conference speakers was Bill Fletcher, coauthor of *Solidarity Divided*, ex–education director at SEIU, and former assistant to John Sweeney at the AFL-CIO. After seeing four thousand UHW members march through downtown San Mateo shouting anti-trusteeship slogans, Fletcher was interviewed by Juan Gonzalez and Amy Goodman on *Democracy Now!* He predicted, accurately, that:

> If SEIU goes forward with this ridiculous idea of trusteeship, they are going to have to dedicate many staff to dealing with this situation, because the members of that local are very, very clear: they're not accepting a trusteeship. So what that means is that people that could otherwise be around the country working on various campaigns are going to be tied up in trying to impose this trusteeship. This is going to be absolutely horrible.

Two academic observers on the scene, Eileen Boris from the University of California, Santa Barbara (UCSB) and Jennifer Klein from Yale, were equally impressed by the spirit and determination of the home health aides and nursing home employees in the crowd. As Klein reported later, "long-term care workers didn't want to leave UHW" because the jurisdictional realignment sought by SEIU would sever their connections to fellow members in hospitals. According to Klein, "the problem with Stern's model of a pure long-term care local is that it just admits and accepts that home care is a dead-end job." She warned of creating a demobilized and divided workforce at a "moment of great political and fiscal crisis" for home care providers and their clients in California.[23]

During the first round of trusteeship hearings held shortly thereafter, more than seventy health care workers were just as vehement about not wanting their UHW officers removed by Stern. While they waited for hours to speak at microphones set up in the San Mateo convention center, six thousand of their fellow members rallied outside in the largest of all the anti-trusteeship demonstrations organized by UHW. Even surrounded by his SEIU entourage, eighty-year-old Ray Marshall should have been moved by the intensity of emotion and extraordinary degree of rank-and-file engagement on display. (Instead, in an interview a year later, he seemed slightly peeved that UHW "brought the big crowds" and made him the target of "a big letter-writing campaign" by its rank-and-file members. In contrast, he noted, "nobody from SEIU made any effort to influence my decision."[24]) Local unions suffering from the kind of corruption, incompetence, political paralysis, or other dysfunction that requires "temporary administration" don't generally have much rank-and-file mobilization capacity. When Tyrone Freeman was ousted by SEIU from the presidency of Local 6434, few of his members bothered to rally around him. Only those about to be removed from the union payroll themselves or deprived of other forms of patronage were sad to see him go. Everyone knew there was good cause for that trusteeship.

The retired University of Texas professor picked by SEIU to decide the fate of UHW was, like Leonard Page, somewhat less than impartial.[25] Marshall had past financial ties to the law firm presenting SEIU's case for trusteeship; he had served as a paid witness for SEIU on several occasions. For his UHW hearing and report-writing work, SEIU paid him another $200,000, even though portions of his final decision were actually drafted by Stern's own lawyers. Under oath, Marshall later admitted that he also showed an initial draft to Stern, changing it upon request. Unable to complete the trusteeship proceeding in September, he scheduled more hearing time after Obama's election in November 2008. At that second session, one witness for UHW was labor historian Nelson Lichtenstein from UCSB. In Lichtenstein's expert opinion, there were no grounds for trusteeship because UHW lacked corrupt or self-serving leaders. Lichtenstein described the trusteeship target as a healthy, democratic, and extremely multicultural organization, telling Marshall, "I wish there were more unions like UHW."

When Marshall finally issued his 105-page decision on January 22, 2009, it was a Solomon-like exercise in last-minute cutting and pasting (at the behest of his client).[26] UHW succeeded in persuading him that the Patient Education Fund flap was just an old accounting dispute.[27] Whatever its purpose, the $3 million transfer involved was authorized by the UHW executive board, per arrangements common in other locals. SEIU had created similar nonprofit entities itself and funded them with dues money. After Stern singled out this particular transaction for politically motivated scrutiny, the money was returned to the UHW local treasury anyway and the PEF was folded. As Marshall told me in 2010, "it became a trivial issue. Nobody lost any money."

Thus, there were no current financial irregularities or other grounds developed during the hearing that justified a UHW takeover. However, as a concession to Stern, Marshall discovered new grounds for trusteeship. He recommended that UHW be seized if it failed, within the next five days, to transfer its 65,000 long-term care workers to another SEIU entity (nonexistent then and now) that would also include members from Local 6434. There was just one problem: Marshall's conditional reprieve exceeded his authority as the hearing officer. Unlike Leonard Page, he wasn't asked to address home care jurisdiction matters and that issue wasn't part of the evidentiary record he was limited to considering. SEIU's latest attempt to force long-term care workers out of UHW occurred after the trusteeship hearings ended. Indeed, the SEIU executive board resolution to consolidate all California long-term care workers into a new megalocal with 240,000 members wasn't adopted until January 9, 2009, long after the trusteeship hearing record was closed and only days before Marshall rendered his decision.[28]

A Chance for Compromise?

Tainted as it was, the Marshall Report gave a few fence-sitting progressives an opening to seek a last-minute compromise between the warring parties.

SEIU board member Stephen Lerner worked the phones, trying to get friendly professors (mainly those who didn't sign the May Day letter to Stern) to pressure UHW to accept Marshall's ultimatum. Despite his liberal reputation, Lerner was in the vanguard of trusteeship planning and preparation; in mid-2008, Stern named him one of four international union "monitors" who hovered around UHW, interfering with its day-to-day operations and reporting back to headquarters. When Lerner contacted Nelson Lichtenstein about signing this new letter, the historian asked him what guarantee there was that SEIU wouldn't go ahead and impose a trusteeship on UHW anyway—for other reasons, later on—even if Marshall's terms were accepted. Lichtenstein pressed for some assurance that SEIU would, in the future, recognize the "legitimate opposition" of UHW. He urged, in particular, that its health care "negotiating strategy be respected or at least given some weight." In the absence of such SEIU concessions, Lichtenstein balked at adding his name to the proposed letter to Rosselli and Stern. Privately, however, he wondered whether it might be better just to acquiesce and try "to preserve UHW, even if as a smaller entity."[29]

Right before Marshall's five-day deadline expired, eight other academics, including Peter Dreier, Ruth Milkman, Catherine Fisk, and Kim Voss did support this Lerner-engineered appeal. Their letter hailed Marshall as "a nationally recognized figure in the field of labor-management relations and union governance." They argued that acceptance of his report could lead to "a renewed dialogue that might allow a vibrant local union and an effective international union to reach a point of common purpose which can sustain SEIU's organizing dynamism." If UHW members would just obey Marshall, their act of submission might even "inspire the SEIU International Executive Board (IEB) to take creative steps to arrive at collective settlement of any outstanding issues beyond the jurisdictional dispute."[30] For his part, Marshall still believes that "if the UHW leadership had been of a different disposition, this could have worked out very well for them." From his perspective, "the basic issue—the showdown issue—was a no-brainer. If you're going to be part of SEIU, you have to obey its constitution and executive board."

More than five thousand members of UHW met in five locations on January 24, 2009, to ponder the consequences of further disobedience. They were far less sanguine about SEIU good will or creativity in the area of dispute resolution than SEIU's friendly professors. Those with major contracts coming up wondered how long it would be before Andy Stern used his new constitutional powers, granted in San Juan, to deprive them of elected representation on the multistate bargaining committees dealing with Tenet and other employers. A resolution adopted at all five UHW mass meetings left the door open for further negotiations with SEIU, but insisted on a democratic vote before any membership transfer.[31] At the same time, many UHW stewards were completely fed up with SEIU and its behavior. They were not inclined to compromise further.

When Sal Rosselli addressed the media on Monday, January 26, to report on the weekend meetings, he made a final bid for reconciliation. He proposed that UHW's sixty-five thousand at-risk members be allowed to vote on their transfer, after getting guarantees that Stern's new long-term care local would be democratically structured and responsive to its huge statewide membership. This was a process that would require outside mediation, a longer timeline than five days, and other safeguards. Rosselli ended his last press conference as an elected SEIU official with a carefully worded statement declaring that UHW members would resist trusteeship by all means, up to and including SEIU decertification. SEIU's response was, of course, to put UHW under trusteeship the very next day, removing its one-hundred-member executive board. According to Stern, he was forced to act "to restore democratic procedures" and "protect the members' interest."[32] The embattled UHW board met in an emergency session. As Rosselli recalled their discussion later:

> For three years, we had been saying "SEIU is our union, and we have to reform it," when our members were saying, "why do we have to take this, why don't we just leave?" after seeing the incredible assault being paid for with their dues money. At that meeting, our leaders voted unanimously to turn the page—it was no longer possible to reform SEIU and realize our vision within SEIU. So we decided to leave."[33]

Martial Law in Oakland

It is not easy to seize a labor organization with thousands of rebellious members, twenty-two offices, four hundred staff people, and three hundred and fifty separate contracts. Imposing the labor movement equivalent of "martial law" on this scale was not cheap either. It required a huge misallocation of staff time and membership dues dollars. When the invasion of UHW was finally launched on January 27, 2009, SEIU parachuted in an occupation force composed of national and local union staffers from around the country. Their mission was to seize UHW offices and notify employers that they were no longer to deal with anyone but the international union. Before, during, and after the invasion, SEIU was aided by professional security personnel from the OSO Group. These former employees of the FBI, CIA, U.S. Secret Service, and local police departments normally provide surveillance, intelligence, counter-terrorism protection, and other services to multinational corporations. According to a lawsuit OSO later filed against SEIU (for failing to pay all of its $2.2 million in back bills), the firm established a 24/7 "command post" at a hotel in Oakland to "coordinate the large amount of manpower and logistics" required for the military-style takeover of UHW.[34] The OSO Group also provided twenty-four-hour security coverage for Mary Kay Henry and her partner in their San Francisco home during the first four months of the occupation, a special benefit not made available to ordinary SEIU foot soldiers.

The UHW invaders were recruited from SEIU affiliates on both coasts and many in between. Some locals contributed personnel under duress; others were happy to demonstrate their fealty to Stern. Only a few refused to participate in this debacle, fearing, correctly, that it would divert resources from worthwhile SEIU causes like campaigning for EFCA.[35] At a pre-trusteeship meeting of national union staffers involved in healthcare organizing, some participants balked at being assigned to the UHW takeover. According to John Marshall, a strategic researcher for SEIU who attended the meeting, Mary Kay Henry stood up and applauded those in the group willing to serve in California as union "warriors." Marshall soon resigned in disgust and believes that SEIU was guilty of blatant political hypocrisy. "Nowhere else but in California did SEIU attempt splitting long-term care and acute care workers into different unions," he pointed out later.[36] Other resignations flowed in from talented organizers like Audra Makuch, who worked for SEIU in New York City; Dana Simon, the former UHW staffer who was aiding 1199's successful Caritas hospital chain organizing in Boston; Andrew Tripp, who coordinated SEIU home care worker organizing in many states; and Fred Ross Jr., who spent years working on the Santa Rosa Memorial campaign for UHW and SEIU. Former SEIU board member Jerry Brown assailed the trusteeship as "a painful, horrible development for SEIU and the entire labor movement," urging financial support for "the thousands of courageous UHW members who have stood up to SEIU."[37]

Labor historian and activist Cal Winslow, whose daughter Samantha resigned as a UHW staffer after the trusteeship, provided the most vivid firsthand account of what it was like. Winslow was present when Kaiser workers like Emily Ryan, Angela Glasper, and Mel Garcia, who had been sleeping in UHW offices for several nights, personally confronted SEIU's takeover crew. The out-of-town staffers who showed up in Oakland were "30, maybe 40-strong—a nicely dressed group of white men...led by a young female lawyer, with a couple of nasty ex-cops in tow, just in case. They used bolt cutters to get through the parking-lot gates in back; they smashed their way through a second-floor window and pushed their way to the front. There, they opened the doors and let in the rest...evicting members of UHW from their own union hall." Anticipating trouble, Oakland cops provided backup. As cotrustee Dave Regan assured a local reporter, "The police came and we sorted it out."[38]

At the last UHW redoubt, a field office in San Jose, SEIU came knocking, both lawyered up again and equipped with a crowbar. A videotaped standoff ensued, with Kaiser Santa Clara steward Lisa Tomasian waging a high-decibel defense of the premises. SEIU's chief spokesperson was a grim-faced, preppy-looking fellow in a sports jacket who refused to identify himself when challenged by Lisa and her coworkers. He disclosed only that he was a "person with a lawful right to the property" who was "waiting for the police to come." On YouTube, I immediately recognized my old UMW coworker Edgar James—in his current incarnation as the high-paid Washington, D.C., lawyer who was part of Bill Ragen's "implosion" planning committee. In the seventies, Ed worked with Miners for Democracy, which fought UMW trusteeships that deprived members of elected leaders. Now, Lisa Tomasian, cursing like a coal miner, told him to his face: "You have no idea what the labor movement is about." Obviously perturbed, Edgar shot back: "I've been in the labor movement a lot longer than you, lady." Soon, the men in blue arrived, tipping the property dispute in Edgar's favor.[39]

Nurses to the Rescue (but Not for Long)

With the trusteeship formally in place, SEIU had to decide what to do with scores of UHW reps and organizers of dubious loyalty to the new regime. Those who hadn't quit already were put on paid "administrative leave." In the Bay Area, they were ordered to report, in several shifts, to a hotel in Oakland, where Dave Regan assured them that SEIU really did care about serving its members and doing "the real work of the union." A phalanx of international union officials stood by, waiting to interrogate UHW staffers, one-on-one, about their job assignments and willingness to serve the trustees. As a UHW staff union steward, my daughter Alex sat in on multiple interviews. Not surprisingly, her own didn't go very well; when she asked who was going to take over a discharge case she was handling, she was told to have the fired nursing home worker (who was still calling her every day) contact UHW via its new 800 number instead. Still in limbo about her status a week after the invasion, Alex went with other staff union activists to the SEIU office in Alameda after hearing about an "all-staff" meeting there. This facility had been visited by angry members and some staffers (including Alex) before the trusteeship, so OSO protection was tight. When Alex and her friends returned, the front doors were barred, burly Ray-Ban-wearing security men were posted on the inside, video cameras started rolling, and, per usual, the local police were called. The locked out group of fifteen or twenty chanted and sang until diminutive UHW deputy trustee Debbie Schneider came outside briefly to address them.

Once a feminist activist in Karen Nussbaum's 9to5 organization, Schneider stood with a row of Alameda cops behind her. When Alex, a young labor feminist, and her fellow stewards peppered Debbie with too many questions, she threatened to have them arrested if they didn't disperse immediately. By that evening, Alex and her fellow stewards were fired.

A few days later, Alex and other cashiered staffers dropped off their Blackberries at UHW headquarters in Oakland (where they were met by more guards at the door). They then headed down Thomas Berkley Way for a bit of solace and solidarity from the California Nurses Association. The UHW refugees met with thirty CNA staffers and got an encouraging pep talk from Rose Ann DeMoro. When Stern first threatened UHW with trusteeship for allegedly conspiring with her organization, Rose Ann disputed this claim in a backhanded kind of way. (She noted that Sal was "very loyal to SEIU" and had only recently "begun speaking out against backroom deals which undercut his own members' standards.") When the boom was finally lowered on Rosselli, DeMoro denounced Stern's "dictatorial receivership" and his nearby deployment of Dave Regan. CNA declared that Regan's appointment as UHW trustee was a "slap in the face for Californians" and a direct threat to "the workplace protections and contract standards of CNA/NNOC members."[40] The CNA staff union generously pledged to pay the cost of COBRA (or extended group medical) coverage for their now-jobless counterparts at UHW who were already volunteering for NUHW, with little pay or just their unemployment benefits to support them.

Without public acknowledgment, the CNA was also in the process of loaning NUHW $2 million to aid SEIU decertification activity. (Even more money was reportedly offered, but declined on the NUHW side because of the organizational strings that might have been attached.) The NUHW card-signing drive got off to an impressively fast start, thanks to several thousand rank-and-file volunteers, all furious about the removal of their elected leadership. Within six weeks, a majority of workers had signed cards or petitions seeking NLRB or public sector representation elections covering 350 UHW workplaces and 91,000 members. Decertification petitions filed in two of the local's largest units—at Kaiser (with more than 45,000 employees) and Catholic Healthcare West (with 14,000 workers)—were dismissed after the NLRB ruled that SEIU could only be challenged when their contracts expired. Tens of thousands of workers in public sector units, like Fresno home care, also petitioned to leave SEIU. This huge wave of organizing activity swamped the NLRB in California. The board is incapable of expediting union representation votes even when the objecting party is just an employer. All the elections sought by NUHW ended up being delayed for periods ranging from five to twenty-two months as a result of management-style legal stalling by SEIU. The incumbent union often worked in concert with employers to block or delay voting.[41]

Unfortunately, further official collaboration between CNA and NUHW was soon curtailed. Rose Ann DeMoro craftily used her hefty investment in the breakaway union as a bargaining chip in CNA-SEIU truce talks that had been under way, behind the scenes, for some time. CNA's March 2009 cessation of hostilities with SEIU caught many by surprise. I got a bit of advance warning after DeMoro asked me in mid-February 2009, for "any comments" on the draft version of a blistering new CNA pamphlet. It was entitled *Andy Stern's Playbook for Conquest* and recounted SEIU's history of "Hostile Takeovers of Unions and Workers" (a record later documented by UNITE HERE in a research report called, *Growing Pains: SEIU Campaigns Against Other Unions*). When I visited the CNA in Oakland a few weeks after getting this draft, I asked its communications director Chuck Idelson when the new pamphlet would be coming out, only to learn that it was "on hold." The reason for that became clear on March 18, 2009. In a press briefing conducted with Andy Stern, DeMoro announced: "We have buried the hatchet."[42] The two union leaders unveiled a "transformative cooperation agreement" in which they committed to "set aside our differences" and focus instead on coordinated hospital chain organizing "with CNA/NNOC as the lead union for RNs and SEIU as the lead union for all non-RNs." Their joint press release lauded the unexpected peace pact as a boon to labor's campaign for EFCA and lobbying to get more states "to adopt single-payer health care systems."[43]

In a separate press release, SEIU emphasized the "no-raiding" provision of the agreement, particularly its ban on "supporting other organizations that engage in such activities—including the so-called 'NUHW.'" One senior CNA official admitted to me that, in some ways, it was "a bad time to settle, because you've got the HERE war and the UHW war." But more than a decade of bilateral conflict with SEIU was a big organizational drain on CNA, which had larger ambitions in the form of the soon-to-be-created alliance with RN unions in Massachusetts, Maine, Minnesota, Pennsylvania, and other states. "The deal with SEIU is a great deal for CNA," I was told, because SEIU would have to "cede a whole sector" of the industry and "this is phenomenal for our nurses."[44] A few months later, CNA co-president Deborah Burger was equally transactional in her account of how and why the truce came about. "Getting an all-RN union nationally—getting that from SEIU is no small feat. We, as nurses, are not going to jeopardize that," Burger told *Labor Notes*. She predicted that "Andy and Sal will do what they need to survive" and "can work out their own deal." In the meantime, "other unions will help NUHW. And we'll all move forward together."[45]

A Different Kind of Union

With large-scale funding from one natural ally suddenly curtailed, "the so-called NUHW" began operating more like a guerrilla band than a well-supplied battalion in Stern's "Purple Army." Before the trusteeship, UHW boasted a public relations department that was a veritable chip off the old purple block—slick, well funded, and multimedia savvy. At SEIU's San Juan convention, UHW set up a media center, run by its own staff and aided by outside consultants, that equaled the convention press operation of an entire national union like CWA.[46] Deprived of the treasury that funded this cutting-edge PR machine—and other formidable union programs—ousted foes of Stern went low budget and grassroots in creative new ways. The hapless denizens of "Zombie UHW," as the *Perez Stern* blog called them, soon faced embarrassing daily scrutiny by pesky, provocative, whistle-blowing bloggers. The pioneer in this field was the anonymous but always well-informed "Perez." He or she hilariously mimicked the celebrity gossip site PerezHilton.com to chronicle every bureaucratic miscue of SEIU anywhere in California or the world. Perez began trolling for inside dope with the following mission statement, born of the bitterness of expulsion:

> Andy Stern and his appointees love to think they're rich, famous, powerful, and accountable to no one. A member-led union just doesn't fit in with their plans for stardom! They like to drive around in SUVs with tinted windows, acting like they (literally) own the place. So if they want to be famous, let's help them! If you're an SEIU member or employee, tell Perez what the SEIU trustees and appointees are up to, and help them feel just like Paris Hilton.

Perez was later joined by the equally informative Sierra Spartan at *Adios, Andy!*, Keyser Sose at *Sonoma Red Revolt*, and Tasty Stern Burger at *Stern Burger with Fries*.[47] These undercover UHW members (or former staffers) started off with excellent rank-and-file sources and, thus, access to a steady stream of embarrassing videos, photos, SEIU internal documents, and correspondence. (One early discovery was a letter sent to UHW vendors signed by Eliseo Medina but with the words "Dennis Rivera, Trustee, SEIU UHW-W" typed under Medina's signature. Perez took this as confirmation that Dennis, as rumored, had originally been scheduled for UHW takeover duty but, at the last minute, wisely backed out—after form letters were already prepared for his post-trusteeship use.)[48] Once the insurgent bloggers got up and running, their sites were a magnet for leaks from angry dues payers, disgruntled trusteeship staffers, and other jilted payrollers anywhere in the country. As Sierra confessed to her readers, "Little did I realize that SEIU would be such a self-destructive font of information."

SEIU's darker side was often revealed on the blogs when emissaries of the trusteeship, like Richard Rubio-Bowley, ventured forth from what Perez called their "Green Zone" and onto the contested turf of "Californiraq." Rubio-Bowley was an older Filipino nursing home rep. He helped my daughter Alex get oriented when she was new on the job in 2008, familiarizing her with important UHW rules like the one about staffers not conferring with nursing home managers without a steward present. Unfortunately, Richard was not in good health. When the trusteeship was imposed, he was unable or unwilling to make the considerable financial sacrifice of quitting his job or getting fired, like many others did. Richard and Alex were then sadly pitted against each other, vying for the hearts and minds of workers at places like the Convalescent Center Mission Street (CCMS), an inner-city nursing home owned by the Foresight chain. Now representing NUHW, Alex had the linguistic edge over Richard among Spanish speakers at CCMS, but her Tagalog certainly lagged behind his among the Filipina majority. Plus, Richard had the OSO Group on his side and access to a building Alex was excluded from. As Perez reported on February 14, 2009, with typical snark, Richard rolled up Mission Street:

> with an entourage of three Neanderthal body guards in dark sunglasses to escort him into a nursing home of approximately 50 workers. He'd already tried to bar the former UHW rep from entering the facility. Given that she's 24 and weighs 120 lbs. soaking wet, one could see the need for 3 thuggish guards. When the same rep tried to enter the break area and ask for a fair debate about the merits of SEIU vs. NUHW, one guard wouldn't let her in. Richard, realizing the absurdity of the measures being taken, stated that the only reason for his "Krew" was that he was getting harassing phone calls. Richard said that he'd be right out to debate. After waiting outside for 30 minutes, the old UHW rep walked in again, only to discover that Richard was having the meeting he really wanted: alone, behind closed doors with the boss.

Throughout the now-occupied UHW, there were many Keystone (renta-)Kop episodes like this. Tragedy outweighed comedy when workers got fired or suspended for their pro-NUHW activity. In one of the most infamous examples of SEIU collusion with management to purge a rank-and-file critic, Sutter Health acted on a complaint by trusteeship staffer Erica Duffy and fired Beverly Griffith. Griffith is an African American housekeeper with thirty-one years of service and a long history of UHW activism. A hearing officer from the NLRB ordered her reinstated with full back pay, a ruling that Sutter then appealed to the board in Washington, D.C. (As of late 2010, Griffith was still awaiting a final decision on her case.) The hearing officer also found that Sutter security guards were deployed in plain clothes to photograph, surveil, and intimidate NUHW supporters at Alta Bates Summit Medical Center who had petitioned to decertify SEIU.[49]

The "threat" posed by rank-and-filers like Beverly Griffith and Brenda Washington, and volunteer organizers like Alex, became the basis for the damage claims made by SEIU in its $25 million lawsuit against twenty-eight former UHW officers or staffers. Among those sued were Alex's old nursing home division comrades John Vellardita and Gabe Kristal. Due to their efforts and the work of ousted steward Marilyn Aquino, a majority of CCMS workers quickly signed up to leave SEIU in February 2009. Thanks to the NLRB, and SEIU blocking charges, it took fourteen months for their election petition to be processed. On April 23, 2010, the CCMS workers finally got to choose between SEIU and NUHW. By a vote of 23 to 16, they stuck with the new union, despite weeks of propagandizing against it by multiple organizers from SEIU who had management backing and complete access to the facility. SEIU immediately filed thirty-three frivolous objections to the election that were not dismissed until four months later. During that time, CCMS was able to avoid dealing with NUHW because it was not yet certified by the NLRB. SEIU staffers ceased providing any representation when they lost the election and they never returned to CCMS. Marilyn Aquino continued to build NUHW by helping with its organizing at another nursing home nearby.

NUHW on Trial

After SEIU's organizational coup d'etat failed to crush the spirit of workers like those at CCMS, SEIU tried to administer a follow-up coup de grace. One way to avoid losing NLRB elections, when you face another union on the ballot, is to put your rival out of business. So that was the real goal of Andy Stern's federal court lawsuit filed against twenty-eight founders of NUHW shortly after the trusteeship. As noted above, SEIU's legal theory had been tested before, but was found wanting when Charlie Wood and Karen McAninch were sued by Stern's trustee in Local 134 in Rhode Island. In California, SEIU had better luck after finding a friendlier judge, William

Alsup. The cost of its April 2010 courtroom victory was greatly disproportionate to any conceivable membership gain, even if you sympathized
with the purposes of the litigation and cheered its outcome. As estimated
in chapter 10, SEIU legal costs for this case were at least $10 million. (Low-
balling the cost, as usual, SEIU said it spent only $5 million through the
trial stage.) The defendants were an honor roll of UHW veterans, none of
them affluent and all still working then to build NUHW. They included
Sal Rosselli, John Borsos, John Vellardita, Gabe Kristal, Emily Gordon,
Laura Kurre, and Joan Emslie in Northern California, plus Barbara Lewis
and Jorge Rodriguez in Los Angeles.[50]

The gist of SEIU's case was that the connection between a national
union and any of its local affiliates is just like the Bank of America's relationship with branch banks. (This analogy was a favorite of the union's
lead counsel, Gary Kohlman, and Judge Alsup.) If the parent company
wants to reorganize a branch or change its management in any way, there's
no legal basis for objecting. In the union context, local officers, even
though elected by the membership, owe a greater "fiduciary duty" to the
international union than to anyone else. They must comply with any headquarters directive, even if local union dues payers—the workers they represent and who pay their salaries—believe it to be erroneous. In this case,
the legal basis for compliance with corporate headquarters was clear. As
Kohlman reminded the jury: "The SEIU constitution does not require a
local members' vote on being assigned to a different local."[51]

For the defendants' breach of their fiduciary duty to ignore the wishes
of UHW members, SEIU originally sought $25 million in damages from
them personally, as well as from NUHW, the organizational expression of
their disloyalty and conspiracy. SEIU was nevertheless open to settlement.
Two months before trial, its lawyers offered to drop the case in return for
only $13 million—and the disbanding of NUHW, which by then had won
bargaining rights for nearly thirty-five hundred workers. After a two-week
trial, the amount of damages the judge would even allow the jury to consider
awarding was just a fraction of the original amount claimed. The largely
white-collar jurors were fairly clueless about unions in general; on that front,

Judge Alsup didn't help matters by restricting NUHW's defense in many of his rulings, and then instructing the jury not to consider "which side has the better labor philosophy or would better represent workers." When the verdict was finally returned, the jurors decided that NUHW owed SEIU $724,000. Sixteen of the defendants were ordered to pay another $780,000, in individual amounts ranging from $36,000 to $77,000. Members of the "NUHW 16" were primarily held liable for their own salary and benefit costs during January 2009, when they allegedly focused more on fighting off trusteeship than doing their regular jobs. Also assessed were damages for diversion of UHW resources, dues revenue soon to be lost to an organization not yet functioning prior to the trusteeship, and a paltry $20,000 worth of increased security for SEIU.[52] (Even if collected someday, that last sum won't cover much of SEIU's disputed $2.2 million bill from the OSO Group.)

Despite its huge cost, unjust verdict, and confused (but still under appeal) damage award, the trial did provide an opportunity to explore a central mystery of "The Mother of All Trusteeships." During his cross-examination of soon-to-be SEIU president Mary Kay Henry, NUHW attorney Dan Siegel asked a very relevant question: If the stated reason for trusteeship was the failure of UHW to transfer its long-term care workers into another local, per order of the SEIU executive board, why were all sixty-five thousand still in UHW fourteen months later? By its own inaction in removing them, was SEIU belatedly acknowledging that acute care and long-term care workers are better off united in the same local? Mary Kay was not very forthcoming on this topic. All she would acknowledge, under oath, was that there had been no dismemberment of UHW—despite all the damage done to workers during SEIU's earlier pursuit of this goal.

Acting as president several months after she testified, Henry extended the UHW trusteeship so there would be no election of new officers until early 2011. According to Henry, more time was needed to stabilize collective bargaining relationships and develop new bylaws.[53] Few observers expected SEIU EVP Dave Regan to return to his old local in Ohio. Any change in the bylaws of UHW would be engineered to facilitate his election as its first post-trusteeship president. Regan would have a handpicked slate running with him for the executive board. It seemed likely that they would be elected at large, just like 1199 does back east. Any opposition candidates will face questions about their membership status (since they are likely to be connected to NUHW in some way). While this 2011 vote was still pending and perhaps well into the future, the sixty-five thousand long-term care workers in UHW could count on staying right where they wanted to be before the trusteeship, but in a local that's now very different than the old UHW.

Chapter 7

Ivy League Amigos No More

*"When you look at SEIU's body of work in recent years it's terrify-
ing. If that's where the labor movement is headed, we're finished."*
— UNITE HERE president John Wilhelm, January 15, 2010[1]

Right after April Fools' Day in 2009, Andy Stern ventured into what Bob
Dylan once called "the green pastures of Harvard University." Andy was,
no doubt, expecting a bigger audience than the seventy-five to a hundred
people who came to hear him at the Kennedy School of Government. After
all, even John Sweeney, the aging president of the AFL-CIO, attracted a
crowd twice that size in the same venue a year earlier. Unfortunately, there
was a very big name appearing simultaneously on the other side of town.
Massachusetts's own Noam Chomsky—always a huge draw at home and
abroad—was speaking at a forum on student-labor action over at North-
eastern University. Plus, SEIU Local 615 was hosting an annual "Labor
Seder" at its union hall in downtown Boston.

So, on this particular Passover evening, those welcoming their national president tended to be dutiful SEIU functionaries rather than working members. Among them I spotted Joe Buckley, the portly, red-faced

SEIU international rep who so helpfully arranged my brief audience with Andy's predecessor, George Hardy, more than three decades before. Buckley, SEIU board member Celia Wcislo, and a few other Stern loyalists were joined by local Change to Win staffers, Harvard students and professors, and a smattering of Boston-area labor activists, including campus workers who belong to AFSCME. Since I live just fifteen minutes away from Harvard Square myself, I arrived early in order to make the most of this rare opportunity to reconnect with the union leader I hadn't seen since SEIU's convention in San Juan. Stern's talk was titled "A Country That Works" and drew on his 2006 book by the same name, which touted CTW as a bright new departure from the dreary dysfunction of Sweeney's AFL-CIO.

In the run-up to this Harvard visit, there had been an embarrassing falling out among the Ivy League graduates who formed CTW. Its founding fathers included Stern, who attended the University of Pennsylvania, Bruce Raynor, a Cornell man, and John Wilhelm from Yale. When the "three amigos" forged their "New Unity Partnership" in 2004, as a prelude to the seven-union CTW defection from the AFL a year later, it was an article of faith among them that "size matters." Raynor insisted that the AFL-CIO's fifty-plus affiliates should consolidate into just ten to fifteen mega-unions, with less overlapping jurisdiction and a better focus on "core industries." He dismissed union democracy as a troublesome impediment to this visionary restructuring.[2] To demonstrate how progressive unions could supersize themselves overnight and grow faster, Raynor and Wilhelm formed UNITE HERE. This "marriage of equals," with 440,000 members overall, was wildly applauded by labor-oriented academics who had been steering students toward one union or the other for years.

Always a contrarian, I found the celebration a bit premature. In my own experience, as a veteran "M&A" guy for CWA, union "mergers and acquisitions" sometimes became more problematic, in their actual implementation, after the honeymoon period of hyping them to the members. Amalgamation was definitely not a panacea for labor. For that reason and many others, it's always best to have an "escape clause" handy, in case the separate "union cultures" just don't mesh. Even if the relationship does endure, just merging union bureaucracies does not by itself make members any stronger. "Building power for workers"—a favorite SEIU mantra—requires far deeper organizational changes. The mere linking of acronyms is the least of them.[3]

Labor's War of the Roses

In the hopefulness (or hubris) of the moment, Wilhelm and Raynor didn't negotiate such a prenuptial agreement back in 2004. A mere five years later, the UNITE HERE merger had transformed into the labor marriage from hell. The union's "co-presidents" were locked in a legal and public relations struggle reminiscent of the *War of the Roses*. In that film, a deeply estranged couple, played by Michael Douglas and Kathleen Turner, fight for control of the McMansion of their dreams, only to destroy it piece by piece. The real-life equivalent of the fancy chandelier swinging high above their main stairwell (a source of truly fatal attraction in the film's final scene) was the Amalgamated Bank in New York City. This $4.5 billion "family jewel," inherited from the garment worker side of UNITE HERE, was much coveted but not easily divided.

In a lengthy *New York Times* account of the fight over the bank, Steven Greenhouse described Wilhelm and Raynor as "hyper-articulate heavyweights." Yet his article contained little of the higher-toned "discourse" generally favored by the *Times*; instead, it read like a gossip column in the tabloids, about a very messy Hollywood divorce. As told to Greenhouse by John, Bruce had become a "dictator" out to "destroy the union" by "creating chaos and strife." Bruce, in turn, declared he would not "be held captive" by a bunch of "thugs," "jerks," and "hijackers" led by John. Bruce claimed that John was spending too much money on organizing, with "few recent successes" to show for it.[4] John's side countered with an email blast exposing the high cost of keeping Bruce on the payroll. His car service and other perks added nearly $100,000 to his salary of $254,000, and what union of "poor workers" could possibly afford that in 2006 or any other year?[5] In a bid to restore peace and quiet within the second "house of labor," United Food and Commercial Workers president Joe Hansen became a CTW marriage counselor—an unsuccessful one. Two former Wilhelm-Raynor colleagues, from the days when they all served together on the AFL-CIO executive council, then tried peer intervention from the outside. In a letter jointly addressed to John and Bruce, Ron Gettelfinger of the United Auto Workers and Leo Girard of the United Steelworkers warned that "the continuing public escalation of your internal battle…threatens members' interests and reforms that would benefit the entire labor community."[6]

In any crisis, there is always opportunity. Wherever there's a divorce in the making, a marriage "on the rebound" may be just around the corner (although not highly recommended). Our guest speaker at Harvard announced in early 2009 that his union, SEIU, stood ready to unite with either or both of the feuding partners, as long as the Amalgamated Bank was part of the dowry. Just as private eyes are sometimes hired in domestic relations cases, Stern, Raynor, and SEIU advisor Steve Rosenthal arranged for the Investigative Group International (IGI), run by well-known corporate security consultant Terry Lenzner, to investigate Wilhelm and, according to the target, conduct "a fishing expedition" into his personal affairs.[7] The apparent objective of deploying a private investigator (once used by Ivana Trump to dig up dirt on her matrimonial rival Marla Maples) was to force a settlement of the emerging legal dispute over the bank. Spurned by a furious Wilhelm, who had no intention of settling on terms unfavorable to UNITE HERE members, Stern rushed Raynor to the altar instead.

At a hastily convened meeting of four hundred and fifty people in Philadelphia on March 21, a new SEIU affiliate named "Workers United" (WU) was unveiled to the world. It claimed to represent one hundred and fifty thousand workers, mainly from local unions that were premerger pieces of UNITE. Raynor and several top allies joined the ever-expanding SEIU executive board. A divorcee himself, Stern waxed philosophical when he welcomed the delegates to SEIU. Like most bad marriages, he said, the disagreements between John and Bruce had developed gradually over the previous two or three years. Stern suggested that, in retrospect, UNITE and HERE may not have been right for each other from the very start, although that's not what he said publicly when the two got married. But then, Andy was not in Philly to dwell on the mistakes of the past. "I'm here," he said, "to talk about how we can build a partnership to organize more workers."

Wilhelm struck back with press releases that denounced the "messianic mindset" of "Czar Stern" and accused his one-time "New Unity Partner" of "brazen interference" and "breath-taking imperialism." According to Wilhelm, Raynor's "splinter group" left in violation of the UNITE HERE constitution and without taking any kind of valid membership vote. Raynor himself breached his fiduciary duty to the entire membership by secretly disbursing $16 million to his local union supporters to encourage their defection. Andy Stern was now launching a "hostile take-over of UNITE-HERE jurisdiction," replete with SEIU staff invasions of its workplaces and "mud-slinging mailers to members' homes worthy of anti-union corporations like Wal-Mart and Cintas." The struggle for control of the Amalgamated Bank would continue in the courts, Wilhelm vowed, where the faction representing a majority of the membership was laying rightful claim to it. "This is not democracy," Wilhelm said. "This is electoral fraud. We're not going to let this happen."[8]

A Laundry Worker's Story

Stern's appearance at Harvard, coming just ten days after SEIU's shotgun wedding with WU in Philadelphia, prompted more than the usual amount of Kennedy School security for a potentially controversial speaker. Organizers of the event feared that local hotel workers or officials from the old New England Joint Board of UNITE, which sided with HERE, might show up and make a fuss. They had good reason to protest (even though they did not appear that night). According to Joint Board manager Warren Pepicelli, Raynor and SEIU were already colluding with TJX Companies, Inc., a major retailer, to woo thousands of workers away from UNITE HERE at Massachusetts warehouses supplying Marshall's, T.J. Maxx, and other big stores.[9]

Marshall Ganz's glowing Kennedy School introduction of Stern gave no hint of the conflict unfolding in UNITE HERE workplaces just a few miles from Harvard Yard. Equally unmentionable was the UHW trusteeship recently imposed in California. Instead, the former UFW organizer, who now teaches courses on "moral leadership" at Harvard, praised Stern for "leading the way in introducing young people to the labor movement." After showing some stirring video footage of SEIU's 2008 convention (sans San Juan riot police and FMPR protestors outside), Andy then stepped up to the mike, energetic as always, with his dress shirt collar open and his sleeves rolled up, ready to rock the crowd.

He began with an upbeat report on labor's legislative progress in Washington. To much applause, he declared that the prospects for enacting EFCA during Obama's first year in office looked very good. He wanted everyone to know that SEIU was still growing just as fast as ever, and had just scored its latest "organizing win," even without the help of labor law reform. To put a human face on that triumph, Stern invited Shirley Cheeseboro to join him on stage. Shirley is an earnest, heavyset, African American woman from New York City who has been a laundry worker for nearly three decades. She started out, she told me later, as a member of the old AFL-CIO Laundry & Dry Cleaning Workers Union. But, in the mid-eighties, the Laundry Workers merged with SEIU. Then, SEIU decided it didn't want laundry workers any more and spun them off to the Amalgamated Clothing and Textile Workers (ACTWU). ACTWU later merged with the ILGWU (International Ladies Garment Workers Union) to become UNITE, which later joined forces with the hotel workers to become UNITE HERE. That, like a left-wing sect, spawned the UNITE HERE "majority faction," led by Wilhelm, and the smaller WU group, headed by Raynor. Shirley's bargaining unit stuck with Bruce so she was now back in SEIU again. Andy Stern had been her new national union president for less than two weeks.

Andy, of course, didn't recount any of this fascinating merger history. So some members of his audience were left with the impression that Shirley had just helped organize a nonunion laundry. Also not explained in his talk was how workers in the garment, textile, laundry, distribution, and hospitality industries fit into SEIU's three self-proclaimed "core jurisdictions." In the past, when staking out health care, property services, and government employment as his union's exclusive areas of concentration, Stern had urged other unions to follow SEIU's example and stick to their own knitting. Stern's right-hand man, Stephen Lerner, often preached against "non-strategic mergers" with unrelated groups, which led to weak and unfocused "general worker unionism."[10] If necessary for proper alignment of membership, SEIU recommended that workers be transferred to other, more appropriate unions (which is what SEIU did when it shipped Shirley and her coworkers off to ACTWU two decades before).

Puzzled by this new SEIU contradiction, I took the mike during the question period to remind our speaker, politely, that one of the founding principles of CTW was building union strength based on appropriate jurisdiction, instead of ranging too far afield or, worse yet, poaching on the occupational turf of another organization. Could Stern's current designs on hotels, casinos, and food service contractors be the reason why his former ally John Wilhelm was now calling him a "brazen, imperialistic, messianic union czar"? In his answer, Stern tried to make light of these labels, joking that this was "just what John calls me on a good day!" He then explained, in rather convoluted fashion, that a recent convergence in corporate ownership of hotels and other commercial real estate ventures had created a fortuitous (for SEIU) overlap in jurisdiction with the hotel workers. With a look of complete innocence and sincerity, Stern professed to have "no desire to compete in organizing hotels." Instead, he foresaw a bright future in which SEIU and UNITE HERE would one day be working together again, "just as we do with AFSCME in home care."

Marshall Ganz was allowing just one question per customer so there was no opportunity for a follow-up query about union harmony in home care. A few questions later, a Harvard library employee tried to prod Stern into a populist stance on impending campus job cuts. The worker wanted to know why SEIU's president wasn't demanding that President Drew Gilpin Faust cut her own $600,000 a year salary before laying off janitors, librarians, and clerical workers making fifteen times less. Perhaps with a future, longer-term stay at the Kennedy School in mind, Stern did not favor "equality of sacrifice" by President Faust and carefully refrained from criticizing her. "I really don't like pitting people against each other," he said demurely.

Up Against "Big Purple"

When I caught up with John Wilhelm ten months later, we met at a New Haven café near the scene of the strike and organizing battles at Yale, which shaped his career in the labor movement. Wilhelm graduated with a degree in history and belonged to Students for a Democratic Society. In 1969, he was driving an industrial laundry delivery truck, trying to avoid the draft, and doing SDS-influenced community organizing in "The Hill" section of the city. Needing a better job, he noticed "a weird ad" in the *New Haven Register*. It read: "Labor leader trainee wanted, willing to work long hours for low pay . . . Must be unmarried." Sorting through the few replies, including Wilhelm's, was Vincent Sirabella, a charismatic union militant with a ninth-grade education and a passion for organizing the unorganized. Sirabella chose Wilhelm, even though he was not single, to become his apprentice business agent at the Hotel Employees and Restaurant Employees (HERE). Under Sirabella's tutelage, John helped blue-collar workers at Yale battle the university throughout the seventies and then, in the following decade, built a second campus local composed of twenty-five hundred clerical and technical employees. HERE Locals 34 and 35 formed one of the strongest alliances of students, campus workers, and community supporters anywhere in the country. Within several decades, Wilhelm succeeded his mentor as HERE national organizing director and then surpassed Sirabella's career in the union by becoming its secretary-treasurer, and later president, prior to the hotel workers' merger with UNITE.[11]

When we met at Café Romeo, Wilhelm was still using harsh words to describe Andy Stern's very pronounced habit of "pitting people against each other." That habit had, in fact, been widely criticized at UNITE HERE's national convention, held in Chicago three months after Stern appeared at the Kennedy School. At the convention, Wilhelm was elected president, replacing Raynor, and he delivered a speech denouncing SEIU as "the bosses' lackey union." Hotel Employees Local 2 president Mike Casey from San Francisco reported that his members were "battling both SEIU and the employers." Speakers from other unions also condemned SEIU's encroachment on hotel worker jurisdiction. "For another union to come onto your turf and take advantage of what you've built, that is piracy on the seas of organized labor," thundered Gerry McEntee, president of AFSCME. "What SEIU is doing is bullshit," McEntee shouted, before leading delegates in a chant of "Bullshit! Bullshit! Bullshit!" In his convention speech, Vince Giblin, president of the Operating Engineers, repeatedly referred to Stern as the "Darth Vader of the labor movement." Guest critics from the AFL-CIO were joined by Terry O'Sullivan, president of the Laborers and a fellow CTW founder. He told the delegates: "What happens in this fight we have with SEIU will determine what kind of labor movement we have…We didn't join Change to Win to raid and hijack another union's members."[12]

Top officers of the AFL-CIO also weighed in on Wilhelm's behalf. More than twenty labor councils, including those in Los Angeles and San Francisco, adopted resolutions critical of SEIU's behavior. Twenty-seven national labor leaders from both CTW and the AFL-CIO affiliates—representing more than ten million workers—released a public statement pledging their full "support, both materially and morally," against any poaching of UNITE HERE members by SEIU. Among the signers were James P. Hoffa of the Teamsters, Joe Hansen of the UFCW, and Douglas McCarron of the Carpenters, along with O'Sullivan—which left only one small CTW affiliate still in SEIU's corner, the six-thousand-member UFW. Forty recent college and university graduates—all of them former campus activists now employed by UNITE HERE—sent a letter to their labor-oriented undergraduate friends denouncing "the corporate-style takeover campaign that Stern is running against our members." UNITE HERE operatives even solicited a solidarity pledge from twenty-five labor organizations in sixteen other countries, including two unions in Albania.[13]

After the UNITE HERE convention ended, Wilhelm held a conference call for reporters and I was among those participating. He again denounced SEIU for its "outrageous and unprecedented assault on a fellow North American union" and predicted the demise of CTW. He accused Raynor and Stern of conspiring to steal or sequester more than $300 million in UNITE HERE assets. Despite SEIU being ten times larger and having a huge resource advantage, Wilhelm was confident his union would "do quite well against Big Purple." He said the "key to fending off SEIU" was rank-and-file organizers. He highlighted changes in UNITE HERE's structure, just approved by its convention delegates, that would make the union "more bottom-up, not top-down," ensure greater financial transparency, and give members veto power over local union mergers. "I am proud of our union's new constitution," he said. "It stands in stark contrast to the top-down, autocratic manner in which SEIU has approached our union and its own members."[14]

Wilhelm also put the latest inter-union conflict in a broader context, reminding the listening reporters that SEIU was responsible for past aggression against "smaller unions like the teachers in Puerto Rico, which most of you failed to cover." He described "the extraordinary struggle between UHW and SEIU as a harbinger of the difficulties we've been facing lately." In response to a question about the possibility of greater UNITE HERE support for NUHW, Wilhelm said a decision about that was pending. By the time we met in January 2010, UNITE HERE was not only supplying volunteer organizers but hundreds of thousands of dollars worth of loans and grants to NUHW. This infusion of money, combined with the initial funding received from CNA, was keeping the new union afloat until it could develop a dues-paying membership base of its own.[15]

Making Sense of the Craziness

At Café Romeo in New Haven, Wilhelm and I were surrounded by a bustling crowd of blue-collar workers on their lunch breaks and Yale students tapping away on their laptops, books piled high next to their cappuccinos and pastries. The chubby, graying sixty-four-year-old UNITE HERE president was casually dressed in a blue shirt, white pants, a leather jacket, and a pair of Dockers. As Wilhelm reflected on his original student, labor, and community organizing four decades earlier in the same city, he often flashed a toothy grin and seemed even more confident of victory over SEIU than he was the previous June. He had just returned from a triumphant march through downtown San Francisco with Rich Trumka, president of the AFL-CIO, which had welcomed the hotel workers back a few months earlier. Wilhelm, Trumka, Mike Casey from HERE Local 2, and Sal Rosselli from NUHW were part of a crowd of a thousand that converged on the Hilton Hotel in Union Square, where more than a hundred union supporters were arrested for blocking traffic. Closer to home, in New England, workers at TJX warehouses, aided by SEIU defector Dana Simon (who now worked for Hotel Workers Local 26 in Boston) were beating back a faltering raid conducted by WU/SEIU. And, in Philadelphia, UNITE HERE Local 634 had recently scored a decisive two-to-one win against SEIU in a representation vote involving twenty-three hundred cafeteria workers in the city's public school system.

In our wide-ranging conversation, Wilhelm reflected on his organizing roots in New Haven, recent SEIU-related conflicts, and how mystifying this collection of controversies must seem to union outsiders. As if on cue, our talk was briefly interrupted by a fellow Roma patron, longtime Connecticut political activist Paul Wessel, who stopped by to ask Wilhelm: "How goes the craziness?" After we both laughed and said hello to Paul, Wilhelm admitted to being "schizophrenic about this fight. I didn't choose it and very much regret and resent the wasted resources and diversion of focus involved." He still found it hard to believe that SEIU was behaving in such scorched-earth fashion. The idea that a fellow labor organization would act like a corporate adversary and hire a private eye to investigate him was hard to fathom. His friends assured him that any IGI operative assigned to pry into his personal life was going to be very bored. "I don't even drink," Wilhelm said, explaining that he quit that occupational hazard of the hospitality industry more than thirty years ago.

In several interviews with the press, prior to our talk, Wilhelm had warned about the impact of union infighting on labor's legislative agenda in Washington. In the *Las Vegas Sun*, he blamed SEIU for "the likely failure of the Employee Free Choice Act" because of the mixed signals Stern was sending to Congress about labor law reform:

> When you add up Andy Stern's efforts to stifle local unions and undermine contract standards, his fight with UNITE HERE and the corruption issues of SEIU in California, it's doing a lot of damage. The

business community has drawn a line in the sand and Republicans
are standing firmly behind them. There is a significant number of
Democrats who don't support two key provisions—card check and
binding arbitration—and I think SEIU is one of the major causes for
their wavering.[16]

Absent EFCA and more organizing rights agreements achieved
through bargaining, strikes, or union leverage campaigns, private sector
membership recruitment wouldn't get any easier, Wilhelm predicted. In
2005–06, his own union's "Hotel Rising" campaign resulted in neutrality
agreements that netted thousands of new members.[17] However, in 2009,
UNITE HERE's "organizing of new members was way down," he told me.
Hotel industry organizing conditions were "getting brutal," as more employers resorted to subcontracting schemes for union avoidance. Wall-
to-wall hotel unionization becomes more difficult, legally and
organizationally, if every part of the workforce—housekeeping, restaurant
staff, laundry workers, bellhops, and even valet car parkers—has a different employer, rather than a common one. This arrangement permits the
real boss, who owns or operates the hotel, to cut costs and shirk direct responsibility for employment conditions.

Despite such organizing obstacles, "our mindset has always been we
can grow," Wilhelm said. "There's a lot of opportunity for those willing to
fight." Wilhelm's generational cohort in HERE didn't spend their careers
"closing places," as he put it, because gaming and hospitality were always
expanding fields. He contrasted that organizational consciousness with the
more limited expectations and aspirations of his former UNITE colleagues,
who had "to deal with a dying, offshoring industry," either textile manufacturing or garment-making. Raynor, according to Wilhelm, did "remark-
able organizing in the South" in the seventies, but his union success was
often followed by long first-contract fights and then plant shutdowns. The
three predecessor unions of UNITE were once more than a million members strong.[18] Now their battered remnants, inside and outside of WU,
amounted to less than 150,000 workers versus UNITE HERE's 265,000.[19]
"Bargaining in that environment, the objective is often just to figure out

what level of concessions to make to keep the plant open for another three years." The experience of "losing for their entire career" had to be scarring for UNITE veterans, Wilhelm speculated.

As for Stern, Wilhelm's perception was that, "for reasons we can all relate to, he got very impatient with our failure to grow. Some of us are still trying to build the labor movement through workers' power. But Andy thinks that's an outmoded notion." Wilhelm was adamant that SEIU growth strategies in the public sector "manifestly won't work in the private sector...We're never going to do mass organizing via political deals." He agreed that unions do need to debate how best to grow while maintaining wages and benefits for existing members. But he questioned how much "we can organize if we by-pass workers and fail to uphold contract standards." He argued that SEIU doesn't "fight for people once they're in the union," echoing the complaints of Stern's own dissident members and other SEIU critics.

The Food Service Fight

Disagreements over how hard to fight for people already in the union contributed to the unraveling of the SEIU/UNITE HERE joint venture known as Service Workers United (SWU). SWU was formed as an organizing vehicle for employees of three food service contractors—Aramark, Compass, and Sodexo. Nationwide in scope, it was set up like a staff-run SEIU megalocal, complete with call center servicing, and a membership covered by NHA-type template contracts. SWU promised management that workplace activity would be restricted—both at contract expiration (when workers were barred from striking) and during the contract term (when worker leafleting, picketing, or community outreach was also limited as part of the quid pro quo for employer neutrality and union recognition based on card check). Both Raynor and Stern defended this experiment and the tradeoffs involved, which included keeping some parts of their deal with management confidential. "The old ways aren't working," Stern explained. "We're trying to find different relationships with employers that guarantee workers a voice...These workers have no unions; that's where we start from." Raynor hailed the SWU approach as a major advance for labor because it "resulted in tens of thousands of workers getting unions."[20]

Criticism of SWU started among student allies of food service workers, seven months before its national union sponsors had their own falling out. In May 2008, fifteen undergraduate activists affiliated with United Students Against Sweatshops in California and North Carolina sent an open letter to Stern demanding that SEIU "fight for a better deal with Aramark, Compass, and other multi-service contractors." According to the signers, SWU members had "no effective voice" in their nationwide "local." When they had a job problem or grievance, they were told to contact "the SWU 'Member Resource Center,' an out-of-town call center established as a lower cost alternative to replace union organizers and representatives." The letter writers criticized SEIU for using "students and campus workers as little more than pawns." In particular, they cited SEIU's abrupt abandonment of organizing efforts at UNC–Chapel Hill, after hundreds of students rallied on behalf of dining hall employees in 2005. Over the summer break, union supporters learned that SEIU had reached a recognition agreement with Aramark covering "only a small percentage of its workers across the country" without any "significant improvements in wages and benefits." Even worse, "the deal ensured that UNC workers could not join SEIU" because Aramark got to decide which of its work locations would be organized and how many employees would be involved.[21]

As in the case of the NHA, union membership gains were less than expected, despite the compromises made. By 2009, when food service became another battlefield in labor's civil wars, SWU was reporting only six thousand actual members to the Department of Labor, while publicly claiming to have organized as many as eighteen thousand. At the UNITE HERE convention, a cafeteria worker named Daqwell Carrasquillo, employed by Sodexo in New York City, presented a petition signed by a thousand fellow SWU members. They objected to having "no union democracy," an "800 number that doesn't work," and "leaders who cut deals behind our backs and make decisions with little input from the members." Carrasquillo's own experience illustrated these complaints. He signed a union card in 2005 and immediately came under a prearranged agreement. Four years later, conditions hadn't improved much, he hadn't had a raise since 2007, and members with salaries of only $20,000 a year were required to pay $400 a month for family health coverage. Attempts to file grievances about contract violations through the SWU national call center were fruitless. In negotiations on a second contract, management's standard response was "SWU already agreed to boilerplate contracts and we can't change that." When Carrasquillo and his coworkers violated the SWU agreement by leafleting outside their building, calling for contract improvements, Sodexo called the police on them.[22]

For organizers from the original HERE, the stakes in this fight were high. When it merged with UNITE in 2004, HERE already represented sixty thousand food service workers and had just won a coordinated campaign against Sodexo.[23] In big cities on both coasts, hotel worker locals had some food service bargaining units with fully paid family health coverage. These were soon undercut by Raynor-engineered SWU agreements with the same employers in the same markets that required workers to make huge premium contributions. Jim Dupont had to deal with this problem, first as an SWU negotiator and now as UNITE HERE's Laundry and Food Service division director. "SEIU's definition of partnership is you do what the company wants," he told *Labor Notes*. "Our definition is, you're treated as an equal… We're not going to let them enter this jurisdiction and be the companies' favorite cheap alternative. They want to be the Wal-Mart of unions."[24]

A Pink-Sheeting Controversy

The "Wal-Mart of unions" and its new WU franchise looked for any leverage they could find in their legal, public relations, and workplace war with UNITE HERE. Among the issues exploited by Raynor was a dark side to the formidable organizing culture of HERE that soon came to light in unflattering fashion. Again, the initial whistle-blowers were concerned young organizers who were not sympathetic to either SEIU or WU. They spoke out against a controversial practice, originating on the hotel union side of UNITE HERE, known as "pink-sheeting." Pink-sheeting and the organizational behavior associated with it summoned up memories of "the Game" that was used so objectionably by Cesar Chavez and his inner circle to maintain their grip on the UFW.

In an open letter to other labor activists, Tenaya Lafore, Lohl Berning, Crystal Stermer, and Sean Abbott-Klafter described pink-sheeting as a "system of control…designed to keep those involved in the union's work from straying from the directives of the leadership." All four had been Bay Area "salts" for UNITE HERE, volunteers who took jobs in nonunion hotels to help organize them from the inside. They objected to a process in which "union staff gather sensitive personal information about the lower level staff that they directly supervise, as well as unorganized workers and members, in order to discover their personal weaknesses. This information is then used at a later point to 'push' them to follow the union's program." The four organizers depicted "pushing" this way:

> A lead organizer will share personal struggles they have experienced in their life and then ask a new organizer about hardships they have experienced…The information that the new organizer shares is then remembered by the lead (and in many cases, actually recorded on a form that was originally pink). Down the line, if the organizer is told to do something on a campaign that they feel uncomfortable doing, the lead will put this information to use. They will bring up the sensitive information to convince the new organizer that, by following the lead's direction, they are confronting their fears and insecurities and becoming a stronger person, just like when they dealt with personal hardship in the past.[25]

The letter from the "salts" was followed by damaging coverage in the *New York Times*, based on Steven Greenhouse interviews with more than a dozen past or present UNITE HERE organizers with similar complaints. A staff-union dispute about pink-sheeting was already under way inside UNITE HERE, before this flurry of unwelcome publicity.[26] The issue was originally taken up by the Federation of Union Representatives (FOUR), which ended up representing just WU employees, after the majority of UNITE HERE researchers and organizers formed a new staff organization called the Union of UNITE HERE Staff (UUHS).

Even prior to the Wilhelm-Raynor divorce, Jerry Hairston, president of FOUR and a former textile worker, filed a grievance/arbitration case over pink-sheeting. In Hairston's view, higher-level management in the merged union clearly condoned this lower-level supervisory practice of "demanding that we 'tell our stories,' exposing the most intimate and personal details of our lives, including family issues, sexual orientation, marital relationships, and the like." Hairston objected to his "members being judged by their ability to elicit this information from rank-and-file workers on house visits or while building [organizing] committee leadership." He noted, in an email message about the grievance, that many of these workers "are minorities and women without a ton of formal education facing a well-organized cadre of college-educated staff."[27]

Former FOUR members, who still work for UNITE HERE but now serve as leaders of UUHS said they too condemned any invasion of staff member privacy. But they believed Hairston was "sensationalizing" the pink-sheeting issue. In their experience, contrary to the claims of some former organizers, UNITE HERE "fosters our ability to think and critique, contributes intelligently, and creates space for us to challenge and discuss key decisions of the union."[28] For his part, Wilhelm declared that he had "zero tolerance for inappropriate intrusions into people's private and personal lives. I have not personally used these techniques, and I have taken a very strong stand against them."

One Casualty of War

A year after Andy Stern spoke at Harvard and several months after my chat with Wilhelm, one former UNITE HERE staffer found himself bizarrely entangled in both its divorce case and the controversy about pink-sheeting—long after he had left the union's employ. The experience of twenty-three-year-old Elvis Mendez wasn't what he expected when he joined the hotel employees union because it seemed more "worker-led than others." Mendez grew up in Framingham, Massachusetts, the son of immigrant parents from Puerto Rico and the Dominican Republic. He went to the University of Massachusetts in Amherst, where he majored in social thought and political economy and was a student government leader. After graduation, he became a hotel boycott organizer for UNITE HERE in California until the spring of 2009, when he was sent to Phoenix "on special assignment relating to the SEIU conflict," as he put it in a later memo.

In Arizona, UNITE HERE was making a frenetic retaliatory thrust at SEIU in the public sector. State workers had recently won new "meet and confer" rights, thanks to an executive order signed by Governor Janet Napolitano, in response to union lobbying, before she left to join the Obama administration. This deal fell far short of full collective bargaining rights. But public employee unions were using it to expand their workplace activity. When Mendez and several coworkers arrived in Phoenix, SEIU was signing up members and seeking representation votes in places like Pinal County. UNITE HERE had no intention of getting on the ballot and competing with SEIU. Instead, its young organizers were sent to government office buildings and directed to hand out flyers that merely asked whether the money SEIU was devoting to "needless fights" with other unions elsewhere might be better spent on public worker representation in Arizona.

If leafleting like this had been done in California or Massachusetts, among members of well-established SEIU bargaining units, there would have been far less risk of feeding local anti-union sentiment. However, in the more hostile environment of a right-to-work state, where public sector unionism had just gained a helpful new foothold, the impact of UNITE HERE's intervention was a little different. Mendez noticed right away that managers were among the most avid readers of his anti-SEIU flyers, apparently eager for any new information that they could use against SEIU as well. "I was essentially union-busting in a place where workers needed a union," Mendez recalls. "And I didn't feel good about undermining another union's work, even if I didn't particularly like SEIU."

When Mendez and two other boycott staffers expressed discomfort about what they were doing, on workdays that lasted from 7 a.m. to 11 p.m., their Harvard- and Yale-educated union supervisor directed them to attend a special staff meeting. One of the three had already resigned in protest by the time this meeting was held. During it, there was little discussion of the substantive objections they had raised. Instead, Mendez and a fellow boycott organizer were subjected to personal questioning and guilt-tripping by a union group that included supervisory staff, more experienced organizers, and rank-and-file members on leave from their bargaining unit jobs.

The UNITE HERE state-level official presiding over the session first invited personal testimony from the rank-and-filers about the difficulty of their lives and the sacrifices they had made for the union. During the repetitive questioning that followed, both Mendez and his coworker were "pushed" to share similar personal information, while everyone around them expressed doubts about their lack of leadership and commitment to the cause. Mendez recognized the group dynamic that unfolded as a form of activity now officially disavowed by the union. In a formal complaint filed afterward, he described the meeting as "stressful and inappropriate," full of "hostility and tension," and "an unhealthy and unprofessional work environment." At one point, the group reduced Mendez's fellow dissenter to tears. Even though he was crying and saying, "Shame on me, shame on me," no one present "offered him any reassurance or tried to console him as he was asked the same questions again and again."

In UNITE HERE's new "Employee Privacy Policy"—introduced after the FOUR grievance mentioned above—union managers and supervisors are prohibited from subjecting employees to "pink-sheeting, the Game, or other similar practices which purportedly build loyalty and increase motivation by unwelcome inquiries into personal information." The policy defines "unwelcome requests" as "behavior that is not welcome, is personally offensive, and fails to respect the rights of others." According to the policy, "repeating requests or otherwise persisting in seeking information in the face of staff's reluctance to answer indicates the request is unwelcome." In his internal complaint, citing this document, Mendez wrote: "The direct result of the meeting was that I felt horrible about myself, and partially ashamed that I had brought up concerns about our strategic direction because of the sacrifices others had made. I felt stressed and torn between work that I found morally objectionable and feelings of loyalty and guilt."

He emphasized that it was not his "desire to hurt our union...but rather to ensure a productive and healthy work environment and the strengthening of our union through the enforcement of our privacy policy." When UNITE HERE higher-ups failed to respond to his complaint, Mendez decided to quit, along with five other young boycott organizers who shared his concerns. He returned to UMass, enrolled in its labor studies program, and became president of the two-thousand-member UAW-affiliated graduate student employees union on campus.

An April Fools' Day Deposition

On April Fools' Day, 2010, Elvis was not where he wanted to be, which was in western Massachusetts helping his fellow teaching assistants. Instead, as the recipient of a recent subpoena, he was sitting uneasily, in his best dark suit and olive tie, in front of a video camera in the cramped conference room of a downtown Boston law firm. There, surrounded by three out-of-town lawyers from big corporate firms, a videographer, a stenographer, and several of his own friends and legal advisors, he was about to be deposed in the (then) still-unresolved legal dispute over the Amalgamated Bank and other UNITE HERE assets.

When Elvis was working long hours for UNITE HERE, he was paid about $33,000 a year. Yet, the seven-hour proceeding he was about to undergo cost union dues payers about half his old salary, when all the lawyers' fees and related expenses were totaled. And this was just the price of a single pretrial deposition among dozens. The fifty-two-page federal court complaint filed by Raynor and other plaintiffs against Wilhelm and his supporters, not to mention the twenty-four-page counterclaim filed by the latter, raised many different and complicated factual issues, requiring wide-ranging "discovery," which included the taking of pretrial testimony under oath.

Mendez had good reason to wonder why he was being dragged into this mess. He is not now and never has been a national executive board member of UNITE HERE or either of its predecessor organizations. He had absolutely nothing to do with the souring of John Wilhelm's relationship with Bruce Raynor. He doesn't know either of them and they don't know him. While working for their union, he certainly never got any perks like the one hundred thousand dollars' worth of sports tickets, chauffeur services, and director fees that Raynor received in 2008 as chairman of the Amalgamated Bank. Mendez doesn't even have a checking account there.

Yet, while serving unhappily as a foot soldier in labor's civil wars, Elvis Mendez made the mistake of raising some conscientious objections to the campaign tactics and personnel practices employed by UNITE HERE. And, for that admirable display of principle, he now had the pleasure of being grilled all day by lawyers whose other clients, in addition to Bruce Raynor, included MasterCard, T-Mobile, Lazard Freres, and Wyeth Laboratories. At one point in this strange proceeding, Mendez's own representative inquired: Was there really any more dirt to be dug up on pink-sheeting? And, if there was, what bearing could it have on which UNITE HERE merger partner should be awarded control of the Amalgamated Bank?

One of Raynor's lawyers solemnly explained that "these types of practices are one example of the real differences" that existed between UNITE and HERE, in the run-up to their divorce. Therefore, Elvis Mendez might have information relevant to the pending judicial determination of who gets what joint property. In his own questioning of Mendez, Wilhelm's lawyer did his best to reduce the union's Game-playing to the realm of unsubstantiated rumor. Perhaps, he suggested, what Mendez perceived to be emotional manipulation was really just a good-faith effort by an overzealous supervisor to help improve his job performance? Mendez didn't think so. Both sides were very interested in Elvis's future career. He was asked whether he had any desire to work for either of the competing unions. With the video camera rolling, the lawyers scribbling away on their yellow legal pads, and the stenographer taking down his words as well, Elvis Mendez quietly told his interrogators that he had no such plans.

Chapter 8

The Progressive Quandary

"Academics should refrain from inserting themselves in disputes among unionists. If they choose to do so, they should at least make sure that they act in a fair manner, on the basis of full information."
—Joshua Freeman, labor historian, City University of New York

By late spring 2009, it was "déjà vu all over again" for labor-oriented academics and other progressives. SEIU's messy internal dispute with UHW had been followed by the disconcerting rift within CTW that turned one-time union friends into bitter enemies. The UNITE HERE divorce was not just throwing young organizers like Elvis Mendez into unwanted battles with their SEIU counterparts. Once again, college professors, public officials, community leaders, and members of the clergy throughout the country were being asked to choose sides as well.[1] Cornell University researcher Kate Bronfenbrenner lamented that this new clash was occurring between "two groups of people who actually share so much," noting that "at least 200" of the combatants were her own former students.[2] Just twelve months after a hundred intellectuals beseeched Andy Stern to spare UHW from trusteeship—and some, like Bronfenbrenner, were then pressured by SEIU to disavow that appeal—a group of professors gathered in Chicago to consider writing to SEIU again.

Their discussion took place around a long table at an Italian restaurant near Roosevelt University, during the annual conference of the Labor and Working Class History Association (LAWCHA). Nancy MacLean, a well-known historian from Northwestern University, welcomed the dinner crowd of forty by expressing her personal anguish about the "division and crisis" within CTW. "We always thought of these unions as our friends and allies," she said. Now it was "very scary to all of us committed to a progressive labor movement" to see SEIU raiding UNITE HERE locals and disrupting their activities. Enormous resources—needed for health care reform and EFCA campaigning, plus union organizing and contract fights—were clearly being squandered.

Many of those present, like Jennifer Klein from Yale, were past supporters of SEIU—when the union seemed to be advancing the interests of oppressed workers. In her introductory remarks, Klein recounted her own positive interaction with the "women, immigrants, and people of color" who belonged to UHW in California. She expressed dismay over their subsequent fate because, according to Klein, Andy Stern's trusteeship "reflected total disrespect for the 'social world' they had created." Klein lauded UHW for its "strong shop steward system" and a "vision that was not merely local." By way of contrast, Klein described a recent visit to Yale by Anna Burger, who boasted to undergraduates about all the management consultants used by SEIU. Klein was not impressed with SEIU restructuring schemes that reflected "the corporate model." That model is "a disaster in politics and economics," she pointed out, "so why should we embrace it in labor?"

After Klein finished, three speakers from UNITE HERE provided an update on its current troubles. Andrea van den Heever, a former Yale clerical worker, led off with an urgent plea for help. Born in South Africa, van den Heever came to the United States to escape apartheid. In the early eighties, she helped create HERE Local 34 in New Haven through organizing and strikes that she described as "radicalizing and transforming." Now, in her old bargaining unit, hundreds of members were being bombarded with "robo-calls," mailings, and leaflets urging them to leave the union they had built, through many years of struggle, with John Wilhelm's help. These anti-HERE messages, paid for with dues money diverted by Bruce Raynor before he defected to SEIU, was just one front in a nationwide assault on her union, van den Heever said. In the hotel industry and other HERE jurisdictions, "SEIU is going in and becoming a company union, making sweetheart deals. Whether UNITE HERE survives is up in the air." A former student of MacLean's, now working as a hotel union organizer, and an African American shop steward from Chicago sadly corroborated Andrea's account of life on the front lines of labor civil warfare. As the litany of SEIU sins grew longer, the expressions of many listeners became pained. Others looked down at their plates of spaghetti. A few squirmed in their seats.

The question before the body, when the presentations were over, was what to do about this troubling information? Attending as a LAWCHA conference participant, I briefly tried to remind everyone about some unfinished business from the year before, involving solidarity with UHW members. In California, at that very moment, SEIU was using management-style tactics to block or delay NLRB elections involving thousands of health care workers. Since many in the room had already taken a strong public stand in favor of "employee free choice," why not support the elections sought by NUHW *and* a cessation of hostilities against UNITE HERE? My friendly amendment was not well received. The organizers wanted to stay focused on SEIU's latest misadventures and they were right. Overcoming the reluctance of some of their colleagues—to speak out again—was a big enough challenge for one evening.

Leading off the discussion was LAWCHA president Mike Honey, who signed the May 2008 letter to Stern. He reminded the group that "we got all kinds of calls from SEIU" after UHW, unbeknownst to the signers, ran the letter as an ad in the *New York Times*. (Even MacLean was still upset about seeing the UHW ad in "a boss paper;" it left her feeling "violated and betrayed," she told me.) SEIU's message to academics the year before was: "You don't know what you're talking about." Honey predicted that anyone signing another letter would be hearing that mantra again because this new controversy was even more complicated and LAWCHA, of course, could take no official position on it.

Seated next to me was Leon Fink, a University of Illinois professor and editor of the LAWCHA journal *Labor*, who seemed to agree with Honey. Also a May Day letter signer, Fink cautioned his fellow historians about inserting themselves this time in the crossfire between "serious strategic concepts." Joe Berry, a longtime labor educator (since retired), argued that there was "plenty of blame to go around" for the overlapping SEIU-related disputes. All the top union officials involved are "democracy challenged," he contended, and none should be "romanticized." Another labor educator and author from Chicago, whose spouse works as an SEIU consultant, agreed that the union's behavior at Labor Notes and "what SEIU is doing now with HERE" was "repugnant." But, he said, "what I'm hearing tonight is that SEIU is the devil incarnate—worse than the Carpenters or Machinists." He could not accept those characterizations. He urged everyone to remember that "Justice for Janitors is one of the greatest movements we've had in the last twenty years. The strike of janitors at the University of Miami was brilliant and Stephen Lerner is one of the most brilliant organizers in the country." Reminded of the Miami campaign, another LAWCHA member defended UHW cotrustee Eliseo Medina as "an honest militant" who deserved respect because of his heroic role in the UFW forty years ago.

The conversation around the table was not going well, from the standpoint of follow-up action. The drift of it seemed to be that SEIU should not be criticized in the present because of what the union had accomplished in the past. Whatever its errors lately, SEIU still stood head and shoulders above the rest of the union pack. Individual SEIU organizers were worthy of admiration. Blame for progressive union misbehavior must be shared equally by all sides. Nobody has clean hands.

Eileen Boris, from the Feminist Studies Department at UCSB, was among those who favored acting but tried to identify with the mixed feelings in the room, which might prove paralyzing. "Part of our dismay is that so many of us were in awe of SEIU," she observed. Friends of labor "expect bad behavior of the Teamsters," Boris said, but "doing things to hurt people" was not something previously associated with SEIU officials because "they were progressive." Another professor immediately corrected Boris. "They *are* progressive!" she insisted. And so it went, back and forth, until Klein and MacLean finally read their draft "letter of concern." It stated in part:

> SEIU's concerted efforts to undermine UNITE HERE belie the progressive ideals that SEIU has upheld for decades...The attempts to discredit UNITE HERE leaders, to lure workers out of UNITE HERE and into SEIU, and to interfere in the constitutional process of UNITE HERE will not help the cause of democratic unionism and progressive reform. On the contrary, we are concerned that these actions are undermining the principle of union democracy and dividing the progressive movement at a critical moment in history.[3]

Recalling her own experience at Yale with professors prone to splitting hairs over the wording of faculty resolutions, van den Heever urged everyone present to endorse the Klein-MacLean draft, as written. There just wasn't time for a lot of tinkering, she said. Perhaps a third of the diners provided their signatures before leaving the restaurant. Thanks to the follow-up efforts of MacLean, Klein, and Nelson Lichtenstein, along with UNITE HERE itself, the list of endorsers eventually reached three hundred in all. The signers included faculty members from colleges and universities throughout the United States, Canada, and the United Kingdom.

Despite the organizers' careful efforts to avoid procedural, if not substantive, controversy of the type that occurred the year before, objections were registered anyway. Joshua Freeman, a labor historian from the City University of New York (CUNY) who didn't attend the dinner, professed to be "startled" that anyone could be asking "LAWCHA members to sign a letter criticizing SEIU for its actions." He immediately contacted eighty other academics with a last-minute appeal not to endorse this "partisan attack." Freeman likened it to "throwing oil on a fire," arguing that:

> Academics should refrain from inserting themselves in disputes among unionists. If they choose to do so, they should at least make sure that they act in a fair manner, on the basis of full information...

Over the past fifteen years, there has been enormous progress in deepening the relationship between organized labor and progressives in the academic world. The moral presumptuousness and factional purpose of this letter can only harm that relationship.[4]

Freeman's intervention seemed to have little deterrent effect. In a strong riposte, Dan Clawson from UMass questioned whether the CUNY professor, who was close to Bruce Raynor, was really being "neutral" himself. Said Clawson:

> I don't dispute your right to be partisan, nor your right to choose not to be involved, but in this case I think you ARE actively involved, and are making a partisan appeal to oppose the side supported by the letter writers, and support the SEIU analysis, argument, etc…[A]lthough we may have been told, as scholars, to stay out of internal labor disputes…the world at that time also involved unions not leading raids on each other, trusteeing locals for disagreeing with the national leadership, and so on."[5]

Labor's Academic Alliance—in Happier Days

The often uneasy relationship between organized labor and intellectuals—on display at the LAWCHA conference dinner—has a long back story.[6] As noted earlier, the New Left activists who remained in academia, like those who went into unions, were estranged from the AFL-CIO for years. Its hawkish stands on foreign policy issues and insensitivity to women and minorities made coalition building difficult, if not impossible. There was near universal rejoicing when our sixties generational cohort, on campus and off, had the opportunity to reunite during John Sweeney's AFL-CIO presidency. Among those ousted by Sweeney's "New Voice" slate in 1995 were cold war conservatives long hostile to the left on campus and in labor. In contrast, Sweeney and his running mates, Richard Trumka and Linda Chavez-Thompson, welcomed the assistance of student activists and sought the advice of their professors. Many campus progressives, in turn, were eager to help make unions a more effective force for social justice. "In the euphoria of those days, life was simple for radical academics," Herman Benson observed. Everybody seemed to be on the same side finally so "little debate was in order; everything would surely work out; labor was newly on the march; it was enough to rally support."[7]

Both Dan Clawson and Josh Freeman were among the founders of SAWSJ, which hailed "the new wave of hope and energy surging through the AFL-CIO" and pledged to do research and writing supportive of the "remobilization" of U.S. unions. Leaders of the group, like historian Steve Fraser, began organizing "teach-ins" to support labor causes, including one in New York City where Sweeney was a featured speaker. Speeches made there were later published in book called *Audacious Democracy*, a volume edited by Freeman and Fraser.[8] Subsequent books in a similar upbeat vein often showered praise on SEIU, either for its own accomplishments under Andy Stern or the role played by the many former SEIU staffers employed at AFL-CIO headquarters by Sweeney. The personal affinity that existed between academics and the "new AFL-CIO" was even stronger in the case of SAWSJ ties to leaders and staffers of SEIU, UNITE, and HERE. In 1999, Stern, Wilhelm, and others from key "organizing unions" joined their allies at one of the biggest conferences ever organized by SAWSJ.[9]

At this gathering on the campus of Yale, there was still a strong sense of common purpose among the hundreds of students, professors, labor activists, and full-time union officials who came to New Haven for the weekend. The AFL-CIO's Organizing Institute had, with SAWSJ's help, just published a manual called *Faculty@Work*, for academics who wanted to defend the right to organize. This seventy-four-page guide "offered a wide-ranging program of activism; classroom inspiration for students, opportunities for internships and jobs in unions, unionization of teachers in universities." Above all, *Faculty@Work* urged "educators to use their prestige to rally community support for union organizing campaigns, and put pressure on anti-union employers." As part of the conference, HERE hosted a reception in a building facing the New Haven Green for young people interested in getting staff jobs; among those acting as recruiters were ex-Yalies already employed as organizers or researchers for Wilhelm's organization.

At an informal social gathering at the nearby Omni Hotel later adversaries like Stern and Rose Ann DeMoro chatted amiably in a group that
included Labor Party founder Tony Mazzocchi and political scientist
Adolph Reed, who had steered some of his own students toward jobs with
SEIU. At the conference itself, largely organized by Dan Clawson, Stern
appeared on a panel about health care issues with DeMoro and Boston-
based journalist Suzanne Gordon. After the panel, Stern remained in contact with Gordon about her work, putting her in touch with SEIU
headquarters staffers who work on nursing issues. He later agreed to blurb
her next book, *Nursing Against the Odds*. When that Cornell ILR Press title
appeared in 2004, he sent the publisher a check for $75,000 to buy five
thousand copies for distribution to SEIU members and nonunion RNs.
Soon, Gordon was a regular speaker at SEIU Nurse Alliance rallies and
conferences in Washington, D.C., New York, Florida, Iowa, and Washington State. She was also asked to assist organizing campaigns like the Maine
Medical Center drive, described in the second chapter.[10]

Stern's personal interest in Gordon's work and subsequent patronage
was not unusual. During his presidency, SEIU made a systematic effort to
cultivate academics, journalists, political activists, and filmmakers by providing financial support for their books, blogs, research projects, movies,
magazines, conferences, or single-issue campaigns. This organizational
generosity paid off in many different venues, including Hollywood. Alone
among American unions, SEIU was depicted favorably in a feature film,
Ken Loach's *Bread and Roses,* about the recruitment of Latino janitors in
Los Angeles. It was the first such cinematic boost for labor since Martin
Ritt's 1979 film *Norma Rae,* which earned Sally Field an Oscar for her role
as a textile union organizer in the South.

In media circles, Stern was able to burnish his reputation as "the most
articulate and heterodox union leader in American labor," whose organization could be counted on to "fund more progressive groups and causes
than any other institution in liberal America."[11] When well-known author
Barbara Ehrenreich needed $100,000 to launch United Professionals, a
short-lived effort to promote online networking among white-collar em-

ployees, SEIU was there, checkbook in hand.[12] An appreciative Ehrenreich reciprocated with a plug for *A Country That Works*. On its jacket cover, she called Stern's 2006 book "a glimpse into the heart of a man who has devoted his life to the struggle for a better deal for American working people." She lauded Andy's "bold vision" and "vital agenda for change."

In New York City, the most reliable source of union bulk-order sub-scriptions for the *New Labor Forum* (*NLF*) has always been United Healthcare Workers East, SEIU's largest affiliate. One of 1199's former of-ficers, Gerry Hudson, serves on both the SEIU executive board and *NLF*'s own editorial board. Published by CUNY's Center for Labor, Community, and Policy Studies, *NLF* has regularly featured major articles by SEIU strategist Stephen Lerner, Stern himself, and academics sympathetic to the union.[13] *NLF*'s annual editorial board meeting brings together a mixed labor-academic crew that includes Hudson, Josh Freeman, Steve Fraser, Kate Bronfenbrenner, and, a recent addition to the board, Janice Fine from Rutgers. Another longtime SEIU ally, United Students Against Sweatshops, has likewise been a longtime beneficiary of purple largesse. Before the union's approach to organizing food service workers became controversial in local USAS circles, SEIU paid for scores of students, in-cluding many USAS members, to come to its 2004 convention in San Francisco. There, they mixed with delegates and happily participated in convention-related activities like a march across the Golden Gate Bridge for health care reform. Four years later, liberal bloggers were flown down to Puerto Rico at union expense. One of them sent back a breathless dis-patch to the Huffington Post, headlined: "SEIU Convention—These Are PROGRESSIVE People!"[14]

During the Stern years, SEIU investments in good will, good works, and good publicity required small sums of money compared to its overall spend-ing on electoral politics and, in 2008–10, labor civil warfare. Nevertheless, the results were highly valued at the top of the organization. The damaging internal and inter-union conflicts initiated by SEIU's president put a major strain on relationships with students, professors, and other political allies. As concern increased about UHW, SEIU corruption in California, and then the conflict with UNITE HERE, headquarters staffers spent a lot of time brainstorming about "how we repair/build relations with the progressive left community."[15] In academic circles, this meant presenting SEIU's side of the story—what Stephen Lerner called its "left narrative"—but never in joint forums or face-to-face debates with progressive union adversaries or critics. Any informational briefings would always be one-on-one, with small invited groups, or, in a real pinch, take the form of promised audiences with President Stern himself. On campus, SEIU reminded already-vulnerable labor educators that any criticism from their quarter would jeopardize support for labor studies programs. (Most of them got the message rather quickly.) The union also relied on its investment in a few friendly academics who sometimes failed to disclose which side they were on, financially speaking— a strategy that led, in one notable case, to further campus controversy.

Presenting a "Left Narrative"—Online and over Lunch

Between SEIU's turbulent 2008 convention in Puerto Rico and its takeover of UHW eight months later, the union's leading ambassador to academia, out front and behind the scenes, was IEB member Stephen Lerner. Lerner had to fight fires on several fronts, as the practice of sending nettlesome "open letters" to Andy Stern began to catch on and press coverage of SEIU took a nosedive in the Golden State. Working with SEIU media relations director Michelle Ringuette and Matt Witt (the consultant who urged Stern to "play offense, not defense" on ethics), Lerner developed multiple "talking points" for use with outsiders now "questioning SEIU, its program and leadership." Lerner's messaging was fine-tuned with the help of trusted campus friends who could act as surrogates. His pitch was delivered personally, as needed, to targeted audiences around the country. To get more SEIU officials out on the road, peddling the party line, he proposed that a "Leadership Speakers Bureau" be created. It would help develop "a standard rap" for local officers with "expertise or credibility to speak" on critical issues.[16]

For example, in the wake of Tyrone Freeman's widely publicized embezzling, a broad cross-section of SEIU allies in California were now clamoring for a course correction. Solicited by UHW, more than 240 state legislators, city council members, county supervisors, and community leaders wrote to Stern, sharing their "distress at the recent financial scandals that have arisen in SEIU and the damage these may cause in achieving our common priorities."[17] Another very similar letter arrived soon afterward from fifty California writers, professors, and workers' rights advocates. They warned that SEIU's internal problems were "impeding much-needed political action to defend state worker jobs in health, education, and other services."[18] So Lerner needed to find campus experts willing to put SEIU's recent behavioral problems in the proper perspective. In late summer 2008, he reached out, via phone calls and email, to various vacationing professors, including Fine, Milkman, Bronfenbrenner, her Cornell colleague Richard Hurd, and Bob Bruno, director of labor studies at the University of Illinois.

Milkman, then director of UCLA's labor center, had already been helpful when asked by the *Wall Street Journal* whether mishandling of dues money was becoming more common in SEIU. "Overall, it's had a very clean record in the last few decades," she asserted.[19] After sounding Milkman out further, Lerner emailed Ringuette with the encouraging news that Ruth would, if requested, continue to repeat the mantra "that SEIU doesn't tolerate corruption."[20] Peter Dreier, another SEIU stalwart at nearby Occidental College, was similarly "on message" in the dark days of August 2008. Dreier opined in the *Los Angeles Times* that Freeman's downfall was "a tragic situation." But one had to remember, SEIU was just another "organization with human beings in it, some of whom are selfish and corrupt." According to Dreier, it was unfair to pass judgment based on a few "rotten apples." He expressed confidence that "if SEIU cleans house and does what's necessary, the union can continue to thrive."[21] When a reporter from New York telephoned Kent Wong, Milkman's UCLA colleague, Wong seemed exasperated by the wave of campus and community criticism directed at his former employer. "I don't agree with everything Stern says and every contract they sign, but there has to be some perspective on this," he said. "You think Andy Stern is the biggest problem in the American labor movement? Give me a break."[22]

The peripatetic Lerner popped up next at MRZine, where he reassured online readers of the Marxist journal *Monthly Review* that SEIU, not UHW, was the proper choice for progressives. In a lengthy exchange with two California labor radicals, Dave Bacon and Warren Mar, joined by soon-to-be-removed UHW vice president John Borsos, Lerner dismissed the threat of a UHW trusteeship as a "myth" propagated by Borsos, Rosselli, and others in UHW. "This simply isn't true, no matter how often repeated," Lerner wrote. He blamed UHW for spreading "misinformation" that distracted everyone from "the vibrant, open honest debate" that SEIU wanted to have.[23]

In an email to Stern before his MRZine piece was posted, Lerner confided that he was trying "to develop a left narrative for this debate." But first he had to come up with a good name for the "ideology behind the current critique of SEIU." Lerner proposed to the SEIU president that UHW be denounced for its *"neo-business unionism."*[24] He wanted to expose Sal Rosselli's retrograde focus "on servicing and defending remaining islands of unionization (i.e., local union interests)" while at the same time indulging in "left rhetoric about militant struggle, better contracts...and greater local autonomy."[25] Stern liked this new label very much, particularly since it might be linked, in left-wing readers' minds, to "neoliberalism and neoconservatism," neither of which are popular at *Monthly Review*. On July 2, 2008, Lerner's boss OKed his draft article in a typically terse email: "Very good. Neo Business unionism."[26] Two other SEIU board members (and fellow in-house lefties) took the same tack in their online debate with Herman Benson from the AUD. Responding to a Benson article in *Dissent*, Jerry Hudson and Tom DeBruin tried to convince readers of the social democratic journal that the real threat to workers was not SEIU's undemocratic practices or collaboration with employers. It was UHW's misguided "business union model... built on servicing and defending remaining islands of union strength in cities like San Francisco."[27]

One would think that a good place to have "an open, honest debate" about such claims would be right on campus. The free exchange of information, opinions, and ideas is, after all, supposed to be a hallmark of intellectual life among students and professors, even in university-based labor studies centers. Borsos, who has a doctorate in history, had been trying for months to get any labor program in the country to sponsor an educational event featuring representatives of UHW and SEIU. Lerner and other Stern loyalists repeatedly claimed to be in favor of airing different points of view on the same platform. Yet, when invited, they refused to participate in any public forum with internal or external critics. Instead, they arranged their own invitation-only conference call briefings or closed-door meetings. At one such gathering in Chicago, Lerner, Local 1 president Tom Balanoff, and Local 880 president Keith Kelleher promised to field any "tough but fair" questions from twenty invited students, professors, and community organizers. As one participant reported, "most of the folks in the room just wanted everybody to get along." They were "upset at all this fighting among labor progressives and hesitant to take sides, but nobody was drinking the [purple] Kool-Aid anymore."[28]

Throughout the country, no one was more "hesitant to take sides" than the staff of university-based labor education centers. Labor studies specialists depend on labor lobbying to keep their embattled programs afloat, particularly in the face of growing attacks from university budget cutters and conservative legislators.[29] As UMass Amherst Labor Center director Eve Weinbaum told me, programs like hers "are often asked to weigh in on intra-union or inter-union conflicts and usually decline." If they don't remain neutral, labor program staff—even ones with more secure academic appointments—can easily find themselves without union support for their teaching, writing, and research. Offending a key player like SEIU can result in loss of access to unionized workplaces, fewer consulting opportunities, and not as many union members signing up for classes and seminars. Weinbaum and the handful of other labor educators who bravely endorsed the May 2008 letter to Andy Stern were quickly reminded of those risks when that missive appeared in the *New York Times*. Under pressure from SEIU, twenty-five endorsers of the original sent a follow-up letter to the editor of the *Times* that was never published. The second letter said: "We signed [the letter to Stern] as part of an internal debate within the labor movement about strategies, tactics, and our vision of the future. We did not intend to choose sides, only to express ideas and concerns." As Weinbaum explained later, this mea culpa "was instigated by Labor Center people, who felt that they were in a different situation from other academics who study labor but aren't directly involved with workers/unions."[30]

Sadly, the "we can't choose sides" excuse extended even to hosting a debate or participating in a discussion with both sides represented and no institutional endorsement of either position. In the fall of 2008, for example, sixty left-wing intellectuals and activists from throughout California met in McCone Hall on the UC Berkeley campus. There, they hoped to hear from health care workers in UHW and officials of SEIU about their disagreements. Although UHW provided some funding for travel expenses, the group assembled was not a partisan one; it even included local labor educators like Karin Hart, Vivian Price, and Bill Shields, who had no desire to alienate SEIU. The meeting organizer, Cal Winslow, tried unsuccessfully to get UC Berkeley's Center for Labor Research and Education (CLRE) to participate, because of its past research focus on home care and health care issues. Its director Ken Jacobs indicated that he and his fourteen-member staff were too busy to attend. So the Geography Department had to arrange space for the meeting instead. No one from CLRE came. SEIU was invited but, as usual, failed to appear or even respond to the offer of equal time.

While ducking such public forums, SEIU opted for a much cozier, if more costly, one-on-one approach. Nelson Lichtenstein, a participant in the McCone Hall discussion, was among the Stern letter signers who started getting SEIU-related phone calls from Jo-Ann Mort in New York. A former garment union newspaper editor who still serves on the *Dissent* editorial board, Mort runs a PR firm called ChangeCommunications. Its impressive roster of clients includes the Ford Foundation, the Carnegie Corporation, the AFL-CIO, and the Open Society Institute funded by George Soros. In 2007–09, the firm was paid $700,000 by SEIU for consulting work that included having its founder and CEO invite intellectuals to lunch so she could explain the union's controversial actions to them.[31]

Mort's outreach shifted into high gear when SEIU took over UHW and there was a danger that progressives might sympathize with NUHW. To provide detailed guidance in this area, Mort sent all her campus contacts a press release in early February 2009 that denounced the new union as a "rogue organization" whose attempt to "destabilize UHW" was "both reckless and feckless."[32] In her accompanying email, Mort reported that she and SEIU leaders were putting together "an ongoing mechanism for dialogue between the academic community and SEIU to make certain that we combine the best of intellect and activism to take advantage of the Obama presidency." As for SEIU controversies in California, "I'm sure that you are as anxious as we all are to move past the UHW trusteeship situation," she said.[33]

A Dialogue Derailed

Moving on, in 2009, wasn't so easy because of Andy Stern's worsening dispute with John Wilhelm. (For Mort, who reportedly charges $1,600 a day for her services, that conflict did have the virtue of generating more billable hours for ChangeCommunications.) As noted above, SEIU's conflict with UNITE HERE ignited another round of campus controversy that, on the East Coast at least, hadn't been anticipated by Stern. In March 2009, the SEIU president confided to *BeyondChron*'s Randy Shaw that progressives in New York, unlike those on the West Coast, actually favored SEIU absorption of WU. As reported in the previous chapter, not only did the vast majority of UNITE HERE members reject SEIU's overtures; Wilhelm was strongly supported by other CTW and AFL-CIO unions, with three hundred academic "letter of concern" signers trailing helpfully in their wake.

Stern responded to his growing political isolation by taking out several full-page ads—in the *Nation*! In July 2009, he spent more than $20,000 to buy the whole back page of the magazine for two successive issues to inform its one hundred sixty thousand readers—most of whom are not even union members—that "the conflict between UNITE HERE and Workers United/SEIU" was all John Wilhelm's fault. Readers were urged to go to www.putworkersfirst.com and sign an online statement supporting SEIU's position in the dispute, a petition never seen or heard from again.[34] Randy Shaw—a prolific blogger, author, San Francisco community organizer, and lawyer—was one *Nation* subscriber who didn't approve of the ad or Stern's raiding activity. He denounced SEIU for its "self-destructive strategy" of "waging war on progressives," as symbolized by the union's threat to withhold funding from the California Democratic Party in retaliation for its chairman, John Burton, attending an NUHW fundraiser. Shaw also took aim at other journalists, academics, and publications, like the *Nation* itself, which, in his view, had been "troublingly silent" about SEIU misbehavior for too long. According to Shaw, *Washington Post* columnist Harold Meyerson and Steven Greenhouse of the *New York Times* were among those who have "spent so many years promoting SEIU as the vanguard of a revitalized labor movement that they cannot accept, or publicly acknowledge, that the union has changed."[35]

In addition to making its case to *Nation* readers, SEIU needed to respond to the letter that Klein and MacLean circulated. So Mort, Ringuette, and SEIU board member Javier Morillo began brainstorming together, online, about how to deal with this new "academic/lefty" initiative. As noted in chapter 5, Yale-educated Morillo abandoned his own college teaching career in Minnesota so he could become a rising star in SEIU. In an email to Mort and Ringuette, he argued for a dose of tough love. The professors should get a response from SEIU that "shames them just a little bit for signing onto something without knowing all the facts…Nothing guilt trips an academic more than reminding them how isolated they are from the world of policy, politics, and activism." Morillo took it upon himself to contact Nancy MacLean directly. While looking forward to "opening a dialogue" with MacLean that might avert future "misunderstandings," Morillo made it clear that he was "saddened" and "disappointed" by her letter about SEIU. He upbraided MacLean and her colleagues for failing to do the kind of "research and fact-checking you require, when producing work in your own fields."[36]

Meanwhile, Mort was encouraging Morillo to engage other faculty members "about moving forward in a serious fashion." She recommended targeting a few of the notables on the UNITE HERE letter signers list for special attention. As for the rest, "most of these academics really are not worth it," she asserted. "I just went through that list on the most recent letter and most of them are Labor Notes-types."[37] Ringuette then joined this private exchange with a report on discussions at SEIU headquarters about "setting a few workers loose," on MacLean and other professors. "I know these aren't high value targets," she told Mort and Morillo. "But I firmly believe people should not be permitted to do 'drive bys.' They are all getting a letter [from Andy Stern] this AM and they all bought a spot on our spam list."

Morillo forgot to delete these attached emails from Mort and Ringuette when he sent his condescending message to MacLean.[38] Needless to say, when the other professors learned from MacLean (and *Perez Stern*) that they were going to be shamed, spammed, or treated as mere "Labor Notes-types," some were pretty miffed. MacLean certainly did not regard their appeal to Stern as the literary equivalent of a drive-by shooting. So she sent a blistering reply to SEIU that rejected any further dialogue with Mort and Ringuette because of their "contemptuous" comments. She reminded Morillo that the letter signers were "not as clueless and unconnected as your email exchanges imagine." However they were labeled by SEIU now, MacLean wrote:

> [T]he truth is that the faculty who organized and signed this letter have long been your supporters and allies, and have used every occasion possible—until recent events—to hold up SEIU (along with UNITE HERE) as the best hope for the labor movement…We have done this in our scholarship, in our public lectures to community as well as academic audiences, in our relations with foundations and public officials, and in our teaching and mentoring of students, which has brought you many a staff member and student ally.[39]

Within three days, Andy Stern was on the phone himself, personally apologizing to MacLean (as Ringuette did also, via email). MacLean reported that the prospects were now good for a "meeting with Stern and Bruce Raynor to discuss our concerns about their conduct and the broader issues at stake." Based on Stern's assurances, MacLean was also more optimistic than before that "our voices mattered to SEIU's leadership."[40] A few months later, Lichtenstein and Klein did have a short discussion with

Bruce Raynor in Manhattan, a session attended by Raynor's friend Josh Freeman from CUNY. Little was accomplished in the exchange, according to one participant. By the time Stern retired from SEIU in May 2010, he had managed to avoid his own promised meeting with MacLean and other academics who defended UNITE HERE.

Independent Scholarship or Work for Hire?

When the dust settled from Javier Morillo's embarrassing email blooper, Nancy MacLean and other outspoken LAWCHA members were apparently still in need of reproach by someone with academic credentials. Josh Freeman took his best shot, unsuccessfully, before the open letter about UNITE HERE was sent to SEIU. Morillo's intervention after the letter arrived turned into a minor disaster. So, in September 2009, Janice Fine stepped forward to challenge SEIU's campus correspondents. Fine used the occasion of the American Political Science Conference in Toronto to chide her colleagues for their public criticism of SEIU leaders, indicating that private communication would have been far more productive.

In her conference presentation, the Rutgers professor characterized the rift between Andy Stern and "labor intellectuals" as one centered on union governance issues. SEIU, she explained, "justifies certain decisions it has taken on the grounds that they are the result of democratic processes, while its critics on the other side feel equally strongly that some of these same processes are undemocratic." Fine described herself as an "independent scholar" whose "perspective is colored by the fact I was an organizer for many years." She disclosed that, during her prior career, she had never "worked at a truly democratic organization—staff and elected leaders always exercised power." As a result, she believes labor researchers should be "exploring dilemmas of union structures and processes and cultures with a tone of inquiry rather than judgment." They should "elucidate how hard it is to achieve 'union democracy'...or, for that matter, what union democracy even is, or what its varieties are, or whether they are even possible to achieve." According to Fine, SEIU officials need "less heat and more light" from the Ivory Tower. "I think we lessen our ability to really talk to and

influence labor leaders when they feel we are publicly calling them out…
as opposed to when we use the relationships we have with them to privately tell them what we honestly think and push them, but do it out of
the limelight."[41]

According to one member of the audience, Fine failed to disclose
some relevant information about her own labor leader "relationships." The
same union she urged other professors to refrain from criticizing paid
Rutgers $127,000 for consulting work that she, Adrienne Eaton, and Saul
Rubinstein performed on its behalf. In addition, between 2005 and 2009,
the fourth member of their research team, Allison Porter, received another
$300,000 from SEIU for her own SEIU consultant activity.[42] Their 2009
report *Organizational Change at SEIU* is chock-full of useful statistics but
hardly a model of independent scholarship in many other ways. Like
equivalent products of corporate consulting, the Rutgers study provides
SEIU managers with much positive feedback on their past decisions and
plans for the future. The authors definitely favor less, rather than more,
"union democracy"—music to the ears of this particular client. When Fine
and her colleagues tried to evaluate Stern's takeover of UHW, arguably the
most costly and disastrous management mistake by SEIU during the period studied, that part of their 67-page report was redacted—at least in
the version unofficially circulated. There are few recommendations in the
publicly available version of *Organizational Change* that "push" SEIU leaders in any new or unapproved direction. Because the authors, by their own
account, interviewed no rank-and-file members, they failed to note the
grassroots backlash against call center servicing; in fact, their report recy-
cles the claim that MRCs will "free up resources for member engagement
and leadership development," while SEIU's own internal analysis concluded otherwise.[43]

In early 2010, I contacted Fine about her SEIU consulting work and
tried to confirm what she did or did not tell her Toronto conference audience. She refused to discuss the matter by phone but explained, via
email, that she had "studied SEIU on and off since 1992." Citing "relationships of long standing among staff and leaders at all levels of the union,"

she told me "what I discuss with them is none of your business." She
added that:

> Three years ago, SEIU commissioned Rutgers to conduct an academic
> study of its organizational change process. Funding for that study went
> to the school. In the few academic presentations we have made of this
> work, we have been forthright about having received funding from
> SEIU and will continue to do so. I have also told reporters when they
> contacted me about the study and who has funded it and will continue
> to do so as well.[44]

During her work on this "academic study," Fine has been quoted by
a number of reporters about SEIU-related matters, but not identified as a
paid consultant to the union. For example, when asked by the *Las Vegas
Sun* about the wisdom of nurses changing bargaining representatives at
three Nevada hospitals in 2008, Fine—described as "a professor of labor
relations at Rutgers University"—offered the SEIU-friendly opinion that
switching to CNA was a mistake. "There are some instances where having
competition in the labor movement is a good thing," she said. "This is not
one of them."[44] (Not coincidentally, the nurses in question were fleeing
from SEIU Local 1107, then run by Jane McAlevey, a close friend of Fine's
whom we met in chapter 5.)

Since Steven Greenhouse has also quoted Fine as an academic expert,
I contacted him about what disclosures she had made to the *Times* about
her work for SEIU. I also inquired about Greenhouse's frequent use of
quotes from Richard Hurd, a Cornell professor who had been a consultant
for the union in the past. SEIU has long been a major institutional client of
the School of Industrial and Labor Relations (ILR), where Hurd teaches.
According to other Cornell staff members, 1199SEIU has paid the ILR extension program hundreds of thousands of dollars for union training, staff
time, and consulting services over the years.[46] In March 2010, Stern lectured
at Cornell as its "Alice B. Grant Labor Leader in Residence." Yet, when Greenhouse quoted Hurd in SEIU-related stories, his personal and institutional
ties to the union were never noted. In a *Times* story, like the one in which
Hurd predicted that Andy Stern was likely to prevail over Sal Rosselli be-

cause Stern was "the bigger bulldog," it seemed to me that readers might want to know about Hurd's closer connection to that particular dog.[47]

Greenhouse explained that he generally tried "to avoid quoting people when I know they have financial ties to a union (or some other entity I'm writing about) or to identify those financial ties if I do indeed quote them." For that reason, he was no longer quoting "folks from the UCLA Labor Center" because he knew that Ruth Milkman and Kent Wong "have contracts with the SEIU." In the cases of Hurd and Fine, he confessed:

"I didn't realize that they had contracts with the SEIU when I quoted them. If I had, I certainly would have mentioned that when quoting them. (I learned, I think last year, that Janice is doing a big research project on SEIU, but I didn't learn until quite recently that SEIU was funding it. I had thought it was an academic project financed without any assistance from SEIU.)"[48]

In Fine's view, of course, she and her coauthors *were* engaged in an "academic project." But, as Greenhouse correctly notes, there's a difference between research "financed without any assistance from SEIU" and a union-funded study, produced for internal consumption (even if the results are later recycled in academic circles as the Rutgers study apparently will be).[49] Under *New York Times* reporting guidelines, the client relationships of a union consultant should be acknowledged when that person is quoted as an "expert" on matters related to the institution that has employed him or her. A *Times* reporter may even decide that a particular expert's union financial ties constitute a sufficient conflict of interest that he or she, like Wong and Milkman at UCLA, shouldn't be quoted at all.

How academics are identified in connection with their SEIU "work for hire" became a big issue at the University of Maryland Public Policy School.[50] At the same time that SEIU consultant Fred Feinstein's views were being disseminated to Kaiser workers in California—as those of an independent expert—his lucrative financial ties to the union were kept in the dark. As a result, Maryland publicly reprimanded Feinstein for a "legal opinion" he wrote on SEIU's behalf that "violated University procedures by misusing campus stationery and his title."[51] Feinstein is a labor lawyer, former general counsel of the NLRB under Bill Clinton, and a member of the UAW Public Review Board. He serves as an adjunct professor and senior fellow at the University of Maryland. Using its letterhead and his academic title, Feinstein provided a letter to SEIU organizers that was used, unsuccessfully, to discourage Kaiser workers in Southern California from switching to NUHW in January 2010. The letter was reproduced with Feinstein's picture on a flyer headlined: "Top Labor Expert Explains What Happens to Our Contract If We Vote to Change Unions."[52]

Prominently identified as a former high-ranking NLRB official, Feinstein warned Kaiser workers that, if they exercised their legal right to switch unions—and management bargained to impasse on a new contract with NUHW—their employer would then be free to "implement a proposal containing terms less favorable than those in the current contract negotiated by the decertified union." In addition to not disclosing his financial relationship with SEIU, Feinstein neglected to mention that the same worst case labor relations scenario was possible if the incumbent union retained bargaining rights. Subject to an inevitable legal challenge, Kaiser was equally free to impose, on SEIU members, the terms and conditions of any concessionary "final offer" if negotiations with SEIU dragged on long enough for the employer to declare "impasse." While Feinstein's pro-SEIU letter-writing was deemed "unrelated to his university work," it was his "lack of transparency" that got him into trouble. According to Dean Donald Kettl, his action did not reflect well on "the academic integrity and the high standards of scholarship" at Maryland. "We are taking strong and immediate steps to set this right," Kettl declared, "to avoid a repeat of this breach by any of our employees."[53]

As *Inside Higher Ed* noted, SEIU and CTW both reported their payments to Feinstein, totaling $240,000 in 2007–08 filings with the U.S. DOL. However, the university's reprimand suggested that mere disclosure of outside institutional relationships in such public documents was not sufficient "transparency," as Feinstein apparently assumed. For there to be real openness about financial ties that might influence "expert opinion," *Inside Higher Ed* agreed that academics should feel obliged to acknowledge actual or potential conflicts in their writings and publications.[54] And, one might add, in their academic conference presentations.

Neither Fred Feinstein's controversial Kaiser flyer nor the organizational ego massage that SEIU received from Rutgers met all of the union's new "work for hire" needs. In mid-2010, Mary Kay Henry, SEIU's just-elected president, was trying to give the union a PR makeover. As part of that effort, SEIU unveiled a slick $25 coffee table book called *Stronger Together: The Story of SEIU.* This 276-page illustrated history of SEIU appeared to come from a progressive publisher called Chelsea Green. In the halcyon days, not so long ago, when SEIU was less enveloped in controversy, the union could count on the professoriate to write favorably about its activities in books published by prestigious university presses. Studies like Ruth Milkman's *L.A. Story* or *Working for Justice: The L.A. Model of Organizing and Advocacy,* or Steven Henry Lopez's *Reorganizing the Rust Belt,* burnished SEIU's reputation and informed a broader audience of its positive accomplishments, all with an academic seal of approval.[55]

Although its production values were very high (thanks to the large amount of membership dues money spent on it), *Stronger Together* was more of a vanity press book. It barely received its first published review when even Chelsea Green Press was distancing itself from the project (in an email to *Labor Notes,* which ran the review). This took some doing because the Vermont publisher's name appears on the back cover of *Stronger Together,* its spine, title page, and promotional material. Plus, the author, Don Stillman, thanks Chelsea Green for being his publisher in the acknowledgments. Au contraire, Chelsea Green is (according to Margot Baldwin, its president) only "distributing" the book, not really publishing it.[56]

Chelsea Green's sudden self-demotion was understandable. *Stronger Together* is a self-congratulatory account of past SEIU glory produced, with lots of headquarters help, by a labor scribe married to Judy Scott, the union's general counsel. As usual, anyone interested in finding out what Scott's spouse was paid for his work will have to wait until SEIU files its next LM-2 form in March 2011. But the union's report for 2009 reveals that someone named Don Stillman received $90,000 for his "support for organizing." Prior ghostwriting and editing, for Stern's *A Country That Works* and an earlier SEIU-backed book, earned Stillman a previously reported $210,000. In a little footnote on page 275 of *Stronger Together,* there is "full disclosure" of the author's personal connection to Judy Scott. Close readers will learn that she fully "recused herself" from SEIU's "legal review of the book" and assigned that task to six lawyers who work under her. But that arrangement doesn't really address Scott's broader role in the union. One of the more factually challenged chapters of *Stronger Together* deals, not surprisingly, with Andy Stern's strong-arming of California health care workers. In Stillman's retelling, the takeover of UHW rescued its members in the nick of time from Sal Rosselli's secret plotting, after which UHW became "a member-focused union that was winning major gains." The legal mugging of UHW (and then NUHW) by SEIU is recounted in much favorable detail. Missing from Stillman's account is the fact that his wife was a key architect of the UHW trusteeship and personally profited from litigation related to it in 2008–09.

Scott's law firm, James & Hoffman, was one of four involved in the civil suit against Rosselli and other NUHW founders. (As noted earlier, one of the firm's partners, Ed James, even personally participated in the UHW takeover.) The case against Sal Rosselli and his fellow defendants cost SEIU members approximately $10 million, but resulted in a jury award of only $1.5 million, which is still being appealed. For its billable hours on this SEIU dispute and other cases, James & Hoffman received more than $2 million in 2009. (As of the end of that year, it was still owed another half million.) Scott's personal salary and benefits for the year totaled more than $240,000. Her share of the firm's profits added nearly $90,000 to that. In short, Stillman and Scott are definitely among those who, as the back cover of *Stronger Together* proclaims, "have won a better future for themselves and their family through SEIU." And their income-producing career synergy is not at all unusual at SEIU headquarters, as Paul Pringle revealed in one of his most interesting *Los Angeles Times* reports on SEIU insider dealing.[57]

Of course, none of this relevant financial information from U.S. DOL filings made it into *Stronger Together.* Instead, we see the beatific visage of

Mary Kay Henry on many pages in the book. For those who wondered why and how SEIU came to embrace the color purple so religiously, there is a very interesting chapter on its corporate-style rebranding campaign and related adoption of Pantone 268c as its official shade.[58] Unfortunately for the real publisher, *Stronger Together* won't get far in the outside world as a credible new facelift (regardless of how many copies are distributed within the union). Amid the continuing progressive quandary about SEIU, putting a convincing shine on all things Pantone 268c is much harder than it used to be.

Chapter 9

How EFCA Died for Obamacare

"I think at SEIU we've clearly demonstrated we can stay incredibly focused on the change America needs despite whatever else goes on in our union day to day."

—Andy Stern, speaking at the SEIU-funded Center for
American Progress, January 26, 2010

In 2008, organized labor spent more than $300 million on the election of Barack Obama and other Democrats in a frantic bid to end eight years of Republican rule.[1] SEIU was the largest single financial contributor to this multi-union campaign, reinforcing its claim to have "the most effective political program of any international union."[2] On the road to victory, it was a proud moment for SEIU when not only the union's secretary-treasurer, Anna Burger, but also a rank-and-file member appeared on stage (and national TV) at the Democratic convention in Denver. Pauline Beck, a home care worker from California, stood before thousands of delegates to remind them of her personal connection to Obama.

Beck was there because of a clever SEIU program, rolled out during the primary campaign, called "Walk a Day in My Shoes." Obama and his

255

competitors for the nomination were all invited to spend a day doing the jobs of various SEIU members. Obama reported for duty as Beck's assistant in Oakland, "doing home care work with me," she told the delegates. Her client that day was an eighty-six-year-old former cement mason, a fellow African American named John Thornton. Barack Obama did "Mr. John's laundry, he mopped floors, did dishes and changed the sheets," Beck reported. "Being a home care worker is hard. The wages are low. The hours can be long and the work can be physically challenging. My union, SEIU, is a great help. But workers need a president who stands up for us." Obama, she recalled, "didn't want to talk politics or pose for pictures. That's the kind of president we need. Someone who really understands working people."[3]

By Election Day, more than $85 million SEIU dollars (including 20 percent of the national union's total budget for the year) had been poured into the campaign. Thousands of AFL-CIO and CTW union volunteers and staffers were deployed in key "battleground states" to help Obama defeat Arizona Republican John McCain, who backed right-to-work laws and other anti-union measures. Stern and Burger were among those deployed. Following the Denver convention, they immediately embarked on a "Take Back Labor Day" tour of the Midwest. At each stop, the SEIU officers sounded the theme that Obama's victory on November 4, 2008, would herald a new day for labor. That message later became the basis for a lavish documentary, released on the first anniversary of the president's election. It was called *Labor Day,* cost SEIU more than $1.6 million to make, and chronicled the union's singular contribution to Obama's election. *Labor Day* was produced and directed by two-time Oscar nominee Glenn Silber, a veteran of the sixties antiwar movement at the University of Wisconsin, whose earlier credits included a movie called *The War at Home.* Silber's new project depicted the 2008 presidential campaign as "an extraordinary moment in U.S. history," not only because "of the race and gender" of some of the would-be candidates, but "because of the passions they inspired." One reason Obama inspired such passion in union circles was his ostensible commitment to the two top items on labor's agenda—

legislation that would make it easier to organize and health care reform.[4] Few knew at the time how fatally entangled these priorities would become.

In March 2010, after much lobbying by SEIU and other unions, Congress finally passed the Patient Protection and Affordable Care Act (PPACA). Demonized by conservatives as "government-run" and prohibitively expensive, the president's plan mandated individual medical coverage and greatly expanded the role of private insurance companies in providing it (with the help of huge federal subsidies based on income). "Obamacare" was found wanting by labor activists who favored a "single payer" system, or at least some "public option" for the millions of Americans who will now be herded into the reformed market for private insurance. On the road to overhauling health care, the administration's push for PPACA always left labor law reform next in line. There, it languished in second place for a full year, until the grassroots backlash against Obama's tax on higher-cost health plans helped kill any chance of enacting EFCA, even in watered-down form.

Doubts During the Transition

While running for office, Obama repeatedly informed union audiences (if not the general public) that he favored "employee free choice."[5] Unlike his opponent, John McCain, he was—or so he said—opposed to taxing workers' job-based medical benefits. By the time he was elected in November 2008, the country faced its worst financial crisis since the Great Depression. This gave the Democrats an unparalleled opportunity—the first since the thirties, in fact—to link much-needed changes in federal labor law to broader economic recovery efforts. As progressive economist Dean Baker argued, "If workers are able to form unions and get their share of productivity gains, it could once again put the country on a wage-driven growth path, instead of growth driven by unsustainable borrowing."[6]

In Senate races where Democratic candidates had pledged to support EFCA, business groups spent an estimated $50 million on advertising depicting labor law reform as a desperate "power grab" by "union bosses" that would open the floodgates for new union organizing. As originally drafted, EFCA would compel employers to recognize new collective bargaining units based on a showing that a majority of workers (in an appropriate unit) had signed union authorization cards. Management would no longer be able to insist on NLRB elections, with their accompanying delays and opportunities for legal (and illegal) anti-union campaigning. Workers fired for organizing would be eligible for "treble damages"—three times their lost pay—rather than just "back pay" minus "interim earnings." Other employer unfair labor practices—now penalized with a mere notice posting—could result in a $20,000 fine (if found to be willful or repeated violations of the act). Finally, EFCA would create a Canadian-style process of first contract mediation and arbitration. Unresolved first contract negotiations could, at union request, become the subject of binding arbitration leading to imposed contract terms. This would make it harder for employers to use bad faith bargaining as their second line of defense against unionization—as many do after losing a contested representation election.

Despite being EFCA-baited by big business, key Democratic challengers to the GOP were elected in 2008 anyway, giving labor law reform what then appeared to be fifty-nine possible votes in the Senate and even more supporters in the House (where it was passed by a vote of 241 to 185 in 2007). Labor's best-case head count in the Senate included all the Democrats, two independents, and one Republican—soon to become a Democrat—Arlen Specter. In the flush of victory, many believed labor was only one vote shy of having the supermajority of sixty necessary to thwart a GOP filibuster like the one in 1978 that doomed labor law reform during Jimmy Carter's presidency. All it would take now, under Obama, would be continuing grassroots agitation by union members and a favorable outcome of the Minnesota recount involving Democratic Senatorial candidate Al Franken and his opponent.[7]

Nevertheless, there were early warning signs of presidential-elect ambivalence about EFCA. Michael Mishak reported in the *Las Vegas Sun* on November 30, 2008, about Obama's private fears that any push for EFCA "would be divisive" at a time when he was already planning, as promised on the campaign trail, to go "to great lengths to bridge the partisan rift in Washington that grew deeper" during the Bush years.[8] As Randy Johnson, vice president of the U.S. Chamber of Commerce, pointed out: "The Administration wants to pass the stimulus and they need the business community to do that. Trying to pass card check would be like declaring a nuclear war with the business community. It'd be Armageddon." A key centrist Democrat, Senator Blanche Lincoln from Arkansas, was already in synch with the Chamber of Commerce. She told a home-state newspaper that "focusing on this bill, this issue, isn't paramount" because "the nation has more important issues to deal with," like the state of the economy. She announced that she was still "undecided" on EFCA.[9] Even a staunch labor backer and key member of the House leadership like Representative George Miller (D-CA) began sending out ambiguous signals. In a postelection interview, Miller told the *Chicago Tribune* that EFCA was not going to be "the first bill out of the chute" in the new year, but was "not moving to the back of the train" either.[10]

Some union strategists worried that, if EFCA was not quickly integrated into overall economic recovery efforts, the bill would become vulnerable to attack as narrow "special interest" legislation. Labor's proposed amendments to the National Labor Relations Act would be depicted as postelection "payback" from Obama to his union supporters. The rare opportunity to make organizing rights part of a larger proworker package of tax cuts, home foreclosure protection, extended unemployment insurance, and funding for public jobs would be lost if EFCA was pigeonholed this way. In his lobbying of leading Democrats, CWA president Larry Cohen argued that labor law reform was a proven economic fix, costing taxpayers almost nothing compared to the big federal bailout of banks, insurers, and brokerage firms. Using EFCA-sanctioned "card check" campaigns to win bargaining rights more easily, hundreds of thousands of workers could finally gain a voice in personnel policy decisions. Just as the Wagner Act did during Franklin D. Roosevelt's presidency, EFCA could restore greater balance to labor-management relations and, over time, help workers' raise their living standards again.

The First Hundred Days

In the midst of this postelection EFCA maneuvering, America's second largest union, SEIU, was enjoying the fruits of victory. In a video message to members after Obama's "first hundred days" in office, then president Andy Stern boasted that "SEIU is in the field, it's in the White House, it's in the administration!"[11] Patrick Gaspard, a top political operative for 1199SEIU in New York, became the new White House political director, Karl Rove's old job under George Bush. Craig Becker, the union's associate general counsel, was in line for an NLRB nomination. Another SEIU lawyer, John Sullivan, was tapped to join the Federal Election Commission. Obama's policy of disclosing all visitors confirmed that Stern and SEIU secretary-treasurer Anna Burger were indeed in the White House quite frequently, much to the chagrin of some of their colleagues. ("Andy has better access than anyone else in labor," one complained.[12]) As *Newsweek*'s Jonathan Alter later reported: "Stern spent little time with Obama personally in all those trips to the White House; mostly, he was war-gaming health care strategy."[13] The key to accomplishing labor's goals, Stern explained, was figuring out "how to make sure what the President wants to get done, gets done."[14]

Getting anything done about EFCA soon got much harder, thanks to Arlen Specter. The Republican senator from Pennsylvania was just one month away from becoming a Democrat, much to the joy of Obama and his national party. Locally, Specter had long been regarded as a "friend of labor" by SEIU, the United Mine Workers, Steelworkers, and other unions. In 2007, he supported bringing EFCA to the floor for a Senate vote after it was passed overwhelmingly in the House. But on March 24, 2008, when he was still in the GOP, Specter announced in a major speech that he wouldn't vote for "cloture" on EFCA again. Echoing Blanche Lincoln and other centrist Democrats, Specter declared that "the problems of the recession" made Obama's first year in office "a particularly bad time to enact Employee Free Choice."

But there was more to Specter's speech than bad advice about political timing. The former prosecutor had discovered that, in organizing campaigns where NLRB elections have been bypassed and "card check" used to prove majority support for unionization, workers were being subjected to "widespread intimidation." According to Specter, "union officials" come to their "homes and refuse to leave until cards are signed." The same senator always encouraged unannounced union door-knocking when he was running for reelection. But now he was opposed to such "strong-arm tactics" and wanted to make it an "unfair labor practice," under the National Labor Relations Act (NLRA), for any union organizer to visit "an employee at his/her home without prior consent for any purpose related to a representation campaign." In the same speech, Specter indicated his willingness to work with others in the Senate on a compromise bill that would amend the NLRA in ways more to his liking—an overture that soon led to weakening of labor's original bill.[15]

Stern insisted that card check was still "alive and well," despite Specter's defection. "Sixty votes are required to open and close debate," he noted. "Without Al Franken, one vote is getting to mean a lot more. Arlen Specter switching parties is a positive trend...And if he's red on card check, I couldn't get my members to vote for him. That's like being against universal health care."[16] In November 2008, right after Obama's election, Stern took a similar stance when he and Burger visited the *Nation*'s offices for an interview with its editors. There, Burger confidently declared: "You don't need to rewrite EFCA or compromise." Labor should just "get it through the House, into the Senate, stay in the field, and get it passed." At the *Washington Post* just five months later—at a time when other unions felt it was still premature to entertain EFCA amendments—Stern and Burger started singing a different tune. "We are on the hunt for a solution," Stern assured the *Post* editorial board. He emphasized that expedited NLRB elections would be an acceptable substitute for requiring employer recognition based on card check. Whether it includes majority sign-up or not, Stern said, the final bill just had to minimize opportunities for employer misbehavior and NLRA violations. He was, as usual, extremely solicitous of Obama: "The President has said that he has a series of things—that we agree he needs to get done—which are major for every man, woman, and child, like health care....We respect that we have a job to do to line up enough votes without him. I don't think there's any question there will be a vote, that this bill's time has arrived, and he will do whatever is in his power to bring this home. We just aren't there yet."[17]

A Health Care Summit

Nowhere was SEIU's bond with Obama more obvious than in coalition building related to the fight for health care reform. To "win this war," Stern named as "our General Petraeus," the man who had been "the mightiest labor leader in New York City," Dennis Rivera.[18] The former president of 1199SEIU saw his primary mission as being intertwined with two others—labor law reform and "build[ing] a new relationship and a new paradigm with our employers at the national level."[19] After becoming head of SEIU Healthcare, an alliance of locals in the industry, Rivera played a leading role in enlisting the Greater New York Hospital Association, Kaiser Permanente, and Catholic Healthcare West in a "Partnership for Quality Care," unveiled in Washington in 2007. Two years later, on May 11, 2009, Obama met with these same "partners" at the White House, along with other powerful trade groups representing doctors, insurers, and drug manufacturers. In a buoyant email message sent to SEIU members afterward, Stern declared that the participants at this "game changing" gathering had made "the most significant move toward real health care reform in our nation's history." Stern and Rivera were, of course, the only labor officials present to "jump-start the drive toward real reform"—by coming up with a plan to control costs.

The "cooperation" of America's "medical-industrial complex" didn't come cheap and was shaky from the beginning.[20] Stern's account echoed the official White House version of the meeting, in which representatives of the American Hospital Association, the American Medical Association, America's Health Insurance Plans, the Pharmaceutical Research and Manufacturers of America, and other big industry players came together and, in one day, figured out how to save $2 trillion in health care spending over the next decade. As a result of everyone setting aside "partisan politics,"

America was now "one step closer to putting our country on a sound fiscal footing," Stern proclaimed. Unfortunately, as one Huffington Post contributor noted, there was no "enforcement mechanism or penalty" if anyone involved reneged on their part of this deal.[21] Some participants started backtracking immediately, resulting in this May 14, 2009, *New York Times* headline: "Health Care Leaders Say Obama Overstates Their Promise to Control Costs." According to reporter Robert Pear, industry executives remained very "leery of enforceable cost controls," did not "pledge specific year-by-year cuts," and only "agreed to slow health spending in a more gradual way." The head of the American Hospital Association and Medical Association (AHA) even complained that Obama's misleading spin on the meeting had "caused a lot of consternation among our members."[22]

The competing priorities of health care and labor law reform were discussed at a second, less-publicized White House meeting two months later. This one was a union-only session with Obama, attended by a much broader delegation from the National Labor Coordinating Committee (NLCC). With David Bonior facilitating its work, the NLCC had been launched, after high-level discussions in January, as a joint venture of the National Education Association (NEA) and the largest unions in the AFL-CIO and CTW.[23] The primary reason for their convergence was "the political opportunity that the Obama Administration and the Democratic Congress afforded labor" to achieve goals it had long pursued in Washington with little past success.[24] A secondary objective was to minimize political freelancing like the Stern-Burger trial balloon about abandoning card check. At their joint audience with Obama on July 13, Stern, AFL-CIO president John Sweeney, Gerry McEntee from AFSCME, James P. Hoffa from the Teamsters, and others present were informed by the president, in no uncertain terms, that "fixing health care" had to come first, then EFCA. Some objections were raised about this sequencing. But most in the AFL-CIO/CTW/NEA delegation politely went along with the plan.

Despite this demonstration of "labor unity," there was, by the summer of 2009, a noticeable division between the "growing ranks of single-payer, Medicare-for-all advocates and a new, institutionally weightier coalition of more than a hundred labor unions and other advocacy groups called Health Care for America Now" (HCAN). Created in June 2008, HCAN raised more than $40 million from liberal foundations and labor organizations like SEIU, AFSCME, and the AFL-CIO. As David Moberg reported, HCAN was "promoting a strategy closer to Obama's proposal that would include employer-provided or individually purchased private insurance and the option of a public plan."[25] Even when inclusion of a "public option" still seemed achievable, the SEIU-driven approach was dismaying to many single-payer advocates within labor, including CNA.[26] During its feud with SEIU, CNA had complained of mailings to its members in which Stern's union had criticized CNA for advocating a "government-run health care system," echoing John McCain's own attacks on Obama. Michael Lighty, CNA's policy director, once described Stern as "the single biggest obstacle to single-payer health care in this country."[27]

When the two unions negotiated their 2009 truce, CNA claimed there would soon be joint CNA-SEIU "measures to allow states to adopt single-payer, or an expanded and updated Medicare for all, as a comprehensive, cost-effective healthcare reform."[28] (Their accord was also going to "spur" labor's campaign for EFCA.) CNA itself remained an exemplary source of single-payer agitation, in California and elsewhere. But there was little evidence of any new legislative/political partnering with SEIU, locally or nationally. The much smaller RN union had none of the ready access to the White House that gave SEIU such special insight into what "the president wants to get done"—and when. CNA remained very much on the outside looking in, unhappily, like many others in the single-payer movement who lacked the financial resources of HCAN. "Obama is really the one who is puzzling to us," Rose Ann DeMoro fumed. "We were all supporters of him...It's hard to understand how he can expect us to rally support around a plan that will leave the big insurance companies in charge and keep hurting patients."[29]

Whether you liked Obama's health plan or not, its prospects got worse when a patient named Ted Kennedy died from a brain tumor in August 2009.With Kennedy's death, the Democrats lost the sixty-vote supermajority

they had finally gained the previous month with the long-delayed seating of
Al Franken from Minnesota. Under prior Massachusetts law, Governor Deval
Patrick could have appointed a successor to Kennedy immediately. But, in
2004, the relevant statute had been changed by Democratic state legislators
to make sure that Mitt Romney, Patrick's predecessor, couldn't appoint a replacement for John Kerry if Kerry defeated George Bush for the presidency.
The new method of filling a U.S. Senate seat vacancy required holding a special election, including party primaries beforehand, a process that would
take months. Unless it was modified again, this meant Senate Democrats
and Obama would be one vote shy of the number needed to overcome any
Republican filibuster during the rest of 2009 and early 2010.

So, in the Bay State, Kennedy's own labor activist constituents were
mobilized to assist a frantic national union effort to replace him sooner
rather than later. By late September, despite cries of hypocrisy and growing
public cynicism about the situational "principles" of Democratic Party
leaders, the governor's power of appointment was restored. Governor
Patrick then named Kennedy confidante Paul Kirk to the Senate seat,
which he held for the next four months until the special election on January 19, 2010. As a condition of his appointment, Kirk agreed not to be a
candidate himself, in a Democratic field that soon included state attorney
general Martha Coakley, Congressman Michael Capuano, and two lesser-
known but well-heeled competitors from the private sector. For the Republican primary, a then-obscure state senator and small-town lawyer
named Scott Brown filed petitions as well.

Over Labor Day weekend, many of the same labor activists still signing
up coworkers on petitions demanding card check (or, in Massachusetts, trying to change its election law) were unhappy to see John Sweeney raising
the same white flag on EFCA that Stern and Burger waved at the *Washington
Post* in April. In a farewell interview, the nearly retired (and plenty tired-
looking) AFL-CIO leader "signaled a significant shift to try to move a long-
stalled pro-union bill." Sweeney, the *New York Times* reported, would now
"support speedy unionization elections" in place of "the much attacked card
check provision" of EFCA. In the same article, his soon-to-be-successor

Richard Trumka stopped short of endorsing faster votes—held five or ten days after a representation petition was filed—as a substitute for card check. Trumka stressed the need for three essential elements in any bill—stronger penalties for employer law-breaking, arbitration of unresolved first contract disputes, and some "process in which workers were free of intimidation." Sweeney claimed that EFCA foes would have more difficulty criticizing expedited elections than card check (although there was no evidence, in the *Times* article or anywhere else, that his peace offering or Stern and Burger's earlier one, would reduce business opposition in the slightest). As Sweeney headed out the door after fifteen years in office, he expressed cheery optimism about EFCA. "It's going to pass this year," he said.[30]

The Role of Specter and Baucus

At the AFL-CIO's September 14–17, 2009, convention in Pittsburgh, labor's own mixed signals about EFCA required even more cognitive dissonance. Who was scheduled to speak about labor law reform at the convention? None other than Arlen Specter, the same seventy-nine-year-old senator who had denounced card check in terms redolent of the Chamber of Commerce just six months before. When the wrinkled and cadaverous Specter appeared on stage in the David Lawrence Convention Center, Trumka introduced him warmly. Specter reported that he was working hard on a "robust public option in health care." He said his current stance on "employees' choice"—although not explained in any detail—met Trumka's three minimum requirements ("prompt certification," "tough penalties," and "binding arbitration"). According to Specter, a half dozen senators, including himself, Tom Harkin, and Chuck Schumer, were busy working on a new and more widely acceptable version of EFCA. The bill was likely to be passed by the end of the year and would "be totally satisfactory to labor," he assured the delegates.[31]

After President Obama addressed the same crowd, getting a far more rapturous reception, he and Specter flew off to Philadelphia together. There, Obama spoke at a big fundraiser for the senator, providing him with the same kind of reward for party-switching that the Pennsylvania AFL-CIO later did as well. In the meantime, confusion reigned back in the convention press gallery about whether a compromise on EFCA had been worked out behind the scenes on Capitol Hill. After permitting Specter to update the convention on the status of its own bill—whose key provision he had trashed earlier in the year—the AFL-CIO was immediately bombarded with questions from reporters about the accuracy of his report. In a hurried briefing right after Specter's speech, Trumka claimed that "card check legislation was still in play." This led the *Wall Street Journal* to report the next day that Specter's rollout of a new "road map for putting a long-stalled overhaul of labor law back on track" was "quickly dismissed by leaders of the AFL-CIO." In his capacity as federation organizing committee chair, Larry Cohen did his own media damage control, insisting correctly that, until there were sixty Democratic-controlled votes in the Senate, "we don't even want to finalize a bill, because who are we discussing it with?"[32]

In the weeks following the convention, Cohen and other union leaders soon had worse things to worry about on Capitol Hill than EFCA becoming "EFCA Lite," thanks to Arlen Specter. Democrat Max Baucus from Montana unveiled the bipartisan product of the long (and much protested) deliberations by his Senate Finance Committee.[33] The key financing mechanism of Baucus's bill took direct aim at negotiated medical plans like the ones telephone workers in the Northeast had struck repeatedly to defend. Baucus proposed that expanded coverage be funded, in part, through a 40 percent "excise tax" that would be applied to that portion of the value of any employer-provided coverage that exceeded $8,000 for individuals and $21,000 for families. (The House, meanwhile, was developing a proposal that relied on payroll taxation of employers offering no health insurance, plus an income tax surcharge on individuals earning more than $250,000 a year.) In New England, where medical costs are particularly high and the telecom workforce tends to be older, the medical benefit tab of AT&T and Verizon was reaching the threshold amounts that would trigger the Baucus excise tax. As CWA's Cohen pointed out in the *New York Times* on October 13, "at least half our members would be in health plans subject to the tax in 2013."[34]

CWA's own biggest battle against health care cost shifting occurred two

decades earlier, when sixty thousand workers from Maine to New York went
on strike for four months at NYNEX (the regional phone company later re-
branded as Verizon). To counter the corporate attack on their own superior
medical benefits, CWA and IBEW strikers carefully framed the central issue
in dispute. Their buttons, banners, press releases, and leaflets all made it
clear that the solution to medical cost inflation was "Health Care for All,
Not Health Cuts at NYNEX!" Backed by allies like Jesse Jackson, Citizen Action, and Physicians for a National Health Program (PNHP), the NYNEX
strike became a popular focal point for ongoing public and membership
education about the need for Canadian-style national health insurance.[35]
The enormous sacrifices by IBEW and CWA members paid off—both at
the time and for years to come. In 2009, Verizon workers (at the former
NYNEX in New York and New England) still made no premium contributions for comprehensive individual or family coverage.

Twenty years after battling to keep their own health insurance affordable (while calling for single-payer as a better alternative for themselves
and everyone else), former NYNEX strikers suddenly found their medical
benefits back in the news. What they and many other workers had always
thought was a Chevy—that everyone should have in their garage—was
now being demonized as "Cadillac coverage" by White House economic
advisors and other leading Democrats. In the administration view, high-
cost union benefits contributed to medical cost inflation because they encouraged profligate use of doctors and hospitals. According to Senator
Baucus (and soon President Obama as well), these "luxury plans" should
be taxed for three reasons: to restrain rising health care costs, raise the additional federal revenue needed to expand Medicaid, and subsidize, at
great taxpayer expense, wider private insurance coverage.

As health policy expert Len Rodberg noted, funding "reform" in this
fashion directly penalized companies like Verizon and AT&T which cover
workers, their families, and even retirees to a far greater degree than their
nonunion counterparts. At the same time, Senate Democrats were unwilling to level the playing field by requiring all employers to provide some
job-based medical benefits. (Under their plan, of course, only individuals

would be forced to buy health insurance.) The excise tax would impose an additional cost on unionized employers, providing them with "a strong incentive to cut back on benefits."[36] Workers without collective bargaining rights would just have their coverage reduced unilaterally. At unionized firms, health care cost-shifting guaranteed further labor-management conflict, at a time when union strike capacity was much diminished.

"Don't Tax Our Benefits!"

A political attack on their own benefits was not what labor activists anticipated when they knocked on doors, made phone calls, and cast their ballots for Obama rather than McCain. In 2008, unions hammered away, successfully, at the Republican candidate's nefarious plan to tax worker benefits. Now, a year later, they were forced to lobby against the Senate Finance Committee's embrace of the same idea (albeit in a different form). In response, Obama started working the White House phones to make sure that labor opposition didn't deep-six the Baucus bill. He personally called top union officials with the same message he delivered to the NLCC in July. If health care reform failed, the Republicans would have a victory that would doom EFCA as well. Obama knew how upset his labor friends were now about the excise tax, but that could be fixed "*later in the process,*" he stressed. The important thing was getting a health care bill out of committee and onto the Senate floor as soon as possible, so House-Senate differences could be resolved, final legislation passed, and workers' rights addressed next.

Obama's argument swayed some unions more than others. On October 14, one day after the Baucus bill was reported out of the Finance Committee, the AFL-CIO, AFSCME, USWA, CWA, and other labor organizations ran ads in major newspapers opposing the proposed "new tax on middle class benefits." SEIU was not among them. As Dennis Rivera explained: "Every group has to determine their own strategy and tactics. We believe expressing directly how we feel to the principals is the best way to do that." By then, Stern's "General Petraeus" had a history of holding his fire on the excise tax. When the White House first started floating the idea, Rivera told the *New York Times* that SEIU was "predisposed not to agree to the taxing of benefits," but didn't want to pass judgment until it was clearer how this change might fit into Obama's overall health care plan. "We need to see the total picture," he said.[37] By October 2009, "the total picture" was very clear. Every other major union found medical benefit taxation to be totally unacceptable. They were feverishly mobilizing their members and lobbying on Capitol Hill against this threat. So Rivera was asked again whether SEIU's public reticence about Cadillac tax criticism was related to the fact that many of its members "have no or low-cost healthcare insurance" and, therefore, wouldn't be impacted by the tax. He responded that SEIU did indeed have "pockets of members" who are "in the same situation as other unions." SEIU didn't endorse the anti-excise tax ad because "we chose to communicate our views privately," he explained again. On the prospects for a "public option," Rivera was as optimistic as ever. "I believe we have an excellent opportunity of having a government plan that can bring down the costs of insurance. It's going to be in the bill."[38]

There were several problems with this upbeat scenario—the main one being that the carrot of labor law reform, dangled repeatedly by Obama to keep unions in line on health care, always remained just out of reach, for one reason or another. Meanwhile, labor's costly, time-consuming lobbying against the excise tax did have an impact in the Senate, but Cadillac-bashing remained very much in vogue. When Democratic majority leader Harry Reid brought his own bill to the Senate floor, the "luxury insurance tax" remained intact, in modified form—and only five Democrats backed a GOP move to strike it from Reid's bill.[39] For his part, Obama ended up taking a firm stand in favor of taxing benefits, while simultaneously failing to press for either "a public option or a strong employer mandate to provide insurance."[40]

In my home state of Massachusetts, union members and leaders were not pleased with Obama's flip-flop on benefit taxation. The *Boston Globe* ran a front-page story, headlined: "Stalled Agenda Irks Labor Leaders— Unions See Little Action from Democrats in D.C." Anna Burger was among those interviewed inside the Beltway who preached patience with the president. Obama just needed a little more time on health care so he could "get it finished first," she said. Brushing aside worries about the possible negative impact of "reform" on union members, Burger insisted that "the larger goal of getting closer to universal health care is most important."[41] The new mood of membership frustration and alienation, taking root in the hinterlands, did not bode well for the world premiere of *Labor Day*. The film celebrating how SEIU members and their farsighted leaders worked "passionately for the candidate who could best produce real change" contained little instruction, much needed a year later, on how to hold the president accountable.

To fill theater seats for a preview of the film in Madison, SEIU members had to be bussed in from Milwaukee. "The day after screenings in L.A. and New York, *Labor Day* disappeared from the landscape," one union insider noted. "It was dropped like a stone because it's a political embarrassment now." In a typical review, the *Village Voice* dismissed Glen Silber's film as "strictly members-only viewing"—a "crappy infomercial" devoid of journalistic credibility.[42] Over a period of several years, SEIU paid Silber's firm, Catalyst Media, more than $1 million for *Labor Day* and other projects. But, even with distribution help from Lionsgate Films, a screening at Sundance, and aggressive Internet marketing efforts, *Labor Day* was not destined to be another *Bread and Roses*. (In fact, after retiring from SEIU in May 2010, Stern blamed Silber, his former high school tennis team doubles partner from West Orange, New Jersey, for misleading him about the film's commercial potential. "We would love to have our union be seen in a very positive light by large numbers of people," Stern told the *Washington Post*. According to Andy, it was Silber who sold SEIU on the idea of making "this movie that everyone would want to watch. We believed him and it didn't work."[43])

A Member-Driven Process?

In Massachusetts, union activists roused themselves to keep Ted Kennedy's seat in friendly hands. Representing seventy-five thousand workers in state and local government, health care, and property services, SEIU is the largest combined private/public sector union in the state. As such, its political endorsement is highly valued. The SEIU Massachusetts State Council announced that its Senate candidate would be "determined through a member-driven process that included a candidate forum." More than three hundred people turned out for this pre-primary event on October 3, 2009, showing greater popular participation than many unions have. Although the forum featured presentations by Coakley, Capuano, and their two lesser-known opponents, the contest for SEIU backing came down to a competition between the first two. In the preference forms filled out at the forum, Capuano won by a narrow margin. Before he was elected to Congress, Capuano served as mayor of Somerville. In that role, he developed a reputation for combative urban populism that won him the support of Boston's SEIU janitors' local.

However, officials from 1199SEIU, headquartered in New York City, tend to dominate the SEIU state council in Massachusetts. They did not believe that member sentiment, as measured by the close vote at the forum, should be determinative. They lined up two smaller locals on their side, and delivered SEIU's support to the bland, cautious, and then seemingly unbeatable Martha Coakley. The latter had a decent record of enforcing state wage and hour laws as attorney general and was thought to have greater appeal to female Democrats (particularly those still miffed by Hillary Clinton's loss of the 2008 presidential nomination to Obama).With SEIU dollars, door-knockers, sign holders, and phone bankers at her disposal—plus other union backing—Coakley defeated Capuano 47 to 28 percent.

After the primary, "Coakley started with huge leads in polls as she entered the general election against Scott Brown." Unbeknownst to her supporters, it was all going to be downhill from there. Coakley refrained from stressing economic issues in a state where blue-collar workers were bearing the brunt of joblessness even before the 2008–09 recession made their plight far worse. Except when addressing union audiences, she never mentioned EFCA and she certainly didn't tout collective bargaining as a way to boost workers' wages, where they still had jobs. But the sleeper issue that really had her plummeting in the polls before long—particularly among labor voters—was health care. On January 7, twelve days before the special election, Obama made it clear that he favored "the so-called Cadillac tax as a feature of the health care bill that cleared the Senate on Christmas Eve." Labor was still lobbying for its preferred financing mechanism, which included the tax increase on the wealthy contained in the corresponding House bill. But Obama insisted the two bills be reconciled his way. He "put pressure on the House to drop its approach and adopt the Senate tax as part of a compromise between the two bodies." The media immediately noticed that this new "more active role" was "a change for the White House, which for months gave wide latitude to Congress as it shaped legislation."[44]

A "Working Class Revolt"

In Massachusetts, voters thus had a choice between the candidate of the Democratic Party establishment—eager to get to Washington and be the sixtieth vote for Obama's plan—and an affable, photogenic Republican who promised to vote against taxation of workers' benefits. A former Tufts University basketball player, Brown received the reelection endorsement of the Massachusetts AFL-CIO in 2008 because, as a state senator, he favored building gambling casinos. While Coakley was conducting a kind of Rose Garden campaign—replete with photo ops of her accepting a series of organizational endorsements—Brown was tooling around the state, like a building trades guy himself, in a green GMC pickup truck. Benefiting from gusts of local Tea Party wind, he started to attract bigger and more enthusiastic crowds. In the state legislature, Brown had voted for the bipartisan bill, backed by Romney, the Democratic legislative majority, and SEIU, that created the Massachusetts model for Obamacare. But, unlike Coakley, he was able to exploit the fact that our Bay State experiment with universal coverage had done little to curb cost-shifting from employers to employees, wherever the latter still had job-based benefits, union-negotiated or not.

The Massachusetts plan required other residents, under penalty of a fine, to buy individual insurance policies at their own expense (or with subsidies from the state, if they could qualify for them, based on income). But the high out-of-pocket costs associated with some state-approved plans made them unaffordable for people who had chronic conditions requiring frequent doctor visits and prescription drug refills.[45] At the same time, the proposed excise tax in Washington sent a message to recession-battered "blue-collar workers that you should pay higher taxes and get lower benefits to help finance coverage for the uninsured."[46] From Boston to the Berkshires, this was additionally unpopular because the local "uninsured" had been taken care of already—or so we were told—by the state of Massachusetts. To neutralize labor's continuing resistance to the "Cadillac tax," the White House convened what became a 12-hour bargaining session, ending on January 14. In the run-up to those talks, AFL-CIO president Rich Trumka reminded his fellow union leaders, on Obama's behalf, that any derailing of health care reform now, due to labor opposition, would be a victory for the GOP and, thus, the death knell of EFCA.[47]

The bargaining committee, composed of national union presidents from the AFL, CTW, and NEA, was pleased with the changes it wrung from the White House: exemption of union-negotiated plans and those covering state and local government employees until 2018, higher dollar thresholds for when the 40 percent tax would kick in, carve-outs for particular occupational or demographic groups, and other concessions. A CWA message to local union leaders emphasized that delaying the effective date of the tax would "give us at least one and, in some cases, more than one round of bargaining to address the impact on our members." This scenario was not reassuring, given current trends in medical cost inflation and related concession bargaining.[48]

For organized labor as an institution, the public perception created or enhanced by this White House settlement was hardly positive (and came much too late to alter the Senate election results in Massachusetts). As *American Prospect* coeditor Robert Kuttner pointed out, administration deal-making with "special interests"—as exemplified by the Stern/Rivera-assisted session at the White House in May 2009—resulted in "exactly the wrong framing" for Obama's health care reform campaign. "The battle should have been about the president and the people versus the interests," argued Kuttner. Instead, by pursuing an "interest group strategy" (that greatly limited the scope of proposed reforms, no matter how popular they were), "more and more voters concluded that it was the president and the interests *versus* the people."[49] And now, it seemed, unions had cut their own insider deal too, making them appear to be just another "special interest." Rather than standing up for all workers, as CWA did twenty years earlier during the NYNEX strike (and other contract struggles), organized labor negotiated a complicated agreement with Obama that left wage earners without collective bargaining rights far more exposed to the excise tax.[50]

With Brown no longer considered a long shot, out-of-state money poured into his campaign. Between New Year's Day and January 19, 2010, he raised an astonishing $14 million. So local Democrats and their labor allies began to panic. Obama himself flew up to Boston on Sunday, January 17, for an election eve rally and voter pep talk on Coakley's behalf. In the closing days of the race, national labor, feminist, and environmental organizations unleashed "the most blistering assault of late attack ads the state has ever seen."[51] SEIU contributed $685,000 worth of negative advertising to this Washington-directed "air war." They were dark, gloomy TV warnings that Brown was "out of step with the mainstream," accompanied by music seemingly lifted from a horror film soundtrack. As one disgusted former SEIU organizer observed, this huge ad buy was like a "*Saturday Night Live* parody of bad political advertising," completely out of touch with the electorate and "an insult to its intelligence." In every mainstream media postmortem on the election, the "desperate multimillion dollar carpet-bombing" of Brown was deemed to have hurt labor's candidate more than it helped her.[52]

By Election Day, most labor voters still hadn't gotten the good news from Washington about their eight-year exemption from the "Cadillac tax." Or they had simply decided to strike a blow—with a vote for Brown—against benefit taxation altogether. Forty-two percent of those who cast ballots on January 19 believed that Obama wanted to tax their health insurance, and those voters favored Brown by a two to one margin. "Sizeable majorities of Brown voters saw the Democrats' plan, if passed, as making things worse for their families, the country, and the state."[53] In a state where union-endorsed candidates for federal office regularly get 65 percent of the labor vote, Coakley only got 46 percent to Brown's 49 percent, losing 47 to 52 percent overall. Among Massachusetts voters who are not college graduates, Obama beat McCain by a 21 percent margin just fourteen months before; Coakley lost just as badly to Brown in this same group, reflecting a huge forty-one point net swing away from the Democrats among predominantly blue-collar voters.[54] Overall, Coakley received 850,000 fewer votes than Obama, while Brown only got 50,000 more than McCain—an indication of the huge stay-at-home voter factor, particularly in urban, blue-collar Democratic Party strongholds, that enabled the challenger to win.[55]

To explain this defeat, the AFL-CIO highlighted the results of a post-election voter survey by Hart Research Associates. The pollsters declared that a "working class revolt" had occurred in Massachusetts. It was an embarrassing finding indeed, given the fact that labor's own Senatorial candidate, plus its friend in the White House, were key targets of the revolt and the national GOP the revolt's main beneficiary.

The Death of EFCA

The combination of union hubris, political gullibility, compromise, and miscalculation that helped seal the fate of EFCA was the subject of much right-wing derision. "Scott Brown pulled off a miracle for non-union employers!" crowed one anti-union lawyer on his blog. "Those Democratic politicians blew the best chance Big Labor ever had to see real changes in the law that would keep Big Labor from becoming extinct, just like the dinosaurs."[56] Not only did the Democrats lose their Senate supermajority—needed to pass EFCA in any form—but the Senate's quick seating of Brown meant that the nomination of SEIU lawyer Craig Becker to serve on the NLRB was in additional trouble. On February 10, just fifty-two senators supported his appointment, with Blanche Lincoln from Arkansas joining Brown in voting no, along with Democrat Ben Nelson from Nebraska, who claimed that Becker was too pro– "card check."

This development left *Washington Post* columnist Harold Meyerson nearly apoplectic. He declared that the first year of Obama's presidency was "close to an unmitigated disaster" for labor. The "Senate's inability to pass EFCA" was particularly "devastating and galling" because, in Meyerson's view, the compromise that jettisoned card check "had a shot at winning"— if it had been brought to a vote in late 2009, when Ted Kennedy's seat was still filled by Paul Kirk. Instead, Obama and Reid asked the unions, yet again, "to wait until health care reform had passed."[57] In Washington, D.C., labor circles, labor law reform was, by now, an awkward topic. In late January 2010, the AFL-CIO's legislative director Bill Samuel told *Workers Independent News* that "We don't see it being dead...We're obviously re-evaluating our strategy." Speaking at the Center for American Progress, SEIU's Anna Burger waffled as well."If we really want to get this economy going again, we need to figure out a way to pass the Employee Free Choice Act," she said. "Does 60 matter? Sure it matters. Is there a way that we can try to make the Senate understand that we have to do what's good for America, what's good for working families? I don't know. That's the challenge we have."Obama might have helped with this challenge just a day later when he delivered his 2010 State of the Union address to Congress. Instead, he never once mentioned EFCA (or the state of unions), thus signaling to the assembled solons that the time for labor law reform had come and gone again.

In the past, under Jimmy Carter or Bill Clinton, the consolation prize for labor when the Democrats failed to enact NLRA changes, was at least a more worker-friendly NLRB. One quarter of the way through Obama's first (and perhaps only) term, the five-member NLRB was still operating with just two decision makers, one a designee of the Democrats and the other holding a seat reserved for a GOP nominee. Their "bipartisan" handling of five hundred "noncontroversial" cases, during the previous two years, faced a Supreme Court challenge by employers (who soon won their claim that a minimum of three members was necessary for NLRB rulings to be enforceable by the federal judiciary). CWA's Cohen pointed out that, with just two active board members, "thousands of fired workers can get no justice and hundreds of thousands have no bargaining rights as every critical case at the national level is frozen."[58] Thanks to the Supreme Court's ruling in June 2010, many two-member cases had to be redecided, creating additional delays.

Obama responded to this unfolding debacle by failing to use his first opportunity to name Becker and upstate New York labor lawyer Mark Pearce to the board without Senate approval. CWA and other unions began a phone calling and emailing campaign urging the White House to use the next round of recess appointments to restore the board to something resembling normal functioning. In late March, Obama finally named both Becker and Pearce to the NLRB for limited terms ending in December 2011. (Pearce was later confirmed by the Senate to serve longer.[59]) The board's new prolabor majority did finally reverse some bad decisions issued by their predecessors.[60] The NLRB also asked for public comment about possible Internet voting as an alternative to mail ballots or workplace votes. In the meantime, quicker board elections—the "EFCA Lite" substitute for card check embraced by some in Congress and labor—did not become any more common (as California health care workers learned during their interminable waits for SEIU decertification votes).[61]

CWA, SEIU, USWA, and other unions spent between five and ten million dollars on a Democratic primary challenge to Blanche Lincoln in Arkansas, as payback for her EFCA opposition (even though her opponent, Bill Halter, distanced himself from card check too). Although forced into a close run-off vote, Lincoln won the nomination after getting strong support from both Obama and Bill Clinton. The contested race for the Democratic senatorial nomination in Pennsylvania became, according to the state fed president there, "the first primary election in a long time where we've gone all out."[62] Unfortunately, the AFL-CIO, SEIU, and other unions went "all out" for the wrong candidate—Arlen Specter, who didn't just oppose card check, but also "singlehandedly killed the entire bill," in the words of one embittered ex-SEIU staffer.[63] It was left to Democratic primary voters to punish the Republican-turned-Democrat, who lost (46 to 54 percent) to Congressman Joe Sestak. (Both Sestak and Lincoln then lost to Republicans in the general election.)

In late March 2010, President Obama was finally able to use the budget reconciliation process to get his Patient Protection and Affordable Care Act through Congress, while denying the Republican minority in the Senate any filibustering opportunities. Labor reactions were generally favorable. "We did what generations have hoped to do," Andy Stern proudly stated. "We changed our nation and declared healthcare a right."[64] In turn, the Obama administration was glad to acknowledge that Stern "helped shape the strategy that ultimately won passage of the health-care overhaul legislation."[65] In an interview shortly before he stepped down as SEIU president in April 2010, Andy defended whatever tradeoffs were necessary for victory. "Any decent country that wants to have basic opportunity for people has to have a health-care system," he said. "So that's why we've never tried to imagine having Free Choice or anything that we're interested in come before health care."[66]

John Wilhelm, president of UNITE HERE, was less forgiving of SEIU's Obama-oriented prioritizing of labor's top demands. In an angry speech to the AFL-CIO executive council in February 2010, he accused his one-time CTW ally of "providing cover for gutting our key priorities" and being a "willing participant with Democrats who engage in divide and conquer." Said Wilhelm:

> Health care reform was knocked off the rails right from the beginning when Stern bargained deals first with the hospital industry and then helped with Big Pharma. Having thus walled off two of the most profitable players, is it any surprise that the Administration went looking for sources of money to pay for reform and found taxing our member's health plans? And how about card check? Stern gave the OK to strip our card check bill of card check before the rest of us even discussed that.[67]

With both EFCA and even "EFCA Lite" off the table now, Wilhelm was not alone in bemoaning labor's lost political opportunities, circa 2009–10. His NUHW ally, Sal Rosselli, offered a similarly blunt assessment:

> Labor put so much money into electing the Democrats and Barack Obama, and look what the result is. It was a huge opportunity, at our position of greatest strength—theoretically. And we got no labor law

reform and a shitty health care plan. All the dreams we have of establishing a progressive majority and dealing with all the other issues that are important to working people—are never going to be accomplished unless there's a bottom-up movement that forces government to level the playing field, just like the civil rights movement in the '60s.[68]

Another AFL-CIO national union president, long active in the fight for EFCA and health care reform, was less willing to single SEIU out for any special blame or criticize the PPACA so harshly. But he didn't disagree that workers' rights had lost again. "It's the end of labor law reform for another generation," he said.[69] And the problem with that timeline was well noted by Harold Meyerson: "When the next chance to rewrite labor law comes around, the rate of private sector unionization could be down to trace elements."[70]

Chapter 10

Labor Day: The Sequel

"My election was the healing process."
> —New SEIU president Mary Kay Henry in a
> radio interview with Tavis Smiley, May 22, 2010[1]

Andy Stern was always a fan of the blogosphere. So it was quite fitting that news of his departure from SEIU in mid-April 2010, first appeared on several blogs. The most influential and high-profile union leader of his generation bid SEIU members adieu, officially, a few days later (on a YouTube video, of course). By then, the initial unconfirmed reports of Andy's resignation had become major news in the *New York Times, Wall Street Journal, Washington Post,* and other national papers. The ensuing flow of economia and criticism summed up much that was good or bad about Stern's career. The White House saluted his role in shaping "the strategy that ultimately won passage of its health-care overhaul legislation."[2] In appreciation for services already rendered, President Obama appointed Stern to be labor's only representative on his bipartisan Deficit Reduction Commission. Andy pledged to serve as the "voice of ordinary working Americans," although few of them will retire, as he did, with a pension worth more than $200,000 a year.[3]

Stern's "insight, experience, and leadership, particularly his under-standing of how our federal government works" was also much in demand by Dr. Eric Rose, CEO of SIGA Technologies, Inc. SIGA's major stakeholder is billionaire Ron Perlman. Stern and Perlman met when the latter's private equity firm owned AlliedBarton, a security company that negotiated an organizing rights agreement with SEIU. Eager to "complement the skill sets" of his existing board members, Rose made Stern a director of SIGA two months after his resignation from SEIU.[4]

In the mainstream media, Stern's faithful Boswell at the *New York Times*, Steve Greenhouse, penned a tearful farewell that strung together trib-utes from past and present recipients of SEIU largesse (only partially iden-tified as such, of course). Ron Pollock, director of Families USA, the Washington advocacy group that has received large donations from SEIU over the years, praised its "practicality" and "steadfast role" in supporting Obama, saying much of the credit for that "goes to Andy." Howard Dean, whose failed presidential campaign in 2004 drew strong backing from Stern, declared that, even without Andy at the helm, "SEIU will very likely con-tinue to be a change agent for the country and the labor movement." Steve Rosenthal, the political consultant paid half a million dollars to orchestrate pro-SEIU attacks on UNITE HERE, praised Stern's "courage" for stepping down "at the pinnacle of his career," unlike "a lot of people in these jobs." Rosenthal, who shares a beach cottage with Andy in New Jersey and is mar-ried to an SEIU executive board member and top headquarters staffer, ex-plained that his friend didn't "want to be one of the people who stay past their prime." Ben Sachs, a thirty-eight-year-old former SEIU lawyer now teaching at Harvard Law School and serving on the union's Ethics Review Board, told the *Times* that Stern "breathed new life into the labor move-ment, especially for my generation. He gave a new generation of people rea-son to care about unions and to think that they're relevant."[5]

Washington Post columnist Harold Meyerson hailed Stern, for the umpteenth time, as "the leader of liberalism's most effective political or-ganization." Now finding Andy to be a "figure of Dostoyevskian complex-ity" as well, Meyerson argued that he "has done more than any other to build a nationwide progressive infrastructure."[6] Meanwhile, over at the *Nation*, its editor expressed—and not for the first time either—her gushing admiration for Stern's singular charisma, pragmatism, and vision. According to Katrina vanden Heuvel, Andy's "push for dramatic structural change, his openness to remaking labor's traditional ties to the Democratic Party and creating new institutions and alliances for working people, and his urgency, even desperation, about the future of labor" made him a "bold and heretical reformer." Katrina did acknowledge that, on Stern's watch, "SEIU waged bitter battles" within organized labor. One of the nastiest just "turned in SEIU's favor," she informed *Nation* readers (with no further comment on the punitive federal court verdict against NUHW activists).[7]

At *American Prospect*, Tim Fernholz also alluded, in passing, to Stern's penchant for "creating or exacerbating conflicts." But according to Fernholz, this was little more than "a distraction from his broader mission."[8] On his blog, *Nation* contributing editor Marc Cooper defended Andy against any final round of sniping from the left. Stern may have been "abrasive," "divisive," and uncaring about "whether he made a lot of friends—or enemies," Cooper conceded. Nevertheless, the SEIU leader "embodied the best hope for labor's renewal" and was never "a ruthless and power-hungry ego-tripper who ran roughshod over a noble rank-and-file."[9] Over at the *New Republic*, John Judis feared that Stern's departure might be "another step in labor's descent" because so many union leaders who remained in office were just "managing the decline of their membership."[10]

In a long "exit interview" with Ezra Klein at the *Washington Post*, Stern dismissed recent coverage of SEIU-related conflicts as the work of people who "misconstrue what goes on every day" in the labor movement. "Our union's never been stronger," he insisted. "Obviously, there's a long history of unions competing and it's only because we're so big and prominent that there's even any attention on it...I think it's an interesting subject for the press, but it doesn't really occupy a lot of the union's time and the proof is in the results."[11]

Among those commenting most perceptively on Andy's departure were two adversaries not sorry to see him go. John Wilhelm characterized

Stern as a "brilliant man of enormous ability" who, unfortunately, "got captured by the notion that, by being part of the inner circle of discussions in Washington and rubbing shoulders with people with power, he himself was powerful." Said Wilhelm: "I know that I have zero power if I'm disconnected from my members. And that's what happened to Andy—he couldn't have gotten more disconnected. That's the kiss of death."[12] Rosselli observed that "Stern's multi-million dollar fights have diverted resources away from healthcare reform and employee free choice, weakening the former and scuttling the latter. These wars of choice have taken a toll on the union's finances as well as on Stern's credibility." According to Sal, Andy left behind "a workers' organization in disarray, undemocratic, unable to pay its bills, and unwilling to defend its members, with a crisis of leadership from top to bottom."[13]

The Cost of Civil War

One count in the Wilhelm-Rosselli indictment of Stern was simply incontestable: the staggering cost of SEIU-instigated (or perpetuated) conflict. At the time of Stern's resignation, I did my own preliminary tally of the tab Andy left behind. Here are the estimates I came up with, as subsequently revised upward, based on further union spending:

1. SEIU's direct-mail pounding of the much smaller CNA in 2008, and prior staff-intensive "ground campaigns" cost "tens of millions," according to one CNA headquarters source. The mounting financial burden of this conflict, for the nurses' union, was a major factor in its 2009 settlement with SEIU.

2. The ill-fated Andy Stern–Dennis Rivera raid on FMPR, described in the introduction, cost $20 million according to the militant teachers who successfully resisted that onslaught. Their estimate seems a bit on the high side. The teachers themselves spent about $50,000. I believe that because they no longer have the big organizational budget that automatic dues check off from forty thousand members once provided. As vocational school teacher Edgardo Alvelo told me: "Our

money was very hard to obtain, but it was enough to win. It was our people in the schools who did the job."

3. Laying the groundwork for the "Mother of All Trusteeships" over UHW cost SEIU at least $10 million in 2008 alone. As noted in chapter 6, these costs included pretrusteeship litigation, opinion polls, robo-calling, repeated mailings to 150,000 UHW members, relocating scores of national staffers to California, employing Ray Marshall (for $200,000), and hiring corporate security firms that billed SEIU for several million dollars' worth of work. The union's California hotel bill alone during 2008–09 was $2.5 million—a fivefold increase over what it spent on temporary staff housing in 2007. To resist Stern's takeover, the UHW was forced to spend what former leaders say was about $6 million on membership mobilization and publicity, legal fees, and other organizational expenses.

In *Stronger Together*, Don Stillman claims the real number is almost twice that, since UHW spending "against SEIU" on lawyers and PR alone amounted to more than $4.2 million.[14] Whatever the actual amount, this was money that the embattled members and elected leaders of UHW would have much preferred to spend on new organizing, contract campaigns, and political action, instead of institutional self-defense. Their successors at UHW spent little time on organizing the unorganized. Between February 2009 and late August 2010, the trusteeship staff didn't have a single representation election victory at a nonunion health care facility.[15] (During the same period, NUHW organized more than twice as many nonunion workers.)

4. As previously noted, total campaign spending—including salary, transportation, housing, and per diem costs for the nine hundred full-time and part-time SEIU organizers from around the country sent to Fresno, California, for a single home-care workers' election—was about $10 million.

5. In 2009, the overall cost of the UHW trusteeship grew far beyond any initial SEIU projections, as workers resisted the takeover by forming

a new union. The four high-priced law firms involved in winning the monetary judgment against the "NUHW 16" billed SEIU $9.8 million in 2009 alone, helping to drive the union's overall legal expenses up 64 percent over the previous year. And that was, of course, before the case went to trial in March 2010 and got really expensive. (On the day of final arguments, all the SEIU lawyers involved showed up in court at the same time, and they numbered nearly twenty.) SEIU efforts to block or delay NLRB representation votes sought by NUHW created thousands of additional billable hours for their firms and others. Prior to trusteeship, the once flourishing and financially healthy UHW, sent about $20 million a year in per capita dues to SEIU in Washington. After twelve months of trusteeship, UHW was $6 million in arrears on such payments—adding yet another SEIU local to the long list with a mounting per capita dues debt to the international. At the time of Stern's departure, much of SEIU's $188 million in assets consisted of IOUs from cash-strapped local affiliates. Its own national union debt was then about $121 million, leaving it far more in hock than most other unions.[16]

6.   SEIU's disastrous meddling in UNITE HERE was not a boon to any-one's balance sheet. By the spring of 2010, Andy Stern's intervention was responsible for about $40 million in divorce-related disbursements. This total includes the $16 million improperly transferred by Bruce Raynor to internal organizational allies while he was still president of UNITE HERE with a fiduciary duty to all its members—but already plotting with SEIU to defect with as many as he could bring with him. The resulting schism led to millions more being spent on legal fees, security expenses, and costly competitive organizing campaigns. In those battles for bargaining rights, a union one-tenth the size of SEIU emerged as the winner on the ground. While WU/SEIU claimed, at its founding, to have 150,000 members, the actual number was well under 100,000 by mid-2010. In 2009, its rocky first year, WU was able to send only $10 million in per capita dues to SEIU, while spending $19 million. SEIU had to make up the difference via millions

in dues rebates, salary reimbursements, and a big loan. The high price SEIU ultimately paid to settle the dispute, in July 2010, was "not as costly as an ongoing conflict," according to its new president.[17]

7. Before SEIU finally sued for peace under Mary Kay Henry, John Wilhelm's side was forced to keep many high-priced lawyers very busy. In 2009 alone, UNITE HERE spent $6.5 million on legal expenses, and the meter was still running when the sprawling Amalgamated Bank litigation ensnared Elvis Mendez and others. Wilhelm estimated that the total tab, for that case and other divorce-related legal disputes, could reach $12 million—money he would have much rather spent on the fight against the Hyatt Hotel chain or any other anti-union employer.[18]

8. SEIU's unresolved conflict with NUHW was even more costly, although the incumbent union far outspent its new rival. During all of 2009, NUHW operated on less than $3.5 million. This money was raised through individual dues and contributions, grants, and loans (mainly $2 million from CNA and $1.3 million from various UNITE HERE entities). The big-ticket item facing both SEIU and the NUHW in 2010 was the series of NLRB elections held at Kaiser, in various bargaining units. During the first half of the year, UNITE HERE continued to aid NUHW efforts by loaning organizers, providing office space, and donating additional money so NUHW could hire more help of its own.

    The contest to replace SEIU as the largest union at Kaiser (described further below and in the conclusion) made the $10 million fight over Fresno home care providers look low-budget in comparison. For the mail ballot vote that ended in October 2010 SEIU spent heavily on phone-banking, robo-calling, expensive mailings, advertising, and full-time staff flown in from all over the country. NUHW estimated that SEIU's campaign cost $25 to $40 million. SEIU's new president told the *Wall Street Journal* that the $40 million figure was "nowhere near the ballpark." UHW trustee Dave Regan claimed that only $4 to $5 million was budgeted to beat NUHW, an estimate that few observers credited. *Labor Notes* called it "the most expensive union election ever held." In his *BeyondChron* blog, Randy Shaw likened SEIU's per-capita spending at Kaiser—which ranged from an estimated $455 to $910 per voter—to ex-eBay CEO Meg Whitman's attempt to use her personal fortune to buy the governor's office. *In These Times* reported that NUHW spent "less than $2 million at Kaiser."[19]

Totaling up all the above, while the meter was still running, was like tracking the real cost of America's wars in Afghanistan and Iraq. The bills for SEIU's multiple interventions just kept piling up from one budget year to the next, despite a truce here, a rumored settlement there, a possible de-escalation of conflict somewhere else. Contrary to Stern's upbeat "state of the union" report at the time of his departure, SEIU membership growth in 2009 had clearly slowed. After gaining 300,000 new members between 2006 and 2008, SEIU sent an LM-2 report to the U.S. DOL in March 2010 that showed only 50,000 workers joining the union during the first year of Obama's administration, for a total of 1,857,136. (In his farewell video, Andy boasted that SEIU was now "2.2 million strong," just a month after he signed the DOL filing which reported 342,864 fewer actual dues payers; for PR purposes, he preferred to count agency fee payers and workers, in right-to-work states, not paying any money to the union as "members," too.)[20]

SEIU was definitely not on track to add a half million more members between its 2008 and 2012 conventions, the goal proclaimed in Puerto Rico. And, the "deep cuts in organizing staff"—required both by the union's deficit spending on the 2008 election and subsequent cost overruns in battles with NUHW and UNITE HERE—certainly left it with less national union organizing capacity than before.[21] "SEIU—once the fastest growing union in the United States—has hit a wall," contends Fred Ross, its former strategist at Santa Rosa Memorial. According to Ross, SEIU "has abandoned organizing campaigns at five major health systems around the country, after spending millions of dollars, leaving pro-union activists vulnerable to management retaliation."[22]

In all the effusive tributes to Stern, no one mentioned how many millions he squandered on "progressive" union mayhem. Instead, he was lauded for the $85 million that SEIU poured into the election of Obama and other Democrats, pursuant to its San Juan convention plan to transform American politics. Even when combined with the $10 million allocated for a postelection lobbying campaign (known as "Change That Works"), SEIU's total political spending in 2008 was much less than the total tab for labor's civil wars, circa 2008–10. I estimate that amount to be about $140 million, which is why the *Washington Post*, upon his retirement, correctly highlighted Stern's "mixed legacy." In an interview with the paper, even Andy agreed that these expenditures were "a tragedy." But then, echoing George W. Bush, he justified the overall cost based on the seriousness of the threat posed by SEIU dissenters. In America, Stern said, "there is not enough money you can spend…to protect us from terrorists. As you know, sometimes you have to spend money to protect the integrity of the institution from its own version of self-righteousness and terrorism."[23]

A Struggle for Succession

In his farewell video, Andy wanted to assuage any popular grief over his sudden departure. So he quoted from a favorite Dr. Seuss story he often read to his children. "Don't cry because it's over," he advised SEIU members. "Smile because it happened." In the top ranks of the union, little time was wasted on tears. Like the mischievous Cat in the Hat, four SEIU executive vice presidents immediately launched a campaign against Stern's proposed successor—Anna Burger, his close associate for four decades. Eliseo Medina, Dave Regan, Gerry Hudson, and Tom Woodruff favored their fifty-two-year-old colleague, Mary Kay Henry, who proved to be "a pretty slick dudette" (as one friend called her) in her unexpected bid for office.[24]

Burger's frantic attempt, in April 2010, to get a majority of the seventy-four IEB members on her side was backed by Dennis Rivera, who appealed, unsuccessfully, for "leadership unity." By this, Rivera meant that Henry should bide her time and take the secretary-treasurer job instead while Burger served out the two years remaining in Stern's term. But even Rivera's old local, the one-time 1199 now known as United Healthcare Workers East, endorsed Henry, leaving Burger with supporters like Tom Balanoff, Mitch

Ackerman, Javier Morillo, and the embattled Bruce Raynor.[25] The whole process of replacing Stern was about as transparent as the College of Cardinals' method of picking a new pope in Rome. Instead of waiting for color-coded smoke signals from the Vatican, SEIU-watchers were reduced to deciphering messages, from one side or the other, as they got posted on the Internet. The gang of four EVPs who favored Henry took a different—and, as it turned out, more effective—tack when courting their board colleagues. Their public letter of support acknowledged growing internal concern about SEIU's loss of focus on real organizing (as opposed to poaching members from other unions) and its alienation of past labor-community supporters around the country. It read in part: "Many of you have expressed the need to return to organizing as our top priority…We've also heard many of you say it's time to restore our relationships with the rest of the union movement and our progressive allies."[26]

All four signers bore considerable responsibility for the SEIU misadventures, recounted in this book, that disrupted and diverted resources from real organizing, while alienating union supporters. Nevertheless, their letter implied that Henry was more likely than Burger to undertake a discreet "rectification campaign" that would be familiar to anyone living in a one-party state. There, just as in SEIU, the "party line" can suddenly change, but without any acknowledgment that the top leadership (or, at least, anyone still part of it) ever made a political mistake in need of correction.

Henry's initial plaudits in the press were similarly disconnected from reality. In the *New York Times*, she was hailed as "someone fresh and new." In fact Mary Kay is a prototypical product of the SEIU managerial class recruited and installed by Stern or his predecessor John Sweeney without the benefit, in her case, of ever having been a working member of SEIU, a shop steward, or an elected local officer of any kind. The headline on the same *Times* story referred to Henry as the "Grassroots Choice." In fact, her brief palace coup of a presidential campaign was about as far from the grassroots as skyboxes are from the field in any big league stadium.[27] David Moberg reported, with greater accuracy, that Mary Kay was "more collegial and solicitous of others' opinions" than the "stiff and arrogant" Anna

Burger. This led him to hope that, in "troubled times" when "SEIU is facing a growing number of difficulties," Henry might be "a soothing leader."[28] Over at the AFL-CIO, Rich Trumka, ever hopeful of reconciliation, pronounced Henry to be a "quality leader." He invited SEIU and other CTW unions to follow UNITE HERE back into the AFL-CIO fold—a path that Henry, once in office, quickly spurned.[29]

Lacking enough support to win, Anna Burger withdrew from the race several weeks before the scheduled vote. She insisted there had been no "rejection of the Stern-Burger agenda." Announcing her decision to stay on as secretary-treasurer, Burger explained that: "We women have a special knack for putting our egos aside and keeping our eye on the bigger picture and the common good."[30] On May 8, 2010, the IEB met and chose Mary Kay by acclamation. "Today's meeting was much more participatory and inclusive," one vice president reported afterward. "Mary Kay has a very inclusive style, which excites people at a lot of different levels in the union," agreed Bruce Raynor. "More people will be involved in our decision-making," a third leader predicted. "Mary Kay ran and won on that."[31]

Henry concluded the session with a special "blessing" of all SEIU leaders, members, and staff. "Grant us the gift to listen to each other with mutual respect, and when we disagree, to do so respectfully," she intoned. "Grant us the strength and wisdom to bridge the divides and heal the wounds that have separated us within SEIU and with other unions. May we reach across the chasm and recover that which unifies us and makes us strong."[32] In a postelection interview, Los Angeles talk show host Tavis Smiley pressed Henry on how she was going to "heal the rifts" created by "the bloody legal battle with former SEIU members who have now formed an independent union." "My election *was* the healing process," she regally informed him.[33]

SEIU's new "president emeritus" pronounced himself satisfied that both contenders for his job—and his largely handpicked IEB—were all going to pull together and "build on what's happened here in SEIU, not tear it down and change it."[34] Henry and Burger didn't put their egos aside for too long. In August of 2010, Burger announced she was leaving SEIU and CTW. In the case of the latter, she departed just a few days before the Laborers did; with the Carpenters, UNITE HERE, and now the Laborers gone, Andy and Anna's five-year-old labor federation was left with only four affiliates—SEIU itself, UFCW, the Teamsters, and tiny UFW. In her own farewell video, Burger looked tired and subdued. There was no clever invocation of Dr. Seuss. Anna announced that she would be acting as a paid "consultant" to SEIU for the next several years, while working with its "progressive partners." She assured members that they will see her "in the streets, turning up the heat."[35]

Healing Together at Kaiser?

Among many Kaiser workers in California, the distant passing of the torch at SEIU headquarters definitely had the feel of continuity, not change. And that's because Mary Kay Henry was widely remembered—and not fondly—for her high-profile role in the seizure of UHW in January 2009. In SEIU press releases about her election, Henry was hailed as a key figure in the formation of the national labor-management partnership at Kaiser Permanente. Yet, when Henry visited Kaiser workplaces in the early months of the UHW trusteeship, her warm and fuzzy "partnership" style was nowhere to be found. In fact, among rank and filers critical of SEIU, she and her fellow headquarters "warriors" displayed little interest in "debate about the future direction of our union."[36] When Henry and other SEIU officials took over UHW, they immediately began purging hundreds of stewards opposed to the trusteeship in hospitals, nursing homes, and other clinics throughout California.

At Kaiser's Walnut Creek Medical Center, Lover Joyce, an African American medical assistant, was removed as an elected UHW steward because he, like many others, balked at signing the new "loyalty oath" required by SEIU. At a meeting of SEIU dissidents in Detroit the year before, Lover had explained why it was better for workers to have an elected steward than an appointed one: "When you have people who are appointed to things, their loyalty isn't to the membership, it's to the people who appointed them." In response to his removal, other Walnut Creek stewards called an emergency meeting and passed a resolution refusing to recognize SEIU's dismissal of Lover and another coworker. When Mary Kay Henry and SEIU staffer Angela Hewitt showed up for the next monthly meeting of the stewards' council in March 2009, Lover came into the hospital on his day off so he could participate as well. He was told he couldn't and the Walnut Creek Police Department was called for backup. As *Perez Stern* reported at the time: "Fortunately, the police had a far better understanding of union democracy than Mary Kay or her assistant. After hearing what happened, the police told the SEIU staffers: 'We can't arrest this guy. He works here at the hospital. And he's a union member. How can we arrest him for coming to a union meeting?'"[37]

In other similar confrontations, Kaiser steward council members in Modesto and Manteca challenged Stern's newly appointed Kaiser Division coordinator, Greg Maron. At a March 2009 meeting in Manteca, Maron stormed out after telling the worker representatives that their council meetings were "suspended until further notice." In Modesto, he announced that, henceforth, all steward council meetings would be planned by newly assigned staff representatives at each facility and the trustees would have time allocated on each agenda. On March 17 in Oakland when the trustees convened a statewide meeting of Kaiser stewards to discuss upcoming bargaining about pension issues, some of the hospital workers who had traveled two or three hours by car to attend were prevented from entering their own recently seized union hall. While private security guards barred the door, the stewards already inside confronted Maron and out-of-state SEIU staffer Mary Grillo about the lockout of their coworkers. Cotrustee and SEIU EVP Dave Regan was called in, from elsewhere in the building, to quell the rebellion, but his stonewalling only led to insistent group chanting: "Let them in! Let them in!" The SEIU officials' next move was the same as in Walnut Creek: they called the police on their own members. As *Perez Stern* reported, "Soon there were seven squad cars and a dozen cops from the Oakland Police Department, armed with guns and tasers, in front of the union hall, along with one of SEIU's hired security consultants, walkie-talkie in hand, consulting with the OPD sergeant."[38]

In Stockton, Kaiser's collusion with SEIU in the harassment of NUHW supporters became so severe that more than a hundred workers held a protest picket in late May 2009. "We used to take pride in the labor-management partnership between Kaiser and the union, but that has gone away," said Tamika Edwards, a nine-year Kaiser employee, upset about the lack of management neutrality in the dispute between the two unions. NUHW activist Jeff Taylor told the *Stockton Record* that conditions in the facility had become "very chaotic. Kaiser is mistreating its workers and favoring SEIU because SEIU won't fight for better wages and worker rights. We just want Kaiser to back off and let us organize. They should not be breathing down our backs."[39] Inside the hospital, at the same time, the new SEIU rep, assigned by the UHW trustees, was busy tearing NUHW flyers off employee bulletin boards, urging the human resources department to "get members under control," and sending a gift basket to the hospital security director as a token of her appreciation for his cooperation with the incumbent union.[40]

Kaiser Stewards versus the Staff

In SEIU's largest private sector bargaining unit in California, the interunion battle for the hearts and minds of Kaiser workers felt like David versus Goliath. In the first round of voting by Kaiser workers trying to switch unions, NUHW beat the giant by a decisive margin. In three separate Southern California units, a total of 1,652 workers voted for the new union in January 2010, while only 254 chose to stay with SEIU.[41] Among those taking sides—opposite ones this time—were two backers of SEIU's failed attempt to organize RNs at the MMC ten years earlier, the campaign recounted in chapter 2. Martha Baker, president of Local 1991 in Miami, loyally urged Kaiser Sunset Medical Center nurses to stick with SEIU, while her journalist friend from Boston, Suzanne Gordon, recommended that they choose NUHW.

For Paul Krehbiel, aiding SEIU decertification activity was a labor of love. As a staffer for SEIU, sixty-two-year-old Krehbiel actively encouraged steward activity within Local 660 in Los Angeles. When 660 became part of Local 721 and Annelle Grajeda was named interim president, Paul got the axe, along with nineteen other field reps. Now he was working for NUHW. He attributed the new union's staying power, despite its lack of resources and official status at Kaiser, to just the kind of autonomous workplace structures that Grajeda, Henry, and other SEIU officials care little about. As Krehbiel observed:

> After Stern put UHW into trusteeship and removed the elected officers and board members and later hundreds of Kaiser stewards, most of the old steward networks continued to function, even without recognition by the employer, as NUHW stewards councils at the worksites. These unofficial bodies—some were called organizing committees—conducted NUHW's campaign among their coworkers. Because these worksite leaders were known, trusted and elected by the other workers prior to the trusteeship, they continued to have their support. That was key to winning, and winning by such a large margin.[42]

Prior to the initial Kaiser decertification votes among Southern California nurses and other professionals in January 2010, there were already "pitched battles over getting access to workers, with SEIU and KP managers teaming up to keep NUHW out," Krehbiel reported. Where NUHW lacked an active rank-and-file presence, the workplace access that SEIU commanded, as the legally recognized bargaining agent, was a huge advantage. SEIU tried to win with negative campaigning built around the message that switching unions would result in a loss of pay and benefits plus exclusion from the larger coalition of Kaiser labor organizations. Krehbiel's main job as an outside organizer was to get accurate information "into the hands of stewards and organizing committee members so they could counter these charges by talking to their coworkers, on the job, and keeping their support." Where NUHW had well-informed, experienced workplace supporters, they were the "key to stopping SEIU's intimidation and scare tactics."

Marshall Ganz's *Why David Sometimes Wins* describes a different California union battle that occurred nearly forty years ago. Yet it offers additional insight into the underdog strengths of NUHW. Ganz describes how the United Farm Workers defeated a much bigger, better funded, and more employer-friendly foe, the International Brotherhood of Teamsters, because, in its heyday, the UFW had superior "strategic capacity." After a

series of bloody battles, UFW bested the IBT in the fields "because the motivation of its leaders was greater than that of their rivals; they had better
access to salient knowledge; and their deliberations became venues for
learning." According to Ganz:

> The greater an organization's strategic capacity, the more informed, cre-
> ative, and responsive its strategic choices can be and the better able it is
> to take advantage of moments of unique opportunity to reconfigure it-
> self for effective action. [Strategic] capacity is a function of who its lead-
> ers are—their identities, networks, and tactical experiences—and how
> they structure their interactions with each other and their environment
> with respect to resource flows, accountability, and deliberation.[43]

This is, in fact, a very good description of how NUHW organizers, with
their longstanding workplace connections and credibility, and a far greater
willingness to interact creatively and productively with rank-and-file members, were initially able to counter SEIU's huge advantage in money, man-
power, and trusteeship-created incumbent union status.

Unlike the posttrusteeship UHW—with its cumbersome crew of appointed staffers and dysfunctional culture of political conformity—
NUHW cadre have far "better access to salient knowledge" about the
contested terrain in California health care. Prior to the trusteeship, Richard
Flacks, a now-retired University of California sociology professor, met with
a group of UHW rank and filers, and some of their labor and community
supporters, in Berkeley. Flacks had been invited to this campus gathering
because he was among the intellectuals who urged Andy Stern to refrain
from putting UHW under trusteeship. After the exchange, he identified
what he believed was a major weakness of "top-down organization," as per-
sonified by SEIU. To Flacks, the SEIU "model is not just morally problematic (on the grounds that democracy is better than oligarchy)," it is also
"likely to fail from a practical point of view since it prevents top leadership
from having the local knowledge and close-up experience needed for making both internal decisions and external political strategy."[44]

In contrast, even with its own internal flaws and megalocal sprawl,
the pretrusteeship UHW "did a good job of building a healthy and vibrant

union," Krehbiel contends. UHW leaders "dealt with members' problems and issues effectively—including negotiating very good contracts; they involved members in a meaningful and empowering way in the work and life of the union; and they built an internal union structure—based on stewards at the worksite level—that gave the union a permanent presence on the job as a democratic, member-driven union."[45]

Help from a Management Partner

In the summer of 2010, confronted with this still formidable legacy of shopfloor organization, SEIU began to lean more heavily on its partnership with Kaiser. When Southern California Kaiser workers were on the verge of switching unions, the SEIU-dominated Kaiser union coalition announced that NUHW would not be permitted to join the Labor-Management Partnership—just as the Alameda call center workers who voted for CWA were once excluded. When that threat failed, there was a noticeable increase in Kaiser unfair labor practice activity, which benefited SEIU. Most significantly, KP management punished the 2,300 nurses and other professionals who ditched SEIU in January by denying them a scheduled 2 percent wage increase in April—a version of the dark scenario envisioned by SEIU's favorite law professor, Fred Feinstein. Even the slow-acting NLRB contradicted SEIU's claim that everything in the old contract became "null and void" with the union switch. The board's regional director in Los Angeles issued a complaint against the HMO. It accused Kaiser of failing to maintain the terms and conditions of its existing contract while NUHW negotiated a new one.

In some facilities, KP managers or security guards even interfered with distribution of NUHW literature. They tried to evict eighty-year-old Dolores Huerta from several hospital cafeterias open to the public when her lunchtime meetings with pro-NUHW workers were disrupted by groups of chanting, yelling, and table-pounding SEIU staffers. In Kaiser-Modesto, one SEIU supporter told the UFW founder that she should "go back to the fields," while hospital security hovered in the background. During Huerta's visit to Kaiser Baldwin Park Medical Center, SEIU organizer Tiffany Ford threatened to kill two NUHW supporters and pushed a third. A Los Angeles Superior Court judge issued a restraining order against Ford. The NLRB forced Kaiser to post a notice promising not to discriminate against employees advocating for NUHW on their own time in nonwork areas.[46] So much SEIU campaigning was being done on Kaiser-paid time—by employees involved in labor-management partnering—that nine workers finally sought an injunction against this unlawful management assistance to the incumbent union.[47]

After the belligerent behavior of Angela Hewitt, Mary Kay Henry's companion at Walnut Creek, was captured in a video posted on YouTube, Huerta called a press conference to denounce SEIU's "workplace campaign of intimidation and bullying and trying to scare people." (In a strategy memo, Hewitt urged SEIU supporters to "create WWIII inside Kaiser Hospitals" so NUHW would "know that they have no right to be here, and this is UHW territory."[48]) Huerta sent an open letter, addressed to "Sister Henry" that likened SEIU misconduct to the Teamsters' use of violence and intimidation against UFW members in the seventies. "Today, it is your staff and appointed local leaders who are responsible...Will you use your authority as president to put a stop to these tactics?"[49] Henry did not respond.

NUHW's workplace-based approach required hundreds of volunteers to supplement its own skeletal, low-paid staff, plus organizers on loan from UNITE HERE. Danielle Estrada, a patient coder at Kaiser Baldwin Hills, took her own time off—a whole vacation week—to help circulate NLRB election petitions. She visited almost every Kaiser facility in Southern California. "It's not been done by magic," she said. "It's been members on committees, members going out, recruiting, going from department to department, shift to shift, member to member. I took that week because we have to talk to the workers, every one of them, one by one. How can we not do this? Consider the alternative, stuck with SEIU. And the prize— a union of our own!"[50]

SEIU also tried to squelch decertification activity by negotiating a tentative deal with Kaiser on a new three-year contract—four months before the old contract expired. This wage settlement was reached after just four bargaining sessions that included no negotiating about local issues (of the type UHW had conducted in the past to address workplace problems). Ignoring the existence of an obvious internal rift, UHW trusteeship staffers proclaimed, in a press release, that "unprecedented unity" had enabled them to win 3 percent across-the-board annual pay increases with "no takeaways."[51] They then orchestrated a quick ratification vote, which favored the agreement by a 94 percent margin—20,118 to 1,219.

To NUHW supporters, the trustee-negotiated contract only bolstered their case for a new union that would return to the bargaining table and do better. They viewed it as the latest in a series of contract setbacks at Kaiser that began when SEIU seized UHW. "Kaiser is truly in bed with SEIU," said ousted UHW leader Ralph Cornejo. "Relationships that our stewards had built with the administration ended from one day to the next, when the trusteeship was imposed. Kaiser felt they could do just about anything, and get away with it." Even though KP had profits of $2.1 billion in 2009, management first went after retirement benefits. Replacing the old UHW's open bargaining approach with secret meetings with management, trusteeship staffers approved a 25 percent reduction and phaseout of lump-sum payouts that saved KP $242 million in pension plan costs. There was no debate, discussion, or membership vote on this important midcontract benefit change. Instead, as Lisa Tomasian recalled, "SEIU brought four stewards to meet with Kaiser after the deal was made. They were told to just listen and ask no questions. SEIU appointees claimed that, by including these four people, democracy was served. Meanwhile, our lump sum payout will get smaller and smaller until it's gone as an option altogether in 2012."[52] Next, SEIU contract administrators failed to defend the no-layoff clause in the 2005–10 Kaiser agreement. Again, with no membership vote, UHW trusteeship staff secretly agreed with management to "streamline operations," cutting 1,700 jobs. When this contract change proved to be even more controversial than ditching lump-sum pension payouts, SEIU hurriedly organized informational picketing to pressure Kaiser to find jobs for those no longer protected by the contract's now undermined employment security language.

The 2010 settlement provided the lowest wage increases in fifteen years, despite first quarter Kaiser profits of $600 million. And most ominously for UHW members and others affected by this contract pattern, it included a side agreement obligating the union to support health insurance cost-cutting—a "takeaway" to be determined later by a new "Partnership Committee" composed of experts in medical benefit cost and design but no Kaiser workers. The committee's proposals would not be subject to membership approval. NUHW supporters like Danielle Estrada ignored the UHW-conducted Kaiser ratification vote and focused instead on gathering the (30 percent or more) signatures needed among 44,000 coworkers for the largest NLRB vote since 1941.[53]

Old Enemies Organize Together

Prior to SEIU's new contract, the most vocal past critic of labor-management partnering at Kaiser quietly upheld its end of the political truce negotiated in 2009. In the twenty months after the UHW trusteeship, as NUHW supporters struggled to build a new union seemingly more compatible with its own professed politics, the CNA stayed out of NUHW-SEIU battles. In shared workplaces at Kaiser and other hospital chains, individual RNs who disliked SEIU often went out of their way to aid NUHW organizing. But the CNA leadership and staff kept their eye on the prize of organizational expansion elsewhere. Their self-proclaimed "RN Super Union"—the CNA-dominated NNU—now boasted a combined multistate membership of one hundred fifty-five thousand. RN organizations affiliated with NNU in Pennsylvania and Minnesota were conducting high-profile strikes around CNA's signature issue, nurse-patient staffing ratios.[54]

On the organizing front, CNA and SEIU organizers were working side by side in nonunion hospitals run by Hospital Corporation of America (HCA) in Texas, Kansas, and Florida. The initial success of this HCA drive showed that private sector worker recruitment was still possible—even in an EFCA-less world—if union pressure on an employer could produce more optimal conditions for an NLRB vote. The SEIU-CNA Election Procedure Agreement (EPA) negotiated with HCA in 2009 was the product of leverage campaigning. Strategic union interventions hampered HCA financing and expansion plans to such a degree that management was persuaded to crack the door open for further unionization, outside of California—but at times and places of its own choosing. The two unions agreed with HCA on a list of five hospitals in Texas, thirteen in Florida, and one in Kansas City where they would have windows of opportunity in 2010–11 to sign up RNs and other hospital staffers so election petitions could be filed in their respective proposed bargaining units. The workplace access granted under the EPA to CNA and SEIU could only be used "in a positive and non-disruptive manner." The unions pledged "not to engage in negative campaigning which disparages management." In turn, HCA agreed that the question of union representation "is one that employees should answer for themselves." Each side was obligated to submit all campaign literature to the other for "pre-screening." The unions will refrain from organizing at any HCA hospitals not on the agreed-upon list until 2014 (unless a third labor organization initiated a campaign, in which case they are permitted to intervene); they also promised to forgo any corporate campaigning against HCA for an even longer period.

Rio Grande Regional in McAllen, Texas, was one of the first HCA hospitals where CNA's National Nurses Organizing Committee achieved a "card majority" among RNs. One of the organizers making a big difference on that campaign was a south Texas native named Marti Garza, who just happened to be an ex-staffer of UHW and a member of the "NUHW 16." Working alongside representatives of the union that had sued him (and won a $36,600 damage award still under appeal) wasn't easy for thirty-five-year-old Garza. So he quit the NNOC-Texas/NNU drive to return to California and aid NUHW at Kaiser, shortly before a labor board election was held at Rio Grande Regional. In May 2010, the nurses there prevailed, defeating "No Union" 172 to 153. By early June, after elections at four other hospitals, the CNA-backed NNOC-Texas won bargaining rights for nearly two thousand nurses in all. (SEIU won fewer elections in the same facilities, and now represents about fourteen hundred workers.)[55]

With typical political flourish, CNA hailed these HCA victories as the realization of "the long-held dream of working people to organize the South," a goal that was, in its view, "central to promoting the growth of unions and the advance of social reforms in the U.S."[56] Both unions had their next big opportunity to organize about two thousand HCA workers each in Florida. [57] Unfortunately, SEIU's Florida campaign got under way more slowly because so many organizers were dispatched to fight NUHW at Kaiser.

Meanwhile, during contract negotiations with HCA back in California, members of UHW and Local 121/RN discovered that SEIU had signed a secret "peace accord" with management. This side deal was never disclosed to workers in existing HCA bargaining units. They never voted on the agreement and some feared it might limit their ability to engage in collective action when their hospital contracts expired. Nurses and others on the HCA bargaining committee demanded a copy from the SEIU staff but were denied access to any details. This stonewalling led to an internal union appeal (as a prelude to possible legal action involving the U.S. DOL). According to attorney Arthur Fox, SEIU was again negotiating "secret, back-room riders which materially altered members' rights under their contracts and operated to waive their fundamental statutory rights," in violation of Section 104 of the Labor Management Reporting and Disclosure Act.[58]

Just as food service workers covered by confidential union-negotiated contract language were left in the dark about what action they could or could not take to win better conditions, HCA workers now had to challenge their own union while bargaining with their employer to get information they were entitled to under federal law. If this situation raised questions about what deals SEIU might cut during first contract negotiations with HCA in Texas, Kansas, or Florida, CNA/NNOC organizers professed to be unconcerned. "SEIU is going to do what SEIU does so we're likely to end up on our own bargaining with HCA," one told me. In an interview with *Labor Notes*, former United Electrical Workers organizing director Ed Bruno, who now works for NNOC/NNU, insisted that a template agreement was not part of the HCA organizing rights deal. "Bargaining will be what it always is, a relationship of power," he said.[59]

However, NNOC/NNU and SEIU did not seem to be equally focused on postelection union-building in their respective HCA units. As *Labor Notes* reported, "although a majority of workers voted the unions in, many are apparently waiting to see what will come of bargaining before they decide whether to join"—which in right-to-work states like Texas and Florida is entirely voluntary.[60] "The neutrality model may produce impressive membership growth, but some organizers question what kind of unions are left behind after quickie campaigns." As one former CNA staffer in Texas warned: "Collective struggle is hard to foment when you cannot critique the boss and paying dues is seen as a way of buying representation and raises, as opposed to building and supporting an organization that can maintain real power in these shops." Karleen George, who is leading NNOC/NNU's first contract negotiations with HCA in Texas, described the organizational challenge in one hospital this way: "We had the beginnings of a committee, but there wasn't a lot of time to test the committee. The fights that strengthen [our] committee didn't happen during the campaign, but in the postelection period."[61]

Back at Kaiser in California, CNA president Deborah Burger's confident 2009 prediction that "we'll all move forward together"—even if CNA stopped supporting NUHW—was definitely not panning out. In fact, many Kaiser nurses believed that SEIU undercut them with the contract negotiated in the summer of 2010. At a meeting with CNA's Kaiser coordinator Jim Ryder in June 2010, RNs argued that SEIU's health care cost-shifting study committee at Kaiser would have a negative impact on their own bargaining in 2011. In a later internal memo, Ryder agreed. With the largest union at Kaiser "already committed to cost containment guarantees," he predicted that CNA faced a major fight "unless other forces successfully intervene to push back against Kaiser's clear plan to implement health care takeaways." Ryder was deliberately vague about what intervening force he was referring to—since NUHW was the only candidate for the job. The CNA official left it up to individual members "to determine

who they want to cover their back in our upcoming bargaining." He urged
them to support NUHW or SEIU, "based upon facts, not me telling nurses
what to do."[62]

The Achilles Heel of Home Care Unionism

If hospital organizing in Texas (and reorganizing in California) was experiencing an uptick in 2010, things weren't going so well for home care
workers anywhere. In Fresno, scene of the costly inter-union slugfest in
2009, the county board of supervisors negotiated with SEIU for a year on
a new contract. Then they voted to implement "a last, best, and final" offer
that would eliminate health benefits for many workers and slash their
hourly rate from $10.25 to $8 an hour, effective July 1, 2010. SEIU was
able to get a temporary restraining order from a federal judge to block the
move.[63] In October 2010, UHW trustees convened a statewide stewards'
meeting in Fresno, so out-of-town union visitors could help stump for
county supervisor candidates more sympathetic to home care. At the same
time, Governor Schwarzenegger was pushing for a new state budget that
would drastically cut funding for In-Home Supportive Services (IHSS)
and curtail state-funded child care throughout California.

Many other states were also limiting home-based care for the aged and
disabled, due to Medicaid spending restraints.[64] Lack of funding for subsidized day care for low-income families was forcing many mothers off work-
fare and back onto welfare, if they qualified, because cash assistance
programs gave them greater access to child care.[65] For thousands of home
care and child care providers, this safety net collapse meant fewer hours,
less benefit coverage, lower pay, or no job at all. In New York, the 1199SEIU
health care trust reduced its total enrollment of home care workers by half.
Starting January 1, 2011, thousands of their children were scheduled to be
dropped from the plan due to "a dramatic shortfall between what employers contributed to the fund and the premiums charged by its insurance
provider."[66] Adding to the general insecurity, the National Right to Work
Committee filed lawsuits in several states, seeking to rescind recently-won
collective bargaining rights.[67]

In April 2010, Labor Notes convened an urgent meeting of home-based worker organizers. Their discussion was supposed to focus on the question posed by Illinois SEIU organizer Matthew Luskin: "How do we avoid building paper tiger unions with a lot of money but no real members, leaders, or activity?"[68] While participants did share ideas about that challenge, they also discussed the right-wing counterattack that could deprive unions of money and members, whether active or not. Despite some newer election victories, like the SEIU-AFSCME win among twelve thousand home care attendants in Missouri, unions faced new legal threats to employer recognition and dues collection. In Michigan, where a new unit of child care providers was created by executive order but not nailed down through follow-up action by the legislature, these arrangements seemed particularly vulnerable.[69] In New Jersey, CWA and AFSCME were able to get the child care unit recognition, originally granted by Governor Jon Corzine, reaffirmed by New Jersey legislators during a "lame duck" session held after Corzine was defeated for reelection. But in 2010, they faced tough bargaining on a second contract for day care providers because New Jersey's new GOP governor was seeking concessions from all state workers. As Eileen Boris and Jennifer Klein noted, the recession, state budget crises, and right-wing legal challenges have exposed

> an Achilles heel of the organizing model established by SEIU and copied by other unions...Deals made at the top are vulnerable. The sector and the work are insecure and unstable, with constant turnover. Workers themselves have to be able to build the union. There has to be a social depth and culture of the union that enables it to live on when workers move in and out, or the political deals fall apart, and that sustains political activism at the state house where the budget and wages take shape.[70]

In Northern California, the unraveling of past home care gains made by the pretrusteeship UHW was particularly frustrating for Sal Rosselli. After the close vote in Fresno, SEIU slammed the door on further home care election challenges in other counties by ramming through quick contract settlements or overwhelming NUHW with staff and money. "We can't do home care organizing now because it's so resource-intensive," Rosselli lamented. "You have to do mail and house calls because there's no worksite. SEIU will spend millions of dollars preventing these workers from having a fair election." Any wage cuts to the level of eight dollars an hour would leave home care workers in Fresno and elsewhere near the minimum wage after SEIU's 2 percent dues were deducted from their checks. (Even NUHW's 1.5 percent formula would be a burden for many.) For Rosselli, the ongoing budgetary threat to all California home care workers was exacerbated by "paper tiger" unionism. Even though SEIU filed a lawsuit, which secured an injunction blocking the state from reducing its contribution to the pay of IHSS workers in 2009, the NUHW leader argued that not enough was being done to mobilize the three hundred thousand caregivers affected, along with their clients and communities. "They are organized top down—there's no movement whatsoever," Rosselli said. "So their numbers might be reduced to half, and the other half will be making minimum wage or slightly over that in some counties. That's the future of SEIU, because of the way they've been organizing."[71]

A Union Divorce Gets Settled

While home care workers struggled to survive and some "free and fair" elections were being won by CNA and SEIU, the UNITE HERE divorce case finally got settled in July 2010. In his cease-fire announcement, John Wilhelm declared simply, "We have won our union back."[72] The consensus of opinion was that UNITE HERE did prevail, while SEIU "wound up paying a pretty high ransom for peace."[73] According to the settlement that ended their costly lawsuit (and averted more deposing of innocents like Elvis Mendez), WU/SEIU got to keep the Amalgamated Bank. UNITE HERE received a twenty-eight-story building in Manhattan worth $85 million and $75 million more in cash and other assets that had been frozen for the duration of the now-ended litigation. The two unions agreed not to compete with each other in hotels and gaming for the next twenty-four years. In food service, UNITE HERE also got the lion's share of the turf; workers in public school, college, and university cafeterias would still have a choice between SEIU and

Wilhelm's union. SEIU was given jurisdiction over hospital food service operations (where NUHW was nipping at its heels in California).[74]

In his public statement, Wilhelm graciously credited Mary Kay Henry "for personally devoting her energy to making this agreement." For the sake of workers and the labor movement, I hope that this is the first step in making SEIU the great union it can be under her leadership," he said. In a memo addressed to the "UNITE HERE Family"—a document clearly not intended for internal distribution alone—Wilhelm's tone was a lot more unforgiving. He recounted how merger problems morphed into a new front in labor's civil wars, with UNITE HERE as a target and the "'labor visionary' Andy Stern directing the attack in order to get our jurisdiction…On the ground every day for nearly two years, the organized power of our members, leaders, staff, and attorneys wrestled our union back in the face of local union office lockouts, physical intimidation, smear tactics, private investigators, a PR blitz by labor's biggest PR machine, and employers delighted to cozy up with our opponents." The end result: "SEIU has withdrawn from the field, Bruce Raynor is no longer a union president, and Andy Stern resigned."[75]

The UNITE HERE president thanked a long list of allies and supporters who "rallied to our cause," including the three hundred professors who backed the appeal to Andy Stern launched at the 2009 LAWCHA conference. Wilhelm noted that one impetus for settlement, on the SEIU side, was the fact that "health care workers in California challenged our opponent in its home base." Just like in Stern's peace talks with CNA a year earlier, Mary Kay Henry sought a provision in the agreement curtailing further contributions to NUHW. "For her, that was the bottom line, clearly," Wilhelm said, even though "the support we provided NUHW pales in comparison to what SEIU brings to the fight."[76] After the settlement, NUHW moved out of several UNITE HERE offices. In the Bay Area, some key operatives for Hotel Employees Local 2 stayed with NUHW, so they could continue "the fight," at Kaiser at least. UNITE HERE and NUHW financial disclosure forms, due at the U.S. DOL in March 2011, were expected to confirm more funding from Wilhelm in 2010—of the sort NUHW already received in 2009.[77] No one in either union would say, even off the record, how much NUHW received in the months before the settlement. "We're just very happy that UNITE HERE beat back SEIU's takeover of them," Sal Rosselli said.[78]

Bruce Raynor was definitely not happy with the deal and reportedly voted against it. The settlement left Raynor with what one UNITE HERE organizer dismissively called a "landlocked union." By that he meant WU/SEIU was destined for further membership decline in the needle trades, with little potential for growth elsewhere. Raynor should have been cheered by the discontinuation of UNITE HERE efforts to seek criminal charges against him. Further investigation of Raynor was recommended by the union's Public Review Board (PRB) just a few months before the settlement. This panel was created after a lengthy federal investigation of HERE labor racketeering, which concluded in the nineties; its mission today is the further elimination of any internal corruption. In early 2010, review board members asked the U.S. Departments of Justice and Labor to investigate whether "Raynor and the union officials who acted with him" violated federal law with their unauthorized $16 million spending spree. The PRB found that Raynor was "engaged in a conspiracy" to "transfer large amounts of inter-national union funds to affiliates loyal to him" to facilitate their secession.[79] One "wrongful payment" cited was $460,000 spent by Raynor on Stern's friend Steve Rosenthal for direct mail and robo-call assaults on local affiliates aligned with Wilhelm. This was, of course, the multimedia blitz described by Yale union activist Andrea van den Heever when she sought the help of labor-oriented academics gathered in Chicago in late May 2009.[80]

In her public comments, Henry welcomed the settlement because "we cannot be spending our time fighting one another over workers who are already represented"—a stance that clearly did not apply to her war with NUHW at Kaiser. In a July 26, 2010, internal memo to SEIU staffers, Mary Kay acknowledged that "significant compromises and sacrifices" were made by "our sisters and brothers in Workers United." She admitted that SEIU board approval of the settlement was not unanimous. ("Some of our leaders agreed; others did not.") By then, even her predecessor was having second thoughts about getting involved with Workers United.[81] In one postretirement interview, Andy Stern likened his ill-fated acquisition to "going into Iraq," thinking "we'll be out in a month," only to wind up still engaged in a war six years later. "Now everybody gets 20-20 hindsight," he noted testily. "I made a decision based on what I thought was going to happen."[82]

The Hard Slog of SEIU Reform

Six months to a year after ousting Stern supporters in their respective locals, the SEIU reformers we met earlier in this book were not sorry they ran for election. But they were struggling with the burdens of union office in a terrible bargaining climate on both coasts. New leaders like Roxanne Sanchez, Sin Yee Poon, and Larry Bradshaw in California Local 1021 and Bruce Boccardy in Massachusetts Local 888 had to deal with multiple budget crises afflicting their public sector members. They also faced lingering rank-and-file resentment over the megalocal problems they inherited and now had to solve. In 888, Boccardy had some success persuading the disenchanted to give SEIU another chance. In three small units, members pursued decertification anyway. His local now tries to keep everyone better informed with regular newsletters, flyers, and an e-bulletin called the *Spark*, which is reaching three thousand members at their personal email addresses. Worker participation in bargaining, organizing, and political action has been actively encouraged and, unlike his aloof and imperious predecessor, Boccardy makes frequent workplace visits—without a staff entourage. He has cut his own salary, empowered the 888 executive board, and invited members and their families to visit the union office. He has also worked hard to repair 888's damaged relations with a wide range of community-based organizations, including Jobs with Justice, the workers' rights coalition abandoned by his predecessor. "Our goal," Boccardy explained, in a message to his members is to "transform [888] into a model for other SEIU locals…We believe that none of our goals and objectives will be realized without a highly active membership."[83]

Despite postelection overtures from Local 1021, a large majority of its fifteen hundred members in Marin County voted to leave SEIU and join

an independent union in May 2010. The original Marin Association of
Public Employees (MAPE) affiliated with SEIU in 1983 and became Local
949. After getting jammed, unhappily, into Northern California's ten-local
creation in 2007, Marin County workers no longer had a nearby union office. According to former steward Christine O'Hanlon from San Rafael,
"the level of service plummeted," while Marin County workers continued
to send more than a million dollars in dues over three years to 1021's new
Stern-appointed officials. When workers had a problem, said Maya Gladstern, an organizer for the revived MAPE, "we were calling someone in
Oakland or Santa Rosa. Then the SEIU had us use a call center in Pasadena.
So you'd be talking to someone who didn't know our contract with the
county." When MAPE started circulating decertification petitions, the old
leadership of 1021, backed by the international union, suddenly became
much more attentive—but only by sending organizers out to knock on
members' doors, which further alienated them from SEIU. In Gladstern's
view, "the people who are now heading 1021 are very nice, good people,"
but their national union was not getting a second chance in Marin.[84]

SEIU then tried to get those same "good people" to divert Local 1021
resources to the war against NUHW. Harry Baker, the convention delegate
who bravely picketed with the FMPR in San Juan, now serves on the 1021
executive board. He took the lead in opposing this new waste of money. He
noted that the previous leadership of 1021 contributed $500,000 to SEIU's
Fresno campaign war chest. "Andy Stern's actions to crush NUHW and strip
hundreds, if not thousands, of UHW stewards of their authority have dis-
graced our union," Baker said. "I am passionately opposed to giving one
dime of our dues or one minute of our organizing department's time to assist UHW." The rest of the executive board agreed, voting 24 to 2 against al-
locating a proposed $2 million to the anti-NUHW campaign at Kaiser.[85]

In Massachusetts, John Templeton's old local dutifully went along
with SEIU headquarters and sent six 509 staffers to California. (As one
SEIU local official in Boston explained, "we are resisting within the box.
If the international union suspects opposition, they will hurt us and we
are not ready yet for that fight.") Templeton went out to California as a

volunteer to work for NUHW at Kaiser. Undeterred by reform setbacks at the 2004 and 2008 SEIU conventions, John was already planning for the next one. In *Union Democracy Review*, he urged concerned SEIU members and locals to contact him about reintroducing Local 509's now six-year-old proposals to curb "politically motivated trusteeships." If adopted at the 2012 convention, these constitutional changes would, Templeton argued, help "restore SEIU's credibility and luster in the eyes of its own members, the union movement, and the nation."[86]

Meanwhile, down in San Diego County, Monty Kroopkin was trying to restore the luster of Local 221 by ousting Sharon-Frances Moore's appointed successor. Thanks to Reform221's successful appeal of the 2009 election results, members of his local got a Labor Department supervised rerun in September 2010. This rerun pitted Monty against Eric Banks, a former SEIU political operative and Moore's chief of staff. As Kroopkin tallied up the whole four-year legacy of appointed leadership—interrupted by six months of an elected president (who then resigned and sued the union)—there was a lot that needed fixing. According to Monty, the local union merger that spawned Local 221:

> resulted in a culture of no accountability; grossly overpaid senior staff; a severe reduction in the amount of information members got about anything; weak to nonexistent enforcement of our contracts; a steady decline in our membership numbers; loss of four bargaining units to decertification and independent unions; loss of agency fee in another bargaining unit (and loss of most of the members there); an internal union trial to expel a leading dissident steward; staff yelling at and threatening stewards and chapter officers; the railroading of an unworkable and unrepresentative constitution and by-laws; executive board members with improper use of closed executive sessions; and suppression of [rank-and-file] members' access to the roster of stewards and chapter officers.[87]

With this record to defend, even Banks ran away from it. In a letter to 221 stewards, his incumbent slate claimed that union staff were "more active and present in our worksites." In addition, members could now contact a Local 221 "advocacy center, here in San Diego, *not a far-away call center*" (emphasis added). The "top-notch representation" provided by union reps answering the phone locally—with overflow calls still going to the Pasadena MRC—was apparently not good enough for many 221 members. Kroopkin doubled his vote from the previous election, losing to Banks 423 to 522. (Only 13 percent of the membership voted, a slightly better turnout than the previous election.) The Reform221 slate did best among San Diego county workers, who elected four of its members to the executive board. DOL oversight helped level the playing field a bit, by enabling the rank-and-file challengers to send campaign literature to sixteen hundred members, via an email list maintained by the local. Banks and his team still had the advantage of full-time officer and staff visibility out in the field. They conducted a flurry of preelection meetings and workplace visits that Kroopkin claimed were not just incidental to "normal union business." In late October 2010, yet another postelection challenge was filed with the U.S. DOL, seeking a third vote because of this alleged "illegal use of unions funds by Banks and his slate."[88]

Dissenters like Monty, who still support SEIU Member Activists for Reform Today, tried to stay in touch, share information, and support each other's local union election activity. But shorn of its pretrusteeship funding from UHW, the SMART network remained small and geographically contained. Its main sympathizers were the successful and (so far) unsuccessful challengers to California megalocalism, with a few rank-and-file contacts widely dispersed in the United States and Canada. Reformers from three California "property services" locals—security guards in Locals 24/7 and 2006, along with janitors in Local 1877—came together in the fall of 2010 to protest the creation of a new statewide forty-thousand-member megalocal called "United Service Workers West" (USWW). "From the standpoint of democracy, the proposed constitution for USWW is a disaster," reported San Francisco security officer Catherine Cox. In 2009, Cox narrowly lost her own bid for the presidency of six-thousand-member Local 24/7 when the Labor Department ordered an earlier election rerun. (Not long afterward, she was fired by her employer, Securitas.[89]) In the usual SEIU fashion, creation of USWW was approved in a pooled vote—dominated, in this case, by thirty-thousand-member Local 1877. As part of the merger deal, the dues of 24/7 members will be raised to 2.3 percent of their pay, an increase previously rejected when they were able to vote on it in their own local.

USWW will, of course, operate under the appointed leadership of former Local 1877 president Mike Garcia until 2013. To gain reelection as head of the Los Angeles–based Justice for Janitors local, Garcia went to great lengths in the past to discourage Latino janitors from challenging his administration. Union staffers helped build support for him and overly restrictive candidate eligibility rules narrowed the field of members able to run. As one former 1877 staffer told me: "Like the home care workers in Local 6434, the majority of 1877 members are spread out over huge geographic areas. In 2006, Garcia and his lieutenant Andrea Dehlendorf, a protégé of Stephen Lerner, made it virtually impossible for a rank-and-file reform movement (the "Allianza") to pose any kind of electoral threat."[90] Garcia was reelected by a margin of more than 2 to 1.

Three years later, a better organized group of Garcia foes tried to run for office, under the banner of "California United Janitors" (CUJ). Not surprisingly, one of their main concerns was "forced implementation of Member Call Centers" and the already emerging plan to "merge all of us into one giant local." Said the CUJ: "We are concerned that this will have a negative impact on our contracts and on our local with regards to member input and participation. As dues paying members, we expect to speak to a representative that visits our facility and works directly with us on filing grievances or other worksite complaints."[91]

CUJ's challenge was thwarted when Local 1877 disqualified thirteen of twenty-three opposition candidates. Allegedly, their membership status was deficient or the janitors who signed their nominating petitions were not eligible to do so. (In contrast, when SEIU staffers, who have never been working members, run for local union office, they quickly get a headquarters waiver of any troublesome rule regarding their membership standing.) Among those excluded from the ballot in 1877 was CUJ activist Oscar Alonzo, who was running against Garcia for the presidency. A fellow "reformista," Jose Escanuela, then president of SEIU Local 2007 at Stanford, was so disgusted by this injustice to janitors that he sent Garcia an e-mail likening the latter's election practices to those in Mexico. Escanuela's widely circulated message lauded the "testicular fortitude" of the rank-and-filers who dared "to stand up and tell everyone that they have something to offer to make their union stronger."[92] He accused Local 1877 of "working endlessly to create an illusion of democracy, while secretly ridiculing and working to quell all those that have opposing views and choose to run for office."[93]

Running for office in their own local (or the demands of office, when they succeeded) left SEIU reformers with little spare time, energy, or money for broader movement building. In addition, some feared retaliation from SEIU headquarters if they aligned themselves openly with SMART. By mid-2010, SMART was more of a listserv than an incipient SEIU version of TDU, the uniquely durable thirty-five-year-old rank-and-file caucus in the IBT. SMART lacked dues paying members, an office, and any full-time organizer. As TDU's experience has shown, all are essential to getting a reform group off the ground nationally.[94]

SMART's low profile wasn't unrelated to its "objective conditions." The traditional strategy of union reform—pursued most vigorously during the seventies and by TDU to this very day—appears to have little chance of success in SEIU, above the local union level. Even there, would-be reformers must win over members who believe, with some basis in fact, that internal challenges are futile in locals with 40,000 or 160,000 or even 350,000 members. In the view of many disgruntled dues payers, the only strategy that makes sense is getting out of SEIU. Yet, as thousands of California health care workers have discovered, changing unions—instead of changing SEIU—is not easy either.

A Purple Parting of Ways with ACORN

In the case of Wade Rathke and his SEIU Local 100, going independent was not a voluntary decision, thanks to the troubles of the community organization he founded, ACORN. As noted in chapter three, a right-wing media campaign to discredit the group reached its peak in 2008–09. As described by John Atlas in his recent ACORN history, this staunch ally of labor for four decades got dropped like a hot potato by its private and public funders.[95] Acting on behalf of SEIU, a longtime financial backer of ACORN, Anna Burger was among these fairweather friends. At a Congressional hearing on September 30, 2009, she reassured a concerned North Carolina Republican that "SEIU has cut all ties to ACORN."[96]

According to Rathke, the news that SEIU was also purging Local 100 came by phone from a union executive board member. There was no prior notice that charter revocation was under consideration, no opportunity for a hearing on the matter, and apparently no way to appeal the decision. At SEIU headquarters, Michelle Ringuette told reporters that Local 100 consisted of an "odd mix of workers," who were no longer a viable entity or, at least, one that SEIU wished to subsidize any further. "Local 100 never fit any strategic model that made sense to the union," she said, airily dismissing a twenty-five-year organizational relationship that had obviously benefited SEIU in the past. Like Local 509 (under John Templeton) and many other dutiful SEIU affiliates, Local 100 had always transferred members, upon request, to other locals—three thousand in all—whenever SEIU headquarters decided that made strategic sense. Ever the organization man, in his own way, Rathke was not the least bit sympathetic when thousands of health care workers resisted a forced transfer out of UHW, triggering a retaliatory trusteeship. "I am crystal clear that UHW president Sal Rosselli brought this all on himself," he declared on his blog in 2009.

Now, his own four thousand remaining dues payers in Louisiana, Arkansas, and Texas were being abandoned like an old house in post-Katrina New Orleans. So Rathke tried to make the best of ending up outside of SEIU, too. He professed to be happy that United Labor Unions Local 100 was back in business, as an independent, considering the alternatives. "These days, I think finally that's a great decision…much preferable to being trusteed or forced into a merger."[97] In an interview with me several months later, he was still calling SEIU "a truly amazing institution" while lamenting the fact that, even on the progressive wing of labor, "nobody's got an organizing program with a vision." He was particularly chagrined by the fate of his Wal-Mart Workers Association (WMWA), a five-year project that, at its peak, signed up a thousand members in thirty-four stores, mainly in Florida, as an experiment in "non-majority" unionism.[98] Initially, this campaign had joint backing from the AFL-CIO, SEIU, and the UFCW. The CTW split led the AFL to drop out, and then tensions developed between UFCW and SEIU over Andy Stern's dealings with Wal-Mart CEO Lee Scott regarding health care reform. The lead organizer for the project, a former TDU activist named Rick Smith, was laid off by SEIU and now works with its public sector members in Florida instead of Wal-Mart workers. Before union and foundation funding dried up, the WMWA's total budget was a pittance compared to the sums spent on any single battle—over existing members, rather than nonunion workers—in labor's subsequent civil wars. The WMWA didn't survive long enough to be a direct casualty of SEIU's resource-squandering. Yet, to Rathke, the collapse of union backing for Wal-Mart worker organizing was collateral damage nevertheless. "You can't organize these things without a united labor movement," he said.[99]

A Puerto Rican Lesson

At a conference in New York City not long after Wade Rathke was booted from SEIU, Rafael Feliciano joined Sal Rosselli and Andrea van den Heever on a panel discussion about the experience of FMPR, NUHW, and UNITE HERE, respectively, in the civil wars of 2008–10. Speaking in English, which wasn't easy for him, the FMPR leader movingly recounted the story of the 2008 strike by forty thousand teachers in Puerto Rico. He reported that their union still lacks a clear legal route to regaining the bargaining rights yanked away by Acevedo Vila, the former governor, in collusion with Dennis Rivera, that wayward native son of Aibonito, Puerto Rico. FMPR has been able to keep its battle-scarred boat afloat, with voluntary contributions from eleven thousand teachers—about a third of those once covered by its now canceled contract, which required everyone to pay dues to the union. Rafi described his own personal history as a socialist and union activist, making an earnest plea for linking labor and community struggles, as the teachers did during their historic contract fight. He talked about FMPR's term limits for officers and the importance of union leaders being paid no more than the members they represent. He argued that FMPR was able to defeat SEIU in the one-choice balloting for a new teachers' union because "a union's militants are more important than money." (In the fall of 2008, they certainly were the key to FMPR's low-budget but successful "Vote No" campaign.[100]) Rafi urged other labor organizations to rely less on staff and more on elected rank-and-file leaders, arguing that real union power could only be developed in the workplace from the bottom up. "Workers," he insisted, "must always be the people who have day-to-day control over their union."[101]

Conclusion

Signs of a New Workers' Movement?

"If there is going to be change, real change, it will have to work its way from the bottom up, from the people themselves. That's how change happens."
—Howard Zinn, in his last interview, *New York Times*, January 2010[1]

The stereotypical union battles of the past were fought by burly working-class heroes, on the picket line and the proverbial "shop floor." Think of the tough-looking guys, wearing scally caps (and wielding baseball bats, when necessary), who marched along San Francisco's waterfront in 1934. Their enemies were many—the longshore bosses and shipping companies, the courts and politicians, a corrupt and management-friendly East Coast union that sought to undercut their walkout and bargain behind their backs. They shut down the port anyway, and others along the West Coast. They rallied fellow workers, briefly triggered a general strike, and ended up breaking away to form a new union, under far greater rank-and-file control. It was the depths of the Great Depression—the kind of economy in which you don't want to take risks, as SEIU warned Kaiser workers in 2010. The founders of the International Longshore and Warehouse Union (ILWU) took risks anyway, along with many casualties. But, in the end, they won a historic victory, making life better for themselves and future generations.

In September 2010, the long-awaited showdown between NUHW and UHW/SEIU was most visible not in the streets, but in Kaiser cafeterias where union members wear hospital scrubs and lab coats or, if they work in the operating room, what looks like a shower cap on their heads. In hundreds of Kaiser facilities across California, purple-clad SEIU loyalists and red standard-bearers of NUHW vied for the hearts and minds of their coworkers. At lunch and on breaks, they gathered around union information tables like members of rival fraternities or sororities competing for new members during rush week. (At Kaiser, the analogy is not that far-fetched since workers often call their place of work "the campus.") Service, maintenance, clerical, and technical employees already "pledged" to one union or the other could be easily identified based on the lanyard around their necks, the buttons and stickers that adorned their various outfits, or what color they were sporting in response to a scheduled day of union T-shirt wearing. Those still sitting on the fence (or concealing their preference) blended in more easily with scores of nonbargaining unit employees, like doctors or administrators, and other union members, such as nurses, who all came together in the same eating and meeting place, along with Kaiser patients and their visitors.

A Purple Pizza Party

In every Kaiser facility I visited during the mail ballot voting period, SEIU and NUHW stalwarts had staked out separate turf at lunchtime, eyeing each other suspiciously. One mid-September day at the big Kaiser Medical Center on Geary Boulevard in San Francisco, there was little intermingling—except when lines formed for the "free" food offered by SEIU. Befitting the high culinary standards of the city, the incumbent union fare was high-end pizza, with thin crust and exotic toppings like pineapple.[2] Boxes of these pricey pies were piled high next to campaign flyers warning workers that, if they voted to switch from SEIU to NUHW, they might lose the contract wage increases recently negotiated by the SEIU trustees who replaced the old leadership of UHW. Not coincidentally, one of those ousted leaders—in fact, the former president of UHW, Sal Rosselli—stood next to the NUHW table, warmly greeting a stream of rank-and-file visitors of every race and nationality. In his familiar goatee, a tan sports jacket, khaki pants, and thick-soled shoes, Sal looked buoyant as always. In a news story about the Kaiser campaign just a few days before, Steven Greenhouse of the *Times* reported that Rosselli was "using brass knuckles on his former colleagues at the Service Employees International Union." The day I dropped by the same hospital as Greenhouse, there was no sign of NUHW coshing or coercion.[3] With a handshake, a hug, or friendly pat on the back, Rosselli urged Kaiser workers to get a piece of SEIU pizza first and then come back to talk. "After all," he said with an impish grin, "your dues money paid for it!"

Among those backing the new union, on her own time, was Julia Tecpa-Molina, a unit clerk in cardiology. A native of El Salvador, Julia came to California in 1989 as a civil war refugee when she was twelve years old. She has worked for Kaiser for eleven years, lives in Richmond in the East Bay, and wanted to be with her coworkers on their big "wear red" day. Her husband urged her to stay home because she was not scheduled to work; she made up a story about having to vote at the hospital, instead of by mail, and headed for the BART train with her two-year-old daughter in tow. At the time of the trusteeship, Tecpa-Molina's hospital had sixteen hundred UHW bargaining unit members. A subsequent "rebalancing" of the statewide workforce (Kaiser jargon for cutting seventeen hundred jobs) has reduced the head count at Kaiser's San Francisco Medical Center by nearly 10 percent, leading to job combinations, speedup, understaffing, and reassignments that would have violated the old contract. "Seniority doesn't count for anything anymore," Julia told me. "SEIU hasn't helped us so we don't believe in them."[4]

Julia's friend Gladys Cortez-Castillo, who sat next to us in the cafeteria, was out on Geary Boulevard leafleting at six in the morning before work. She described how understaffing in the ICU leaves its unit assistants badly overstretched. "We need something better to protect us, the kind of union it was before. With these people, we don't have a chance," she said, casting a contemptuous glance at the SEIU staffers from out of state who were busy serving pizza purchased with money deducted from her paycheck.

Red T-shirt wearers far outnumbered the SEIU crowd on this particular day and at this KP location. The mood was upbeat, in part, because RNs in the hospital had just weighed in with a strong letter on NUHW's behalf. In a message to their fellow CNA members, Donna Goodman, Pamela Fulton, and Pascal Wilburn declared that "we cannot afford to stand on the sidelines...We are asking nurses to wear their CNA red this Friday to show our coworkers that we are standing with them. The leaders of NUHW have a proven track record. For years, the old UHW was a strong member-run union, very much like CNA."[5]

The full-time staffers manning the SEIU table, with a handful of workers at their side, looked a bit tense and beleaguered. A thin, bespectacled, and bearded young UHW rep named Mathew Nicholsen arranged for me to interview Gabriella Padilla, the "contract specialist" for the hospital. She was one of thirty-five workers—off the job full time, at Kaiser expense— who assist the "labor-management partnership." Their alleged NLRB election activity was already the subject of a lawsuit filed by NUHW and would become part of the latter's postelection challenge because soliciting votes for SEIU on company time violated federal law. Padilla insisted that she was only campaigning during her breaks and lunch hour. (NUHW supporters claimed that those lasted all day.) "I want somebody who has power," she explained, citing SEIU's claimed North American membership of 2.2 million. "If NUHW wins, how are they going to get a contract?" She hinted darkly that the rival union was "planning to go on strike," but "they don't want to tell members that because it would turn them off."

Scoundrel Time at Kaiser

The impressive degree of rank-and-file volunteerism involved in the NUHW get-out-the-vote effort stood in sharp contrast to the multimillion dollar "blitz" already under way on the SEIU side. Estimates vary, but probably about a thousand national and local union staffers and "lost-timers" (stewards on leave from their own jobs in other SEIU bargaining units) were flown in from around the country to reinforce the anti-NUHW message delivered by in-house supporters like Padilla. SEIU's out-of-town army stayed in hotels, drove around in rental cars, and worked out of union offices throughout California, making thousands of house visits and phone calls. Many were issued the same Kaiser ID badges that non-employees representing UHW need to gain access to workers in patient care areas. Among the canvassers assigned to visit members at home were laid-off U.S. census workers and others with little or no union background who were hired through a temp agency called TruCorps, which lists former SEIU official Jim Philliou as a "strategic advisor."[6]

Their carefully scripted "talking points" were lifted right from the "Vote No" handbook of anti-union employers.[7] SEIU door-knockers and phone-bankers stressed the same themes as Maine Medical Center managers when they scared nurses into sticking with the status quo ten years before. Kaiser workers were told, over and over again, that change was too risky in a bad economy. "Switching to NUHW Would Wreck Our Future!" one flyer declared. If workers voted the wrong way, they might end up worse off, losing their existing wages and benefits. ("Kaiser employees who switched to NUHW in January lost their 2% raise in April.") Anyone who abandoned SEIU would be "bargaining from zero" with little or no clout. They might even be forced out on strike, putting their jobs in jeopardy.[8] Plus, they would end up paying dues to "corrupt" officials who had already been "convicted" of mishandling workers' dues money.

The most mendacious and despicable of these warnings was the last. SEIU's relentless demonization of the pretrusteeship UHW leaders, who were responsible for past membership growth in California and union gains at Kaiser, required a radical rewriting of their personal biographies. Some of the most dedicated and self-sacrificing organizers in the country were labeled (and libeled as) "crooks," thanks to SEIU's $1.5 million jury verdict in the "NUHW 16" case. At Kaiser Walnut Creek, where Mary Kay Henry once called the police on NUHW supporter Lover Joyce, SEIU organizers were handing out a red flyer the day I was there. It had a mug shot–type photo of former UHW organizing director Glenn Goldstein.

Goldstein has spent the last thirty years helping hospital workers win bargaining rights in dozens of SEIU campaigns, including the six-year struggle at Santa Rosa Memorial. The headline above Glenn's picture declared in sixty-point type that "this person" was "GUILTY" and personally owed $73,850 in damages for "putting our contract and our jobs at risk." At Kaiser in Roseville, thirty-five-year-old Marti Garza, who left the CNA-SEIU campaign at HCA to aid NUHW members once again, came under similar attack. In the fall of 2010, the soft-spoken, neatly groomed, cowboy boot–wearing Texan was earning about $36,000 a year working for the new union—the same amount he owes SEIU as a member of the "NUHW 16." As the main Kaiser election approached, 25 percent of Garza's modest wages were about to be garnisheed for the first time. This is a monthly payroll deduction that will continue until he satisfies his portion of the federal court judgment, posts an expensive bond, or gets the jury verdict against him overturned on appeal. In its anti-NUHW propaganda in Roseville, SEIU turned Garza's civil liability—for courageously helping UHW members resist Andy Stern's trusteeship—into a criminal act, a "theft" of union treasury funds, as one organizer claimed in front of Kaiser workers during a presentation by representatives of both unions. Garza patiently explained his side of the story, pointing out that he was not in jail and was guilty only of "insubordination" to national union directives opposed by the workers who paid his salary. Impressed with his personal sacrifice and commitment to the membership, this particular Kaiser Roseville work group decided collectively to support NUHW.

As some observers of the campaign noted, SEIU fear-mongering was profoundly disempowering.[9] It sought to lower rather than raise worker hopes and expectations by stoking insecurity. In areas of union weakness at Kaiser, it simply reinforced existing (partnership-assisted) tendencies toward workplace passivity and acceptance of management initiatives. In its campaign, NUHW tried to project an ambitious multistep plan for postelection rebuilding of the union, through mobilization of the membership and renegotiation of the three-year contract. The UHW stewards and bargaining committee members who broke its way in the run-up to the vote declared their independence from the trusteeship with gusto.[10]

In contrast, SEIU emphasized that its own recently concluded bargaining with KP required no muss and fuss—so why rock the boat now? UHW staffers and supporters seemed personally and politically averse to any form of activity—even traditional grievance filing—that might challenge management or disrupt the Kaiser LMP. For example, when I asked one recently appointed UHW staff rep, DeJohn Williams, what he intended to do about two custodial workers (both with considerable seniority) who had just been dismissed earlier in the day of my visit to Kaiser in downtown Richmond, he displayed little sense of urgency about their situation, implying that they might have been guilty as charged (of violating a hospital rule related to break time). "It's hard to get fired at Kaiser," he told me, a claim that is clearly no longer true, if it ever was.

At Kaiser in Roseville, environmental services worker Jonathan Welch had recently been dismissed after fifteen years. He was accused of failing to follow new safe needle disposal procedures he had never been properly trained in. While actively supporting NUHW, Welch was trying to get UHW representatives to take his discharge case to arbitration. When I visited the Roseville "campus," all grievance handling seemed to have been put on hold for the duration of the NLRB election campaign. A new steward in the OB/GYN department explained why her coworkers sided with the international union—at the time of the trusteeship and afterwards. "We weren't angry and don't have many issues with management," Danielle Wanger told me. "Mostly, it's the angry people who support NUHW. Those of us who are pretty content are not willing to risk change."[11]

The twenty-three hundred Kaiser nurses and other professionals who did risk change in January 2010 received only belated help from the NLRB. On October 1, with only three days left in the mail ballot voting period for Kaiser's forty-four thousand service and technical workers, the board's regional director in Los Angeles decided that KP's six-month-old violation of the NLRA was sufficiently serious to warrant seeking what's called a "10(j)" injunction. As noted by the union-funded American Rights at

Work (ARAW), the NLRB can seek 10(j) orders "when there is strong evidence that an employer has committed unfair labor practices" and "swift relief" is needed to "mitigate the damage of the employer's actions." Each year, the NLRB seeks only a handful of 10(j) injunctions against the most egregious violators of the NLRA. In this case, getting one would force management to pay NUHW-represented workers more than a million dollars in back pay, while their case against Kaiser was still being litigated and their first contract negotiations continue. Per usual with the NLRB, this uncommon remedy—which requires getting a federal judge to actually issue the injunction—was too little, too late. Previously feted by ARAW itself as a model employer, Kaiser once again worked to undermine any group of employees opting for a union outside its approved club of labor "partners." Taking their lead from SEIU (and reprising their performance when CWA was fighting Kaiser, unsuccessfully, six years earlier), the whole national coalition of Kaiser unions remained silent.[12] And this, along with the NLRB's delay, helped Kaiser get away with unlawful conduct long enough to make a "free and fair" election impossible in its biggest bargaining unit.[13]

Waiting for Lefty or the Democrats?

Around the country, the results of the Kaiser vote count, which began on October 5, 2010, were eagerly awaited by many who had no connection to NUHW or SEIU. How you reacted to the outcome (and, before that, which side you were on) was kind of a Rorschach test of how you felt about labor's civil wars. In the view of many labor insiders, the lingering health care workers' revolt was just an unfortunate hangover from the Stern era. Within the labor officialdom, there was never much sympathy for NUHW, except in the Bay Area and Los Angeles, where it retained some staunch local union allies. As an organizational project, decertifying an incumbent labor organization, whether AFL-affiliated or not, creates a most unwelcome precedent. The NLRB vote at Kaiser may have been the biggest in private industry in nearly seven decades. But it was definitely not an approved form of "employee free choice."

Many friends of labor, understandably, just wanted everyone to get along so a "united labor movement" could concentrate on rescuing endangered Democrats at the polls in November, despite their disappointing performance during Obama's first two years in office. For those weary of internal conflict, SEIU's midsummer settlement with UNITE HERE was a promising sign, just as Rose Ann DeMoro's unexpected truce with Andy Stern brought a collective sigh of relief the year before. With CTW downsizing by the day, and several of its former affiliates returning to the AFL-CIO, "labor unity" seemed possible again. The AFL-CIO had no love for the SEIU leaders who spearheaded the 2005 split, and cost them many millions of dollars in lost per capita dues payments. But the two SEIU ringleaders were gone now (although hard to forget given the press coverage still garnered by Andy Stern, due to FBI probing of higher-level SEIU complicity with the crimes of former Los Angeles SEIU leader Alejandro Stephens).[14] Stern's successor was less divisive and much easier to work with; SEIU and the AFL-CIO even made plans to coordinate their $88 million worth of new political spending on the midterm elections.[15]

One sign of renewed cooperation—as the Democrats' November 2010 wipeout neared—was the mobilization of two hundred thousand workers and their allies in our nation's capital. This widely praised "One Nation" rally on October 2, 2010, drew many participants from CTW and AFL-CIO unions, plus more than four hundred other sponsoring groups. As a response to the right-wing populist threat of the Tea Party, some on the left found the rally's timing to be a little late and its content too tepid. Even union rank and filers less overtly political wondered why those disappointing "friends of labor" elected in 2008—and now threatened with defeat by two, three, many Scott Browns—didn't merit just a hint of public criticism? A month before Election Day, "labor's big threat to punish misbehaving Democrats" had "largely evaporated," as unions tried to stir up member enthusiasm for incumbents denounced not long ago as betrayers of labor's agenda.[16]

CWA president Larry Cohen shared his few minutes on the podium with Barbara Elliott, a union supporter at a Xerox-owned call center on

Staten Island. With CWA help, Elliott and her coworkers had been trying to bargain with their employer for more than two years. Like Kaiser today, Xerox was once widely acclaimed for its union-friendly behavior. The Rochester, New York, company did its own labor-management partnering with a predecessor union of UNITE. But now, listening to Elliott at the rally, one could hear echoes of health care employee complaints in California. At Kaiser, Santa Rosa Memorial and many other places, workers' aspirations for a more effective "voice at work" were thwarted not just by management (acting like Xerox) but a national union allied with their own employers, and a federal agency seemingly incapable of fulfilling its original Wagner Act mission, under any administration, Republican or Democrat.

"We need jobs with justice," Barbara Elliott told the One Nation throng. "We need real organizing rights, not the imaginary rights of the National Labor Relations Act. Along with a majority of my coworkers, I voted 'union' fifteen months ago…The NLRB ruled that the election was conducted fairly, and management's objections had no merit. Management has yet to negotiate with us but has spent huge amounts on lawyers to delay and deny us our rights…Our laws don't protect workers like me. The company controls virtually every aspect of the organizing process."[17]

In its NUHW variant, the similar appeal for workplace fairness in California health care continued to resonate, on the labor left, in the run-up to the Kaiser vote. In 2009–10, hundreds of concerned trade unionists—small donors all—attended NUHW fund-raisers in Massachusetts, New Jersey, Pennsylvania, Vermont, Wisconsin, Minnesota, Oregon, Illinois, Missouri, and Washington State.[18] Despite SEIU consultant JoAnn Mort's warnings about the dangers of "rogue unionism," labor-oriented intellectuals—or at least the "Labor Notes types" among them—continued to identify with the new union cause. In a widely circulated piece for *In These Times*, entitled "SEIU's Civil War," Nelson Lichtenstein and Bill Fletcher declared optimistically that "the ideas contained in the NUHW insurgency are contagious." The attempt by NUHW members to create "a structure of democratic participation is not just a moral imperative," they wrote, "but an organizational weapon that sustains struggle and ensures that the union remains part of a larger movement for social justice."[19] Sociologist Dan Clawson stuck with the new union too. "If democracy and a larger vision are central to unions, NUHW's challenge could be the best news we've had in years," Clawson wrote. "And perhaps—as happened in the 1930s—a battle between unions, combined with the greatest economic crisis in a couple of generations, will again lead to a labor upsurge."[20]

An October Surprise?

The results announced on October 7 did not reflect upsurge so much as steady erosion of NUHW support during the twenty months between Andy Stern's takeover of UHW and the long-stalled vote involving Kaiser workers trying to flee SEIU. When NUHW first circulated election petitions in February 2009, more than twenty-nine thousand KP employees signed up.[21] Their exit was then blocked by the NLRB's subsequent ruling that no vote could be triggered until their five-year contract was almost expired the following year. In June 2010, when that "window period" finally arrived, more than fifteen thousand signed up again—no longer a majority of the service and technical unit, but far more than the 30 percent required to obtain an election. As one SEIU organizing veteran accurately summed up the impact of the intervening delay:

> This decertification election has been on and off too long to allow the challenger to maintain the momentum against the incumbent. In regular organizing, that means the company wins more than two-thirds of the time that the election is over sixty days from the filing. *In this case, the "company" is SEIU.* Its ability to tie up the challenger means that, just on the numbers, before any work was done, if normal odds prevailed, SEIU's chances of winning were at two-thirds.[22] (Emphasis added.)

Four months later, *after* SEIU's "work was done" with Kaiser assistance, NUHW received about four thousand fewer votes than its total number of second-round decertification card or petition signers. The NLRB tally was 18,290 for SEIU, 11,364 for NUHW, and 365 for no union. Explained Roy

Chafee, a call center worker in Vallejo and past UHW board member: "Most people couldn't get past the fear. Unless they saw something from a government agency saying clearly and plainly that you weren't going to lose anything, they weren't going to take any chances."[23] To UHW trustee and SEIU EVP Dave Regan, his union's victory was "a huge achievement." According to Regan, "NUHW is now, for all intents and purposes, irrelevant. We're thrilled."[24] Still preparing to run for president of UHW, when the trusteeship was finally lifted in early 2011, Regan expressed confidence that "we can put this chapter behind us, and not have the union turn into a circus for arcane political arguments among people who ought to know better."[25]

The challenge to SEIU was not about to disappear. But even NUHW partisans were forced to admit that, for the time being, "Goliath has won again."[26] NUHW attorneys filed objections to the election, seeking to have it overturned because "management worked closely and illegally with SEIU to influence the outcome."[27] Not everyone thought a rematch was feasible, even if ordered, because NUHW's resource disadvantage would be even greater in the future.[28] Meanwhile, NUHW organizers quickly rebounded in November 2010 with an encouraging election victory among 1,500 Kaiser mental health professionals and optical workers. With bargaining rights for nearly four thousand Kaiser workers in all, the new union hoped to at least maintain a foothold within California's largest health care employer. Clearly, SEIU foresaw a different outcome. Its press spokesman, Steve Trossman claimed that "NUHW faces member defections and possible decertification by two units of Kaiser professionals" who voted to join NUHW in early 2010.[29] Clearly nothing would make SEIU happier than to see these workers experience the same first contract frustration that led to CWA's ouster from the Alameda call center in 2006. And Kaiser management, with its demonstrated hostility toward NUHW, seemed eager to help history repeat itself.

NUHW also soldiered on where it had already won bargaining rights for about thirty-two hundred non-Kaiser workers. But until new contracts were negotiated for them and more dues-paying members recruited via NLRB votes delayed nearly two years, the new union faced big financial challenges.[30] The eighty-person staff NUHW still boasted during the main Kaiser campaign was not sustainable beyond October 2010. Generous outside funding from UNITE HERE ended with the settlement of its war with SEIU; Hotel Employees Local 2 operatives, who left their own union to assist NUHW during the Kaiser campaign, returned thereafter, and other longtime UHW/NUHW organizers, like Barbara Lewis in Los Angeles, were forced to take jobs elsewhere.[31] Still confident of success "in the long term," Sal Rosselli saw many opportunities for continued shop-floor struggle at Kaiser, even if the organizational form it might take was not immediately clear.[32] There will be "more layoffs," he predicted. "Reorganizing. 'Flexibility' that will disrupt peoples' lives. Every week that goes by, people will see what SEIU is about in terms of lack of representation, lack of accountability, and its deals with managers."

In a postelection interview with Lee Sustar, Sal noted that workers at other hospitals were already suffering from UHW's feeble defense of job security. "In Daughters of Charity Health System, where we hadn't had a layoff in 15 years because of our contract language, SEIU just agreed to over 100 layoffs. And at Salinas Valley—where we won an election by a 2-to-1 margin several months ago, but where SEIU is interfering with certification, so they still represent the folks—they agreed to 160 layoffs. That's who SEIU is."[33]

At Salinas Valley, the 860 licensed vocational nurses, clerks, and nursing assistants threatened with this downsizing had good reason to be mad at both management and SEIU. The hospital reported $14 million in profits in 2009. As thirty-six-year LVN Marilyn Benson said, "These cuts are going to put patients at risk and eliminate dozens of good union jobs at a time when families are hurting from a weak economy." On October 21, 2010, more than one hundred Salinas Valley workers spent their lunch hour doing some spirited, self-organized informational picketing. The union still collecting dues from them—even after being voted out—opposed their protest. A staff person for SEIU, still assigned to the hospital, "scurried around telling workers they would be fired if they joined the picket line."[34]

Lessons of Labor Civil Warfare

Much of the conflict described in this book, culminating most dramatically in the 2010 Kaiser decertification elections, grew out of the once-promising (and still necessary) union strategy of trying to neutralize employer inter-ference with organizing. Union advocacy for the Employee Free Choice Act may have been fatally derailed inside the Beltway during Obama's first year as president (and rendered completely null and void by Democratic losses during the midterm elections). Yet the demand for labor law reform did not just emanate from national union headquarters and their Capitol Hill lobbyists. Labor's EFCA campaign started at the grass roots and grew out of organizing work by model unions like the pretrusteeship UHW. Most of the resulting membership gains required strikes, contract fights, and comprehensive campaigns with the common goal of securing an easier path to bargaining rights than contested NLRB elections. With mandatory "card check" recognition and arbitrator-imposed first contracts as the new legal remedy for union-busting and bad-faith bargaining, respectively, unions hoped they could become less reliant on private organizing deals. Securing management neutrality (which EFCA did not address) would still require considerable labor and community pressure on many employers, but there would be far less need for questionable quid pro quos to win card check procedures or "free and fair elections." With passage of EFCA, union leverage would be strengthened and the temptation to give away the store when "bargaining to organize" (by signing off, in advance, on weak first contracts) would be reduced.

That was, at least, the thinking in 2009 about how the great wave of EFCA-aided organizing was going to sweep the country, with SEIU, UNITE HERE, CNA, CWA, and other unions riding it to new membership heights.[35] The expectation was that everyone would do just swimmingly under the new law, as 1199SEIU was able to do at Caritas hospitals in Mas-sachusetts and CNA-SEIU have been doing outside of California, as a re-sult of their own prior organizing rights campaigning. In these campaigns, election ground rules were negotiated without apparent harm to existing contract standards (although those were hard to find in Texas). Employee free choice was exercised in a way that's usually impossible wherever management conducts a full-blown anti-union campaign in health care or other industries.[36]

Organizing Without EFCA

In the EFCA-less world that confronts unions today, it's back to Plan B. Under the now badly-wounded Obama administration, the NLRB is only slightly less dysfunctional than it was before under George Bush. If large-scale membership recruitment is the goal, the NLRB is still to be avoided. As one AFL-CIO union president grimly observed, "Our ability to extend bargaining rights in the private sector will be determined by workers' willingness to wage major fights against the worst corporate management in the world."[37] As we've seen in this book, lots of workers, already in a union and some just trying to form one, have been willing to fight and stand up for their rights—at Catholic Healthcare West, Tenet, Kaiser, Sutter, Santa Rosa Memorial, and tiny Convalescent Center Mission Street in San Francisco. Outside health care, many have been a collective profile in courage at Hilton and Hyatt hotels, Aramark and Sodexo, and many other companies. In the public sector, home care workers in Fresno and teachers in Puerto Rico both stood up against a multimillion dollar assault that many found astounding, in its cost and scale, because the funding source was their own or fellow workers' dues money.

What animated all these struggles, against formidable odds, was a strong sense of organizational ownership, a willingness to take risks and make sacrifices because the union that workers were trying to build, extend, defend, or reclaim inspired strong allegiance based on relationships of trust and mutual respect. The very same dynamic has fueled SEIU reform campaigns described in this book, where the immediate adversary was not a union-busting boss, but a blundering, bullying local (or national) union bureaucracy that behaved much like a second boss. Workers do not unite and fight—for organizing rights, a first contract, a better contract, or a better functioning and more democratic union—unless they have reason to believe in each other and the leadership that has emerged from their own ranks. Few will go the extra mile for an entity that leaves them feeling personally abused, collectively disempowered, and forced to pay the salaries of people who actively work against their interests, in concert with their employers. Likewise, as John Wilhelm warns, union growth campaigns that bypass affected workers, while bypassing the NLRB, won't succeed in the long run. Tough decisions about what to concede now to become organizationally stronger later must be made by workers themselves, not just full-time officials. Keeping workers in the dark about negotiated agreements that may limit their ability to struggle for future contract improvements adds insult to injury. It's not the way forward in bargaining or organizing, now or ever.

A related observation about membership morale and motivation may seem very small bore, in the era of globalization and at a time when so many of our national unions, not just SEIU, face "big picture" problems. But I think it is relevant also, based on the experience of various union rebuilders we've met in this book. If the shop steward elected in your own workplace can be removed by higher-ups in the same union—like an "employee at will" can be fired by management in any nonunion workplace—you're on the road to more serious organizational malfunctioning. There are always people who, for one reason or another, will go along with such an exercise of union authority or explain why it's necessary to achieve "justice for all." But they are not to be trusted calling the shots in national or local contract bargaining, labor-based political action, or contract enforcement in a single workplace (where that task doesn't get any easier with unelected shop stewards). The idea that we can have an effective labor movement resting on a base of disgruntled, disengaged, and call center–serviced workers who can't even choose their own shop steward (or, in the case of many home-based workers, barely know they are in a union) is simply fraudulent.

Remaking the World of Workers?

Even a cursory examination of key episodes in twentieth-century working-class history confirms the sad truth of this claim. In my search for a theoretical framework that might help explain the recent implosion of

U.S. labor's progressive wing, I consulted Yale professor James C. Scott's *Seeing Like a State: How Certain Schemes to Improve the Human Condition Have Failed.*[38] It's not a neoconservative tract about the impossibility of ever making things better for the workers of the world in rich or poor countries. Instead, it's a cautionary tale of what happens when utopian thinkers and political vanguards decide what's best for "the masses," with little or no input from the people impacted by their plans.

Scott's book contains several revealing case studies in what he calls "authoritarian high modernism." He examines forced collectivization in the Soviet Union, "compulsory villagization" in Tanzania under Julius Nyerere, and the damage done to urban communities, at home and abroad, by a host of well-intentioned architects and city planners. In each instance, a "planned social order" became highly dysfunctional (if not always fatal for millions of people) because it was constructed without regard "for the values, desires, and objections of those subjected to it."[39] The attempt by certain progressive trade unionists to remake the world of workers *for* them—in modern day America and without the benefit of state power, of course—contains a distinct echo of post-1917 political failures and disappointments in Russia.

Fans of the largely forgotten Russian revolutionary Alexandra Kollontai and her better known Berlin comrade Rosa Luxemburg will recognize their insights in Scott's critique of the process of change overseen by Lenin (and taken over the cliff by Stalin). At various times and in different ways, both women challenged unhealthy tendencies that emerged in the theory and practice of Russia's vanguard party. And they did so in the early years of the revolution, when Bolshevism still enjoyed widespread (and largely uncritical) support among working-class radicals everywhere.

In her famous retort to Lenin's *What Is to Be Done?* plus other writings and speeches, Luxemburg chided her fellow German and Russian revolutionaries for substituting the party for the proletariat—a substitution, as Scott notes, that ran counter to their professed goal, which "was to create a self-conscious workers movement, not just use the proletariat as instruments." Luxemburg understood that the cost of centralized hierarchy—in the Bolshevik Party and then, after it seized power, in the Soviet state—

"lay in the loss of creativity and initiative from below." If workers are merely viewed as "troops to be deployed" by a "command center" of "specialists," whose "unitary answer" to every problem has already been worked out in advance, the party will never achieve its putative goal of leading "a creative, conscious, competent, and empowered working class."[40]

As a pioneering radical feminist and "Workers' Opposition" sympathizer in the early twenties, Kollontai "clearly saw, as did Luxemburg, the social and psychological consequences of frustrating the independent initiatives of workers." Both were convinced that "the practical experience of industrial workers on the factory floor was indispensable knowledge" that the new class of managers and experts running Soviet industry needed to utilize and respect as part of "a genuine collaboration" between workers and the party. Instead, this collaboration was thwarted by what Scott calls the "pathology of group 'commandism'"—the top-down directives of officials accountable only to their organizational superiors and not to the workers under them.[41]

Oppositional Heresy, Then and Now

If you substitute the word "union" for "party," Kollontai's condemnation of top-down control and political conformity in the young Soviet Union describes the worst tendencies within SEIU today: "Every independent thought or initiative is treated as 'heresy,' as a violation of party discipline, as an attempt to infringe on the prerogatives of the center, which must 'foresee' and 'decree' everything."[42] As Scott points out, the harm done to the construction of democratic socialism in postrevolutionary Russia—and what we could call "civil society" today—came not just from the fact that Soviet technocrats were more likely, by themselves, to make bad and sometimes disastrous decisions. Authoritarian rule, in workplaces and society at large, "smothered the morale and creative spirit of the working class." In their frustration at the specialists and bureaucrats, observed Kollontai, "the workers became cynical and said, 'Let the officials themselves take care of us.'" An arbitrary, myopic, but exceedingly loyal officialdom developed and entrenched itself, presiding over a disempowered and dispirited workforce.[43]

The spread of political corruption, spying, informing, purging, jailing, and myriad other Soviet-era abuses was not far behind (although salved, we should note, by a social safety net sorely missed in Russia today). Yet the scene of revolutionary socialism's initial triumph retained much political cachet for decades to come. Every May Day, the "mobilization of the masses" continued like clockwork, almost to the fall of the Berlin wall and the crackup of the system.[44] The Soviet cause rallied its dwindling band of admirers, on those and other occasions, by hoisting high the red banners of "workers' power" and "anti-imperialism." Unfortunately, the content of the polity had changed, for the worse, long before.

Some readers may protest, at this point, that my analogy is getting strained or was never appropriate in the first place.[45] Andy Stern, the biggest corporate CEO-wannabe in U.S. labor, exposed as a secret Bolshevik? Mary Kay Henry, a devout Catholic, revealed to be a Politburo member? Dave Regan, local ally of the Chamber of Commerce, outed as a flaming socialist from Ohio?[46] Sounds a bit Glenn Beckish, for sure. But we're not trafficking in right-wing fantasies here or demonizing any one person for Tea Party purposes. The problem, in both authoritarian high modernist contexts, the old Soviet Union and the new SEIU, is not just the maximum leader of the moment; it's the organizational machinery and how it operates (as a party/state/union) in the name of workers but with little of their active consent.

Clearly, the modest, reformist agenda of SEIU is unrelated, in content, to any revolutionary politics. The union may be a reliable supplier of rally rhetoric against corporate America (at the same time it mimics many of its practices). But there's not much in the real creed of SEIU that smacks of "anticapitalism," since that's the first cousin of "class struggle unionism," already abandoned as a useless artifact from the last century. The glue for twenty-first-century labor-management partnering is unbridled pragmatism, not utopian ideology. Some SEIU insiders may have started out with a different political perspective, rooted in the social upheavals of the sixties. But their attitude toward radical politics today is best reflected in their private contempt for left-wing professors who send them "letters of concern" about undemocratic practices or attacks on other unions.

800-Number Unionism Is Not the Answer

Looking at the troubled interior life of SEIU, not just its polished exterior, one can't miss political "commandism" at work again, albeit in contemporary union form. Whether creating SEIU megalocals (or collectivizing Soviet agriculture), the leadership style is much the same; the bureaucracy always knows best, no matter how costly the mistakes it makes or how many real people get trampled in the process. So, with the caveats mentioned above, I rest my case with James C. Scott and one final piece of damning evidence: SEIU's extraordinary use of public and private police forces against its worker opponents. When you have to defend your transformative vision with the Puerto Rican riot squad, the high-priced OSO group, the Oakland and LAPD, the Alameda and San Jose police, and other cops throughout California, you're already "seeing like a state"—and the wrong kind of one at that. When a union relies so much on borrowed muscle to have its way (with those who "just don't get it," as Andy Stern would say), is the problem really the backwardness of workers? Or is SEIU's own organizational model, while seemingly so effective, actually deeply flawed?

One can only hope that the creativity, tenacity, and courage of California health care workers—who stuck to their guns when the political artillery of others fell silent—points the way toward a better model of worker organization. Until there is broader rank-and-file militancy, the NUHW struggle will remain an inspiring example and necessary experiment in independent unionism, in a situation where the road to internal union reform was hopelessly blocked. Sustaining a fledgling labor organization, with few resources but a resilient rank and file, has not been—and will not be—easy. The path taken by NUHW members was born of internal union strife occurring at a bad time for union organizing in general. It was not a path freely chosen. As they continued their lopsided competition, NUHW and SEIU both insisted they would much prefer to be working on other campaigns and causes instead of battling each other. And that is true. At Kaiser, as previously noted, SEIU spending on NLRB election activity in the fall of 2010 pushed the total cost of recent labor civil warfare above $140 million (when the contributions of all parties are counted). That's a lot of dues money that didn't get spent on organizing the unorganized, bargaining stronger contracts, electing or holding politicians accountable, and building more community-labor alliances to accomplish any of the foregoing.[47]

If, from the ashes of the old and out of the organizational carnage of the last few years, a better union model does emerge, it will not look like SEIU's pyramid of purple power. Its initial rave reviews notwithstanding, that chimerical structure has proven itself to be the inverse of what's actually needed. Instead of unions that are top down and top heavy, too employer friendly and detached from their base, we need more that are lean and mean at the top, plus strong, broad, and deep at the base. If there's partnering to be done, it should be the kind of collaboration between workers, their elected leaders, and allies that makes the union an independent workplace presence with its own agenda, not a mere appendage of management.[48]

If the latter is the only permissible form of existence for America's remaining labor organizations, union and nonunion workplaces will become increasingly indistinguishable. The more that happens, the less management will have to do to prevent unions from spreading beyond the 7 percent of the private sector workforce they already represent. The damage done to organized labor's prospects for revival will become, at least partially, self-inflicted. And the downward spiral of union density will continue to the point where workers have nowhere to go but up.

Notes

Preface

1. For a good exchange on what to do about these political setbacks, which got even worse on November 2, 2010, see "The Mid-Terms: Prophesying Our Political Future," *New Labor Forum* 19, no. 3 (Fall 2010): 9–21. In this issue of *NLF*, Adolph Reed explains "Why Labor's Soldiering for the Democrats Is a Losing Battle," while my former coworker at CWA Bob Master argues that unions must continue "engaging with Democrats," by building a movement "in the streets and at the polling places," which can push them "from below."

2. SEIU's media relations department would not even respond to simple fact-checking queries related to this book As the union's chief spokesperson, Michelle Ringuette, explained, SEIU "doesn't want to add to its legitimacy" because "we see the whole thing as fundamentally flawed." Phone interview with the author, November 24, 2010.

3. Kris Maher, "Unions See Members Fall by 10 Percent," *Wall Street Journal*, January 23, 2010.

4. For more on this unusual form of artistic engagement with union politics, see Ellen Dillinger, "Life Under SEIU Trusteeship," *Labor Notes*, online edition, December 18, 2009.

Introduction: From the Sixties to San Juan

1. Al Richmond, *A Long View from the Left: Memoirs of an American Revolutionary* (Boston: Houghton Mifflin Company, 1973).

2. Max Fraser, "Labor's Conundrum: Growth vs. Standards," *New Labor Forum* 18,

no. 1 (Winter 2009): 49–57.

3. Steve Early, "A New Generation of Labor Leftists," *Nation*, May 5, 1984, 543–46.

4. See interview with Matthew Kaminski, "Let's 'Share the Wealth,'" *Wall Street Journal*, December 6, 2008.

5. Robert Cohen, "West Orange Native Leads Major Shake-Up in Labor Movement," *Newark Star Ledger*, February 27, 2008.

6. Andy Stern, *A Country That Works: Getting America Back on Track* (New York: Free Press, 2006), 46. "Early on," writes Stern, "I began to suspect that the structure of the union provided the staff with disproportionate authority for decision making, as opposed to the more democratic empowerment of the members that I thought was in the true spirit of the labor movement." Stern's commitment to "democratic empowerment of the members" tended to wane over the course of his subsequent career.

7. Aaron Bernstein, "Can This Man Save Labor?" *Business Week*, September 13, 2004.

8. See Kate Thomas, "In 2008, More Than 88,000 Workers United in SEIU," January 29, 2009, posted at SEIU blog, www.seiu.org.

9. For more on *A Country That Works*, see Steve Early, *Embedded with Organized Labor: Journalistic Reflections on the Class War at Home* (New York: Monthly Review Press, 2009), 231–40.

10. Ruth Milkman, op-ed, "A More Perfect Union," *New York Times*, June 30, 2005.

11. SEIU International Union, "Thousands of Workers from Around the World Arrive in San Juan for SEIU's First 'Green' Convention," press release, May 30, 2008.

12. Steven Greenhouse, "Union Linked to Corruption Scandal," *New York Times*, December 12, 2008. See also Andy Stern, interview by Michael Mishak, *Las Vegas Sun*, May 10, 2009.

13. See May 5, 2008, letter from Medina and Hudson to a hundred labor-oriented intellectuals who sent a May 1, 2008, letter to Andy Stern protesting his threatened trusteeship over United Healthcare Workers West, headed by Sal Rosselli.

14. Juan Gonzalez, "New York Labor Leader Dennis Rivera in Shady Puerto Rico Union Deal," *New York Daily News*, February 29, 2008.

15. Other Local 1021 delegates later produced a flyer for distribution inside the convention hall, which urged SEIU to stop its raid on the FMPR. Several were told by SEIU staff members that they would be brought up on internal union charges for supporting a rival union. For another firsthand report from the San Juan convention scene, see Mark Brenner, "Puerto Rican Teachers Challenge the Purple Lockdown," *Labor Notes*, online edition, June 1, 2008.

16. CNA brochure, *SEIU International: A New Model of Corporate Unionism. Why Union Members and Progressives Should Be Wary*, 2008. Document in possession of author.

17. George Raine, "Unions Battle Over Health Care Workers," *San Francisco Chronicle*, December 7, 2008.

18. UHW advertisement, "Attention SEIU President Andy Stern," *New York Times*, May 2, 2008.

19. As quoted by Mark Brenner, "SEIU Reformers Challenge Union's Direction at Puerto Rico Convention," *Labor Notes*, July 1, 2008.

20. Herman Benson, "AUD Proposes Democracy as a Weapon Against Corruption," *Benson's Union Democracy Blog*, September 3, 2008.

21. Juan Gonzalez, "Union Fighting Over Bank," *New York Daily News*, February 20, 2009.

22. Paul Pringle, "SEIU President Says He Will Seek Aid from Labor Reform Groups," *Los Angeles Times*, September 4, 2008. The fifteen-member ethics panel Stern appointed included two retired judges, three law professors, a professor of organizational behavior, an ethicist, and a well-known African American minister from North Carolina who is both a civil rights activist and an advocate of workers' rights. Stern also announced he would "seek opinions" from an even more "diverse group of people," including past critics not on the commission like Herman Benson from the AUD, Nelson Lichtenstein from UCSB, and Ken Paff, national organizer for TDU. In June 2009, SEIU adopted a new set of ethical standards and practices, initiated a program of ethics training, created a three-person Ethics Review Board, and named a retired judge from New Jersey to be its first "Ethics Officer." See SEIU, "SEIU Code of Ethical Practices and Conflict of Interest Policy," press release, June 15, 2009.

23. Student-labor activists at UNC Chapel Hill, Stanford, Santa Clara University, and UC Irvine, "An Open Letter to Andy Stern and the Leadership of SEIU," *Nation*, online edition, May 2008.

24. J. Justin Wilson, managing director of the Center for Union Facts, as quoted by Steven Greenhouse, "Most Union Members Are Working for the Government, New Data Shows," *New York Times*, January 23, 2010.

25. Donna Brazile, former presidential campaign manager for Al Gore, as quoted on the back of *A Country That Works*.

26. According to Kim Fellner, Schultz's meeting with the SEIU board "went well and both leaders seemed pleased to have made the connection." She explains why the Starbucks founder and union foe was invited: "[Stern] wants to do for labor what Howard Schultz has done for coffee—turn it into a respected brand, market it, and popularize it throughout the country to change the status quo in his field of influence." Kim Fellner, *Wrestling with Starbucks: Conscience, Capital, and Cappuccino* (New Brunswick, NJ: Rutgers University Press, 2008), 154, 239.

27. For an account of UFCW picketing of one of Stern's joint appearances with Lee Scott from Wal-Mart, see Liza Featherstone, "Andy Stern: Savior or Sell-Out?" *Nation*, July 16, 2007.

28. Stern's lavish praise of Gingrich can be found on pages 99–102 of *A Country That Works*. The Gingrich quote is from his latest contemplative work of scholarship, *To Save America: Stopping Obama's Secular-Socialist Machine* (Washington, D.C.: Regnery Press, 2010). Stern's affection for GOP notables has been reciprocated, most recently, by Alan Simpson. In late September 2010, the deficit commission cochair and former Republican senator from Wyoming rushed to defend his "fine friend Andy Stern" when various news outlets reported that Stern was being investigated for his possible role in a "no-show" consulting deal arranged for former Local 660 president Alejandro Stephens. Simpson opened a commission session bemoaning the fact that Andy was "now the subject of anonymous allegations and

retribution from fellow union members." As quoted by Holly Rosenkrantz, "Former SEIU Chief Says FBI Probe Reports False," *Bloomberg News*, September 2010.

29. Ray Abernathy, "Say Hello to Mary Kay Henry," *West Bank of the Potomac* (blog), posted April 25, 2010, www.rayabernathy.com.

30. For the best analysis of the limits of SEIU's "soft power," and details of its actual contract bargaining record in building services, see Kim Moody, *U.S. Labor in Trouble and Transition: The Failure of Reform from Above and the Promise of Revival from Below* (New York: Verso, 2007).

31. At various points in *Civil Wars*, I mention what other national or local union officials were paid, on an annual basis, during 2008–10. In the interest of fairness, my own salary history with CWA should be fully disclosed. In December 1980, I was hired to be a CWA national organizer for $20,000 a year. I maxed out at the top international rep rate of about $85,000 a year when I left the staff union bargaining unit in late 2004. For thirty months thereafter, I was administrative assistant to the CWA national vice president in charge of 175,000-member District 1. As verified by the always invaluable (for this purpose) Center for Union Facts (unionfacts.com), my higher annual salary until retirement in March 2007 was $102,574.

32. For more information on those CWA efforts, see Hetty Rosenstein and Robert Master, *No Shortcuts: Mobilization and Politics Must Drive Labor's Revival from the Bottom Up*, an unpublished paper available from either author at CWA District 1, March 2006.

33. Dan Clawson, *The Next Upsurge: Labor and the New Social Movements* (Ithaca, NY: Cornell University Press, 2003), 46. In Clawson's view, because recent decades have not been "a period of upsurge," these sixties-inspired organizing directors did not gain their later union positions "as leaders of social movements from below, but rather by working their way up through the bureaucracy. They...were able to win power because key players recognized the labor movement was in crisis and needed talented individuals with fresh ideas." To varying degrees and in different ways, the "talented individuals with fresh ideas" in SEIU, UNITE HERE, and CWA did try to change the culture and membership composition of their respective unions through new organizing.

34. See Early, *Embedded with Organized Labor*.

35. Kim Voss and Rachel Sherman, "Breaking the Iron Law of Oligarchy: Union Revitalization in the American Labor Movement," *American Sociological Journal* 106, no. 2 (September 2000): 303–49.

36. Lowell Turner and Richard W. Hurd, "Building Social Movement Unionism," in *Rekindling the Movement: Labor's Quest for Relevance in the 21st Century*, Lowell Turner, Harry Katz, and Richard Hurd, eds. (Ithaca, NY: Cornell University Press, 2001), 17.

37. Ruth Milkman and Kim Voss, introduction to *Rebuilding Labor: Organizing and Organizers in the New Union Movement*, Ruth Milkman and Kim Voss, eds. (Ithaca, NY: Cornell University Press, 2004), 7.

38. Ken Paff as quoted by Paul Pringle, "A Year of Triumphs and Scandals for SEIU," *Los Angeles Times*, December 31, 2008.

39. Steve Early, "Member-Based Organizing," in *A New Labor Movement for a New Century*," Greg Mantsios, ed. (New York: Monthly Review Press, 1998).

40. Steve Early, "Thoughts on the 'Worker-Student Alliance'—Then and Now," *Labor History* 44, no. 1 (2003); "Reutherism Redux: When Poor Workers' Unions Wear the Color Purple," *Against the Current* 112 (September/October 2004): 31–39 ; and "Labor Debates How to Rebuild Its House," *Tikkun* 20, no. 3 (January 2005): 45–48.

41. Herman Benson, *Rebels, Reformers, and Racketeers: How Insurgents Transformed the Labor Movement* (New York: Association for Union Democracy, 2005).

42. For more on the life and death of UMW dissident Jock Yablonski, see Paul Nyden, "Rank-and-File Movements in the United Mine Workers of America, 1960s–1980s," in *Rebel Rank and File: Labor Militancy and Revolt from Below During the Long 1970s*, Robert Brenner, Aaron Brenner, and Cal Winslow, eds. (New York: Verso, 2010).

43. As quoted in Early, "Reutherism Redux," 35.

44. Bevona was John Sweeney's successor as president of 55,000-member SEIU Local 32BJ. He "made himself the highest paid union leader in the country" presiding over a local of doormen and janitors, while keeping Sweeney on his payroll as a $70,000-a-year "consultant" for a decade after the latter left to become president of SEIU. When Stern forced him out in 1999, Bevona was earning $450,000 with several relatives on the payroll as well. Three years earlier, he had tried unsuccessfully to run for secretary of the national union. See Douglas Martin, "Gus Bevona, Ex-Union Chief, Dies at 69," *New York Times*, September 24, 2010.

45. Early, "Reutherism Redux," 36.

46. Ibid., 37.

47. Katrina vanden Heuvel, "Andy Stern on the New Moment," Nation.com, *Editor's Cut* (blog), posted November 25, 2008.

48. Andy Stern, "Are Unions Relevant?," interview with Kris Maher, *Wall Street Journal*, January 22, 2007.

Chapter 1: The Quest for Union Renewal

1. The larger economic and political context for U.S. labor's long-term decline—and the organizing strategy changes described in chapters 2 and 3—are beyond the scope of this book. For much relevant detail on the national and international trends that have decimated unions and undermined private sector collective bargaining, see two excellent studies by Kim Moody, *Workers in a Lean World: Unions in the International Economy* (New York: Verso, 1997), and *U.S. Labor in Trouble and Transition*.

2. Steven Greenhouse, "Most Union Members"; Kris Maher, "Unions See Members Fall"; and Bureau of National Affairs, "AFL-CIO Membership at 8.5 Million in 2009," *Labor Relations Weekly* 24, (March 13, 2010): 387.

3. See Pew Center for the People and the Press, "Favorability Ratings of Labor Unions Fall Sharply," survey report, February 23, 2010. A Gallup poll in the summer of 2010 wasn't quite as grim but almost. It found that 52 percent of Americans viewed unions favorably—but that was still the second lowest level of support reported since Gallup began polling on this question seventy years ago.

4. Peter Levy, *The New Left and Labor in the 1960s* (Chicago: University of Illinois Press, 1994).

5. Tom Hayden, *Writings for a Democratic Society: The Tom Hayden Reader* (San Francisco: City Lights Books, 2008), which contains the Port Huron Statement on pages 57–59.

6. Ibid., 58.

7. Ibid., 59.

8. Paul Buhle, *Taking Care of Business: Samuel Gompers, George Meany, Lane Kirkland, and the Tragedy of American Labor* (New York: Monthly Review Press, 1999), 27.

9. Robert H. Zeiger, *American Workers, American Unions* (Baltimore, MD: Johns Hopkins University Press, 1994), 172.

10. Michael Honey, *Going Down Jericho Road: The Memphis Strike, Martin Luther King's Last Campaign* (New York: W.W. Norton, 2007).

11. Vanessa Tait, *Poor Workers' Unions: Rebuilding Labor from Below* (Boston: South End Press, 2005), 27–28.

12. Ibid., 28.

13. As suggested by the thumbnail sketch of Andy Stern's career in the introduction, another important gateway to activism in SEIU was government employment in human services and other fields. SEIU's development as a public sector union is far beyond the scope of this book. For an excellent California-focused study of that topic, readers should consult Paul Johnston, *Success While Others Fail: Social Movement Unionism and the Public Workplace* (Ithaca, NY: Cornell ILR Press, 1994), specifically 45–46 for the quote below. Before becoming an academic, Johnston was a UFW organizer, a Vietnam-era draftee active in the GI antiwar movement, and, then for ten years, a local union representative in the public sector. In 1982, Johnston had the distinction (no longer unusual today) of being fired by SEIU for being "associated with adversarial labor relations, public service strikes, and related mobilizations."

14. Interview with the author, July 27, 2007. For more on the history of 9to5, see Karen Nussbaum, "Working Women's Insurgent Consciousness," in *The Sex of Class: Women Transforming American Labor,* Dorothy Sue Cobble, ed. (Ithaca, NY: Cornell University Press, 2007), 159–76.

15. SEIU District 925 was later disbanded and its bargaining units merged into other SEIU locals. Nussbaum left SEIU in 1993 to become director of the U.S. Department of Labor's Women's Bureau. Since 1996, she has worked for the AFL-CIO, most recently as director of its Working America project. For more on the organizing work of Nussbaum, Debbie Schneider, and other 9to5ers, see Don Stillman's *Stronger Together: The Story of SEIU* (White River Junction, VT: Chelsea Green Press, 2010), 81.

16. Stillman, *Stronger Together,* 17.

17. For a detailed account of the young organizer culture that developed at SEIU during the 1970s and '80s, see Kim Fellner, "In Search of the Movement: 1960s Activists in Labor," in *Union Voices: Labor's Response to Crisis,* Glenn Adler and Doris Suarez, eds. (Albany, NY: SUNY Press, 1993), 121–30.

18. Biographical details and all quotes are from Wade Rathke lecture at the Williams College Club, New York City, December 3, 2009, and interview with author, December, 4, 2009. For more on his background and organizing career, see John Atlas, *Seeds of Change: The Story of ACORN, America's Most Controversial Anti-Poverty Community Organizing Group* (Nashville,TN: Vanderbilt University Press, 2010).

19. Wade Rathke, *Citizen Wealth: Winning the Campaign to Save Working Families* (San Francisco: Berrett-Koehler Publishers, 2009), 177.

20. Randy Shaw, *Beyond the Fields: Cesar Chavez, the UFW, and the Struggle for Justice in the 21st Century* (Berkeley and Los Angeles: University of California Press, 2008), 8.

21. For more on Justice for Janitors, see Stillman, *Stronger Together*, 18–23, 25–33.

22. Marshall Ganz, *Why David Sometimes Wins: Leadership, Organization, and Strategy in the California Farm Worker Movement* (New York: Oxford University Press, 2009), 22–52.

23. Former UFW activist Frank Bardacke, author of the forthcoming *Trampling Out the Vintage: Cesar Chavez and the Two Souls of the United Farm Workers* (New York: Verso, 2011), reports that Chavez "kept the UFW neutral on the war until 1969 when the Defense Department started buying up boycotted grapes. His first public opposition to the war was in October 1969, when he supported the Vietnam Moratorium." Email to the author, October 21, 2010.

24. Shaw, *Beyond the Fields*, 21.

25. Ibid., 265.

26. See Frank Bardacke, "The UFW from the Ground Up," chap. 5, in *Rebel Rank and File: Labor Militancy and Revolt from Below During the Long 1970s* (New York: Verso, 2010) and Bardacke's definitive work of UHW history, *Trampling Out the Vintage*, which reflects his own firsthand experience as a farm worker in California and UFW activist.

27. Miriam Pawel, *The Union of Their Dreams: Power, Hope, and Struggle in Cesar Chavez's Farm Worker Movement* (New York: Bloomsbury Press, 2009), 305–307.

28. Michael Yates, *In and Out of the Working Class* (Winnepeg: Arbeiter Ring Publishing, 2009), 122–44. See also Yates, "The Dubious Legacy of Cesar Chavez," review of *Beyond the Fields* in *Left Business Observer* (April 25, 2009). This review of Shaw's book notes that, when Yates published an article in the *Nation* in 1977, criticizing the union's internal practices, UFW lawyers threatened to sue the magazine.

29. Ganz, *Why David Sometimes Wins*, 254.

30. Marshall Ganz as quoted in Shaw, *Beyond the Fields*, 257.

31. Ganz, *Why David Sometimes Wins*, 254.

32. Steve Early, "This Labor Day, Let's Salute All Union Stewards—and Their Cutting Edge in California," *Working In These Times* (blog), August 23, 2010.

33. See Tasty, "The CHW Scoop," *Stern Burger with Fries* (blog), July 20, 2010. The post reports on Bustamante's removal of all the elected shop stewards at Saint Francis Memorial Hospital in San Francisco, a CHW facility where NUHW supporters were seeking decertification of SEIU. Before becoming a post-trusteeship staffer of UHW, Bustamante served as vice president of SEIU Local 1877, a statewide janitors local.

34. Shutting things down to reassert leadership control was not uncommon in the UFW. As Frank Bardacke recalls, Chavez "heavily criticized" the editors of *Malcriado*, the UFW newspaper, for running a small amount of antiwar material before he himself came out against the Vietnam War. "His subsequent distrust of them was one of the reasons he allowed the paper to close down in 1967." Email to author, October 21, 2010.

35. As Michael Yates reports, the UFW is now run like a family business. Among the relatives involved are Chavez's son and Arturo Rodriguez, who is the current president and son-in-law of the union founder. See Yates's review of Shaw's *Beyond the Fields*.

36. Interview with the author, February 23, 2010.

37. Andy Stern email, May 1, 2008. This and other SEIU officer or headquarters staff emails, cited later in the book, are documents in the possession of the author. They were sent in 2008 and obtained from an anonymous source in 2010. Some of these leaked messages have been cited in previous SEIU-related reporting by the *New York Times*, the *Wall Street Journal*, and the *Los Angeles Times*.

38. Wilzoch later wrote about the parallels between political developments in the UFW and SEIU for the *BeyondChron* blog. See "After Medina/Huerta Conflict, SEIU Betrayal Complete," May 26, 2010. Another concerned SEIU organizer, on the East Coast, also weighed in around the same time as Wilzoch did in 2008. David Kranz, then director of the Professional and Technical Department of 1199SEIU in New York, didn't write to Stern. But he did circulate a long open letter to his local union colleagues (that ended up being distributed widely outside 1199). To no avail, Kranz urged SEIU reconciliation with Rosselli and UHW. He expressed the hope that his own local would remain "truly neutral" in the California dispute and, along with other Stern critics, worried that the national union was "employing methods that come into conflict with...member involvement and empowerment." See Herman Benson, "On the Eve of the SEIU Convention," *Union Democracy Review* 173, May–June, 2008.

39. All Rosselli quotes are from interview with the author, November 6, 2007.

Chapter 2: Taking the High Road to Growth?

1. Dennis Rivera as quoted by Christopher Rowland, "Union Looks to Organize at Hub's Top Hospitals," *Boston Globe*, August 31, 2005.

2. Clayton Nall, "Gompers's Ghost and Labor's New Look," *Washington Post*, September 4, 2005.

3. For a good statistical summary of the fired worker casualty rate in union organizing campaigns, see Kate Bronfenbrenner, "No Holds Barred: The Intensification of Employer Opposition to Organizing," Economic Policy Institute, May 20, 2009.

4. Peter Dreier and Kelly Candaele, "Why We Need EFCA," *American Prospect*, online edition, December 2, 2008.

5. See Richard Freeman's unpublished paper, "What Can We Learn from NLRA to Create Labor Law for the 21st Century?," available from Freeman, c/o Economics Department, Harvard University, Cambridge, MA. This paper was presented at a

Washington, D.C., symposium, held on October 27, 2010, to mark the seventy-fifth anniversary of the passage of the Wagner Act. Around the same time, Obama appointees on the NLRB ruled that back pay for workers who win their discriminatory discharge cases should include compound, rather than simple interest, and "be compounded on a daily basis, rather than annually or quarterly." While welcome, this increase in potential management liability is still a far cry from the treble damages remedy (back pay times three) proposed as part of the Employee Free Choice Act. See NLRB, "NLRB Remedial Actions," press release, October 25, 2010.

6. See UNITE HERE Strategic Affairs Department, "SEIU Healthcare Organizing: A Report on Issues Related to Growth and Density," available from UNITE HERE.

7. As noted in the preface, Gordon is my wife and the reason I was at this particular SEIU organizing campaign meeting in Maine.

8. Marty Riehle and Kevin Griffin, "Solve Problems Without Divisiveness," *Portland Press Herald*, September 4, 2000.

9. Suzanne Gordon and Steve Early, "Nurses in Unions Can Give Better Care," *Portland Press Herald*, September 4, 2000.

10. One of the key demands of this strike, by seventy-five thousand CWA and IBEW members, was an organizing rights agreement covering Verizon's largely nonunion wireless workforce. For an overly optimistic report on the results of that struggle, see Steve Early, "Verizon Strike Highlights New Union Role," *Boston Globe*, September 3, 2000.

11. About one-third of that number is actually employed in hospitals. In that part of the workforce, unionization is now greater than 14 percent, higher than the overall union density rate and twice the level in the rest of the private sector.

12. *The High Road: A Winning Strategy for Managing Conflict and Communicating Effectively in Hospital Worker Organizing Campaigns*, 1999 SEIU report, copy in possession of author.

13. For an exchange of union views about *The High Road* and a summary of the document itself, see "The High Road: SEIU Rethinks Hospital Organizing Tactics," *Labor Notes*, December 1999, pages 7–9.

14. Mike Elk, "Number of Union Elections, Strikes Continue Steady Decline," *Working In These Times* (blog), July 7, 2010.

15. Steve Early, "Tearing Down the Wall: A Look at Three Strategic Campaigns," *Labor Notes*, April 29, 2007.

16. One of CWA's major setbacks was the failure of its 2000–04 organizing rights agreement involving Verizon Wireless, which became a procedural morass almost as bad as the NLRB. Three call centers covered by it were closed and fifteen hundred jobs moved to parts of the country where it was not applicable. Not a single worker was organized under the deal—at a Verizon subsidiary that employs nearly fifty thousand workers today. See Early, "Verizon Strike Highlights New Union Role."

17. Stern, *A Country That Works*, 90.

18. Ibid., 71.

19. According to one estimate, the different types of SEIU organizing between 2002 and 2006 broke down as follows: "More than half of the new workers organized

were government workers or contractors, such as state-funded childcare providers...16 percent came in through old-style Labor Board elections, 13 percent through corporate campaigns (the stick) and 13 percent through agreements that include various quid pro quos." Esther Kaplan, "Labor's Growing Pains," *Nation*, May 29, 2008.

20. For more on the strengths and limitations of 1199SEIU's joint training fund, see Ariel Ducey, *Never Good Enough: Health Care Workers and the False Promise of Job Training* (Ithaca, NY: Cornell University Press, 2009).

21. Sal Rosselli, "NUHW and the Fight for Union Democracy," interview by Lee Sustar, *Socialist Worker*, May 27, 2010.

22. Thomas Kochan, Adrienne Eaton, Robert McKersie, and Paul Adler, *Healing Together: The Labor-Management Partnership at Kaiser Permanente* (Ithaca, NY: Cornell University Press, 2009). For more on their book, see footnote 48 in chapter 8.

23. Steve Early, "SEIU Civil War Puts Labor-Management 'Partnership' in a New Light," *Dollars & Sense*, September/October 2009, 35–37.

24. For an account of SEIU member unhappiness with the LMP, see William Johnson, "Service Employees Union Mergers Lead to Conflict in California," *Labor Notes*, June 2007, 8–9.

25. Charles Ornstein, "Kaiser Rewarded Clerks for Keeping Patient's Calls Short," *Los Angeles Times*, May 17, 2002.

26. See editorial in the *California Nurse*, entitled "Undemocratic Moves," by then CNA president Kay McVay, August 2002, and Chuck Idelson, "Unions Should Place Public Well-Being Above Self-Interest," *Labor Notes*, June 2002, 11. For more on the history of CNA-SEIU tensions over partnership-related issues, see Kaplan, "Labor's Growing Pains."

27. Author interviews with CWA D-9 organizers.

28. Patrick J. McDonnell, "SEIU Picks Mary Kay Henry as President," *Los Angeles Times*, May 8, 2010.

29. As quoted by Dan Clawson in "A Battle for Labor's Future," *Z Magazine*, June 2009.

30. Tenet's retiree health care and pension coverage remains inferior to those at Kaiser, CHW, HCA, and the Daughters of Charity Health System in California.

31. Cal Winslow, *Labor's Civil Wars in California: The NUHW Healthcare Workers' Rebellion* (Oakland, CA: PM Press, 2010), 40–41.

32. This was how Henry described her Tenet bargaining problems to Max Fraser, "The SEIU Andy Stern Leaves Behind," *Nation*, June 18, 2010.

33. Henry and Aidukas quotes are both from Patrick J. McDonnell, "SEIU Picks Mary Kay."

34. Interview with the author, September 9, 2010.

35. Max Fraser, "The SEIU Andy Stern Leaves Behind."

36. As quoted by Lee Sustar in "Labor Pains," *Socialist Worker*, October 6, 2010.

37. See UNITE HERE Strategic Affairs Department, *SEIU Healthcare Organizing*.

38. Richard Thomas, "Union, Nursing Home Alliance Team Up," *Seattle Times*, March 5, 2007.

39. Matt Smith, "Union Disunity," *San Francisco Weekly*, April 11, 2007.

40.   As quoted in April 11, 2007, press release entitled "Internal Documents Show How Andy Stern Sold Out Nursing Home Workers and Patients," from Court's Foundation for Taxpayer and Consumer Rights.

41.   Stillman, *Stronger Together*, 123. Brown's local union sued GOP governor Rowland, and got a federal court ruling that he had violated nursing home workers' right to strike; two years later, he resigned in a corruption scandal and was later jailed.

42.   The arbitrator, Margaret Kern, denied SEIU's request for a bargaining order. The union argued that a majority of workers had signed cards demonstrating their support for unionization before the employer's campaign of misinformation and intimidation forced 1199 to withdraw from the scheduled secret ballot vote. See "Yale-New Haven Hospital and New England Healthcare Employees, District 1199 SEIU," an arbitration decision issued October 23, 2007. Document in possession of author.

43.   Steven Greenhouse, "Labor Law Is Broken, Economist Says," *New York Times*, online only, October 28, 2010.

44.   All quotes are from Brown's unpublished review of Stern's *A Country That Works* or his later interview with *Dissent* magazine. See Jim McNeill, "Work in Progress: the State of the Unions Two Years After the AFL-CIO Split," *Dissent* (Summer 2007): 36.

45.   UHW, "The California Alliance Agreement: Lessons Learned in Moving Forward in Organizing California's Nursing Home Industry," 2007. UHW document in possession of author.

46.   UHW's Executive Board resolution, May 19, 2007. Document in possession of author.

47.   SEIU United Healthcare Workers leadership letter to home care members, May 29, 2007.

48.   As quoted by Michelle Amber in "SEIU Terminates Controversial Agreement with Nursing Home Chains in California," *Bureau of National Affairs* (hereafter *BNA*), *Daily Labor Report*, June 14, 2007. See also Matt Smith, "Stern Reprimand: SEIU Members in Northern California Challenge the National Boss," *San Francisco Weekly*, June 13, 2007, and Mark Brenner, "Service Employees End Nursing Home Partnership," *Labor Notes*, July 2007, 8–9.

49.   As quoted in "SEIU 2008 Convention Targets Health Care Employers," *Healthcare Employer* 35, no. 1 (Summer). This Jackson Lewis newsletter for the firm's management clients can be accessed at: www.jacksonlewis.com/legalupdates/newsletters/pdf/225.pdf.

50.   Michael Krivosh letter to Anna Burger. Document in possession of author.

51.   As Randy Shaw reported, "SJHS has a long history of violating the rights of workers trying to unionize" with the ILWU, USWA, and CNA. See "New Outrage Exposes Obama's Failure to Help Unions," *BeyondChron* (blog), June 14, 2010.

52.   Through his involvement with the UFW and, later, the community organization Neighbor-2-Neighbor, Ross had many contacts with Sisters of St. Joseph members.

53.   Interview with the author, July 15, 2009. Glenn Goldstein believes that, well before the trusteeship, SEIU headquarters knew "there was a breakthrough pending at SJHS, the largest nonunion Catholic chain in California, and they actively worked against it, behind the scenes, because UHW, under Rosselli, would be credited with

a leadership role in the victory." Email to author, October 31, 2010. Nearly two years later, the CNA was able to negotiate a "free and fair election process" agreement with SJHS that applied, in a limited way, to RN organizing at Queen of the Valley hospital in Napa. Even though CNA suffered a narrow loss in the resulting election, Ross described the ground rules as "a significant breakthrough and precedent for the St. Joseph system."

54.   Fred Ross Jr., "SEIU President Andy Stern Has Crossed the Line," *BeyondChron* (blog), May 7, 2009.

55.   D. Ashley Furness, "Healthcare Unions Clash at Memorial Hospital," *North Bay Business Journal,* October 12, 2009. As Furness noted, after postponing elections for months, "the NLRB has dismissed many such complaints filed by SEIU in other elections involving the NUHW."

56.   Randy Shaw, "SEIU Battles NUHW, Labor Council, and Workers in Santa Rosa," *BeyondChron* (blog), October 6, 2009.

57.   Sam Hananel, "Labor Unions, Catholic Hospitals to End Conflict," Associated Press, June 22, 2009.

58.   John Brenkle, "Labor Wars at Memorial Hospital," *Santa Rosa Press Democrat,* November 2, 2009.

59.   All Eliseo Medina quotes are from his November 2, 2009, memo entitled "Santa Rosa Memorial Hospital Workers," which was sent to Brenkle and other NUHW supporters. Posted at *Sonoma Red Revolt* (blog), November 2, 2009.

60.   For a comprehensive study of the Santa Rosa Memorial workers' struggle and the larger terrain of Catholic hospital union organizing, see Adam Reich's forthcoming book, *With God on Our Side: Labor Struggle in The Catholic Hospital"* (Cornell ILR Press, 2012).

61.   Brenkle, "Labor Wars at Memorial."

62.   Ibid.

63.   At University of Southern California (USC) Hospital a few months later, SEIU had so little support in a decertification election battle with NUHW that it did withdraw prior to NLRB-supervised voting. SEIU spokesperson Adrian Surfas informed the *Los Angeles Times* that management "had created an extremely hostile environment, so that workers who supported unionization feared what was going to happen." Yet within USC Hospital, just as it did in Santa Rosa, SEIU took management's side, actually encouraging its supporters to vote "no union" and give up their rights, wages, and benefits—in an already unionized workplace! In May 2010, NUHW received 393 votes, while only 122 workers voted for "no union." See Patrick McDonnell, "Campaign Underscores Rift Between SEIU and New, Breakaway Union," *Los Angeles Times,* May 25, 2010, and Randy Shaw, "NUHW Defeats SEIU in USC Hospital Election," *BeyondChron* (blog), May 28, 2010.

64.   Fred Ross, "Open Letter to Workers at Santa Rosa Memorial Hospital," *BeyondChron* (blog), December 8, 2009.

65.   Mark Brenner, "NUHW Is Decisive in Santa Rosa, SEIU Tries to Postpone Defeat," *Labor Notes,* December 8, 2009.

66.   In late December 2010, the NLRB in Washington finally certified the results of the election. In a positive move, Santa Rosa Memorial Hospital management sent NUHW a December 29, 2010, letter agreeing to begin negotiations on a first contract.

Chapter 3: A Scramble for New Members

1.   As quoted by Dana Goldstein, "Meet the New Union Boss," Daily Beast, May 6, 2010.
2.   Christopher Hayes, "Healthcare Workers Win Raises," In These Times, February 16, 2004.
3.   Steven Greenhouse, "In Biggest Drive Ever Since 1937, Union Gains a Victory," New York Times, February 26, 1999. See also Beverly Takashi, "Home Care Organizing in California," Working USA (Winter 2003–4): 62–84.
4.   Rosenstein and Master, No Shortcuts: Mobilization, a thirty-three-page paper that critiques Andy Stern, CTW, and various aspects of the SEIU organizing model.
5.   Larry Cohen as quoted in "Building a New Public Employee," National Lawyers Guild Labor Update, October–November 1982. See Steve Early, "Grass Roots Organizing Drive Proves Popular with Jersey Workers," Labor Notes, March 25, 1981, and CWA-SWOC mailer called "The Vote for a State Workers Union: What Difference Does It Make?," document in possession of author. Some SWOC activists also belonged to the NJ Civil Service Association, a smaller independent union that was jointly certified with SEA and, after the 1979 wildcat strike, affiliated in part with CWA.
6.   Anna Burger, "Taking Stock of the State Pension," Newark Star Ledger, December 12, 2002. For New Jersey state workers' response to the privatization scheme backed by Burger, see Charles Webster, "Workers Protest Pension Investment Plan," Trentonian, December 14, 2004.
7.   Larry Cohen email to CWA executive board members, March 25, 2005. Document in possession of author.
8.   For the most comprehensive study of ACORN's rise and fall, see Atlas, Seeds of Change.
9.   Eileen Boris and Jennifer Klein, "We Were the Invisible Workforce: Unionizing Home Care," an essay included in Cobble, Sex of Class.
10.   In a related organizing campaign just involving CWA, Local 1037 later won bargaining rights for a newly created statewide unit of more than a thousand workers paid by the State Division of Developmental Disabilities (DDD) to provide respite care and other home-based services to the disabled and their families.
11.   For a good description of Local 880's organizing model, see Barbara Rose, "Local 880: Labor's New Up-and-Comer," Chicago Tribune, July 5, 2005.
12.   Harold Meyerson, "Labor War in Illinois," American Prospect, March 29, 2005.
13.   Peter Giangreco, Blagojevich's former media consultant, as quoted by David Medell, "What About Me? The United States of America v. Rod Blagojevich," New Yorker, July 26, 2010, 43.
14.   Clare Ansberry, "Blagojevich and Union Go Way Back," Wall Street Journal, December 13–14, 2008.

15. Meyerson, "Labor War in Illinois."
16. Rose, "Local 880."
17. Steven Greenhouse, "Union Is Caught Up in Illinois Bribe Case," *New York Times*, December 11, 2008.
18. Mendell, "What About Me?," 43.
19. Ben Smith, "Blago Disappointed in Wages of Labor," Politico, April 14, 2010.
20. Kris Maher, "Service Union Chief Met with Blagojevich," *Wall Street Journal*, January 7, 2009.
21. John Nichols, "Governor Gone Wild: Blagojevich Busted!" *Nation*, online edition, December 9, 2008.
22. Malcolm Gay, "Successor in Illinois Is the Unassuming, Independent Anti-Blagojevich," *New York Times*, January 31, 2009, 14.
23. See anti-EFCA ad by Americans for Job Security, *Washington Post*, December 14, 2008, page A14, and the Center for Union Facts ad in the *New York Times*, December 15, 2008, page A15. See also Kim Chipman and Jonathan D. Salant, "Blagojevich Case Used by Republican-Allied Foes of Labor Bill," Bloomberg News, December 22, 2008.
24. Deanna Bellandi and Christopher Wells, "Blagojevich a Distraction for Democrats," *Boston Globe*, August 22, 2010.
25. Dan Mihalopouos, "After a String of Political Victories, a Union Has Clout to Spare," *New York Times*, February 26, 2010. The story noted, however, that "politics has not always gone smoothly" for SEIU in Illinois because Tom Balanoff's "close ties" to Quinn's predecessor "would come back to haunt the union when federal authorities arrested Blagojevich and charged him with corruption in December 2008."
26. The election results were reported online by CBS-TV Channel 2 in Chicago in an unsigned article entitled "Home Health Care Workers Choose Not to Unionize," posted at cbs2chicago.com, October 19, 2009.
27. As quoted by Thomas Fitzgerald, "Unions Lead Push for Pennsylvania Democrats," *Philadelphia Inquirer*, October 27, 2010.
28. Ansberry, "Blagojevich and Union Go Way Back."
29. "DOL Investigates Election Violations," *Union Democracy Review* (June/July 2004): 3.
30. Michael Kinsman, "Takeover Blamed on Financial Woes," *San Diego Union-Tribune*, June 16, 2005.
31. SEIU, "New AFSCME-SEIU Pact to Help More Workers Win Voice at Work," press release, September 19, 2005.
32. Interview with the author, October 31, 2007.
33. For a good discussion of this issue, see Mike Parker, "Are Industrial Unions Better Than Craft?," *Labor Notes*, September 2008, 8.
34. Kaplan, "Labor's Growing Pains."
35. Ibid.
36. Ed Bruno and Peter Kellman, "Concessionary Partnerships with Employers Do Not Advance the Labor Movement," *Labor Notes*, June 2008, 7.
37. The continued CLC affiliation of locals that are part of CTW national unions was

and is permitted under the special "solidarity charters" created after the CTW split in 2005.

38. In a 2010 interview with AP reporter Carla Marinucci about Republican gubernatorial candidate Meg Whitman's criticism of CNA salaries, DeMoro said she had never asked for a raise and that her pay is approved by a 35-member board composed of working nurses. See Carla Marinucci, "Nurses Union Leader Embraces Political Fight," *San Francisco Chronicle*, July 13, 2010. This explanation did not satisfy labor journalist Mike Elk, a former organizer for UE where top officials make no more than the highest paid member. See Mike Elk, "High Officials' Salaries Open California Nurses Union Up to GOP Attacks," *Working In These Times* (blog), July 20, 2010.

39. The quoted line was on SEIU Michigan Healthcare's website after Smith's death, but was soon taken down.

40. Steven Greenhouse, "Conflict Between 2 Unions Intensifies," *New York Times*, April 16, 2008.

41. Email exchange in possession of author. Dave Regan's public defense of SEIU's actions at the Labor Notes conference was entitled, "Why We Demonstrated in Dearborn," MRZine, May 2, 2008. In this article, Regan argued that "DeMoro and the CNA had forfeited the privilege of being welcomed within gatherings of principled trade unionists." Within a year, SEIU and CNA were working together on the hospital organizing campaigns described in chapter 10.

42. See video of Regan's May 31, 2009, speech made by Fresno political activist and community newspaper editor Mike Rhodes, posted at *Perez Stern* (blog), June 1, 2009.

43. Cal Winslow, *Labor's Civil War in California* (Oakland: PM Press, 2010), 88–91.

44. As quoted by Holly Rosenkrantz, "What Andy Stern Leaves Behind," *Business Week*, April 17, 2010.

45. As quoted by Paul Pringle, "Service Workers Express Outrage over Alleged Misuse of Funds," *Los Angeles Times*, December 26, 2008.

46. Interview with the author, November 6, 2007.

47. Dana Simon resignation letter. Document in possession of author.

48. Florine Furlow, "Homecare Workers Take Back Their Union," posted on NUHW website, June 1, 2009. Document in possession of author.

49. Eliseo Medina, "SEIU Response to UHW Conflict," posted on *Talking Union*, a labor-oriented website of the Democratic Socialists of America, January 17, 2009.

50. Interview with the author, June 11, 2009.

51. See "Winning in Fresno: Some Tips for Success," a set of SEIU talking points for Fresno home care campaign door-to-door canvassers. Document in possession of author.

52. Document in possession of author, which cites the relevant sections of the Meyers-Milias-Brown Act (MMBA), covering public sector workers in California.

53. Randy Shaw devotes a chapter to this campaign in *Beyond the Fields*.

54. Huerta quote is from her speech to NUHW supporters in Fresno at May 20, 2009, pre-election rally.

55. As reported by Kris Maher, "New Salvo Fired as Unions Battle Over Workers," *Wall Street Journal*, November 12, 2009. NUHW filed charges with the California

Public Employment Relations Board seeking to overturn the Fresno election based on ballot tampering, voter intimidation, and other illegal behavior.

56. As quoted in SEIU/UHW email blast entitled, "Numbers Tell the Story in Fresno," June 6, 2009.

57. Interview with the author, May 16, 2007.

Chapter 4: Dial 1-800-MY-UNION?

1. Steven Greenhouse, "A Union President Presses for Growth Amid a New Round of Criticisms," *New York Times*, June 1, 2008.

2. Andy Stern, as quoted in interview with Kris Maher, "Are Unions Relevant?," *Wall Street Journal*, January 22, 2007.

3. Stephen Franklin, "Democracy Dream Still Eludes Unions," *Chicago Tribune*, April 7, 1997.

4. SEIU Officers, "Recommendations to the SEIU 2008 Convention," 12–14. Document in possession of author.

5. For a positive report on call center servicing involving a Canadian public sector union, see Harvard Trade Union Program (HTUP) case study entitled, "What Do Members Want? The MGEU Resource Centre," August 2008. Available upon request from HTUP director Elaine Bernard.

6. Garcia quote is from her remarks at a UHW press briefing, June 2, 2008, in San Juan, Puerto Rico.

7. Harding quote is from document in possession of author. The UHW blog (at www.seiuvoice.org) was taken down after the February 2009 trusteeship.

8. See *'Justice for All' or 'Control for Just Us'—A First Look at SEIU's Plan to Centralize Decision-Making Power and Financial Resources at the Expense of Union Democracy and Strong Organization Among Members*. Document in possession of author.

9. In 2007, Rosselli was part of a delegation from SEIU that met with the Queensland Public Sector Union (QPSU) and the Health Services Union (HSU) in Australia. He concluded that their "member service center and data base application innovations"— if coupled together and used appropriately—would help his own local become "more efficient and effective," "achieve a more consistent level of representation," and "create permanent and comprehensive membership and employer files."

10. Delegates voting against the Stern administration proposal for expanded MRCs (and other "Justice for All" platform resolutions) numbered about 233. Of those, approximately 150 were from UHW and the remaining ones were mainly dissident members of other California and Nevada locals, including 99, 521, 721, 1000, 1021, and 1107.

11. For a longer discussion of this problem, see Tom Juravich's chapter on Verizon customer service center work in *At the Altar of the Bottom Line: The Degradation of Work in the 21st Century* (Boston: University of Massachusetts Press, 2010), 15–53.

12. For more on Local 1400's membership recruitment at Verizon, see Steve Early, "Membership-Based Organizing," in *A New Labor Movement*, Mantsios, 82–103.

13. Communications Workers of America Education and Mobilization Department, *Mobilizing for Power*, 2006.

14. For a *Labor Notes* published account of how Trementozzi and his slate got elected originally, see Aaron Brenner, "Reformers Take Over CWA Local 1400," under the section "Reform Caucuses & Running for Office," Troublemaker's Website.

15. Steve Early, "Broadband Redlining Targets Rural America," *Nation*, online edition, May 14, 2007, and "FairPoint Mess Puts Three States in Jeopardy," *Rutland Herald*, April 9, 2009.

16. Kate Davidson, "Unions, FairPoint Reach Deal," *Concord Monitor*, March 25, 2008.

17. Interview with the author, August 2, 2008.

18. Stephen Lerner, "Justice for All Unionism vs. Neo-Business Unionism," a response to David Bacon and Warren Mar, "SEIU: Debating Labor's Strategy," MRZine, July 15, 2008.

19. SEIU Officers, "Recommendations to the SEIU 2008 Convention," 15.

20. See Decision and Order in Service Employees International Union, Local 1, AFL-CIO, and Remzi Jaos, NLRB Case 13-CA-41636, available online from the NLRB.

21. All quotes are from interview with the author, conducted by phone, May 14, 2010.

22. As part of her SEIU reform activity, Alexander started a website to keep fellow members informed about developments in their union. Its contents are archived at http://democracy4seiu.blogspot.com.

23. Interview with the author, March 22, 2008.

24. For an account of the broader impact of these merger-related staff layoffs, see William Johnson, "Staffers Get Squeezed in New SEIU Locals," *Labor Notes*, September 2007, 6.

25. See Paul Krehbiel, "Reform Movement Forms in SEIU," *Labor Notes*, April 2008, 1, 4.

26. In 2008, a Yahoo discussion group called "Fightfor347" was created to air the complaints about the transfer of Local 347 members to Local 721. Some staffers—unhappily reassigned to MRC work—joined the discussion as well. One posting complained that "the sheer size and poor planning of the Local 721 merger" produced a backlog of six hundred pending grievances, with "not nearly enough staff to handle them." According to this anonymous blogger, staffers at the "Advocacy Center" in Pasadena responded by staging a "sick-out" in protest. Unfortunately, another workload reduction technique "is to simply tell the rank and file: 'You don't have a grievance, we can't help you.'" See "Fightfor347" group at http://finance.groups.yahoo.com/group/fightfor347/.

27. As early as July 2007, based on interviews with a number of "committed SEIU staff members," the *Nation* reported that Stern's "emphasis on consolidating small locals into larger organizations" is making it "harder for workers to find their union rep or file a simple grievance. If union members don't feel the union is serving them, organizers say, they begin to ask why they are paying dues." See Liza Featherstone, "Andy Stern: Savior or Sell-Out?," *Nation*, July 16, 2007, 9.

28. Ferd Wulkan, "Massachusetts Service Employees Reformers Beat Appointed Leadership," *Labor Notes*, June 2009, 5–6, and Bruce Boccardy, "Members of a Massachusetts SEIU Local Dislodge an Incumbent," *Labor Notes*, August 2009, 6.

29. As quoted by Kaplan, "Labor's Growing Pains."

30. Document in possession of author. All Change 1021 literature was originally posted on the group's now discontinued campaign website.

31. SEIU Local 521 Member Resource Center, Contract Enforcement Team, "Executive Board Report," February 28, 2008, 1, attached to minutes of executive board meeting held on same date. Document in possession of author.

32. As quoted by Jessica Lyons in "Union Shake-up," *Monterey County Weekly*, March 8, 2007, 1.

33. Interview with the author, February 23, 2010.

34. Interview with the author, March 7, 2010.

35. Steve Early, "SEIU's MegaLocal Meltdown," *Working In These Times* (blog), March 1, 2010.

36. "Dear SEIU Local 721 Brother/Sister" letter from Bob Schoonover, dated June 23, 2010, about "Imagine 721" conference in Riverside, California, on July 30–August 1, 2010. Schoonover's MDU critics noted that the meeting was not open to all members and probably cost as much as $150,000 to hold. Kaiser Permanente, one of the major medical care providers for members of the local, was listed as a sponsor of the event.

37. All quotes in this section are from a mid-2010 internal SEIU report entitled *Report and Recommendations from the Member Strength Review Committee*. Its members included Eliseo Medina, Local 32BJ president Mike Fishman, Local 775 president David Rolf, Local 1 president Sharleen Stewart, and John Tanner, a top staff member of Local 721 in Los Angeles. Document in possession of author.

38. In late 2010, a New York City call center, costing SEIU $800,000 or more a year in headquarters subsidies, was closed. According to the Member Strength Review Committee, it previously served members of 1199SEIU until its "steady volume of business" began to suffer from competition from centers outside of NYC with lower operating costs."

39. "Report and Recommendations from the Member Strength Review Committee."

Chapter 5: Who Rules SEIU (and Who Doesn't)

1.   For the rest of the quote, see Steve Early, "Reutherism Redux," 220.

2.   Paul Pringle, "A Year of Triumphs and Scandals for SEIU," *Los Angeles Times*, December 31, 2008.

3.   As quoted by Tony Cook and Mike Mishak, "CNA Tips Status Quo But Doesn't Oust SEIU," *Las Vegas Sun*, May 9, 2008.

4.   See William Johnson interview with John Templeton, *Labor Notes*, January 2005, 8–9.

5.   See Ferd Wulkan, "How and Why SEIU Lost 2,300 Members at the University of Massachusetts," a twenty-eight-page unpublished report in the author's possession. For shorter published versions of the same saga, see Ferd Wulkan, "Quest for Democracy Persists Inside SEIU," *Union Democracy Review*, no. 179, May–June 2009, and a September/October 2004 UDR report entitled, "Mass Merger in Local 888."

6. All Templeton quotes are from phone interviews with the author. Local 509 proposals to the 2004 SEIU convention are contained in a document in possession of author.

7. Adrienne Eaton, Janice Fine, Allison Porter, and Saul Rubinstein, "Organizational Change at SEIU," 1996–2009, 25–26.

8. For more on Sullivan's eventual replacement, Rocio Saenz, see Early, "Reutherism Redux," 224. This Stern-installed SEIU leader from the West Coast came with a more appealing personal biography (and thus greater social movement cachet) than Holway. An immigrant from Mexico with past experience as an organizer for HERE, Saenz also had a Hollywood movie credit on her resume, for her appearance in Ken Loach's *Bread and Roses*.

9. Steve Bailey, "Good Job, Good Wages," *Boston Globe*, April 15, 2009, and a related column on April 29, 2005, entitled, "Good Job(s), Good Wages." NAGE/Local 5000 president Holway continues to wheel and deal in the Massachusetts state legislature to the detriment of other SEIU affiliates in the state. His local refuses to participate in the SEIU State Council. In 2010, council members complained to new SEIU president Mary Kay Henry that Holway used his political connections to sabotage a bill designed to grant collective bargaining rights to home-based child care providers because they were not going to become members of his own local. For more on workplace life inside NAGE, see http://nagemembers-units1-3-6.blogspot.com.

10. Wulkan, "Quest for Democracy Persists," and UDR report entitled, *Mass Merger in Local 888*.

11. Citing earlier work by MIT industrial relations professor Michael Piore, *Solidarity for Sale*, a 2006 book by Robert Fitch, does a good job of describing Stern's affinity for the modern management methods promoted by General Motors executive Alfred P. Sloan. SEIU didn't adopt them haphazardly, Fitch suggests, but rather "opted for business principles and business structure" in a systematic way. According to Piore, "Their single most important source was probably the *Harvard Business Review*. The union hired the American Management Association to do their staff training." See Piore, "Unions: A Reorientation to Survive," in *Labor Economics and Industrial Relations*, Clark Kerr and Paul D. Staudohar, eds. (Cambridge, MA: Harvard University Press, 1994), 528.

12. For example, in the two IEB votes in January 2009 that led to Stern's trusteeship over UHW, only a handful of board members voted no or abstained on the issue of transferring sixty-five thousand long-term care workers out of UHW against their will. On the second vote to approve the UHW trusteeship, there was even less opposition.

13. SEIU's two Canadian vice presidents and two other IEB members from north of the border are elected at the convention, but by Canadian delegates only, in a fairly typical North American union concession to "national autonomy."

14. Harold Meyerson, "Henry Takes Command—Collaboratively," *American Prospect*, May 11, 2010. Previously, several board members had insisted that "Andy Stern does not control all of the ideas and direction of SEIU" and that SEIU operated

with "collective leadership with differing views." See Gerry Hudson and Tom De-Bruin, "A Response to Herman Benson," *Dissent* online only, January 7, 2009.

15. See 2008 SEIU convention flyer distributed by UHW entitled, "The SEIU Loyalty Oath: What's Wrong with That?" Document in possession of author.

16. An up-to-date list of who's who on its IEB is never posted on SEIU's website; only the eight officers and EVPs are listed, along with their bios. SEIU issues press releases when new members are added to the board, but not when others are dropped from it.

17. For the best popular history of the LMRDA and worker attempts to use it, see Herman Benson's book, *Rebels, Reformers, and Racketeers*, available from the AUD at www.uniondemocracy.org/Resources/books/rebels.htm.

18. From "UHW Talking Points," a September 10, 2008, memo prepared by Arthur Fox, when he was hired by UHW to help fend off the trusteeship described in chapter 6. Document in possession of author. See also Herman Benson, "It's Hard to Resist a Repressive Trusteeship," *Union Democracy Review*, September/October, 2009, page 4.

19. Rick Fantasia and Kim Voss, *Hard Work: Remaking the American Labor Movement* (Berkeley and Los Angeles: University of California Press, 2004). See also Voss and Sherman, "Breaking the Iron Law of Oligarchy," 303–349.

20. Any forced departure from the union by Lerner would, of course, create an IEB vacancy that might very well be filled by Courtney, who is a protégé of EVP Dave Regan.

21. As Julius Getman recounts in *Restoring the Power of Unions: It Takes a Movement* (New Haven, CT: Yale University, 2010), on the hotel worker side of the union, organizers recruited from the outside in the 1970s and '80s "now provide the core of its leadership." Yet Getman argues that "the diversity of backgrounds and attitudes has provided an opportunity for HERE's leaders to learn from and teach each other…In fact, the former college students who have risen to positions of authority in HERE—among others, D. Taylor in Las Vegas, Paul Clifford in Toronto, and Henry Tamarin in Chicago—have been meticulous in searching out and recruiting rank-and-file organizers," 313–18.

22. See C. Wright Mills, *The New Men of Power: America's Labor Leaders* (Chicago: University of Illinois Press, 2001), with a new introduction by Nelson Lichtenstein, and Stanley Aronowitz, *Working Class Hero: A New Strategy for Labor* (New York: Pilgrim Press, 1983).

23. For details of this arrangement, see James Parks, "CWA's New Diversity Plan Reflects Strategies from AFL-CIO Diversity Dialogues," *AFL-CIO Now* (blog), July 17, 2007.

24. The newer elements of CWA—including public employees, health care workers, media workers, and other non-telecom groups who joined the union in the 1980s and '90s—were a key part of Cohen's electoral coalition. He was also strongly backed by telephone workers in the Northeast and other parts of the country who had participated in major strikes and organizing activity. Morton Bahr, who was then president of CWA, led the IEB majority that supported Cohen for EVP. See footnote 33 to introduction.

25. Stern's own elevation to the SEIU presidency followed a rare contested race for

SEIU's top position. The union's secretary-treasurer, seventy-four-year-old Dick Cordtz, made a bid to replace John Sweeney when the latter left in December 1995, to become head of the AFL-CIO. During the four months that Cordtz served as president during the remainder of Sweeney's term, Stern was fired as organizing director and forced to run an insurgent campaign against Cordtz and his old guard supporters. By March 1996, Stern had the support of locals representing two-thirds of the union's membership. Cordtz withdrew rather than face defeat at the union's convention a month later. The forty-five-year-old Stern was elected president, without opposition at the convention, and Cordtz retired.

26. Other prominent TDU supporters haven't been so lucky. In 2010, Hoffa backers on the Teamster joint council in Chicago helped engineer the ouster of Local 743 president Richard Berg and secretary-treasurer Gina Alvarez, two reformers elected after a long struggle to reclaim the eleven thousand-member local from corrupt leadership that supported Hoffa. Berg ran on Leedham's slate against Hoffa in 2006.

27. In the usual SEIU fashion, Dale's appointed successor at Local 49 was its organizing director Meg Niemi, a college-educated member of the staff, who has never been one of the seventy-five hundred working members of this health care and building services local.

28. See relevant observation of longtime SEIU local union staffer Paul Garver, "Does SEIU Need an Ethics Commission or Not?," *Talking Union* (blog), September 5, 2008. According to Garver, "there seems to be little doubt that persons of limited talent and character have been promoted rapidly and moved about the country to fill local and regional positions like trusteeships deemed vital to the national leadership."

29. Interview with the author, January 15, 2008.

30. Interview with the author, August 10, 2008. As originally quoted in Steve Early and Cal Winslow, "Tyronegate and Trusteeship: Can SEIU Members Exorcise the Purple Shades of Jackie Presser?," *CounterPunch*, September 3, 2008.

31. See August 10, 2008, statement by Tyrone Freeman posted on his blog on the Local 6434 website and later removed by SEIU after he was forced out and the local put under trusteeship. The "fighting poverty" quote was in Pringle's first story in his award-winning series, "Union, Charity Paid Thousands to Firms Owned by Officials' Relatives," *Los Angeles Times*, August 9, 2008.

32. Barri Boone interview, August 27, 2008.

33. Interview with the author, December 4, 2009.

34. Paul Pringle, "U.S. Investigates L.A.-Based Union's Election," *Los Angeles Times*, August 16, 2008. Six months later, in another Pringle story, SEIU press spokesperson Michelle Ringuette insisted that, "until we read these allegations in the *L.A. Times*, nobody ever brought before us serious credible evidence of wrongdoing" by Freeman. See Pringle, "A Year of Triumphs and Scandals."

35. Document in possession of author. Shaffer's quote also appeared in *New York Times* coverage of the scandal on September 3, 2008.

36. See Herman Benson, "The Sad, Sad Story of SEIU Local 6434," *Union Democracy Review*, November/December 2008, 8.

37. For a full inventory of membership-financed personal extravagance, see Paul Pringle,

"Union Sues Former Executive for $1.1 Million," *Los Angeles Times*, April 1, 2009.

38. See U.S. Department of Labor LM-2 filings for 2008 by SEIU and SEIU Local 721. For more details on the allegations against Stephens that led to Grajeda's downfall, see Paul Pringle, "The SEIU's Top State Officer Takes a Leave of Absence," *Los Angeles Times*, August 31, 2008.

39. See Steve Early, "Reutherism Redux," 227–229.

40. SEIU spent more than $1 million on this campaign, which faced little or no organized opposition. See Andrew Ryan, "Ballot Item Eyes Unions for Day-Care Workers," *Boston Globe*, October 31, 2010.

41. Early, "SEIU's Megalocal Meltdown."

42. Prior to being hired by SEIU, McAlevey worked for several environmental groups, the Highlander Center, and the Veatch Foundation, which is run by the Unitarian Universalist Church. She also worked for the AFL-CIO where she coordinated a promising but short-lived multi-union project in Connecticut called the Stamford Organizing Project. For a sympathetic account of that work, see Clawson, *The Next Upsurge*.

43. J. Patrick Coolican, "New Face of Labor Has Heart, Drive," *Las Vegas Sun*, December 10, 2006.

44. In December 2006, McAlevey told the *Las Vegas Sun* that Local 1107's "membership had grown from 9,000 to 15,000 since her arrival in spring 2004." In a story a year later, the newspaper noted that "the union's filing with the U.S. Department of Labor shows it had 9,124 members at the end of last year" [2006]. See Tony Cook and Mike Mishak, "Union Split Over Leader," *Las Vegas Sun*, December 3, 2007.

45. Email to the author, October 22, 2010.

46. See Herman Benson, "Nurses in Nevada Are Rejecting SEIU Local 1107," *Union Democracy Review*, July/August 2008, 3.

47. Cook and Mishak, "Union Split Over Leader."

48. Ibid.

49. Benson, "Nurses in Nevada," 3.

50. Cook and Mishak, "Union Split Over Leader."

51. Tony Cook and Mike Mishak, "Outcome for St. Rose Nurses Still Uncertain But Union Unrest Is Clear," *Las Vegas Sun*, May 9, 2008.

52. Jennifer Robison, "SEIU Local's Top Executives Set to Step Down," *Las Vegas Review Journal*, June 26, 2008.

53. See Herman Benson, "The Curious Story of SEIU Local 221 in California," *Union Democracy Review*, May/June 2010, 5.

54. Paul Pringle, "Service Union Bans Former California Local President for Life," *Los Angeles Times*, November 26, 2008.

55. When Freeman was replaced, first by a Stern-appointed trustee and then a Stern-anointed successor from the SEIU staff, there was little doubt that the new Local 6434 president would also be a headquarters favorite imported from elsewhere. Laphonza Butler, elected without opposition in early 2010, was previously the Stern-installed secretary-treasurer of the strife-torn Service Workers United, director of SEIU's security guard organizing, and a former staffer for several East Coast locals.

56. Paul Pringle, "Top SEIU Official in California Quits Three Posts," *Los Angeles Times*, March 10, 2009.
57. Dennis Romero, "Alejandro Stephens, Former SEIU Union Leader, Sentenced to Prison," *LA Weekly*, September 2, 2010.
58. Kris Maher and Evan Perez, "SEIU Probed Over Consulting Pacts," *Wall Street Journal*, September 29, 2010.
59. As quoted by Steven Greenhouse, "Ex-Union President Issues Denial of Inquiries," September 29, 2010. As reported by Patrick J. McDonnell, "Ex-L.A. Labor Leader Alejandro Stephens Headed to Prison," *Los Angeles Times*, December 8, 2010, an arbitrator rejected SEIU's demand that the convicted felon return any money to the union because "there was no 'indication what Stephens' specific duties were, or the expectation of SEIU'" regarding work he was supposed to perform. The arbitrator did allow SEIU to withhold its final $75,000 consulting payment to the former Local 660 president because of his fraud and tax evasion conviction.
60. McAlevey's former advisor Jerry Brown contends that her "approach to membership empowerment was the opposite of Stern's" and that she was critical of "the International when it made secret deals with HCA limiting workers' rights." For more on that continuing problem, see chapter 10.
61. For more on the details of Moore's lawsuit, see Eleanor Yang Su, "Service Employees Union Sued Ex-President Over Severance," SignOn SanDiego (the *San Diego Union-Tribune* website), April 12, 2010, www.signonsandiego.com/news/2010/apr/08.
62. Ibid.
63. Bruce Nissen, "Political Activism as Part of a Broader Civic Engagement: The Case of SEIU Florida Healthcare Union," *Labor Studies Journal* 35, no. 1 (March 2008): 72.
64. Only 26 percent of FHU's 7,450 dues-paying members actually participated in the merger vote.
65. Another precondition for the merger between 1199 and 2020 was the dismantling of the latter's longtime staff union. 1199 field reps and organizers in Massachusetts today have no staff union contract like their predecessors had with Local 2020 (and Local 285 before the local was reorganized and renumbered). 1199 has always opposed unionization of its field staff and, during Dennis Rivera's presidency, campaigned aggressively against past organizing efforts by staff members in New York.
66. As quoted by Christopher Rowland, "Baystate Medical Workers Gain Allies," *Boston Globe*, October 17, 2006.
67. Jeff Krasner, "Home Health Assistants Vote to Join Union," *Boston Globe*, November 9, 2007. One Massachusetts 1199 organizer wanted it noted, for the record, that the PCA drive was "a several year campaign that involved the combined work of our political department, the International, and 1199." It took several hundred organizers "from everywhere including other SEIU locals" to collect the necessary union authorization cards and win the representation vote. Email to author, October 25, 2010.
68. As quoted by Christopher Rowland, "Union Looks to Organize Hub's Top Hospitals," *Boston Globe*, August 31, 2005.

69. Robert Weissman, "New Unionization Drive Awaits Big Teaching Hospitals," *Boston Globe*, July 6, 2010.

70. For a profile of Fadel's successor, Veronica Turner, see Weissman, "New Unionization Drive." Doris Turner, the controversial president of District 1199 in New York in the 1980s, is no relation to Veronica from Boston, who became the EVP candidate on George Gresham's slate in 2010.

71. Document in possession of author. Gresham's flyer was issued by the "Committee for the Direct Election of Officers and Organizers" and is part of a collection of 1199 reform movement materials at the Tamiment Library, NYU Wagner Labor Archives. One "Save Our Union" supporter, a working RN at the time, points out today that neither Rivera nor his successor, Gresham, ever changed the 1199 structure established by union founder Leon Davis. "In 1199, the president has always created his own union-wide slate for all board positions because there is no democratic structure of elections in which geographical or occupational groups, like nurses, can elect their own leaders. Then as now, the leader of the RN division of 1199 is elected by the entire membership, not just by RNs." Email to author, October 18, 2010.

72. Leon Fink and Brian Greenberg, *Upheaval in the Quiet Zone: 1199SEIU and the Politics of Healthcare Unionism* (Chicago: University of Illinois Press, 2009).

73. Moe Foner, *Not for Bread Alone* (Ithaca, NY: Cornell University Press, 2002), 113.

74. Stern quotes are from a March 20, 2004, post entitled "Democracy and SEIU Justice@Work," on his now discontinued personal blog.

Chapter 6: The Mother of All Trusteeships

1. As quoted by Michelle Amber, "Work Processes Top Issue Facing Unions," *BNA Daily Labor Report*, April 22, 2010.

2. See Emily Ryan testimony in federal court, as quoted on the *Perez Stern* blog, "Friday in Court," April 2, 2010.

3. William Johnson, "Frustrated by Forced Mergers, SEIU Members Go Independent," *Labor Notes*, October 2004, 5.

4. See Tait, *Poor Workers' Unions*.

5. Document in possession of author.

6. David Bacon, "Hundreds of Union Janitors Fired Under Pressure from Feds," *People's Daily World*, May 21, 2010.

7. Letter to Andy Stern from SEIU Local 134 members, dated June 30, 2002. Document in possession of author.

8. SEIU flyer entitled, "Good Business Agents Gone Bad," March 20, 2004. Document in possession of author.

9. Prior to the NUHW decertification activity in 2009–10, the largest exodus from SEIU occurred in Canada in 2000. There, SEIU lost a quarter of its total membership in Ontario after workers revolted against forced consolidation of eight local unions into one. The Canadian Auto Workers (CAW) petitioned for elections in 180 SEIU bargaining units, eventually winning the right to represent 14,000 members. See Steve Early, "Checking Out of Stern's Hotel California," *CounterPunch*, February 2, 2009.

10. One other significant change from pre- to post-trusteeship UHW was the total compensation of the guy in charge. In 2008, his last full year in office, Sal Rosselli's base pay was $131,344. His additional allowances and expense reimbursements as an elected officer of a local with 150,000 members brought that up to $142,675. His Stern-appointed successor from Ohio, SEIU trustee Dave Regan, was much more costly for UHW members, while delivering what many would describe as less "value." Regan's salary for 2009 was $199,640. He also received more than twice as much in union "allowances," plus "disbursements for official business" that were seven times larger. All of which added up to a total UHW/SEIU EVP compensation of $265,488, nearly twice the cost of Rosselli the previous year.

11. Either directly or as outside lawyers and PR consultants, SEIU employs quite a network of people who were once union reform allies. Among them are MFD-era staffers of the United Mine Workers, like Bob Hauptman, Tom Geoghegan, Edgar James, and Eddie Burke. Hauptman, Geoghegan, and James later worked for United Steelworker dissident Ed Sadlowski. James is now the law partner of SEIU general counsel Judy Scott, who previously served as Teamster president Ron Carey's general counsel. Burke was Carey's 1991 campaign manager and ended up as his chief of staff. Others SEIU has employed include Scott's husband, Don Stillman, who aided both the MFD and Sadlowski early in his career; Matt Witt, who took over from Stillman as editor of the *United Mine Workers Journal* in 1975 and later became Teamster communications director under Carey; and Steve Trossman, a fellow Teamster press staffer during the same period.

12. Sal Rosselli, "Service Employees Union Pushes for More Strategic Focus, New AFL Leader," *Labor Notes*, May 2005, 7.

13. See Kaplan, "Labor's Growing Pains." See also Daniel J. B. Mitchell, "The Collapse of the Schwarzenegger Health Plan in California," *WorkingUSA* 11 (June 2008): 199–218.

14. In the SEIU state council election, Stern stacked the deck against Rosselli by easily lining up votes against him from the appointed "interim" presidents of recently merged locals, and by ignoring per capita dues delinquencies from locals like Tyrone Freeman's. See "Big Local Boycotts SEIU Election as Rigged, *Union Democracy Review*, January/February 2008.

15. Sal Rosselli resignation letter as quoted by Michelle Amber, "Rosselli Resigns from SEIU Executive Committee," *BNA Daily Labor Report*, February 12, 2010.

16. For a longer account of UHW's first anti-trusteeship rally, see Steve Early, "A Purple Uprising in Oakland," in *Embedded with Organized Labor*, 251–255.

17. Document in possession of author.

18. SEIU did succeed in generating some embarrassing publicity for UHW when it rightfully challenged the fact that some of the local's convention representatives had been chosen improperly, in an election process that limited candidates for delegate positions to members already serving as shop stewards. In May 2008, UHW acknowledged this legal impropriety and quickly reran its convention delegate election so any member could campaign to win a trip to San Juan that proved to be no day at the beach.

19. Bill Ragen's "implosion" memo is in possession of the author. Also posted on the *Perez Stern* blog, April 8, 2010.

20. This campaign to undermine UHW's day-to-day functioning became so offensive to some SEIU national union staffers forced to participate that their staff union adopted a resolution in May 2008 opposing any further work on it. Kaplan, "Labor's Growing Pains."

21. For a report on the frustrating attempts by UHW members to coordinate their long-term care bargaining with Tyrone Freeman, see Meredith Schafer, "Industrial vs. Corporate Unionism in Health Care," *Against the Current*, July/August 2009, 4–6.

22. Charlene Harrington, "To Whom It May Concern" letter, July 9, 2008. Document in possession of author.

23. See Boris and Klein's forthcoming *Caring for America: How Home Healthcare Workers Changed the Face of Labor*, from Oxford University Press in 2012.

24. All Ray Marshall quotes in this chapter are from phone interview with the author, October 7, 2010.

25. Marshall, of course, disputes this characterization. He accepted the hearing officer assignment against the advice of his wife, after receiving "conflicting advice" from others about the wisdom of getting involved in the UHW-SEIU dispute. He believed he "had credibility with all sides" that could be deployed in the service of a peaceful settlement. "In my mind," he said, "I could be perfectly impartial in both appearance and reality."

26. Ray Marshall, "Report and Recommendations to the International President," SEIU.org, January 21, 2009, www.seiu.org/images/pdfs/hearingofficerreport.

27. Marshall reports that SEIU "was not happy when I made that decision."

28. For more on the IEB's January 9, 2009, action and the rationale for it, see Eliseo Medina, "Why SEIU Supports Uniting Long Term Care Workers," *BeyondChron* (blog), January 21, 2009.

29. Email message to the author.

30. The letter from academics urging UHW and SEIU acceptance of the Marshall report is a document in possession of author.

31. As Cal Winslow recounts in *Labor's Civil War in California*, 54–55, SEIU conducted its own "advisory vote" in December 2008, on a pooled basis. Most long-term care union members in California boycotted the balloting. Of more than three hundred thousand eligible to participate from three different locals, only twenty-four thousand, or 8 percent, returned their ballots. Maintaining the status quo and remaining within your existing local was not an option. Both choices on the ballot assumed that the forced transfer of long-term care workers from UHW was a done deal. A petition signed by eighty thousand UHW members protested the whole process as a mockery of democracy.

32. For the complete SEIU dossier on what Stern was allegedly protecting UHW members from, see the August 29, 2009, report entitled, *Putting Members at Risk*. In it, SEIU explains, not very convincingly, "how Sal Rosselli and other former officials of UHW misused union dues money, undermined union democracy, canceled union contracts, stole union property, and destroyed critical union

records for their own personal interests." This document can be found at SEIU.org, www.seiu-uhw.org/2009/08/putting-members-at-risk.html#more.

33. Michelle Amber and Joyce Cutler, "Former Leaders of UHW Local Quit SEIU, Plan to Form New Union," *BNA Daily Labor Report*, January 29, 2009.

34. See report from Court House News, "Bodyguards Say SEIU Owes $924,000 for Protecting Bosses During Union Beef," May 3, 2009. See also NUHW press release, "Lawsuit Details SEIU Surveillance Effort," May 6, 2009. Posted at www.nuhw.org.

35. See April 20, 2009, memo from cotrustee Eliseo Medina to SEIU local presidents in California informing them that they "now face hostile and aggressive decertification campaigns from NUHW" that require diversion of staff from their pursuit of the "important goals of Change That Works," SEIU's much-ballyhooed 2009 campaign to hold Obama and the Democrats accountable. Document in possession of author.

36. As quoted by Christopher Cook, "An Inconvenient War," *San Francisco Bay Guardian*, April 9, 2010.

37. Email message to the author.

38. Cal Winslow, *Labor's Civil War*, 59–65. See also his original account, "Stern Gang Seizes UHW Union Hall," *CounterPunch*, February 2, 2009.

39. It was through Ed James, a former UMW headquarters colleague, that I first met Suzanne Gordon in 1978, later to be my spouse and Alex Early's mother. Edgar's legal work for SEIU in recent years has been extremely unhelpful, but I am forever grateful for his role in the chain of events that produced one more foe of his union client in California.

40. See CNA, "CNA/NNOC Criticizes SEIU Trusteeship: Cites Concerns for Disruption of Patient Care in California," press release, January 29, 2009.

41. The legal hurdles faced by NUHW are well described in a letter sent by fifty NUHW supporters in Southern California to NLRB regional directors James Small and James McDermott in Los Angeles. Their October 8, 2009, protest documents the "multiple charges SEIU has filed with the NLRB in an attempt to block elections covering 1,600 hospital workers." To delay representation votes, while the board investigated SEIU allegations of real or imagined employer unfair labor practices, the incumbent union flooded every board regional office in California with scores of "bogus charges." As the signers of the letter assert, this "makes a mockery of the NLRB's duty to safeguard workers' rights to fair and timely elections under federal law." Document in possession of author.

42. Steven Greenhouse, "Two Unions, Once Bitter Rivals, Will Now Work Together," *New York Times*, March 19, 2009.

43. See "SEIU, CNA/NNOC Announce Major Accord—Expected to Spur Campaign for Employee Free Choice Act, Spark Major Drive for Healthcare Union Organizing, and Boost RN Standards and Power for Healthcare Workers," a joint SEIU and CNA press release, March 19, 2009.

44. Not all CNA field staffers were similarly exultant about this sudden leadership about-face. In a March 2009 email to the author, one organizer wrote: "All each side got out of the constant warfare was that it hurt the other side. CNA acts like

it is triumphant but really, considering its size, all it did was just survive. You don't get a national RN union from Andy Stern. You ORGANIZE one."

45. See Mark Brenner interview with Burger, "Quiet on the Western Front? Behind the SEIU-CNA Alliance," *Labor Notes*, May 20, 2009. Writing in *Union Democracy Review* (March/April 2009, no. 178), Herman Benson criticized the fact that nurses were "now for sale, barter, and trade" because both CNA and SEIU abandoned rank-and-file supporters in various places, as they ceded turf to each other under the terms of the agreement.

46. Among those assisting this impressive operation were Jamie Horowitz and Bob Muehlenkamp, both Washington, D.C.–based union consultants with years of experience, whose well compensated work for UHW was no longer affordable after the trusteeship.

47. The still-available postings on these now inactive sites can be found (as of mid-2010) at http://perezstern.blogspot.com/ and http://adiosandy.blogspot.com/. Tasty and Keyser were still alive and kicking at http://sternburgerwithfries.blogspot.com/ and http://sonomaredrevolt.blogspot.com/, respectively.

48. See Perez, "Strange Typo," *Perez Stern* (blog), February 24, 2010, http://perezstern .blogspot.com/2009/02/strange-typo.html.

49. June 16, 2010, decision by NLRB administrative law judge Burton Litvack in Alta Bates Summit Medical Center and NUHW, Cases # 32-CA-24459, 24469, and 24470, NLRB website, www.nlrb.gov/shared_files/ALJ%20Decisions/2010/JD-SF-25–10.pdf.

50. For more on the individual defendants and their background, see Cal Winslow, "No Knock-Out Blow In SEIU's Courtroom Showdown," *CounterPunch*, April 13, 2010.

51. Kuhlman, as quoted by Carl Finamore, "Bloody Nose for NUH, Black Eye for SEIU," *BeyondChron* (blog), April 12, 2010. For an earlier report on the trial by Finamore, see "When a Union Acts like a Big Corporation: A Report from SEIU's Civil Trial Against California Union Reformers," *Talking Union* (blog), March 28, 2010.

52. Joyce Cutler, "Federal Jury Holds NUHW, Leaders Liable for $1.5 Million," *BNA Daily Labor Report*, April 12, 2010. UHW trustees proceeded to use the jury verdict to discourage worker support for NUHW based on the new union being "bankrupt." See, for example, UHW email bulletin entitled, "In New Court Filing, NUHW Reveals It's Nearly Broke," August 23, 2010, www.seiu-uhw.org/2010/ 08/nuhw-reveals-its-nearly-broke.html.

53. A group of UHW members tried, unsuccessfully, to challenge the trusteeship extension in federal court when Henry announced in July 2010, that it would last twenty-four months rather than eighteen.

Chapter 7: Ivy League Amigos No More

1. Interview with the author, January 15, 2010.

2. Steve Early, "AFL-CIO's Organizing Summit Looks at 'Best Practices'—But Leaves Much Unexamined," *Labor Notes*, February 2003.

3. For more on the upside and downside of union consolidation, past and present, see "Working Class Intellectuals" in Early, *Embedded with Organized Labor*, 59–64.

4. Steven Greenhouse, "Two Unions in Marriage Now Face Divorce Talks," *New York*

Times, February 8, 2009, 16.

5. UNITE HERE, "UNITE HERE Statement on Joint Board Actions," press release, March 8, 2009. Document in possession of author. Wilhelm's own reported "total compensation" for 2006—a mere $344,000—didn't lag far behind Raynor's in a union representing many workers who earn, on average, less than one tenth what their then copresidents did.

6. Gettelfinger-Girard letter. Document in possession of the author.

7. John Wilhelm memo to "The American Labor Movement re Private Investigator," May 26, 2009. As Wilhelm noted in his memo, past high-profile "IGI investigations have resulted in news stories alleging wife beating, shoplifting, lying, child abuse, sexual promiscuity, corruption, secret payments, hypocrisy, and resume falsification."

8. See series of March 2009 UNITE HERE press statements issued by John Wilhelm, President–Hospitality Division. In one dated March 8, Wilhelm accused Workers United of leaving "based on the votes of fewer than 1,000 'delegates' some of whom were appointed to their positions rather than elected, and many of whom are paid staff members, not rank and file workers." See also "Statement of UNITE-HERE General Executive Board," issued in Washington, D.C., March 13, 2009.

9. Author interview with Pepicelli and his then consultant on the TJX campaign, the late Tim Costello.

10. Stephen Lerner, "An Immodest Proposal: A New Architecture for the House of Labor," *New Labor Forum* 12, no. 2 (Summer 2003): 9–30.

11. For an excellent history of Wilhelm's career and his early work with Sirabella in New Haven, see Julius Getman, *Restoring the Power of Unions: It Takes a Movement* (New Haven, CT: Yale University Press, 2010).

12. O'Sullivan, Giblin, McEntee, and other UNITE HERE convention speakers were quoted by Randy Shaw, "Labor Movement Backs UNITE HERE Against SEIU Raids," *BeyondChron* (blog), June 30, 2009.

13. "We Stand in Solidarity with Unite Here!" posted at the UNITE HERE website, http://www.unitehere.org/files/InternationalPledge.pdf.

14. Writing in *Union Democracy Review* (no. 182, November/December 2009), Herman Benson applauded the new UNITE HERE constitution for "extending democracy" and "curbing authoritarianism." He noted that it also provided new protections against the imposition of unwarranted and politically motivated trusteeships over local unions.

15. See NUHW LM-2 form for 2009, on file with the U.S. Department of Labor. Form LM-2 refers to the "Labor Organization Annual Report," which private sector unions must file every year with the DOL. These reports are available to union members, along with the general public, and are the source of most union financial data and salary information cited in *Civil Wars*.

16. Michael Mishak, "Wilhelm's Stand: Labor Will Rebuild Middle Class," *Las Vegas Sun*, May 31, 2009. In a separate interview with the same paper, even Bruce Raynor agreed the UNITE HERE dispute was generating unfavorable publicity and having negative political fallout. "It makes the labor movement look bad…It puts Democratic allies of ours in difficult positions and distracts from the real issues," he

said. Michael Mishak, "Card Check Might Be Union War's Collateral Damage," *Las Vegas Sun,* June 3, 2010.

17. Richard Hurd, "Neutrality Agreements: Innovative, Controversial, and Labor's Hope for the Future," *New Labor Forum* (Spring 2008): 35–44. See Getman, *Restoring the Power of Unions,* 79–91, 101–114, for a longer, more detailed account of how HERE-conducted "comprehensive campaigns" won organizing rights agreements with some hotel chains and casino operators.

18. In 1996, ACTWU merged with the ILGWU to form the Union of Needletrades, Industrial and Textile Employees, known by the acronym of "UNITE." ACTWU was itself the product of an earlier merger between separate unions of clothing and textile workers.

19. As Julius Getman points out, Wilhelm's whole career has been spent rebuilding a union that had more members in the sixties than it does today (and lost many of them when big-city restaurants, not connected to hotels or casinos, deunionized).

20. Kris Maher, "Unions Forge Secret Pacts with Major Employers," *Wall Street Journal,* May 10, 2008.

21. See "An Open Letter to Andy Stern and the Leadership of SEIU," from student-labor activists at UNC Chapel Hill, Stanford, Santa Clara University, and UC Irvine, May 2008, posted at Nation.com, www.thenation.com/special/pdf/SEIU/StudentLetter.pdf.

22. Paul Abowd, "Food Service Workers Buck Secret Organizing Deals," *Labor Notes,* September 2009, 14–15.

23. After Sodexo's organizing rights agreement with SWU expired, SEIU mounted its own national campaign against the company, which is ongoing. It organized anti-Sodexo protests, ran ads exposing the company's poor labor relations practices, and lobbied against it getting any federal food service contracts. Sodexo tried to discredit this campaign by attributing it to "an ongoing dispute with rival unions, including Unite Here, designed to attract new members." See Kevin Bog ardus, "Former House Dem Leader Gephardt Hired as Lobbyist by Firm Battling SEIU," TheHill.com, June 16, 2010.

24. Abowd, "Food Service Workers Buck," 15.

25. Sean Abbott-Klafter, Crystal Stermer, Lohl Berning, and Tenaya Lafore, "Open Letter to All Those Concerned About the Labor Movement," September 21, 2009. Document in possession of author.

26. One former staffer, Amelia Frank-Vitale, told Greenhouse that she was very committed to "stopping this creepy, cult-like form of organizing." See Steven Greenhouse, "Some Organizers Protest Their Union's Tactics," *New York Times,* November 19, 2010.

27. Email message, February 4, 2009, from Jerry Hairston, president, Federation of Union Representatives, responding to UNITE HERE's new "privacy policy" issued in response to a FOUR grievance and negative publicity about "pink-sheeting."

28. "Open Letter" from UNITE HERE Local 1 staffer Chuck Hendricks and nine other leaders of UUHS, emailed to the author by Hendricks, November 21, 2009. Two of the UNITE HERE boycott organizers who quit over pink-sheeting, Arlen Jones and Greg Hoffman, had an exchange in *Labor Notes* with Hendricks over this same subject. See "Viewpoint," *Labor Notes,* January 2010, 7.

Chapter 8: The Progressive Quandary

1. Peter Dreier, "Divorce—Union Style," *Nation*, August 12, 2009.

2. Kate Bronfenbrenner as quoted by Jake Blumgart, "The New Terms of the Labor Dialogue," *American Prospect*, online edition, February 26, 2009.

3. "An Open Letter of Concern about SEIU's Interference with UNITE HERE," July 22, 2009, www.unitehere.org/presscenter/release.php?ID=3793.

4. "Dear Friends and Colleagues" email sent by Josh Freeman to fellow LAWCHA members, June 24, 2009. Document in possession of author.

5. Email from Dan Clawson to Josh Freeman and others, entitled "Re: Open Letter about Unite-Here," June 24, 2009. Document in possession of author.

6. For a longer history of this relationship, see Nelson Lichtenstein, "Why American Unions Need Intellectuals," *Dissent* 57, no. 2 (Spring 2010): 69–73.

7. Herman Benson, "After Twelve Years: Where Is That Labor-Intellectual Alliance?," *New Politics* (Winter 2008): 106–116.

8. Joshua Freeman and Steve Fraser, eds. *Audacious Democracy: Labor, Intellectuals, and the Social Reconstruction of America* (New York: Houghton Mifflin, 1997), 277.

9. After its 1999 conference, SAWSJ went into decline and ended up disbanding with some of its leading activists soon playing a role in the formation of LAWCHA. The labor historians network has assumed many of the same campus-labor solidarity functions, and includes, within its membership, many nonhistorians as well.

10. As noted previously, in the preface and chapter 2, Gordon is my wife. After she signed the May Day 2008 letter to Andy Stern that was reprinted in the *New York Times* and the 2009 "letter of concern" to Stern initiated by LAWCHA members, Gordon became persona non grata at SEIU headquarters. She was able to maintain friendly ties with several RN-led SEIU locals.

11. See Harold Meyerson, "Labor's Real Fight," *American Prospect*, February 1, 2009.

12. See Steven Greenhouse, "From Author, Help for White-Collar Workers," *New York Times*, September 14, 2006, or Ehrenreich's personal website. Ehrenreich never responded to an email request that she endorse the May 2008 letter to Stern and did not sign the one about UNITE HERE a year later.

13. *New Labor Forum* has also published exchanges between supporters and critics of SEIU. See, for example, Max Fraser, "Labor's Conundrum: Growth vs. Standards," *New Labor Forum* 18, no. 1 (Winter 2009), which examined the conflict between UHW and SEIU and was followed by responses from partisans of each side.

14. Dave Johnson, "SEIU Convention—These Are PROGRESSIVE People!" Huffington Post, June 2, 2008.

15. Stephen Lerner email to Matt Witt, June 13, 2008. Document in possession of author.

16. Stephen Lerner email to Andy Stern and Anna Burger, entitled "Some Thoughts on Relations with Left Progressive Groups," which contained a memo on "Encouraging New Ideas, Engaging in Debate," June 16, 2008. Document in possession of author.

17. Chris Rauber, "More Than 240 Lawmakers, Community Leaders Urge SEIU to Hold Off on UHW Takeover," *San Francisco Business Journal*, November 17, 2008. See also Randy Shaw, "Progressive Outpouring for Rosselli, SEIU-UHW," *Beyond-Chron* (blog), November 19, 2009.

18. See "Open Letter of Concern to Andy Stern from California Educators, Academics, Writers, and Worker Advocates," November 9, 2008. Document in possession of author.
19. As quoted by Kris Maher, "Spending Issue Raises Concern for SEIU Plans," *Wall Street Journal*, August 16, 2008.
20. Stephen Lerner email to Michelle Ringuette, August 25, 2008. Document in possession of author.
21. Dreir quotes are from Paul Pringle, "U.S. Investigates L.A.-Based Union's Election," and "A Year of Triumphs and Scandals for SEIU."
22. Fraser, "Labor's Conundrum: Growth vs. Standards," 56.
23. Michael Yates et al., "SEIU: Debating Labor's Strategy," MRZine, July 14, 2008.
24. Stephen Lerner email to Andy Stern, May 25, 2008. Document in possession of author.
25. Stephen Lerner et al., "SEIU: Debating Labor's Strategy."
26. Andy Stern email to Stephen Lerner, July 4, 2008. Document in possession of author.
27. Herman Benson, "Hybrid Unionism: Dead End or Fertile Future?," *Dissent* (Winter 2009): 79–85. Hudson and DeBruin's response to Benson was posted on *Dissent*'s website, January 7, 2009, www.dissentmagazine.org/article/?article=1346.
28. Email from participant to the author, September 6, 2008.
29. For more on this problem around the country, see Peter Dreier, "Labor Pains at UCLA," Huffington Post, July 17, 2009; Bob Bussel and Paul Abowd, "University Labor Education Programs Under Fire in Economic Crisis," *Labor Notes*, November 2009, 10; and Stephanie Luce and Mark Brenner, "Labor Studies Under the Gun," *Labor Notes*, September 2007, 10.
30. Email to the author, July 12, 2009.
31. Alec MacGillis, "Andrew Stern Departs SEIU Now Weakened by Infighting," *Washington Post*, May 14, 2010.
32. See SEIU press statement from UHW cotrustee Eliseo Medina entitled, "Rogue Organization's Attempt to Destabilize UHW Is Both Reckless and Feckless," February 5, 2009.
33. Jo-Ann Mort, "Dear All," email, February 6, 2009. Document in possession of author.
34. See SEIU back page advertisements in the *Nation*, entitled "An Open Letter to Friends of the Labor Movement," and "When Unions Fight Each Other, Workers Lose," July 2009.
35. Randy Shaw, "An Open Letter to the *Nation* on the SEIU-UNITE HERE struggle," *BeyondChron* (blog), July 6, 2009. Among those Shaw criticized by name was *Nation* contributor Josh Freeman who, according to Shaw, misleadingly downplayed the role of SEIU in the UNITE-HERE divorce while touting the "social unionism" of the Bruce Raynor–led faction that joined Stern's union. Shaw's own coverage of SEIU has changed in recent years. In 2007, he criticized a "hit piece on SEIU" in a local alternative newspaper. "By attacking Stern," he wrote, "the *SF Weekly* is essentially targeting the leadership of America's progressive labor movement."

Shaw told me that after this *BeyondChron* defense of SEIU appeared, Stern personally called to tell him how much his support mattered. See Shaw, "S.F. Weekly Reaches New Low in Hit Piece on SEIU," April 16, 2007.

36. Javier Morillo, email to Nancy MacLean, July 24, 2009. Document in possession of author.

37. As a thirty-year *Labor Notes* supporter, long familiar with its subscriber list, I can personally attest that most LAWCHA members are not "*Labor Notes* types."

38. The whole Mort-Morillo-Ringuette exchange was forwarded to me by another unintended campus recipient. I passed it along to the always helpful Perez, who posted it in full on July 28, 2009, at the *Perez Stern* blog, http://perezstern.blogspot.com/2009/07/say-what-you-really-think.html.

39. See July 30, 2009, group email from Nancy MacLean entitled "Recent SEIU exchanges about our Open Letter of Concern." Ringuette sent MacLean a note of apology on July 27 for the email Morillo "accidentally" sent to MacLean and for her own "flip tone" and "snarky use of the term 'spam.'" Document in possession of author.

40. Ibid.

41. The relevant portions of Janice Fine's talk to the American Political Science Conference in Toronto were sent to the author by Fine via email, September 10, 2009.

42. See SEIU LM-2s for 2005–09 detailing payments to Rutgers, Allison Porter, or Allison Porter & Associates. According to Eaton, SEIU spent $127,000 on the *Organizational Change at SEIU* report. In a series of email exchanges in November 2010, Porter would not confirm the total amount she was paid by SEIU, as reported by various SEIU entitities to the Department of Labor. She also refused to disclose how much she received as her share of the $127,000 paid to Rutgers for research and writing related to *Organizational Change*. According to DOL records (and the UNITE HERE researcher who helped compile her consulting history), Porter also received nearly $150,000 from UNITE HERE in 2007–08.

43. Despite its supportive tone and content, *Organizational Change at SEIU* did not get much distribution beyond the union executive board. Few local union leaders have ever seen or heard of it and the new national officers of SEIU, who replaced Stern and Burger in 2010, appear less interested in the report than their predecessors who commissioned it.

44. Janice Fine email to author, February 5, 2010.

45. Tony Cook and Michael Mishak, "Union Woos Nurses Amid Rift," *Las Vegas Sun*, April 1, 2008.

46. In a November 6, 2010, email to the author, Hurd reported that he had "no personal knowledge of the dollar amounts of various contracts" between Cornell and SEIU. He explained that his personal consulting relationship with SEIU, as listed in "my vita, which is posted online," involved an affiliate representing state workers in Connecticut.

He argued that SEIU payments to Cornell, as reported on LM-2s "overstate any financial return to our labor extension programs." Because "our labor programs always lose money," Hurd believes it is "simply inaccurate" to "suggest that the money paid to ILR for our labor programs by any union would influence us."

However, only one of Cornell's many labor program staffers, upstate or downstate, was willing to sign the May 2008 letter to Andy Stern protesting his plan to put UHW under trusteeship. After the letter was published, Hurd's colleague Kate Bronfenbrenner quickly demanded that her name be removed from the letter. When I contacted several other Cornell labor educators about signing on before the letter was sent, they expressed agreement with the message but felt they could not afford to be associated with an appeal that might jeopardize Cornell's institutional ties to SEIU or their own personal relationship with its affiliates.

47. Steven Greenhouse, "An Internal Union Dispute Turns Nasty, with a Local in the Balance," *New York Times*, January 18, 2009. The dogfight analogy was Greenhouse's, not Hurd's. Referring to Stern, Hurd told Greenhouse: "You have someone who is arguably the most successful national labor leader who has done a lot of internal restructuring that has worked by and large. I don't see him bowing down or backing down because a strong local labor leader wants another approach."

48. Greenhouse's explanation of the *Times* policy was in an email to the author, February 7, 2010. Greenhouse insisted that, regardless of past or present financial ties to SEIU, "Rick Hurd and Janice Fine [are] among the straightest shooters in the labor relations world" and "continue to view SEIU and Stern with the skeptical, critical eye they view the rest of the labor movement."

49. In a November 10, 2010, phone interview, *Organizational Change* coauthor Adrienne Eaton indicated that she hoped to do some follow-up academic writing based on the report. Eaton was a coauthor (along with three others) of a 2009 Cornell ILR Press book called *Healing Together* about the Kaiser labor-management partnership. As Eaton and her academic colleagues note in the book, "support for the research was provided by the Kaiser Permanente Labor-Management Partnership Trust Fund" over a period of eight years. During that time, they "produced four interim reports on the partnership...written largely for the parties themselves." As part of this LMP consultant role, the authors also provided "periodic feedback and recommendations to the parties on how to address challenges they were experiencing as their efforts unfolded." While fully acknowledging their ongoing relationship with the LMP, Eaton and her coauthors then turned the same partnership-friendly findings into a book for an academic press, claiming that it represented their own "independent" views. The Kaiser-funded LMP trust fund is not required to file an LM-2 form like a labor organization. Neither Eaton nor Tom Kochan, a professor of management at MIT's Sloan School, would disclose what their team was paid for the consulting work with Kaiser that became the basis for *Healing Together*. Based on what Rutgers received from SEIU for a single sixty-seven-page report by four researchers, including Eaton, I estimate that the *Healing Together* authors were paid several hundred thousand dollars (and possibly more) between 2001 and 2008. In an email to the author sent November 22, 2010, Kochan insisted that it was "unfair and inaccurate" to "characterize our role as 'consultants'" or describe their compensation in this fashion. He requested that I accurately report on their "funding as stated in the book"—which, of course, provides no details on the financial "support" received from the Kaiser LMP.

50. This is also a wider issue in academia. See, for example, Robert Gavin, "Silent Part-

ners," *Boston Globe*, November 21, 2010, a report on how some of "the nation's top academic economists—who advise policy makers, testify before Congress, and publish influential papers and articles—are also much sought after by the financial industry as speakers, consultants, and corporate board members." Gavin cites a recent academic study by Gerald Epstein and Jessica Carrick-Hagenbarth from the University of Massachusetts, which found that very few of the economists who "made money from financial institutions...disclosed these connections when writing, speaking or giving interviews on public policy."

51. See January 21, 2010, statement by University of Maryland public policy school dean Donald Kettl, as reported by Childs Walker in "UM Professor Reprimanded for Apparent Conflict of Interest," *Baltimore Sun*, January 23, 2010.

52. Document in possession of author.

53. Walker, "UM Professor Reprimanded."

54. Jack Stripling, "Union's Man," *Inside Higher Ed*, January 21, 2010, www.insidehighered.com/news/2010/01/21/union.

55. See Ruth Milkman, *L.A. Story: Immigrant Workers and the Future of the U.S. Labor Movement* (New York: Russell Sage Foundation, 2006) and Steven Henry Lopez, *Reorganizing the Rust Belt: An Inside Study of the American Labor Movement* (Berkeley and Los Angeles: University of California Press, 2004). For a more recent example of the genre, see also Ruth Milkman, Joshua Bloom, and Victor Narro, eds., *Working for Justice: The L.A. Model of Organizing and Advocacy* (Ithaca, NY: Cornell University Press, 2010).

56. In the interests of full disclosure, I must confess to being that "first reviewer" of *Stronger Together*, for *Labor Notes*, and to being personally confused by its misleading publisher packaging. For a longer critique of Don Stillman's book, see Steve Early, "SEIU Buys Its Own Version of History," *Labor Notes* blog, July 1, 2010.

57. As Pringle reported, SEIU "has paid millions of dollars to consulting firms, political nonprofits and individuals with family ties and other personal connections to some of the labor organization's top officers." See "Union Paid Firms with Family Ties," *Los Angeles Times*, September 26, 2008, which details SEIU spending on Stillman, political consultant Steve Rosenthal, and other spouses of top headquarters staffers.

58. While Don Stillman's once-formidable skills as a labor journalist are misspent on the overall project, *Stronger Together* does have its better chapters—on SEIU history, its University of Miami janitors campaign, and the development of a massive legislative-political operation that's the envy of many other unions.

Chapter 9: How EFCA Died for Obamacare

1. Harold Meyerson, "Under Obama, Labor Should Have Made More Progress," *Washington Post*, February 10, 2010. Some estimates of total 2008 election spending by labor range as high as $450 million.

2. Chris Maher, "SEIU Campaign Spending Pays Political Dividends," *Wall Street Journal*, May 16, 2009.

3. Pauline Beck quotes are from Pauline Beck email message, sent September 2,

2008, from www.seiucope.org, and from 2008 campaign video posted at *The Plum Line* (blog), washingtonpost.com, May 21, 2009, with article entitled "Obama Walked Day in Shoes of Worker Directly Impacted by White House Decision," by Greg Sargent.

4. Maher, "SEIU Campaign Spending."

5. See typical statement by then candidate Obama in the *Chicago Tribune* on March 4, 2007: "We will pass the Employee Free Choice Act. It's not a matter of if, it's a matter of when."

6. Dean Baker, "The Recession and the Freedom to Organize," posted February 6, 2008, on the AFL-CIO's blog, www.aflcio.org/mediacenter/speakout/dean_baker.cfm.

7. For more on labor's impressive and, in many ways, unprecedented 2007–09 campaign of grassroots activity on behalf of labor law reform, see Steve Early, "Back to the Future with EFCA?," in *Embedded with Organized Labor*, 166–176.

8. Michael Mishak, "Tone of Card-Check Support Shifts," *Las Vegas Sun*, November 30, 2008.

9. Jay Newton-Small, "Will Obama Deliver for Organized Labor?," *Time*, December 22, 2008.

10. See George Miller, "Focus on Politics," interview by Dan Morain, *Chicago Tribune*, November 18, 2010. Miller also told Reuters a month later that the deepening economic crisis should take precedence over EFCA. Speaker Nancy Pelosi's later decision not to hold a House vote on labor law reform until after the Senate reached the needed complement for cloture and acted first on labor law reform created an additional procedural problem in January 2010. After Republican Scott Brown was elected in Massachusetts, there was a brief period before his victory was certified and he was sworn in when Democrats could have theoretically moved forward on EFCA, in some form. But, unlike the situation with health care legislation at that point, there was no House version of the bill already passed.

11. Maher, "SEIU Campaign Spending."

12. Interview with the author.

13. Jonathan Alter, "Andy Stern's Legacy: Not All Bad," *Newsweek*, May 14, 2010.

14. Katrina vanden Heuvel, "Andy Stern on the New Moment," Nation.com, *Editor's Cut* (blog), November 25, 2008.

15. See "Specter Speaks on the Employee Free Choice Act/Card Check," full text of floor statement released by his Senate office on March 24, 2009.

16. As quoted in interview with Michael Mishak, "Unplugged: The SEIU Chief on the Labor Movement and Card Check," *Las Vegas Sun*, May 7, 2009.

17. Alec MacGillis, "Stern Considers Alternatives to EFCA," *Washington Post*, April 20, 2009.

18. Steven Greenhouse, "New Yorker Leads Labor Charge for Health Reform," *New York Times*, August 27, 2010.

19. Leon Fink and Brian Green, *Upheaval in the Quiet Zone: 1199SEIU and the Politics of Health Care Unionism*, 2nd ed. (Chicago: University of Illinois Press, 2009), 290.

20. Paul Krugman, "Blue Double Cross," *New York Times*, May 22, 2009.

21. Sam Stein, "Obama and Industry Groups to Propose $2 Trillion in Health Care

Savings," Huffington Post, May 10, 2009.

22. Robert Pear "Health Care Leaders Say Obama Overstated Their Promise to Control Costs," *New York Times*, May 15, 2009. For more background on the May 11 White House meeting, the industry players involved, the subsequent backpedaling of the hospital association, and Obama's deal-making with "Big Pharma," see Jonathan Alter, *The Promise: President Obama, Year One* (New York: Simon & Schuster, 2010), 251–253.

23. See "Joint Statement of International Union Presidents' Meeting," issued January 7, 2009, announcing the twelve-member NLCC's goal of "creating a unified labor movement that can speak and act nationally on the critical issues facing working Americans." As reported by Steven Greenhouse, "Labor Calls for Unity After Years of Division," *New York Times*, January 8, 2009.

24. Harold Meyerson, "Which Union Do I Belong to Now," *American Prospect*, April 9, 2009.

25. David Moberg, "Moving Obama Left," *In These Times*, August 25, 2008.

26. As *Labor Notes* reported, SEIU staffers in the field "actively tried to suppress health care activists in and outside of labor pushing for a more sweeping version of health care reform than SEIU deemed politically feasible." See Mark Brenner, Mischa Gaus, Jane Slaughter, and Paul Abowd, "Andy Stern's Legacy," *Labor Notes*, April 16, 2010.

27. Russell Mokhiber, "California Nurses Bristle at AFL-CIO's Support of Illinois Health Plan," *21 Corporate Crime Reporter* 45, online edition, November 16, 2007.

28. See joint two-page SEIU/CNA press release, issued on March 19, 2009, entitled "SEIU, CNA/NNOC Announce Major Accord at the Expense of the Public Interest."

29. As quoted by Chris Frates in "New Fault Line Forms in Health Care Fight," Politico, December 1, 2008. For a good DeMoro critique of HCAN, see "Why Is Health Care for America Now Giving Up on Real Reform?," Huffington Post, July 10, 2008.

30. Steven Greenhouse, "Union Head Would Back Bill Without Card Check," *New York Times*, September 5, 2009.

31. See Steve Early, "Specter in Pittsburgh: Punishment and Reward at AFL-CIO Convention," *Working In These Times* (blog), September 15, 2009.

32. Melanie Trottman, "Specter, Unions Disagree on Path for Overhaul of Labor Laws," *Wall Street Journal*, September 16, 2009.

33. In May 2009, Baucus held three days of hearings, with twenty-four witnesses, but not one was a single-payer advocate. When representatives of Single Payer Action objected to this at the hearing, Baucus ordered the arrest of thirteen doctors, nurses, and other activists.

34. Steven Greenhouse, "Congress Is Split on Effort to Tax Big Health Plans," *New York Times*, October 13, 2009.

35. For more on the use of strikes and contract campaigns to build support for real health care reform, see Steve Early, "Labor's Health Problem," *Nation*, July 7, 2003.

36. See Leonard Rodberg, "Is There Any Way Out for Obama?," posted on the Physicians for a National Health Program website, October 9, 2009.

37. Jackie Calmes and Robert Pear, "Administration Open to Taxing Health Benefits," *New York Times*, March 15, 2010.

38. Kevin Bogardus, "SEIU Skips Healthcare Ad Despite Shared Opposition to Tax on 'Cadillac Plans,'" TheHill.com, October 18, 2009.

39. Under the Reid version, plans whose premiums exceeded $23,000 a year for families and $8,500 for individuals would be subject to the excise tax. See Bill Salganik, "Tax Would Hit Those with 'Too Much' Insurance," Labor Notes, February 2010, 11.

40. Jane Slaughter, "Anger Boils Over Health Care Bill," Labor Notes, February 2010, 1, 11.

41. Susan Milligan, "Stalled Agenda Irks Labor Leaders," Boston Globe, October 12, 2009, 1.

42. See Vadin Rizov, "Labor Day, a Crappy Infomercial Partly Funded by Its Subject," Village Voice, October 27, 2009. Other reviewers—friendlier to the director—had kinder things to say about the film.

43. MacGillis, "Andrew Stern Departs SEIU."

44. Peter Nicholas, "Obama Backs Health Plan Tax," Chicago Tribune, January 7, 2009.

45. Kay Lazar, "State's Health Coverage Still High," Boston Globe, June 9, 2010. The article cites an Urban Institute survey of Massachusetts residents that found "one in five adults reported they did not receive some medical care in 2009" because of its cost and "about the same percentage said they had problems paying medical bills."

46. See Congressman Jerry Nadler (D-NY) quoted by Robert Pear and David Herszenhorn in "Labor Campaigns Against Tax on Health Plans," New York Times, January 13, 2010.

47. See Slaughter, "Anger Boils Over Health Care Bill," 13.

48. CWA Newsletter, January 15, 2010, which includes the disclaimer that "this is not the [health care plan] we would have written if we were the sole author." Continuing a five-year trend, worker premium contributions went up 14 percent in 2009. This pushed the average employee share of the cost of job-based family coverage up to $4,000, which doesn't include the higher out-of-pocket costs families face when they use these plans. A Kaiser Foundation expert interviewed by Bloomberg News admitted: "At least in the early years, I'm not sure health reform is going to mean that workers are going to face lower contribution amounts." See Drew Armstrong, "Workers Said to Pay 14% More for Health Insurance in 2010," Bloomberg News, September, 3, 2010.

49. Robert Kuttner, "A Wake Up Call," Huffington Post, January 17, 2010.

50. As Jane Slaughter reported in Labor Notes, some union officials, who were not at the White House, even questioned the value of the excise tax agreement for their members. Firefighters president Harold Schaitberger claimed his union didn't ask for the special, higher threshold for first responders and pointed out that it wouldn't benefit firefighters included in the same insurance pools with other public workers. "We're not going to buy into a special deal for us," Schaitberger said. IAM president Thomas Buffenbarger continued to insist that "no bill is better than this bill. We don't care what the amount is they peg it to. Because of inflation, whatever number will be gobbled up pretty quickly." Sean Murphy reported in the Boston Globe that "Health Tax on 'Cadillac Plans' May Wallop Many Communities," April 5, 2010. His article predicted further cost-shifting in the Massachusetts public sector "if high end plans aren't scaled back" before the excise tax kicks in.

51. See Brian Mooney, "Voter Anger Caught Fire in Final Days," *Boston Globe*, January 20, 2010.

52. Ibid.

53. Dan Balz and Jon Cohen, "Brown Rode Anti-Washington Wave," *Washington Post*, January 23, 2010.

54. See Guy Molyneux and Mark Bunge, Hart Research Associates, memorandum on its "Election Night Survey of Massachusetts Senate Voters," January 21, 2010.

55. One top SEIU official in the state believes that, even with a more appealing candidate among urban Democratic voters like Capuano, "Brown's victory would have occurred anyway." Interview with the author, October 18, 2010.

56. Ronald Mason, "Big Labor Agenda Is DEAD—For NOW," *Ohio Labor Lawyers* (blog), February 22, 2010, http://theohiolaborlawyers.wordpress.com/.

57. Meyerson, "Under Obama, Labor Should."

58. *CWA Newsletter*, January 15, 2010. Document in possession of author.

59. Once on the NLRB, Becker quickly backtracked on the scope of his previous commitment to recuse himself on SEIU-related matters. NUHW was particularly concerned about how he would rule on cases that pitted the new union or its members against SEIU. In August 2010, Becker insisted that he should be free to help decide UHW-related disputes, if they arose after his appointment to the board. See Alec MacGillis, "Republicans Seek NLRB Member Craig Becker's Recusal," *Washington Post*, August 17, 2010.

60. In the fall of 2010, the NLRB decided to reconsider the "*Dana* posting" requirement arising from a 2007 case involving Dana Holding Corp. Under that Bush labor board decision, employees were given an additional forty-five days in which 30 percent of them could petition for a representation election—even after management recognized a union based on its card check–demonstrated majority support.

61. See Steven Greenhouse, "Deadlock Is Ending on Labor Board," *New York Times*, April 1, 2010. In May 2010, labor did get a boost from the new, more proworker majority on the National Mediation Board (NMB). The NMB declared that unions seeking certification under the Railway Labor Act only needed to get a simple majority vote among those participating in NMB-conducted representation elections. In the past, many of these elections had been lost due to the old requirement that unions get a majority among all the workers eligible to vote.

62. Marc Levy, "Specter Fights for Votes in New Party," *Boston Globe*, May 14, 2010.

63. Michael Whitney, "Memory Fail: Pennsylvania Unions Endorse Specter," Firedoglake, March 30, 2010.

64. See SEIU, "Hope, Progress, Change...An American Dream," press release, March 25, 2010.

65. Holly Rosenkrantz, "What Andy Stern Leaves Behind," *Business Week*, April 15, 2010.

66. Chris Lehmann, "Andy Stern: The New Face of Labor," *Washingtonian*, March 1, 2010, www.washingtonian.com/articles/people/15093.html.

67. Text of Wilhelm remarks to the AFL-CIO Executive Council. Document in possession of author.

68. Sal Rosselli, "NUHW and the Fight for Union Democracy," interview with Lee

Sustar, *Socialist Worker*, May 27, 2010.
69. Interview with the author.
70. Meyerson, "Under Obama, Labor Should."

Chapter 10: *Labor Day: The Sequel*

1. Mary Kay Henry, interview by Tavis Smiley, Public Radio International, May 22, 2010, www.tavissmileyradio.com/guests10/052110/MaryKayHenry.html.
2. Rosenkrantz, "What Andy Stern Leaves Behind."
3. Christopher Neefus, "SEIU Boss Open to Serving on Obama Deficit Reduction Commission," CNS News, February 25, 2010.
4. Tess Stynes, "Siga Tech Names Former SEIU Leader Stern to Board," Dow Jones Newswires, June 21, 2010. For more on the Stern-Perlman connection, see Ryan Grim, "Andy Stern's Bizarre Alliance with Private Equity and Biowarfare," Huffington Post, October 13, 2010. In July 2010, Stern also became a "senior research fellow" at Georgetown University's Public Policy Institute (PPI). The PPI reported that Stern would "conduct and coordinate research efforts on a number of social policy issues, including wage reform, labor policy, and retirement security." See "Large Union President Joins Policy Institute," Georgetown University, press release, July 23, 2010.
5. Steven Greenhouse, "Andy Stern to Step Down as Chief of Politically Active Union," *New York Times*, April 14, 2010.
6. Harold Meyerson, "Andy Stern: A Union Maverick Clocks Out," *Washington Post*, April 14, 2010.
7. Katrina vanden Heuvel, "Andy Stern Steps Down," *Nation*, April 12, 2010. The same magazine provided a more critical assessment of Stern's legacy a few months later. See Fraser, "SEIU Andy Stern Leaves Behind."
8. Tim Fernholz, "Reading the Tea Leaves: Andy Stern Leaves SEIU," *American Prospect*, online edition, April 13, 2010.
9. See Marc Cooper, "Political Obituary for Andy Stern," *Dissonance* (blog), April 13, 2010.
10. John Judis, "Change to Lose," *New Republic*, online edition, April 14, 2010.
11. Ezra Klein, "Andy Stern: the Exit Interview," *Washington Post*, April 18, 2010.
12. As quoted in Fraser, "SEIU Andy Stern Leaves Behind."
13. From statement by Sal Rosselli, issued by NUHW, April 13, 2010, posted at www.nuhw.org.
14. See Stillman, *Stronger Together*, 237.
15. As UHW/SEIU reported on August 26, 2010, the first such posttrusteeship win was at a nursing home in Santa Cruz—where the workers were recruited on the basis of a strong master contract with other nursing homes operated by the same owner, the Glencare/Mariner chain. That contract was negotiated in 2008 by the UHW officers and staff removed by SEIU.
16. Alec MacGillis, "Andrew Stern Departs SEIU Now Weakened by Infighting," *Washington Post*, May 14, 2010. See also F. Vincent Vernuccio, "Andy Stern's Debts," *Washington Times*, April 23, 2010. As he notes, "the union's liabilities totaled $7,625,832 in 2000. By 2009, they had increased almost by a factor of sixteen,

to $120,893,259. Meanwhile, SEIU's assets barely tripled, growing from $66,632,631 in 2000 to $187,664,763 in 2009. Kim Moody notes also that SEIU's "percentage of member based income shrank from 85% in 2000 to 77% in 2008." Member-based income refers to that portion of the union's annual expenses that is paid for out of dues money collected during the same year versus those operating costs covered with the help of investment income, any cash raised through asset sales, or loans. See Kim Moody, "American Labor's Civil War: the Crisis and the Potential," *Against the Current*, March/April 2010, 8.

17. Mary Kay Henry as quoted by Harold Meyerson, "A Labor War Ended: SEIU and UNITE HERE Come to Terms," *American Prospect*, July 27, 2010.

18. Phone interview with the author, September 20, 2010.

19. Mary Kay Henry quote is from Mathew Kaminski, "California's Union Showdown," *Wall Street Journal*, online edition, August 7, 2010. Dave Regan's campaign cost estimate is cited by David Moberg, "Kaiser's Bitter Labor War," *In These Times*, September 13, 2010. The cost comparison made by *Labor Notes* can be found in Mark Brenner, "Fear Wins as Service Employees Fend Off NUHW," *Labor Notes*, November 2010, 3. Shaw's calculations can be found in "SEIU Uses Fear, Lies and Millions to Sway Kaiser Workers," *BeyondChron* (blog), September 7, 2010.

20. Even counting an estimated 100,000 Canadian members (who may not have been included in the head count for the DOL), SEIU's total membership in 2009 was still several hundred thousand shy of 2.2 million.

21. Alec MacGillis, "At the Peak of His Influence, SEIU Chief Set to Leave a Mixed Legacy," *Washington Post*, April 14, 2010.

22. Fred Ross, "Open Letter to Workers at Santa Rosa Memorial Hospital," *Beyond-Chron* (blog), December 8, 2009.

23. MacGillis, "Andrew Stern Departs."

24. See Ray Abernathy, "Say Hello to Mary Kay Henry," *West Bank of the Potomac* (blog), April 25, 2010, www.rayabernathy.com.

25. Backing the wrong candidate for president got SEIU vice president Rivera demoted just a few months later. While working with Stern on health care lobbying, he had been in charge of the rather amorphous structure known as "SEIU Healthcare." Henry reduced him to the rank of assistant director, under Scott Courtney, who is not even on the IEB yet.

26. See memo to SEIU International Executive Board on "The Future of SEIU" from Gerry Hudson, Eliseo Medina, Dave Regan, and Tom Woodruff, April 17, 2010. Document in possession of author.

27. Steven Greenhouse, "Grassroots Choice Leads Race for Top Union Post," *New York Times*, April 26, 2010.

28. David Moberg, "Post-Stern SEIU: In Upset, Mary Kay Henry Nails Down Presidency, *In These Times*, April 24, 2010.

29. Kevin Bogardus, "Trumka Says Dems' Aggressive Posture Helps Election Chances," TheHill.com, May 4, 2010.

30. See Anna Burger statement to members of the SEIU IEB, April 28, 2010. Posted at *Tapped*, blog of the *American Prospect*.

31.   Harold Meyerson, "Henry Takes Command—Collaboratively," *American Prospect*, May 11, 2010.
32.   As quoted by Kate Thomas, "Mary Kay Henry's Blessing for SEIU," May 10, 2010, seiu.org.
33.   Henry interview with Tavis Smiley, May 22, 2010.
34.   Alec MacGillis, "Stern Deputy Drops Her Bid To Take Over SEIU," *Washington Post*, April 29, 2010.
35.   Chris Cillizza, "Anna Burger to Leave SEIU, Change to Win," *Washington Post*, online edition, August 11, 2010.
36.   See Mary Kay Henry memo to SEIU IEB, entitled "A Smooth and United Transition," April 26, 2010.
37.   "Cops Too Pro-union for Mary Kay?," *Perez Stern* (blog), March 20, 2009.
38.   See *Perez Stern* postings for March 17 and March 20, 2009.
39.   Joe Goldeen, "Kaiser Union Battle Draws Pickets," *Stockton Record*, May 28, 2009.
40.   See "Where's the Gift Basket for Kaiser Workers?," *Perez Stern* (blog), May 29, 2009.
41.   The largest single group of defectors in this initial wave at Kaiser were RNs at Kaiser Sunset Medical Center. See Suzanne Gordon, "Why Kaiser Nurses Should Back NUHW," *BeyondChron* (blog), January 6, 2009.
42.   Paul Krehbiel email to the author, January 28, 2010.
43.   Ganz, *Why David Sometimes Wins*, 8.
44.   Richard Flacks, email to author, January 5, 2009.
45.   From author interview and email communication with Paul Krehbiel.
46.   See June 23, 2010, NLRB Region 21 Settlement Agreement in Southern California Permanente Medical Group, and Kaiser Foundation Hospitals, Case 21-CA-38926 et al.
47.   See NUHW, "Kaiser Charged with Criminal Breach of Federal Labor Law," press release, August 23, 2010. See the full text of the lawsuit at http://bit.ly/kp-charge.
48.   Randy Shaw wrote about Hewitt in "SEIU to Create WWIII to Drive NUHW Out of Hospitals," *BeyondChron* (blog), May 20, 2010. See Huerta's statement criticizing SEIU and clips of the union's Kaiser cafeteria disruptions at "UFW Co-founder Dolores Huerta Bears Witness to SEIU Tactics against Kaiser Healthcare Workers," July 13, 2010, www.youtube.com/watch?v=XsHyLAURzvA.
49.   Dolores Huerta, "An Open Letter to SEIU President Mary Kay Henry," Huffington Post, August 3, 2010.
50.   As quoted by Cal Winslow, "The Battle for Kaiser: SEIU Calls for World War III," ZNet, June 7, 2010.
51.   In a private email, one SEIU health care organizer from the Pacific Northwest objected to NUHW's characterization of the settlement as a "sweetheart deal." Workers saw "less takeaways in that contract than basically any other contract negotiated in the healthcare industry in the western U.S. in 2010," he wrote. "Kaiser folks should feel like their contract is awesome, because it is still the highest bar." Email in possession of the author.
52.   Cornejo and Tomasian quotes are from Steve Early, "SEIU Civil War Puts Labor-Management 'Partnership' in a New Light," *Real World Labor: A Reader in Econom-*

ics, Politics, and Social Policy, Immanuel Ness, Amy Offner, Chris Sturr, and the Dollars & Sense Collective, eds. (Boston: Economic Affairs Bureau, 2009), 200–203.

53. Steve Early, "California Union Rebels Demand Biggest Labor Board Vote in Seven Decades," *Working In These Times* (blog), June 30, 2010.

54. See Lena H. Sun, "Growing National Nurses United Steps Up Strikes in Aggressive New Strategy," *Washington Post*, November 20, 2010.

55. In the fall of 2010, elections in Kansas covered by the HCA agreement also "added 915 members to SEIU's ranks and 600 to NNU's." See Mischa Gaus, "Hospital Unions Make Inroads Through Neutrality Deals," *Labor Notes*, November 2010, 1.

56. See CNA, "Lone Star Rebellion—Nearly 2,000 Texas RNs Vote to Join Nation's Largest Nurses' Union," press release, June 4, 2010.

57. In November 2010, NNOC/NNU won the right to represent 850 nurses at HCA hospitals in Sanford and Kissimmee, Florida. See National Nurses United, "Central Florida RNs Vote by 68% to Join Largest Nurses Union," press release, November 23, 2010.

58. Arthur Fox, email to author, October 14, 2010. At the time of Fox's comments, UHW/SEIU and SEIU Local 121 RN members had yet to receive a copy of the requested HCA-SEIU labor peace accord. On December 6, 2010, SEIU stewards Alicia Taboada and Susan Denardo sent a letter to Alan Weiss, district director of the U.S. Department of Labor's office of labor-management services, seeking DOL enforcement of their legal right to have a copy of any negotiated agreement with HCA that "was made part of our contract and dramatically restricts our rights." Document in possession of the author.

59. Gaus, "Hospital Unions Make Inroads."

60. One former CNA staffer estimated that, as of October 2010, the NNOC was "not above 35 percent in most of these newly organized HCA facilities in Texas. Signing a card for the election or voting for NNOC is not the same as a commitment to join the union or pay dues." Email message to the author, October 24, 2010.

61. As quoted by Gaus, "Hospital Unions Make Inroads."

62. See CNA internal memo, entitled "SEIU/UHW, The LMP, and NUHW," from the union's Kaiser Division director James Ryder, June 2010.

63. UHW Action Update, "Judge Stops Cuts to SEIU-UHW Home Care Members in Fresno," June 29, 2010. In July 2010, the state Public Employees Relations Board (PERB) issued a complaint charging Fresno County "with regressive bargaining and improperly implementing their last, best, final offer." See UHW Action Update, "PERB Takes Action in Fresno," July 22, 2010.

64. Clare Ansberry, "Disabled Face Hard Choices as States Slash Medicaid," *Wall Street Journal*, May 20, 2010.

65. Peter Goodman, "Cuts to Child Care Subsidy Thwart More Job Seekers," *New York Times*, May 24, 2010.

66. Yuliya Chernova, "Union Drops Health Coverage for Workers' Children," *Wall Street Journal*, online edition, November 11, 2010.

67. Eileen Boris and Jennifer Klein, "'Not Really a Worker': Home-Based Unions Challenged in Court," *Labor Notes*, online edition, October 20, 2010.

68. For an account of the Labor Notes meeting, see Wade Rathke, "The Assault on Home Care Workers," *Chief Organizer Blog*, April 26, 2010. See also Matthew Luskin, "Bargain to Organize, Organize to Bargain," *Labor Notes*, September 2010, 12.

69. Dawson Bell, "Caregivers Fight Union Dues," *Detroit Free Press*, April 20, 2010.

70. Boris and Klein, "'Not Really a Worker.'" This article draws on Boris and Klein's forthcoming *Caring for America: Home Health Workers in the Shadow of the Welfare State* (New York: Oxford University Press, 2012).

71. Rosselli "NUHW and the Fight for Union Democracy."

72. Statement of John W. Wilhelm, president of UNITE HERE International Union, on "Reaching Agreement with SEIU to End Dispute," July 26, 2010.

73. Ben Smith, "A Labor Deal," Politico, July 27, 2010.

74. For more details on who got what, see Susan Hobbs, "UNITE HERE, SEIU Reach Settlement to Define Divided Union's Assets, Jurisdiction," *BNA Daily Labor Report*, July 28, 2010. Some unresolved disagreements were left to a process of mediation and arbitration.

75. John Wilhelm, "Memo to the UNITE HERE Family," July 27, 2010. Three months later, Wilhelm announced he was taking a three-month leave of absence and that Las Vegas hotel union leader D. Taylor would be acting as interim president. In this message, he once again reflected on "the long struggle to prevent the Service Employees International Union from hijacking UNITE HERE." During "the last two difficult years," he wrote, "our members, staff, and elected leaders proved we will never let anyone—employers or unions doing the employers' bidding—stop us from our mission." See Wilhelm, "Memo to the UNITE HERE Family," October 21, 2010.

76. As quoted by Mathew Kaminski, "California's Union Showdown," *Wall Street Journal*, August 7, 2010.

77. In Harold Meyerson's more cynical, and inaccurate, portrayal of the negotiations, UNITE HERE only provided "organizers and resources to NUHW as a way to pressure SEIU" until "the pressure worked." In reality, top regional and national UNITE HERE leaders made common cause with NUHW out of genuine solidarity and political affinity, not just to have "one more card to play" in their settlement talks with SEIU. See Meyerson, "A Labor War Ended: SEIU and UNITE HERE Come to Terms," *American Prospect*, July 27, 2010.

78. As quoted by Kevin Bogardus, "SEIU Settles Dispute with UNITE HERE, Turns Its Attention to Breakaway Group," TheHill.com, July 27, 2010.

79. Juan Gonzalez, "Watchdog Group Urges Probe of Union Big Bruce Raynor for $15 Million Transfer," *New York Daily News*, April 30, 2010.

80. Randy Shaw, "SEIU President Henry Faces Test over Raynor Bombshell," *BeyondChron* (blog), May 10, 2010.

81. Smith, "A Labor Deal." The Mary Kay Henry memo to SEIU staff is reproduced in Smith's report.

82. MacGillis, "Andrew Stern Departs."

83. See Bruce Boccardy, "Convenient Scapegoats: Teachers, Firefighters, Parks Workers, Librarians, Hospital Workers, Childcare Workers," *Labor Notes*, November 2010, 1, for a good description of the public sector bargaining climate on both coasts.

84. Paul Jones, "County Workers Shift to New Union," *Marinscope*, May 25, 2010. In late 2010, disgruntled state workers who tried to reform SEIU Local 1000 launched a group called California Professional Public Employees Association (CPPEA), which is also seeking a MAPE-style decertification vote in one or more state bargaining units because Local 1000 "is ineffective at representing its members and irreparable." Its appeals are directed toward 95,000 SEIU members and fee payers. See http://cppea.org/about-cppea/. In San Francisco Local 790, before it was forced into 1021, some dissident members also tried to form independent unions for nurses and other city employees. For an account of that thwarted effort, see Bob English, "SEIU Now and Then: May Democracy Be with You," San Francisco Bay Area Independent Media Center, July 11, 2008, http://IndyBay.org.

85. Harry Baker email message to fellow Local 1021 board members. Document in possession of author.

86. John Templeton, "Time for SEIU to Change Direction?," *Union Democracy Review*, September/October 2010, 6. As advertised in this appeal, John can be contacted at johnboy11@verizon.net for 2012 SEIU convention planning purposes.

87. As quoted by Larry Bradshaw, "Sweeping Victory for SEIU Reformers," *Socialist Worker*, March 3, 2010.

88. See October 1, 2010, "SEIU Local 221 Election Protest," filed with the U.S. Department of Labor in Los Angeles by Reform221 Slate. Document in possession of author and posted at Reform221's website.

89. Cox interview with author, October 22, 2010. For more on her experiences in the San Francisco security guards local, see "Security Officers Watching Their Local 24/7," *SMART/News!*, Fall 2008, 4. Also, Herman Benson, "New Stage in Super Bureaucratization of Labor," *Union Democracy Review*, July/August 2009, 1.

90. Email to the author, September 4, 2008.

91. From undated California United Janitors 2009 election campaign internal memo, entitled "Talking Points, SEIU Local 1877." Document in possession of author.

92. One of the brave immigrant workers involved in CUJ is Hector Rincon, who came to the United States in 2002 as a refugee from death-squad threats against trade unionists in his native Colombia. Rincon worked for Local 1877 for five years before being fired by Mike Garcia for his CUJ sympathies.

93. See October 22, 2009, email message from Jose Escanuela to Mike Garcia and multiple other Local 1877 recipients, posted November 23, 2009, *Stern Burger with Fries* (blog). In early 2010, Escanuela resigned as Local 2007 president, but remains active as a working member and shop steward. So far, Local 2007's fourteen hundred members at Stanford and Santa Clara Universities have managed to avoid direct absorption into USWW, even though their local was part of the earlier district council structure of USWW. This may have to do with their willingness to threaten disaffiliation and/or decertification from SEIU if not left alone.

94. For more information on past and present TDU activity, which illustrates its unusual organizational staying power, see its website at www.tdu.org.

95. For an in-depth analysis of the undoing of ACORN, see Peter Dreier and Chris Martin, "Have the Media Falsely Framed ACORN?," *Editor & Publisher*, November

24, 2009. See also Atlas, *Seeds of Change*, 236–249.

96.	David Moberg, "After Right-Wing Attacks, SEIU Cuts Old ACORN Ties," *In These Times*, October 23, 2010. In 2008–09, SEIU's contracts with ACORN were worth nearly $2 million to the organization.

97.	Moberg, "After Right-Wing Attacks."

98.	For a longer explanation of the Wal-Mart project strategy, see "Majority Unionism: Strategies for Organizing the 21st Century Labor Movement," a paper prepared by Rathke for the SEIU Executive Board in 2003 and reprinted as an article for *Social Policy* 35, no. 3 (Spring 2005). For more specifics, see "A Wal-Mart Workers Association? An Organizing Plan," a chapter by Rathke in *Wal-Mart: The Face of Twenty-First Century Capitalism*, Nelson Lichtenstein, ed. (New York: New Press, 2006).

99.	Not surprisingly, the grassroots organizing activity of the WMWA, even though partially funded by SEIU, is completely airbrushed out of the chapter entitled "Fighting Wal-Mart's Low-Wage America" in Don Stillman's *Stronger Together*. Stillman's account deals only with what was accomplished by SEIU-backed "Wal-Mart Watch," a Washington, D.C.–based watchdog group staffed by political operatives and PR people.

100.	For a good account of FMPR's successful "Vote No" campaign, see Micah Landau, "Puerto Rican Teachers' Union Trounces SEIU," *NACLA Newsletter*, November 24, 2008, https://nacla.org/node/5257.

101.	Rafael Feliciano quotes are from his panel presentation at the Left Forum conference in New York City, March 20, 2010.

Conclusion: Signs of a New Workers' Movement?

1.	Bob Herbert, "A Radical Treasure," *New York Times*, January 30, 2010.

2.	SEIU's statewide budget for vote-buying victuals was not small. See "SEIU Hopes Kaiser Workers Vote with Their Stomachs, Not Their Heads," *Stern Burger with Fries* (blog), September 2010. As *SBWF* reported, the campaign menu included "pizza, chicken dinners, Mexican food, cupcakes, ice cream, fresh fruit, and barbecues...all paid for by workers' own dues money...[A]s one worker arrived at a Kaiser clinic in Antioch he ran into someone delivering thirty-six pizzas to his clinic and many more to nearby facilities. The delivery person showed him the bill: $1,000!"

3.	Steven Greenhouse, "Union vs. Union: Ousted by SEIU, Labor Leader Fights to Lure Its Members," *New York Times*, September 14, 2010. Greenhouse's propensity for bad "framing" was really on display in this much-protested piece. His article transformed a struggle involving thousands of workers into a mere pissing match between rival union officials. Among the workers Greenhouse quoted was Kelela Moberg, an outspoken pharmacy tech at Kaiser San Francisco Medical Center, whom I interviewed several days later. Greenhouse described Moberg as a "Rosselli supporter"—as if she were backing a San Francisco mayoral candidate. "I'm not a Rosselli supporter," she told me indignantly, after seeing the *Times* article for the first time. "I'm an NUHW supporter!" For further negative feedback, see Randy Shaw, "Greenhouse Violates *N.Y. Times* Policy in SEIU-NUHW Story," *BeyondChron* (blog), September 15, 2010.

4. The details of the "SEIU Layoff Agreement" that was negotiated by UHW trustee staffers and significantly modified the contract are given in "EVS—a Department SEIU Has Failed to Represent," NUHW document in possession of author, and other material posted at www.nuhw.org.

5. Undated CNA document in possession of author.

6. Some SEIU staffers conscripted for Kaiser duty clearly wished they were elsewhere. One anguished and anonymous organizer emailed his colleagues in California "to publicly say what many have said privately: this is an assignment we do not believe in...Basically, we're being told to lie to workers. Trying to build a union with lies is like trying to build a house from sand. Soon it will crumble." Posted at *Stern Burger with Fries* (blog), September 12, 2010.

7. As Randy Shaw wrote at the time, citing Marty Leavitt's *Confessions of a Union Buster*, SEIU's campaign "is taking a page from the playbook of professional union-busters." *BeyondChron* (blog), September 7, 2010.

8. For a dramatic example of strike-baiting by SEIU supporters at Kaiser in Roseville, California, see Steve Early, "Scoundrel Time at Kaiser: Hope and Fear Collide in California Healthcare," *CounterPunch*, September 20, 2010.

9. See, for example, an opinion piece by two Kaiser workers, Jessica Garcia and Elaine Monney, "SEIU and the New McCarthyism," *San Francisco Bay Guardian*, August 31, 2010, and Mark Brenner, "Fear Wins as Service Employees Fend Off NUHW," *Labor Notes*, November 2010, 3.

10. See Steve Early, "This Labor Day, Let's Salute All Union Stewards—and Their Cutting Edge in California," *Working In These Times* (blog), August 23, 2010.

11. As quoted in Early, "Scoundrel Time at Kaiser," September 20, 2010.

12. Among the other Kaiser coalition unions are local affiliates of the United Steelworkers, Office and Professional Employees, American Federation of Teachers, AFSCME, IFPTE, the UFCW, Teamsters, and several state nurses' associations in Ohio, Oregon, and Hawaii. In a December 5, 2009, statement, coalition director John August issued a statement rejecting LMP participation by any union engaged in "raiding a constituent member union of the Coalition." CWA's 2004–05 Alameda call center organizing involved nonunion Kaiser workers, not any other union's existing members. Nevertheless, CWA was excluded as well from the coalition and the partnership—a ban that became moot when Kaiser's anti-union activity resulted in decertification.

13. According to statistics compiled by ARAW, the NLRB obtained an average of just sixteen 10(j) injunctions per year between 2001 and 2005. In 2007, even after Kaiser thwarted CWA-backed unionization of its call center in Alameda, California, ARAW gave the HMO an "Eleanor Roosevelt Human Rights Award." When I contacted ARAW in October 2010, to learn whether this workers' rights watchdog organization had been monitoring Kaiser's recent misbehavior, director Kimberly Brown refused to comment or be interviewed.

14. In late September 2010, Andy Stern was back in the news, thanks to Stephens's guilty plea and four-month jail sentence. The *Los Angeles Times*, Associated Press, *Wall Street Journal*, Bloomberg News, *New York Post*, and *New York Times* all re-

ported that FBI agents had been asking questions about who approved the costly "no-show job" consulting payments to Stephens that facilitated the merger of Local 660 in Los Angeles with six other SEIU affiliates. See, for example, Kris Maher and Evan Perez, "SEIU Probed Over Consulting Pacts," *Wall Street Journal*, September 29, 2010. Some of these news outlets also reported that the FBI was investigating the propriety of payments received by Stern himself for his 2006 book, *A Country That Works*.

15. Melanie Trottman, "Unions to Pool Spending for Midterm Elections," *Wall Street Journal*, August 25, 2010. By October 2010, AFSCME was spending nearly $90 million on the midterm elections all by itself. Like the corporations whose "independent campaign" spending dwarfed labor's, the union was freed from the constraints of just using voluntary member contributions to its political action fund by the Supreme Court's Citizens United decision. AFSCME "said it will tap membership dues to pay for $17 million worth of ads backing Democrats in this election." See Brody Mullins and John D. McKinnon, "Campaign's Big Spender," *Wall Street Journal*, October 22, 2010.

16. See Glenn Thrush, "Labor Holds Nose, Backs Former Foes," Politico, October 26, 2010, and David Sirota, "Thank You, Sir: May I Have Another: Labor Leaders Destroy Their Own Ability to Influence Democrats," Huffington Post, October 26, 2010. A week before the midterm elections, AFL-CIO president Richard Trumka sent an urgent message to all union members: "As bad as things are now, they can get a whole lot worse."

17. Not everyone got to hear Elliott's moving duet with Cohen. Back in Massachusetts, two thousand would-be rally goers, from labor and community groups, were left stranded on Friday, October 1. They never got to Washington because of a massive breakdown in rental bus arrangements made by headquarters officials of 1199SEIU. The good news was that 1199 spent an estimated $1.6 million on buses for October 2 and helped initiate the event. The bad news was that fifty or more buses never showed up, thanks to the vendor or broker the union employed. "It doesn't make sense to have things run out of New York," said one leader of a community-labor coalition in Boston that was badly stiffed in the affair. Various organizational apologies for this latest sign of megalocal dysfunction were posted on the website of Massachusetts Jobs with Justice.

18. For more on NUHW fundraising around the country in 2009, see Steve Early, "How a New Union Is Staying Afloat (with a Little Help from Its Friends)," *Labor Notes*, no. 365, online edition, August 2009.

19. Bill Fletcher Jr. and Nelson Lichtenstein, "SEIU's Civil War," *In These Times*, online edition, December 16, 2009.

20. Clawson, "Battle for Labor's Future." See also Clawson's excellent book, *The Next Upsurge*.

21. The exact number of 2009 Kaiser decertification election supporters (29,527) was not claimed publicly in NUHW literature until the following year. The statistic was then confirmed in author interviews with NUHW organizers.

22. Wade Rathke, "Bet on SEIU in West Coast Family Feud," *Chief Organizer Blog*,

September 2, 2010. As other factors favoring the incumbent company/union, Rathke also cited SEIU's willingness and ability to "spend millions again," as it did in Fresno, to "put a thousand or more people on the street in a GOTV effort" that would overwhelm NUHW except in "workplaces where they still have committed workers in place."

23. As quoted by Mark Brenner, "Fear Wins," *Labor Notes*, November, 2010.
24. As quoted by Paul Pringle, "SEIU Defeats Insurgent Group to Continue Representing Kaiser Healthcare Workers," *Los Angeles Times*, October 8, 2010.
25. As quoted by Matt Smith, "Labor Pains," *San Francisco Weekly*, October 18, 2010. Regan's position was seconded, in print, by labor lawyer Jay Youngdahl in an *East Bay Express* article entitled, "NUHW Vote Is a Bloody Nose for the Labor Left," October 21, 2010. While never mentioning the Kaiser unfair labor practices that influenced the election, Youngdahl declared "that the workers have spoken" and "it is time for this country's labor left to listen—including the ingrown left of the Bay Area."
26. Cal Winslow, "How the SEIU Won in California: Big Money, the Big Lie, and Fear," *CounterPunch*, October 11, 2010.
27. NUHW, "Will Illegal and Collusive Behavior by Kaiser Permanente Result in New Union Election?," press release, October 14, 2010.
28. Wade Rathke urged "the upstart union" to focus on organizing the unorganized instead. He argued that this kind of competition with SEIU was more winnable and would make the latter "a better union in California" because it would be forced to "prove its superiority not in statements but in organizing and representation in workplaces." See "Kaiser Win for SEIU, No Rerun Coming," *Chief Organizer Blog*, October 11, 2010.
29. UHW/SEIU, "Following Kaiser Loss…Internal Turmoil, Deep Debt, Defections, Leave NUHW's Future in Doubt," press statement, October 25, 2010. According to Trossman, "more than 120,000 of the 125,000 SEIU-UHW members [NUHW] has attempted to win over rejected them." This oft-cited 96 percent failure rate conflates multiple private and public sector representation election bids, many of which were fatally delayed or lost by some combination of SEIU legal obstruction, labor board foot-dragging, and/or management assistance to the incumbent union.
30. Not the least of NUHW's money problems was the $1.5 million damage award, against the organization and sixteen of its founders. An anonymous benefactor posted a bond for NUHW, shielding it from SEIU collection efforts while the jury verdict against the union is appealed. SEIU has obtained court approval for garnishment of the wages of individual defendants unable or unwilling to post a similar bond, pending appeal, or satisfy the judgment against them. See UHW/SEIU, "Following Kaiser Loss."
31. A member of the "NUHW 16" with her own SEIU damage award to pay off, Lewis went to work for the AFSCME-affiliated United Nurses Association of California (UNAC), which represents RNs at Kaiser, Tenet, and other hospitals in Southern California.
32. For some Kaiser worker speculation about the union's future workplace strategy,

see Brenner, "Fear Wins."

33. As quoted by Sustar in "Challenging SEIU's Collusion with Kaiser," *Socialist Worker*, October 15, 2010.

34. See Salinas Valley picketing report posted at *Stern Burger with Fries* (blog), October 25, 2010. For a longer discussion of UHW/SEIU handling of hospital layoffs, see Randy Shaw, "Hospitals Seize on SEIU's Kaiser Victory to Lay Off Workers," *BeyondChron* (blog), October 14, 2010. On October 28, 2010, Salinas Valley Memorial workers finally got some good news: the state Public Employment Relations Board finally certified NUHW as their bargaining representative, ending forced dues payments to the lame duck SEIU. As a UHW member in 1988, 71-year-old Marilyn Benson was part of the "New Leadership Team," led by Sal Rosselli, that battled the SEIU international union staff in the post-trusteeship election campaign described in chapter 1.

35. CWA/AFA and the Teamsters were able to make some membership gains in 2009–10, thanks to their own efforts and/or the more union-friendly election rules of the Obama-appointed majority on the National Mediation Board, which supervises representation elections in the airline industry. Likewise, the long-delayed extension of limited collective bargaining rights to personnel of the Transportation Security Administration was another boon to membership in two competing federal employee unions, AFGE and the NTEU.

36. After the Democrats midterm election rout in November 2010, the new GOP majority in the U.S. House seemed certain to push legislation curbing private agreements requiring union recognition based on card check. The likely Republican successor to Representative George Miller as head of the House Education and Labor Committee was reported to be Congressman John Kline from Minnesota. Kline was "chief sponsor of the Secret Ballot Protection Act, a bill with 115 House cosponsors that would bar employers from agreeing to unionization through card check." Steven Greenhouse, "Unions Fear Rollback of Rights Under Republicans," *New York Times*, November 1, 2010.

37. Interview with the author, August 26, 2010.

38. James C. Scott, *Seeing Like a State: How Certain Schemes to Improve the Human Condition Have Failed* (New Haven, CT: Yale University Press, 1998).

39. Ibid., 7.

40. All quotations are from Scott, *Seeing Like a State*, 168–174, summarizing the points made by Rosa Luxemburg in "Mass-Strike, Party, and Trade Unions," and "Organizational Questions of Russian Social Democracy," in Dick Howard, ed., *Selected Writings of Rosa Luxemburg* (New York: Monthly Review Press, 1971), 223–70, 283–306.

41. Scott, *Seeing Like a State*, 175–179, 403.

42. Alexandra Kollontai, *Selected Writings of Alexandra Kollontai*, trans. Alix Holt (London: Allison and Busby, 1977), 191, 188, and 190, as quoted by Scott.

43. Scott, *Seeing Like a State*, 177.

44. It should be noted, with all seriousness and due respect, that millions of ordinary Russians did rouse themselves for a heroic defense of their homeland, which

changed the course of the Second World War and helped destroy German fascism. An estimated twenty million died in the process.

45. On the history-minded left, the first point of attack might be the sad subsequent career of Kollontai, which distinguishes her from her martyred comrade in Berlin. In 1919, Luxemburg became the most famous casualty of the Weimar Republic's suppression of the German workers' uprising led by the Spartacist League. Despite Luxemburg's strong critique of certain aspects of Lenin's approach from 1903 to her death, she remained a staunch ally of the Russian Revolution. Kollontai, on the other hand, later decided to make her peace with the party of Stalin (just as some former sixties radicals have ditched their old ideas and found comfortable organizational niches within SEIU).

Beginning in 1923, Kollontai held a series of diplomatic posts for Soviet Russia and remained silent about its political repression and mass murder until her death in 1952. Despite her many contributions to the revolutionary movement, including her focus on women's liberation, Kollontai's subsequent capitulation to Stalin's regime—while a boon to longevity—did tarnish her earlier reputation for courageous and clear-eyed criticism. Luxemburg's tragic and untimely death spared her some hard choices down the road. But as Norman Geras and others have pointed out, she firmly believed in "the essential merit of the Bolsheviks" and unconditionally supported the Russian Revolution of 1917. See Geras, "Rosa Luxemburg After 1905," *New Left Review*, January–February 1975, 46.

46. See Randy Shaw's various accounts of how UHW/SEIU, under Dave Regan's leadership, donated heavily to three Chamber of Commerce–backed candidates for the San Francisco Board of Supervisors who were opposed by "its progressive sister union," SEIU Local 1021, which represents city employees. Two of the three ended up losing. See Shaw, "SEIU Faces Reckoning on Eve of Kaiser Results," Huffington Post, October 7, 2010, and Shaw, "SEIU-UHW Aligns with CPMC in San Francisco Political Endorsements," *BeyondChron* (blog), August 3, 2010. UHW/SEIU participation in the conservative "Alliance for Jobs and Sustainable Growth" was part of its controversial partnering with Sutter Health, described in footnote 48 below.

47. During state budget negotiations and two months before California's gubernatorial and Senate elections, plus key ballot initiatives, political commentator Louis Freedburg noted: "SEIU in general is far less of a presence in the State Capitol than usual, especially in helping to craft and lobby for legislation, and is losing valuable time in turning out volunteers—'boots on the ground'—to work on voter registration and other election year activities." See Freedburg, "Labor Conflict Comes at Bad Time for California Democratic Party," *California WatchBlog*, September 13, 2010.

48. For a current example of health care unionism as an "appendage of management," see UHW/SEIU under trustee Dave Regan. As Randy Shaw noted, UHW has developed "a remarkably cozy relationship with the hospital industry" while in trusteeship. In 2010, UHW broke with CNA, NUHW, and various community groups to support Sutter Health's controversial expansion plans in San Francisco

and Oakland, in return for a "just us" job security deal for SEIU-represented employees. The S.F. project faced opposition from "citywide health care advocates because it is linked with Sutter's plan to reduce acute care beds by 60% at St. Luke's Hospital in the city's heavily Latino Mission District." *BeyondChron* (blog), March 24, 2010, and August 3, 2010.

Index

393

Also from Haymarket Books

Fields of Resistance: The Struggle of Florida's Farmworkers for Justice
Silvia Giagnoni • In Immokalee, Florida, the tomato capital of the world—which has earned the dubious distinction of being "ground zero for modern slavery"—farm workers organized themselves into the Coalition of Immokalee Workers, and launched a nationwide boycott campaign that forced McDonald's, Burger King, and Taco Bell to recognize their demands for workers' rights. ISBN 9781608460939

Live Working or Die Fighting: How the Working Class Went Global
Paul Mason • This is a story of urban slums, self-help cooperatives, choirs and brass bands, free love, and self-education by candlelight. *Live Working or Die Fighting* celebrates workers' common history of defiance, idealism, and self-sacrifice, one as alive and active today as it was two hundred years ago—a unique and inspirational book. ISBN 9781608460700

The Lean Years: A History of the American Worker, 1920–1933
Irving Bernstein • The complex fate of individual American workers, both organized and unorganized, definitively shaped the era of the 1920s and early 1930s. Irving Bernstein's classic text revolutionizes social history, vividly narrating an era of wrenching hardships but also great victories for American labor. With an introduction by Frances Fox Piven. ISBN 9781608460632

The Turbulent Years: A History of the American Worker, 1933–1941
Irving Bernstein • In this groundbreaking work of labor history, Irving Bernstein uncovers a period when industrial trade unionism, working-class power, and socialism became the rallying cry for millions of workers in the fields, mills, mines, and factories of America. With an introduction by Frances Fox Piven. ISBN 9781608460649

Subterranean Fire: A History of Working-Class Radicalism in the United States
Sharon Smith • This accessible, critical history of the U.S. labor movement examines the hidden history of workers' resistance from the nineteenth century to the present. Workers in the U.S. have a rich tradition of fightback, which remains largely hidden. *Subterranean Fire* brings that history to light and reveals its lessons for today. ISBN 9781931859233

The Labor Wars: From the Molly Maguires to the Sit-Downs
Sidney Lens • The rise of the American labor movement was characterized by explosive and sometimes bloody struggles. Lens chronicles the early battles, from Pennsylvania's famous coal martyrs, the Molly Maguires in the nineteenth century, to the crucial workers' victory of the 1930s in the sit-down strikes against General Motors. ISBN 9789131859707

Revolution in Seattle: A Memoir
Harvey O'Connor • In this moving political memoir, O'Connor captures the courage and defiance of workers on the march against the carnage of the First World War and the dramatic inequality that marked the era. ISBN 9781931859745

About Haymarket Books

Haymarket Books is a nonprofit, progressive book distributor and publisher, a project of the Center for Economic Research and Social Change. We believe that activists need to take ideas, history, and politics into the many struggles for social justice today. Learning the lessons of past victories, as well as defeats, can arm a new generation of fighters for a better world. As Karl Marx said, "The philosophers have merely interpreted the world; the point, however, is to change it."

We take inspiration and courage from our namesakes, the Haymarket Martyrs, who gave their lives fighting for a better world. Their 1886 struggle for the eight-hour day, which gave us May Day, the international workers' holiday, reminds workers around the world that ordinary people can organize and struggle for their own liberation. These struggles continue today across the globe—struggles against oppression, exploitation, hunger, and poverty.

It was August Spies, one of the Martyrs targeted for being an immigrant and an anarchist, who predicted the battles being fought to this day. "If you think that by hanging us you can stamp out the labor movement," Spies told the judge, "then hang us. Here you will tread upon a spark, but here, and there, and behind you, and in front of you, and everywhere, the flames will blaze up. It is a subterranean fire. You cannot put it out. The ground is on fire upon which you stand."

We could not succeed in our publishing efforts without the generous financial support of our readers. Many people contribute to our project through the Haymarket Sustainers program, where donors receive free books in return for their monetary support. If you would like to be a part of this program, please contact us at info@haymarketbooks.org.

Order online at www.haymarketbooks.org or call 773-583-7884.

About the Author

Steve Early has been active in the labor movement since 1972.

For twenty-seven years, he was a Boston-based international representative for the Communications Workers of America. Early was involved in organizing, bargaining, and major strikes involving NYNEX, Bell Atlantic, AT&T, Verizon, Southern New England Tel, SBC, Cingular, and Verizon Wireless. He also assisted in CWA public sector organizing, plus mergers with other AFL-CIO affiliates and independent unions. He finished his union career in 2007, after serving as administrative assistant to the vice president of CWA District 1, which represents more than 160,000 workers in New York, New England, and New Jersey.

Early is the author of a previous book entitled *Embedded with Organized Labor: Journalistic Reflections on the Class War at Home* (New York: Monthly Review Press, 2009).

His freelance journalism has appeared in the *Nation, Boston Globe, Boston Herald, New York Times, Washington Post, Los Angeles Times, Newsday, Wall Street Journal, Christian Science Monitor, Philadelphia Inquirer,* and many others.

He serves on the editorial advisory committees for three independent labor publications—*Labor Notes, New Labor Forum,* and *WorkingUSA.* He is a member of the National Writers Union/UAW and a longtime supporter of Jobs with Justice, the Association for Union Democracy, and Teamsters for a Democratic Union.

He can be reached at Lsupport@aol.com.